JOHN MAITLAND

JOHN MAITLAND OF THIRLESTANE
AND THE FOUNDATION OF THE STEWART DESPOTISM
IN SCOTLAND

Princeton Studies in History, 11

John Maitland

OF THIRLESTANE
AND THE FOUNDATION OF THE
STEWART
DESPOTISM IN SCOTLAND

BY MAURICE LEE, JR.

PRINCETON, NEW JERSEY

PRINCETON UNIVERSITY PRESS

1959

✧

Publication of this book has been aided by the Research Fund of
Princeton University and
by the Ford Foundation program
to support publication, through university presses,
of works in the humanities
and social sciences

✧

Printed in the United States of America by
Princeton University Press, Princeton, New Jersey

TO MY FRIEND AND COLLEAGUE,

ELMER A. BELLER,

WITH AFFECTION AND RESPECT.

ACKNOWLEDGMENTS

Grateful acknowledgment is made to the following:

To Princeton University for its generosity with both time and money;

To the Ford Foundation for a grant which helped make publication of this work possible;

To the numerous libraries in which I have worked: the Princeton University Library; the Library of Congress; the New York Public Library; the British Museum; the Public Record Office; the National Library of Scotland; the Scottish Record Office; the Edinburgh University Library; the Library of the city of Edinburgh. I should like to acknowledge especially the great help given me by Mr. Imbrie of the Scottish Record Office;

To the Dowager Countess of Lauderdale for permission to reproduce the portrait of John Maitland, and to the Board of Trustees for the National Galleries of Scotland for permission to reproduce the portrait of James VI;

To His Grace the Duke of Hamilton for permission to examine the Hamilton Manuscripts at Lennoxlove and Holyroodhouse;

To the Dowager Countess of Lauderdale and the Hon. Patrick Maitland, M.P., Master of Lauderdale, for arranging access to the Manuscripts at Thirlestane Castle;

To Sir James Fergusson, Keeper of the Scottish Record Office, Professor W. Croft Dickinson and Dr. Gordon Donaldson of Edinburgh University for their helpful suggestions and advice;

To my colleagues Professors Joseph R. Strayer, E. Harris Harbison, and Jerome Blum of Princeton University, who read the manuscript in whole or in part, to its considerable benefit;

ACKNOWLEDGMENT

To the graduate students' thesis-writing seminar, presided over by my colleague Professor Robert R. Palmer, which subjected portions of the manuscript to a critical inspection;

And finally to my wife, who put up with the usual inconveniences of academic research and writing without complaint and provided encouragement throughout.

Maurice Lee, Jr.

Princeton, New Jersey
October 1958

CONTENTS

CONTENTS

ABBREVIATIONS

APS T. Thomson, ed., *The Acts of the Parliament of Scotland*, III, IV (London 1814-1816)

BUK T. Thomson, ed., *Acts and Proceedings of the General Assemblies of the Kirk of Scotland* (*Booke of the Universall Kirk*), II-III (Edinburgh 1840-1845)

Border Papers J. Bain, ed., *Calendar of Letters and Papers Relating to the Affairs of the Borders of England and Scotland*, 2 vols. (Edinburgh 1894-1896)

BM British Museum

Calderwood D. Calderwood, *The History of the Kirk of Scotland*, ed. Rev. T. Thomson, Wodrow Society Publication, II-V (Edinburgh 1843-1844)

CSP SCOT *Calendar of State Papers Relating to Scotland and Mary Queen of Scots*, II, ed. J. Bain (Edinburgh 1900) ; III-IX, ed. W. K. Boyd (Edinburgh and Glasgow 1903-1915) ; X, ed. Boyd and H. W. Meikle (Edinburgh 1936) ; XI, ed. A. I. Cameron (Edinburgh 1936) ; XII, ed. M. S. Giuseppi (Edinburgh 1952)

CSP SPANISH M. A. S. Hume, ed., *Calendar of Letters and Papers Relating to English Affairs . . . in the Archives of Simancas*, III-IV (London 1896-1899)

Hamilton MSS Manuscripts in the possession of His Grace the Duke of Hamilton, preserved at Lennoxlove and at Holyroodhouse

HMC Historical Manuscripts Commission

NLS National Library of Scotland, Edinburgh

PRO Great Britain, Public Record Office, London

RMS J. M. Thomson, ed., *Registrum Magni Sigilli Regum Scotorum*, IV-VI (Edinburgh 1886-1890)

RPCS D. Masson, ed., *The Register of the Privy Council of Scotland*, 1st series, vols. III-VI; 2nd series, vol. I (Edinburgh 1880-1899)

Salisbury Papers Historical Manuscripts Commission, *Calendar of the Manuscripts of the . . . Marquis of Salisbury*, III-V, XIII (London 1889-1915)

ABBREVIATIONS

SHS Scottish Historical Society publication
SHR *Scottish Historical Review*
SRO Scottish Record Office, Edinburgh

Except for poetry, where the original orthography has been retained, all quoted material in this work has been modernized and standardized with respect to spelling, punctuation, and capitalization.

JOHN MAITLAND OF THIRLESTANE

AND THE FOUNDATION OF THE STEWART DESPOTISM

IN SCOTLAND

ORKNEY
IS.

H E B R I D E S

SKYE

MORAY
Inverness•
Strathbogie
Glenlivat•
Slaines

Aberdeen•

ARGYLL

HIGHLANDS

ANGUS•

Dundee•
•Arbroath

Perth•
St. Andrews•
Falkland•
FIFE

Stirling•
Dunfermline•
Dumbarton•
Musselburgh
Linlithgow•
Coldingham•
Glasgow•
Edinburgh•
EAST
MARCH

Lauder•
Berwick•
Kelso•
MID MARCH
Jedburgh•

ARRAN

Ayr•

WEST MARCH
LIDDESDALE
Dumfries•

•Carlisle

0   10   20   30   40
SCALE OF MILES

CHAPTER 1

SCOTLAND IN THE LATE
SIXTEENTH CENTURY

In October 1589 King James VI of Scotland set out on one of the few romantic adventures of his life. He sailed for Denmark, personally to fetch home his youthful bride, the Princess Anne. The king's departure was a well-kept secret; in the proclamation which he left behind for the edification of his subjects, James explained why. "As I kept it generally close (secret) from all men, so I say, upon my honor, I kept it so from the chancellor, as I was never wont to do any secrets of my weightiest affairs, two reasons moving me thereto. First, because I knew that, if I had . . . [informed him], he . . . [would have] been blamed of putting it in my head, which had not been his duty (for it becomes no subjects to give princes advice in such matters) ; and therefore, remembering what envious and unjust burden he daily bears, for leading me, by the nose as it were, to all his appetites, as if I were an unreasonable creature, or a bairn that could do nothing of myself, I thought . . . [it unfair] to be the occasion of the heaping of further unjust slander upon his head."[1]

The chancellor who thus led the king by the nose was John Maitland of Thirlestane. He was the younger brother of the famous William Maitland of Lethington, the "secretary Maitland" of Mary Queen of Scots, and his historical reputation has been overshadowed by William's spectacular career and close association with the most romantic figure in Scottish history. This eclipse is unjust, because John Maitland was a highly successful statesman, while his brother was a brilliant failure.

[1] RPCS, IV, 428-429.

John Maitland became the principal political adviser of James VI at the moment when the young king assumed the chief responsibility for the conduct of the Scottish government. This was a crucial juncture in Scottish affairs. Protestantism had been dominant in Scotland for a quarter-century; but the full consequences of the religious revolution had not yet worked themselves out. The power of the crown was at a low ebb; but its wearer was intelligent, and his future prospects, if he could realize on them, were dazzling: Queen Elizabeth was over fifty, and he had the best claim to her crown when she died.

Maitland was to remain at the king's elbow for almost ten years. He played a vital part in shaping the mind of King James; it was he who gave to the king his first lessons in what James was later to call "king-craft." Even more important was Maitland's part in reorganizing and revitalizing the institutions of the Scottish state. During most of his career as the king's chief political adviser Maitland was the unchallenged head of the Scottish administrative structure. When he assumed control, this mechanism was functioning very feebly indeed; by the time of his death Scotland, for the first time in its history, had an administration that was in some measure professional. By creating this administration, Maitland laid the foundation for that despotism which was to characterize the government of Scotland in the seventeenth century, and which was not finally to be overturned until the revolution of 1688. Many of the political and administrative changes Maitland set in train were not fully visible by the time of his death. This circumstance helps to explain the neglect he has suffered at the hands of historians. The following pages represent an attempt to do justice, however belatedly, to the achievements of one of the ablest and most constructive of Scottish statesmen.

ii.

The Scotland of Maitland and King James was in many respects the Scotland of the Middle Ages—a poor and backward country, poorer and more backward by Tudor and Valois standards than she had been by those of Plantagenet and

Capetian. The Scottish kings faced much the same problems as their English and French counterparts, but they had not solved them. There was no Henry VII or Louis XI in Scotland, but only a James IV, who wore a hair shirt and died gloriously at Flodden, on a field that should never have been fought. The Stewart kings were not only incapable; they were also incredibly unlucky. Between the accession of Robert III in 1390 and that of Charles I in 1625, every Scottish king, without exception, came to the throne as a minor. These frequent, and often lengthy, minorities naturally weakened the power of the crown; they also provided ample inducement to England to attempt to reverse the verdict of Bannockburn. The constant wars with England impoverished the crown and kept the kings dependent on their nobility for military force. The consequence of all this was that the power of the aristocracy, collectively, and occasionally, individually—though this was rare—was greater than that of the king. The most that the king could hope for, under such circumstances, was to ally himself with one aristocratic faction in order to destroy another, as James II had done in the case of the house of Douglas in the 1450's.

The power the aristocracy thus possessed was preserved by four factors: their control of the land, the pattern of family relationship, the inefficiency of the institutions of the central government, and the weakness of the Scottish middle class. Land was by far the most important source of wealth in Scotland, and the nobles possessed so much of it that the royal resources and the royal domain were not great enough for the kings to cope with them successfully. This state of affairs was perpetuated by the frequent royal minorities, during which the aristocratic faction in power enriched itself at the expense of the crown. The king had the right to revoke all grants made during his minority when he came of age, but it was not always politically feasible to enforce these revocations. The royal resources were further circumscribed by the fact that taxation was still regarded as an exceptional measure, to be employed only in emergencies. Furthermore, the few taxes that were voted, were collected in a manner which has been compared unfavorably with that existing in twelfth-century England.[2] Other sources of revenue, such as the customs, also failed to produce much income, owing to the poverty of the kingdom. The crown was thus constantly tottering on the edge of bankruptcy. It could hardly meet its daily expenses, much less afford the standing army which might have overawed the nobles and at the same time made them less necessary to the state.

On his own land the noble was master, owing to the prevailing system of tenure. "A grant of barony made the landowner the military leader of the men upon his estates, and their judge, with powers of life and death. A grant of regality went much further. It 'took as much out of the Crown as the sovereign could give. It was, in fact, investing the grantee in the sovereignty of the territory.' "[3] There was little that a royal official could do under these circumstances, and, indeed, by the sixteenth century most of the local royal offices, especially that of sheriff, had fallen into the hands of the aristocrats themselves, or of their hangers-on, on an hereditary basis.[4]

The noble's power was further enhanced by the fact that his connection extended, not merely to the tenants on his own estates, but also to all the members of his family. These family ties were particularly important in the highlands, where the head of the clan was generally far more influential than the landlord, in those cases where the two positions did not coincide. Clan sentiment was almost as powerful in the turbulent border areas, and was strong even in the comparatively settled and law-abiding lowlands. Nor was it confined to blood relations. John Knox, of all people, once performed an important political service for the earl of Bothwell, because "my grandfather (i.e., great-grandfather), goodsire (grandfather), and father have served your lordship's predecessors, and some of

2 R. S. Rait, *The Scottish Parliament before the Union of the Crowns* (London 1901), p. 12, n. 1.

3 I. F. Grant, *The Social and Economic Development of Scotland before 1603* (Edinburgh 1930), p. 174. In the interior citation in this passage Miss Grant is quoting Cosmo Innes.

4 For the position of the sheriff in the sixteenth century see W. C. Dickinson, ed., *The Sheriff Court Book of Fife 1515-1522*, SHS, 3rd series, XII (Edinburgh 1928); and C. A. Malcolm, "The Office of Sheriff in Scotland," part iii, SHR, XX (1922-1923), 290-311.

them have died under their standards; and this is a part of the obligation of our Scottish kindness (kinship)."[5]

The greatest nobles, therefore, were those who combined extensive landholdings with a wide family connection. First and foremost stood the house of Hamilton, earls of Arran, the next heirs to the throne should the Stewart line fail, immensely powerful in western Scotland. Not far behind them stood the great highland clan leaders, the earls of Huntly (Gordon) and Argyll (Campbell), whose power lay partly in the lowlands as well. In a similar position, though by no means as powerful as Huntly and Argyll, were the great border clan chiefs— Maxwells and Johnstones in the west, Kers, Scotts, and Hepburns (earls of Bothwell) in the center, Humes in the east. Then there were the great lowland families: the Douglases, not so powerful as they had been in the fifteenth century, but still holding two earldoms, Angus and Morton; the Kennedys, earls of Cassillis, the great family of the south-west; the Erskines, who held the ancient earldom of Mar and whose connection with the royal family was very close; as well as a great many only slightly less important earls and lords whose names it would be tedious to enumerate. Finally, there were the king's own kin, the Stewarts, holders of the earldoms of Athol, Lennox, and Orkney, as well as a good many less distinguished titles.

The king's poverty was his chief handicap in dealing with these over-mighty subjects, but it was by no means his only one. The Scottish administrative machine was extremely inefficient by sixteenth-century standards. The key institution was the privy council, appointed by the crown. The council's powers were theoretically very wide. It was responsible for the day-to-day administration of the government. It controlled the primitive and moribund Scottish Parliament by the peculiar device known as the committee of the articles. This committee was chosen as soon as Parliament met. Parliament then recessed, and the committee prepared a list of enactments, which Parliament was called upon to ratify. Ratification was

[5] W. C. Dickinson, ed., *John Knox's History of the Reformation in Scotland*, II (New York 1950), 38.

virtually automatic. Parliament had thus abdicated its functions to this committee, which by the later sixteenth century had become the only channel by which a measure could be brought before Parliament.[6] It must not be imagined, however, that the committee itself served as a miniature legislature. Scottish parliamentary sessions were very short—that of 1587, for instance, lasted only seventeen days, and this was by no means unusual. The committee of the articles had no time to formulate legislation itself; it simply accepted or amended that presented to it by the government. The methods of choosing the membership of this committee varied in the sixteenth century, but the official element was always predominant, and, indeed, the official record of the Parliament of 1600, "by a suggestive slip of the pen, refers to the lords of the articles as the lords of council."[7]

Such a subservient and easily controlled institution as the Scottish Parliament might easily become an engine of despotism, and this came to pass in the seventeenth century. But as long as the crown was weak, the great theoretical powers of Parliament, and the crown's control over it, mattered very little. Its enactments could be, and were, flouted with impunity. So were those of the convention of estates. This body was a kind of informal Parliament (or greatly expanded *curia regis*), which had virtually all the powers of Parliament, including the right to vote taxes, and to interpret—and thus modify—acts of Parliament, on a temporary basis, until Parliament should meet.[8] The crown possessed ample means of obtaining the legislation it desired. The great problem was not legislation, but enforcement.

In this matter of enforcement the Scottish judicial structure was not much help. Civil cases were in the hands of the court of session, or college of justice, established by James V in 1532. Its fifteen senators were appointed by the king; the government's control was further assured by its right to appoint three or four "extraordinary lords of session" to sit with the regular members, and by the privy council's right to "decide

[6] R. S. Rait, *The Parliaments of Scotland* (Glasgow 1924), p. 373.
[7] *Ibid.*, p. 371.　　　　　　　　[8] *Ibid.*, pp. 151-153.

8

whether a particular case should be dealt with by it . . . and to interpose if, in its judgment, justice had not been done."[9] The crown's control of civil justice was thus fairly extensive. It had much less power over criminal justice. By the sixteenth century the office of justiciar had become hereditary in the earls of Argyll. Since the office of sheriff had also become hereditary, the crown could not depend on these officials, over whom it had very little control; furthermore, the sheriffs' power over the ordinary criminal courts in the shires was declining owing to the practice of making grants of regality to the landed class. This meant that the normal machinery for the administration of criminal justice, save in the burghs, was in the hands of the most lawless elements in the country. The only crime outside the competence of the justiciar and his subordinates was treason. The king's only recourse was the exercise of his right, as feudal superior, to sit in judgment himself, as James VI frequently did, and to rely as heavily as possible on the justice clerk. This official was responsible for the preparation of cases to be tried at the justice eyres. He could at least see that a case was brought into court; if it were mishandled, an appeal could always be taken to king and council. Once a case was formally brought to the attention of the council, it could be dealt with, generally by outlawing the offender—putting him to the horn, in the Scottish phrase. He would then have to find sureties for redress and for future good behavior before he was "relaxed from the horn." The council spent a good deal of time dealing with such cases, as the pages of its *Register* bear witness. The whole process of criminal justice was both cumbersome and inefficient. Thoroughgoing reform was long overdue.

The king's council thus dominated the executive, legislative, and judicial activities of the Scottish government, and whoever controlled the council in effect controlled the government. Such control was worth having, and was often bitterly contested. But in actual fact the powers of the government were nowhere near so extensive as they were in theory. For one thing, there was a shortage of competent officials. This was not merely owing

9 J. Mackinnon, *The Constitutional History of Scotland* (London 1924), p. 252.

to the poverty of the crown; the trained lawyers and bureau-crats simply were not available in sufficient numbers, even if there had been money to pay them. The Reformation, in many ways so beneficial to Scotland, in this respect made a bad situation still worse. Before the Reformation the crown had depended very heavily on the Roman Catholic church for its officials at all levels of government; the list of ecclesiastical statesmen in the annals of medieval Scotland is long, and extends down to that Cardinal Beaton whom Henry VIII thought it worthwhile to have assassinated during the minority of Mary Queen of Scots. The triumph of Protestantism thus deprived the crown of a major source of official talent, and of an important means of rewarding such talent as did exist.

A more serious weakness than the lack of officials was the total absence of reliable armed force. For its armies the crown was dependent on a kind of national levy. Every able-bodied man between the ages of sixteen and sixty was obliged to turn out, fully equipped with weapons and food, on the royal summons. In practice this meant that the men would turn out only at the behest of the local magnate, their landlord and judge. Even the towns were not always dependable. King James was often saved from the unwelcome attentions of some noble ruffian by the loyalty of the burgesses of Edinburgh, but there were times when they, too, rioted against the government's policy. All attempts to form a permanent standing army, or even a royal bodyguard of any size, foundered on lack of money and the implacable opposition of the nobility.[10]

The magnates, therefore, had no objection to the theoretically extensive authority of the crown: in practice the king had virtually no way of by-passing them and exerting any permanent control over their subordinates. The crown's authority in local affairs was so limited that it sometimes could not prevent the illegal practice of electing lairds and noblemen as provosts of burghs, even when the burgh itself complained. In brief, the political, administrative, and social structure of Scot-

[10] See, for instance, A. Lang, *A History of Scotland from the Roman Occupation*, 3rd ed. (London 1924), II, 24-25 for the plan of 1556.

land was still feudal. Very much in evidence was one of the consequences of feudalism, namely, private warfare.

No aspect of Scottish life is better known than the incessant, bloodthirsty feuding and lawlessness of this over-powerful nobility. In the sixteenth century the feuding took the form, less of organized private campaigns, though these were not unknown, than of sudden brawls which arose by chance, varied by occasional murder plots. One example might be quoted. There was a feud between the families of Sandilands and Graham, in the course of which John Graham of Halyards, a violent-tempered member of the court of session, known as "my lord Little-Justice," was killed. In January 1595, about two years after his death, the following occurred in Edinburgh: "Yesterday afternoon, after the king went to the Tolbooth, Sir James Sandilands, returning from him down the street, met Montrose [the earl of Montrose, head of the house of Graham], with whom the chancellor [John Maitland] was going up to the king to the Tolbooth. . . . For the feud of Mr. John Graham's slaughter, both parties began the fray, shooting 40 or 50 pistols and fighting with swords very hotly until the town parted them. . . . The chancellor and Montrose sought to stay it. For this I see no sign of justice, though some townsmen are hurt. . . . The master of Graham, Montrose's son, has fled."[11] This incident was by no means unusual; the fact that it took place in the presence of the highest legal officer in the kingdom, only a few yards from the building in which the king was sitting dispensing justice, simply emphasizes the fact that the usual generalizations made about the lawlessness of sixteenth-century Scotland are by no means exaggerated.

The burgesses of Edinburgh were not pleased by the aristocratic brawls that erupted in their streets, but there was little they could do about them. The Scottish middle class, though growing in size and wealth in the sixteenth century, was still a relatively unimportant part of the community. Scottish commerce and manufacturing lagged far behind those of England and the other economically advanced areas of western Europe

11 CSP SCOT, XI, 527.

—so far behind, in fact, that a great many of the residents in the burghs themselves depended on agriculture for their existence.[12]

There were two principal types of towns, the royal burghs, and the burghs of regality and barony. The royal burghs were by far the more important; there were thirty-five of them about the middle of the sixteenth century.[13] These were the towns that paid taxes to the government; they had a monopoly of foreign trade, of carrying on crafts, and of fairs and markets. Burghs of regality and barony served as local markets only. "So stringent was the monopoly that until 1517 not a single legal fair or market was held outside a royal burgh. One was instituted between 1517 and 1570, and five more between 1571 and 1603."[14]

The merchant oligarchies which dominated the royal burghs were determined to preserve this monopoly, and also to keep the growing craft guilds in a subordinate position within the burghs, and by and large they were successful, thanks to the support of the government. One important consequence was that Scotland remained industrially backward. The rural "domestic system" which flourished in England and elsewhere in western Europe, and which was the principal system of production before the Industrial Revolution, could not develop in Scotland. A measure of the relative weakness of the Scottish middle class is the fact that, on those rare occasions when a national tax was levied, the royal burghs paid but one sixth of the total.

The weakness of the middle class, taken together with the meager resources of the crown, Scottish clannishness, and the great power of the Scottish aristocracy as landlords, amply accounts for the nobles' dominant position. But by the later sixteenth century there were present in Scottish life certain new factors which would bring about a serious weakening in that position, and ultimately reduce the nobles to dependency on the crown. Scotland was not to go the way of Poland or the Holy Roman Empire.

[12] Grant, *Social and Economic Development*, p. 306.
[13] *Ibid.*, pp. 374-375.   [14] *Ibid.*, p. 368.

One of these new factors was an important change in the system of land tenure, with the widespread adoption of the feu farm. A feu was a permanent and heritable lease, and was calculated to meet the chief grievance of the Scottish tenant, insecurity of tenure. It first appeared in the fourteenth century, but did not become widely used until the middle decades of the sixteenth. Church and crown lands were most extensively feued, but a certain amount took place on the estates of the great lords as well.[15]

Among the consequences of the feuing movement was the security of position obtained by large numbers of lesser landholders, who became much less dependent on the goodwill of the local magnate. It virtually turned them into members of the class known in Scotland as lairds—people like the Maitlands. It is difficult to generalize about the lairds as a class, since its members varied very widely in wealth and power, as well as in outlook and behavior. Some, like Douglas of Lochleven, Scott of Buccleuch, or the laird of Johnstone, were as powerful as most earls; others were poverty-stricken smallholders who were often little better than robbers. What they had in common was a legal position: they held land directly of the king, but they were not lords in the sense that they were not summoned individually to Parliament. Their feudal allegiance was to the king, but this did not necessarily mean that they obeyed him. Many of them were much more closely tied to some great lord through family connection; many a laird of the name of Douglas or Hamilton would follow the earl of Angus or of Arran rather than the king. This was particularly true in the highlands and on the border, where clan sentiment was especially strong. Many a laird obeyed no higher law than his own inclination.[16] But many others were becoming heartily sick of the chronic disorder, and would be willing to support a government which seriously attempted to put an end to it.

---

[15] For feu farming see *ibid.*, pp. 265-286.

[16] See, for instance, the account in James Fergusson, *Lowland Lairds* (London, n.d.), pp. 28-43, of Alexander Forrester of the Torwood, who kept Stirlingshire in turmoil for the last thirty years of the sixteenth century.

Much more significant for the future of Scotland was the coming of the Reformation. In the middle decades of the sixteenth century the Roman Catholic church, wealthy and corrupt, was overthrown and a modified form of Calvinism took its place. Protestantism in Scotland, as in many other areas, drew its chief strength and most of its supporters from the ranks of the lairds and the middle class. The great majority of the Scottish towns became solidly Protestant. So did the majority of the lowland and border lairds; the highlands, on the other hand, remained predominantly Catholic, as did a good many of the high aristocracy. A number of great nobles did turn Protestant, though in most cases from greed rather than conviction: they hoped to be able to secure their already considerable hold on the property of the church.

The question of the ultimate disposition of the immense holdings of the ancient church, and the closely allied matter of the polity of the new church, were the two most serious issues raised by the triumph of Protestantism. John Knox and his followers naturally wanted all the property of the old church to pass to the new, chiefly in order to further Knox's laudable charitable and educational projects. But Knox met with an implacable resistance from those very aristocrats whose conversion to the new dispensation had made the overthrow of the old church possible. These nobles wanted the property in question for themselves.

The nobility in fact already possessed a good deal of that property. Beginning in the 1470's, the highest offices in the Scottish church had increasingly become the monopoly of the great aristocratic families, through the appointment of one of their members as bishop, abbot, or (in the case of the monasteries) commendator.[17] The monasteries in particular suffered from this since many of the commendators were laymen, royal favorites, or royal bastards, whose only interest in the monas-

[17] A commendator was one who held a church benefice *in commendam*, that is, in trust or stewardship. Originally commendators were appointed merely to manage a benefice during a vacancy. Later, such appointments became a device whereby a prelate could hold a plurality of livings, or a layman acquire the income of a benefice, while the spiritual office was performed by another on his behalf.

14

tery was the size of its income. The system of feuing made it possible for the great families to make their possession, for all practical purposes, permanent: a scion of a noble house, having obtained appointment to a benefice, would feu its temporalities to his relatives for a very low rent.[18] This process reached its height in the 1550's, when the higher clergy began to fear that the triumph of Protestantism might lead to their extrusion and the confiscation of church lands.[19]

The nobility had no intention of surrendering these lucrative acquisitions to Knox and his cohorts; in fact, they planned to add to their gains by engrossing whatever property of the ancient church had hitherto eluded their grasp. For this purpose the great majority of the nobility, Catholic and Protestant alike, took care to be on the winning side in the brief civil war of 1559-1560 which overthrew that church. But they recognized that something had to be done for the Protestant clergy. The result was a settlement reached in the winter of 1561-1562, shortly after Mary began her personal rule in Scotland. There were to be no confiscations of any kind. The present holders of benefices were confirmed in their possession, but one third of the income was to be paid to the crown, which would support the clergy from this sum, and use any surplus for the expenses of government. Feuars of church lands could obtain confirmation of their feu charters by the crown by paying a fee to the treasury. This arrangement was most distasteful to Knox since it left so much in the hands of the ungodly; it had the further disadvantage of leaving undetermined what would happen to the benefices after the deaths of the present holders. What in fact happened was that the crown assumed the right to appoint successors. Monastic lands came to be treated as nonhereditary fiefs, to which, nevertheless, the heir of the previous holder had a strong claim. The new church soon gave up any serious effort to obtain anything from these save

18 Ample evidence of this statement may be found in the pages of the *Register of the Abbreviates of Feu Charters of Kirk Lands* (SRO).

19 On the question of church lands see Grant, *Social and Economic Development*, pp. 219-27; R. K. Hannay, "On the Church Lands at the Reformation," SHR, XVI (1918-1919), 52-72, and "A Study in Reformation History," SHR, XXIII (1925-1926), 18-33.

the thirds to which it was entitled by law. But the matter of the bishoprics was more complicated, because here the question of the government of the church was involved.

Knox and his friends had no objection to the office of bishop as such, but they had serious objections to the individuals who occupied the Scottish bishoprics. The crisis over the question of bishops began, not with the triumph of the Reformation in the civil war of 1559-1560, but with the end of the civil war of the 1570's which marked the final ruin of Mary's cause. The so-called Concordat of Leith of 1572, arranged shortly before the death of Knox and the end of the war, reflected accurately enough the kirk's attitude at the time. There was no attack on the position of bishops as such; it was simply declared that the kirk as a whole must approve their appointment, and that, with respect to spiritual questions, they were subject to the jurisdiction of the General Assembly of the kirk.[20] But as the decade of the 1570's wore on, the attitude of the kirk began to change. The earl of Morton, regent for the boy King James from 1572 to 1578, used his control of church appointments to enrich his own relatives. As Andrew Lang puts it, "Under Morton . . . the kirk was being reduced to the same condition as the church before the Reformation. Ignorance, profligacy, secular robbery . . . of ecclesiastical revenues, were all returning."[21] This situation opened the door to Andrew Melvill, who, after his return to Scotland in 1574, assumed the place of leadership in the kirk left vacant by the death of Knox. Melvill was, if anything, even more combative and quick-tempered than Knox; he was also considerably more radical in his views of church organization. Melvill believed that episcopacy was unscriptural and ought to be abolished; in its place he advocated the establishment of the presbyterian system. Gradually Melvill converted a number of the younger ministers to his views. Thus was raised a question which was pregnant with future

[20] The General Assembly was the supreme governing body of the kirk. It consisted of both divines and laymen, and met at least once a year, sometimes twice.

[21] Lang, *History*, II, 253.

trouble, and which was not finally to be settled for over a century.[22]

The kirk's attitude toward the Scottish government was generally one of acute suspicion and hostility. The ministers were highly critical of Queen Mary and King James, and they insisted that their criticisms be unquestioningly accepted. Knox and his fellows believed that they were the chosen of God, that in the pulpit God's spirit worked through them, that when they spoke, king and commoner alike must tremble and obey. Their attitude is best summarized in Andrew Melvill's famous outburst to James: "There is [sic] two kings and two kingdoms in Scotland. There is Christ Jesus the King, and his kingdom the kirk, whose subject King James the Sixth is, and of whose kingdom not a king, nor a lord, nor a head, but a member!"[23] In short, the leadership of the kirk believed in theocracy, and only very occasionally, as during the regency of the earl of Moray in the late 1560's, did it find a government with which it was disposed to cooperate.

Nevertheless, despite its balkiness and intransigence on many questions, the kirk was a potential ally of the crown, because it had even more grievances against the Scottish nobility. The ministers favored law and order; the aristocracy was the most lawless element in the state. The ministers wanted the property of the ancient church; the aristocracy stood in their way. The nobility was the class least susceptible to the moral influence of the preachers: sincere Protestants like the regent Moray were the exception rather than the rule among this class. One authority has summed it up this way: "However much the Reformation was dependent on feudalism and influenced by it, there was another aspect of it which led it necessarily to resist the full implications of feudal society. There could be no lasting alliance on the nobles' terms. The Reformation was the revolutionary force within a relatively static and feudally re-

---

[22] On the question of episcopacy see G. Donaldson, "The Polity of the Scottish Church, 1560-1600," *Records of the Scottish Church History Society*, XI (1955), 212-226.

[23] R. Pitcairn, ed., *The Autobiography and Diary of Mr. James Melvill*, Wodrow Society publication (Edinburgh 1842), p. 370.

tarded society. It tended to become the cause of the middle class, the lairds and burgesses, and to awaken something more than preoccupations with monopolies and vested interests. It crossed feudal barriers and feudal ties."[24] And so, as Andrew Melvill's nephew wrote in his autobiography under date of the year 1594, "After good Archibald, earl of Angus [who died in 1588] . . . I . . . [knew of none] of the nobility in Scotland that I could communicate my mind with anent public affairs, let be to have a dealing with in action."[25]

If it could be persuaded to abate its almost chronic suspicion of the government, the kirk could be extremely useful to the crown. The moral fervor the kirk aroused in the majority of its followers, the intrepidity of the ministers in standing up for what they believed to be right, and the influence wielded by these ministers over their flocks, all helped to undermine the position of the nobles because the latter could no longer count on the undivided loyalty of their followers. Knox, Melvill, and their cohorts were quite as ready to denounce publicly any nobleman who displeased them as they were to attack King James. The questions still undetermined as James reached years of discretion were whether the crown and the kirk could come to an agreement with each other at all, and, if they could, on what terms: the crown had no desire simply to change masters.

Another important consequence of the Reformation was a revolution in Scottish foreign policy. Ever since the days of John Balliol and Edward I, England had been the "auld enemy" and France the "auld ally." Scotland had first become conscious of itself as a nation under the repeated hammering of the southern invaders, and Bannockburn is still regarded as Scotland's finest hour. But Protestantism triumphed in Scotland with the aid of Protestant England, and against the wishes of Catholic France, whose troops had to be expelled with English aid. In a religious age a common religious attitude proved to be stronger than the memory of old and recent wrongs. Queen Mary was Catholic and pro-French; her downfall in

[24] D. Nobbs, *England and Scotland 1560-1707* (London 1952), p. 34.
[25] *Autobiography of James Melvill*, p. 315.

1567, followed by the destruction of her supporters in 1573, sealed the victory of the Protestant, pro-English faction, and led ultimately, thanks to Elizabeth's childlessness, to the union of the crowns of the two countries.

But even if that union had never taken place—and it was by no means certain until very late in the day—this fundamental shift in Scottish foreign policy would have meant far more to Scotland than simply the exchange of one ally for another. The major consequence was that after 1560 Scotland was involved in no foreign war. The military threat to the kingdom was ended. This meant that the crown was far less dependent than before on the nobles, who were no longer indispensable to the defense of the kingdom, as they had been in the past. It also meant that, sooner or later, as relations between the two governments improved, the English would abandon their traditional policy of subsidizing a faction among the Scottish aristocracy in order to weaken and embarrass, or even to overthrow, the king. In a sense the triumph of the Protestant faction in the civil war of 1559-1560 had marked the culmination of that policy. With that success the English government gradually changed its objective. Its purpose after 1560 was not to rule over Scotland, not to maintain perpetual turmoil there, but to create a friendly, that is, a Protestant, government. But though the English goal changed, their methods did not, chiefly because these methods seemed to be the most effective means of dealing with the threat represented by the Catholic Queen Mary. Even after Mary's fall Elizabeth's government persisted in this path, continued to support the Protestant faction among the nobility. It was incumbent on King James to persuade his "dearest sister" to stop supporting his Protestant magnates and to support him instead. If this could be done, the king's ability to deal successfully with his fractious subjects would be greatly increased. Then, if ever, would be the time to reduce the overblown power of the nobility, and to try to achieve something like the power wielded by the other princes of western Europe.

King James, as he came to govern his kingdom, was thus faced with a tremendous challenge and a tremendous opportunity. His success in dealing with both, and in obtaining the coveted English throne as well, was impressive. His chief ally in the process, the man who formulated the policy and devised the methods of carrying it out, was the chancellor who led him by the nose, John Maitland of Thirlestane.

JAMES VI IN 1595

"THE GREAT GOD,
THE SECRETARY"

JOHN MAITLAND was born in 1543, the second son of Sir Richard Maitland of Lethington. The Maitlands, an old family of no particular distinction, had long been settled in the area between Edinburgh and the border.[1] Sir Richard Maitland was in many ways a remarkable man, quite different from the ordinary sixteenth-century laird. He was, indeed, typical of a small but steadily increasing number of his class in that he was trained in the law, and, as any conscientious lawyer would, he deplored the disorder and violence which characterized Scottish life. But he was most untypical in that he was also a poet, albeit not a very good one. His poetry was mostly topical, and is therefore worth some consideration since the father's ideas had a good deal of influence on the policies of his two famous sons.

The most pervasive idea to be found in Sir Richard's poetry is his concern for the public welfare—his patriotism, in the best sense of that much-abused word. He was hostile to foreigners, both French and English; he deplored the civil wars which wracked Scotland as a consequence of the Reformation, not only because they were unpleasant in themselves but also because they gave France and England a chance to meddle in Scottish affairs. Chiefly responsible for this unfortunate situation, in Sir Richard's opinion, were the Scottish nobles, the country's natural leaders, who had completely lost sight of the common good, often for the worst of motives.

[1] The Maitland family pedigree, compiled by G. H. Rogers-Harrison, Windsor Herald, is in J. J. Howard, ed., *Miscellanea Genealogica et Heraldica*, II (London 1876), 205-213.

> Nowder for king nor quenis authorite
> Ze strive, bot for particularite,

he wrote, during the civil war of the 1570's.[2]

Sir Richard was himself seriously damaged in more ways than one by the civil wars, but he came gradually to realize that the chief victims were the common people. He had a genuine sympathy for the "poor commons of this land." But he was far from being a social reformer. The proper remedy for the social evils with which Scotland was afflicted was action on the part of the upper classes. It never occurred to Sir Richard to question the existing social structure. In fact, if anything, he was a backward-looking man; it was the happy past rather than the future which claimed his attention. This nostalgic attitude is attributable in part to the fact that he was already an old man when he began to write—sixty at least, and rapidly going blind as well. But age and infirmity are not the sole explanations of Sir Richard's conservatism. He was a cautious man who seems to have disliked the hurly-burly of politics; he never became a prominent public figure until his eldest son William began his meteoric rise to power.

We know how Sir Richard thought a well-advised courtier or official should behave; he wrote a Polonius-like poem of advice on the subject. It is full of the usual platitudes: keep good company, tell the truth, avoid flattery, gambling, and pride, be loyal to the prince. Among these unexceptionable remarks there is one caution which so well sums up Sir Richard's attitude to political activity that it is worth quoting in full:

> Bewar in geving of ane hie counsale
> In materis greit and doutsum speciallie
> Quhilk be the working of ye warld may faill
> Thocht it seme neuer sa apperantlie.
> Behauld ye warldis instabilitie
> That neuer still intill ane stait dois byde
> Bot changeand ay as dois the mone and sie
> He rewlis weill that weill in court can gyde.[3]

[2] "Of Union amongst the Lords," *The Maitland Folio Manuscript*, ed. W. A. Craigie for the Scottish Text Society, i (Edinburgh 1919), 311. For the civil war, see below, pp. 31-35.

[3] "The Laird of Lethington's Counsel to his Son being in the Court," *The*

Here speaks the cautious man, the man afraid to take chances, to accept responsibility. This was an attitude which none of Sir Richard's sons would adopt, fundamentally because none of them agreed with their father that

To gouerne all and reull be not our bent.[4]

They firmly believed that it was.

If his sons did not follow Sir Richard's advice with respect to the desirability of political activity, they did share his view of the most important political issue of the day—religion. Sir Richard was a pious man and a good enough Protestant, but he firmly believed that religious questions should be kept out of politics as much as possible. If they could not be kept out, they must be treated simply as one factor in the total political situation. If they were permitted to become the chief concern of politicians, the result would be turmoil and bloodshed. In short, Sir Richard was a *politique* through and through. Such an attitude was most unusual in sixteenth-century Scotland; this, and his zeal for the public good, were Sir Richard's most important legacy to his sons.

This retiring, cautious, and conservative man must have felt considerable shock at the pushing ambition and dazzling political audacity of his eldest son, William Maitland of Lethington, "the great god, the secretary," as Knox's amanuensis Richard Bannatyne called him.[5] After Lethington's death Sir Richard wrote to Queen Elizabeth, "Very displeasing hath been to me the late proceedings of my son."[6] While it may be argued that this letter was a piece of special pleading, since Sir Richard was asking a favor of Elizabeth, to whom Lethington's behavior had been equally displeasing, there is no doubt that temperamentally, and on many substantive issues as well, father and son were poles apart. Yet it is also true that Lethington inherited some of his father's most important ideas.

Maitland Quarto Manuscript, ed. W. A. Craigie for the Scottish Text Society (Edinburgh 1920), pp. 17b-18.

[4] *Ibid.*, p. 16b.

[5] R. Bannatyne, *Memoriales of Transactions in Scotland*, ed. R. Pitcairn for the Bannatyne Club (Edinburgh 1836), p. 37. Henceforth, for convenience's sake, and in keeping with the custom of Scottish historians, the name "Lethington" will be used to refer to William Maitland.

[6] CSP SCOT, v, 46-47.

Lethington was as much of a *politique* as his father—in fact more so, since, unlike Sir Richard, he seems to have been something of a skeptic. So thought John Knox, who called him a mocker and in later years denounced him from the pulpit as an atheist who had said that heaven and hell were "things devised to make bairns afraid."[7] Knox was exaggerating; he disliked Lethington, who had a sharp tongue, was not afraid to use it against the preachers, and was skillful enough to debate theology with the Reformer on equal terms.[8] Knox was much nearer the mark when he said, in answer to Lethington's claim that he had been brought up in the fear of God, that "it was not education that made a true Christian . . . but the illumination of the soul by God's spirit."[9] Lethington was certainly not "illuminated" in Knox's sense. As a politician he thought exclusively in secular and rationalist terms; he rejected the claim of the preachers to a voice in politics, and thought his own attitude so reasonable that he could not understand why all other intelligent and reasonable men did not share it. Like other rationalist politicians both before and since his day, he seriously underestimated the strength of religious emotion as a political force. It was all very well to scoff at the ministers, and tell them to "bark and blow as loud as they list."[10] But it was not intelligent politics to assume that other men would pay equally little attention to the barking and blowing. It is possible, in a religious age, to be too much of a *politique*.

Lethington also shared his father's view of the Scottish social structure. Sir Richard believed that the upper aristocracy was the only class that counted for anything in Scotland, that all the problems of the country would be solved if only there was "Union amongst the Lords," as he entitled one of his poems. Indeed Sir Richard, possibly owing to his generally backward-looking frame of mind, attributed much more power to the aristocracy than they in fact possessed by the later sixteenth century. The English agent Henry Killigrew was overstating the

[7] Calderwood, III, 231; W. C. Dickinson, ed., *John Knox's History of the Reformation in Scotland*, I, 335.
[8] See Knox's account of their debate, *ibid.*, II, 106-134.
[9] Calderwood, III, 233.
[10] *Knox's History*, II, 104.

case in his oft-quoted remark that the great nobles' power was in decay;[11] but it is certainly true that, relatively, their power was very much less than it had been a hundred years earlier. Sir Richard did not realize this; no more did Lethington. In May 1571, during the negotiations between two parties in the civil war for a possible settlement of the conflict, Lethington insisted that his opponents must take the initiative in making an offer, since "the principals of the nobility of Scotland are here, to whom they that are in the Canongate [i.e., the other side] are far inferior in . . . rank."[12] As his biographer puts it, "With most of the higher nobles on one side—a point on which he never ceased to insist . . . almost as if by itself it ought to decide the controversy—he fatally undervalued the strength of their opponents."[13] This may not have been "aristocratic bias"[14]—there is no evidence that Lethington felt particularly attracted to the aristocracy as a class. It was simply a political mistake, which complemented his other political mistake with respect to the influence of religion. Few aristocrats were sincere Protestants. True Protestant zeal was to be found in the lesser gentry and the townsmen—these were the people who were roused by the preachers' "barking and blowing." Since Lethington underrated the political importance of these groups, it was but natural that he should underrate the political impact of religious considerations.

Lethington inherited his father's patriotism as well as his social outlook. He took a fierce pride in Scotland's heroic past and in her present independence, and he had great hopes of her future. It was this vision of the future that set Lethington off from most of his contemporaries, and that led him on to his destruction. In his opinion Scotland's destiny lay in union with England, through the placing of the crowns of the two kingdoms on the same head in an equal partnership. This idea of union on equal terms was not original with him. It had occurred to Henry VII when he married his daughter Margaret to King James IV. But Lethington, unlike Henry VII, allowed

11 November 11, 1572, Killigrew to Burghley, CSP SCOT, IV, 432.
12 Bannatyne, *Memoriales*, p. 125.
13 E. Russell, *Maitland of Lethington* (London 1912), p. 403.
14 *Ibid.*

the vision to fill his mind and ultimately become an obsession. It is not surprising, therefore, that his religious-minded contemporaries failed to understand him. One authority has summed up Lethington this way:

"That such a man should have been so grossly and so generally misunderstood must be ascribed mainly to the complexity of his ideal and to the extreme fidelity with which he followed it hither and thither through the maze of competing interests, utilizing each of them so long as it would serve his purpose. He did not care greatly for Protestantism, except in so far as it might facilitate the union of the two kingdoms; and he would support no scheme of union which did not secure the honor and the greatness of his native land. Thus he moved in a sphere of his own, apart alike from the mere unionist, from the patriot in the narrower sense, and from the rigid Protestant. . . . To him . . . the country of his birth was neither a pinfold of the universal Church nor a mere province of the republic of letters, but a land most emphatically his own, with a long train of heroic memories behind it, and before it the dawn of a broader day."[15]

Under these circumstances it may seem strange to find that Lethington started his political career in the 1550's as the supporter of the pro-French regent, Mary of Guise, Queen Mary's mother, who appointed him to the office of secretary. The reason is not far to seek. Mary of Guise's policy at first was one of religious peace and conciliation of factions, a policy of which both Lethington and his father, as good patriots, thoroughly approved. But with the shift in her policy to one of open hostility to Protestantism and of the permanent subordination of Scotland to France, Lethington braved his father's disapproval, broke away, and became the chief diplomatic agent of the Protestant party in the Wars of the Congregation. It need hardly be added that he joined the Protestant party, not because it was Protestant, but because it was the patriotic party, fighting for Scottish independence

[15] W. Law Mathieson, *Politics and Religion, A Study in Scottish History from the Reformation to the Revolution,* I (Glasgow 1902), 122-123.

from France. Lethington contributed significantly to the Protestant victory. He was instrumental in obtaining the support of England's new queen, Elizabeth, for the Protestant faction, and this English assistance turned the tide against Mary of Guise and her supporters.

Despite the fact that he had been partly responsible for the destruction of her mother's policy, the young Queen Mary looked with favor upon secretary Lethington after her return to Scotland in 1561, and he became, in fact, her chief adviser, along with her half-brother, the earl of Moray. The Catholic queen's reliance on the leaders of the Protestant party was due to her desire to succeed to the English throne. Indeed, in her own eyes she was already rightfully queen of England, since Elizabeth was a bastard by Catholic standards. But if Elizabeth would acknowledge her claim to the succession, Mary would be content. Her brother and her secretary had committed themselves to obtain that acknowledgement. Mary would let them try; if they failed, she could always adopt the more congenial policy of alliance with the Catholics and open hostility to Elizabeth. This strategy was perfectly acceptable to Lethington, who was willing to use any means to achieve the sort of union he wanted. Therefore, until almost the end of her reign, Lethington, despite occasional fallings-out with the queen, remained her supporter and, as befitted his office, her chief agent in foreign affairs. In January 1567, just five months before Mary's catastrophe at Carberry Hill, the ties between the two became closer still, with Lethington's marriage to Mary Fleming, one of the "Queen's Maries."

The Maitland family was naturally in high favor. Old Sir Richard, despite his blindness, was made an ordinary member of the court of session, and, in December of 1562, was appointed keeper of the privy seal for life.[16] Robert Maitland, dean of Aberdeen, of a cadet branch of the family, was also appointed to the court of session, and was granted a gift out of the temporalities of the cathedral church of Aberdeen.[17] And

16 SRO, *Privy Seal Register*, XXXI, 55.
17 G. Brunton and D. Haig, *An Historical Account of the Senators of the*

it was under these favorable auspices that the young John Maitland began his political career.

John Maitland, like his father and elder brother, was trained in the law. He probably went to the Haddington grammar school; he certainly attended St. Andrews University, where his name is found on the rolls of St. Salvator's College for the year 1555.[18] Thereafter he completed his education in France; when he went, and how long he stayed, we do not know. In the prospective division of the Maitland property on the death of Sir Richard, William was to have Lethington, and John was to receive the barony of Blyth and the old family keep of Thirlestane[19]—which is why William is always known as "of Lethington" and John as "of Thirlestane." He was the recipient of occasional favors from the queen—for example, he and his father were made joint factors of the abbey lands of Haddington in 1563[20]—but he did not become a person of any consequence until early in 1567. On February 7, three days before the murder of Darnley, John Maitland became commendator of the priory of Coldingham. He obtained this by an exchange with Francis Stewart, the nephew of Mary's all-powerful favorite, the earl of Bothwell; Stewart became commendator of Kelso.[21] The income from Coldingham, a thousand marks a year, was to be divided with his younger brother Thomas, which may have been something of a hardship for John, unless Thomas paid his share of the an-

---

College of Justice from its Institution in MDXXXII (Edinburgh 1832), pp. 122-123. SRO, *Privy Seal Register*, XXXIII, 81.

[18] J. M. Anderson, ed., *Early Records of the University of St. Andrews (1413-1579)*, SHS, 3rd series, vol. VIII (Edinburgh 1926), p. 261.

[19] SRO, *Privy Seal Register*, XXX, 14. This was a relatively equal division of the property; in a tax roll of 1554 Lethington was assessed at 10 pounds Scots, Blyth and Thirlestane at 5 pounds each. NLS, MSS 6.2.2. Throughout this work, "pounds" are Scots unless referred to as "sterling."

[20] SRO, *Privy Seal Register*, XXXII, 18-19.

[21] SRO, *Privy Seal Register*, XXXV, 115, XXXVI, 32-33. RMS, III, 439. The evidence as to Maitland's tenure of Kelso is dubious. A member of the Ker family apparently held Kelso as late as August 1566; C. Innes, ed., *Liber S. Marie de Calchou*, Bannatyne Club publication, I (Edinburgh 1846), preface, p. xvi. What probably happened was that Bothwell was persuaded to surrender his nephew's claims to Coldingham, of which the latter's father, Bothwell's brother-in-law, had been commendator, in exchange for the much wealthier Kelso. The nephew was unable to speak for himself as yet; he was only five years old.

nual tax of one-third of the income of benefices, which now began to be collected from Coldingham.[22]

Two months after the gift of Coldingham the newly appointed commendator became an official of Queen Mary's government. On April 20, 1567, Sir Richard resigned as keeper of the privy seal in favor of his son.[23] The office was not an important one—the blind Sir Richard had evidently experienced no difficulty in performing its duties for four years—and it did not mean that young Maitland was going to have any influence on policy. It was simply a way of giving the young man—he was in his mid-twenties—an excellent start on a political career.

The transfer may have taken place at Lethington's suggestion. The secretary was beginning to play a lonely and dangerous political game, and he doubtless felt that his position would be strengthened if his brother, instead of the cautious and reserved Sir Richard, were keeper of the privy seal. For young John was his brother's faithful follower; throughout all the desperate alarums and excursions of the next six years John stayed at the secretary's side, was involved in his ultimate defeat, and learned a good many vital lessons from that defeat, which enabled him, later on, to avoid some of his brother's errors.

Less than a month after she granted the privy seal to young Maitland, who seems to have been in France at the time of the grant,[24] Mary did what Lethington had feared she would do—she married Bothwell, who was universally regarded as the murderer of her husband. To the secretary this was an appalling political blunder; it completely discredited Mary in the eyes of the world at a time when the prospect of a successful solution of the question of the English succession was brighter than ever. At this point, however, Mary was completely irrational. She was in love with Bothwell, and nothing

22 Coldingham paid this tax for the first time in 1568; G. Donaldson, ed., *Accounts of the Collectors of Thirds of Benefices 1561-1572*, shs, 3rd series, vol. xlii (Edinburgh 1949), introduction, p. xiii.

23 sro, *Privy Seal Register*, xxxvi, 41.

24 On this point see Mary's letter of December 19, 1568, in which she speaks of John Maitland as having been in France "a little before our imprisoning." Calderwood, ii, 464.

else mattered. Since the queen could not be brought to see reason, Lethington reluctantly joined the coalition against her. But he had no desire permanently to ruin her; he was the leading advocate of moderate treatment for her after she was captured by the rebel lords at Carberry in June of 1567. He supported the suggestion that Moray become regent for the infant James VI, since Moray also appeared to favor moderation toward Mary. In all this John dutifully followed along; on August 26, 1567, four days after his assumption of the regency, Moray confirmed John in his office as keeper of the privy seal.[25]

Lethington's opposition to Mary was reluctant and temporary. He disliked exceedingly the idea of compelling her to abdicate in favor of her son, since the Scottish chances of obtaining the English succession would be jeopardized. He was confirmed in his opinion by Elizabeth's minatory attitude to the new government and outspoken support of Mary. But as long as Mary remained faithful to Bothwell, nothing could be done. The Maitlands therefore continued to support the regent, and to be rewarded for that support—rewards in which John shared by being elevated to the bench as lord of session in June of 1568.[26] But when, after Mary's escape and flight to England in May 1568, Moray acquiesced in Elizabeth's demand that a virtual trial of the deposed queen be held in England, the secretary turned against the regent. Lethington knew all about the Casket Letters; he knew that Moray would be compelled to produce them at such a trial. Once this was done Mary could never be restored in Scotland without civil war, and probably not even then; worse still, her character would be hopelessly blackened, and all prospect of peacefully obtaining the English succession would vanish forever.

So Lethington worked covertly to wreck Moray's policy at the York-Westminster conference, which began in the fall of 1568 and lasted until January 1569.[27] He failed, but only by the narrowest of margins, and an open break with the regent

[25] SRO, *Privy Seal Register*, XXXVII, 1.
[26] Brunton and Haig, *Senators of the College of Justice*, p. 141.
[27] For Lethington's policy at the conference see M. Lee, Jr., *James Stewart Earl of Moray* (New York 1953), pp. 235ff.

could not be long delayed. It came in July of 1569, at the convention of Perth, which met to consider, among other things, Mary's request for a divorce from Bothwell. The secretary argued vehemently in favor of the divorce, but he was in a small minority. One of his few supporters was his brother. "Lethington . . . opposed mightily, and raged, but prevailed not."[28]

Retribution was not long in coming. In September 1569, Lethington was accused of guilty foreknowledge of the murder of Darnley.[29] His trial was set for November. In the meantime, however, he was protected by his friend Kirkcaldy of Grange, the captain of Edinburgh castle, who carried him off to that fortress by forging the regent's signature to a warrant. Lethington's "day of law" produced a near riot. He had summoned his friends to appear in force at the trial, and they did, led by Lord Hume. The regent postponed the trial; but John Maitland, along with his cousin Robert Maitland, dean of Aberdeen, took the precaution of going to the Tolbooth and claiming that the secretary must be held innocent since no accuser had appeared against him.[30]

Tension between the two factions in Scotland was obviously mounting. Moray might have prevented an outbreak of open violence, but his murder in January 1570, and the subsequent elevation of the king's grandfather, the earl of Lennox, to the regency, made a civil war inevitable. In the struggle the secretary was the driving force behind the queen's party, which would almost certainly have come to terms much sooner than it did had it not been for him. This was recognized by his

28 Calderwood, II, 490. August 5, 1569, Hunsdon to Cecil, CSP SCOT, II, 666-667.
29 Andrew Lang, in his introduction to "The Apologie for William Maitland of Lidington," written by Lethington's son James (*Miscellany of the Scottish History Society*, II, 1st series, vol. LIV [Edinburgh 1904], p. 150), states that John Maitland was present at Darnley's murder as his brother's representative. I can find no evidence to support this assertion, and the fact that John was not accused at the same time as his brother seems to indicate that the regent's party had none either.
30 T. Thomson, ed., *A Diurnal of Remarkable Occurrents That Have Passed within the Country of Scotland*, Maitland Club publication (Edinburgh 1833), pp. 151-152. After Moray's death, early in 1570, a collusive trial found Lethington innocent. T. Thomson, ed., *The Historie and Life of King James the Sext*, Bannatyne Club publication (Edinburgh 1825), pp. 49-50.

opponents, who poured unmeasured abuse on him. His enemy Morton called him "the whole forthsetter of the other side."[31] To George Buchanan he was a "chameleon," inconsistent and treacherous; to Knox's secretary he was the "head of wit, called Michael Wylie [Machiavelli] with his sore feet"[32]—this last a reference to the disease that ultimately killed him.

Throughout the civil war we catch occasional glimpses of John, who looked after the family estates as best he could and was often used by his brother as a negotiator in the frequent efforts made by the two parties to compromise their difficulties.[33] Some of the earliest blows of the war fell upon the Maitlands, whose property was peculiarly exposed to the attacks of their opponents' English allies. In April of 1570, as the war was beginning, the earl of Sussex crossed the border with a sizeable force, and on May 11 occupied Coldingham and proceeded to collect the rents.[34] The barony of Blyth was despoiled by Sussex's men, which caused old Sir Richard to write an indignant poem, punning on the word "blythe."[35] Thomas Maitland, the youngest of Sir Richard's three sons, was captured in May, along with his brother-in-law Sir John Cockburn of Clerkington.[36] Meanwhile, Lethington himself stayed out of reach of his enemies, chiefly in the highlands.

In September 1570 a two-months' truce was arranged; the regent Lennox made use of the breathing-space thus afforded to obtain legal condemnation of the Maitlands. On September 17 the three brothers were put to the horn and dismissed from their offices, and the house and estates at Lethington were seized, in spite of the fact that they belonged, not to any one

[31] Mathieson, *Politics and Religion*, I, 117.

[32] Bannatyne, *Memoriales*, p. 52. Buchanan was a distinguished humanist who became a sort of pamphleteer for the Protestant faction. The *Chameleon* may be found in G. Buchanan, *The History of Scotland*, trans. J. Aikman, I (Glasgow 1827), xci-ci.

[33] July 17, 1570, William to John Maitland, CSP SCOT, III, 265-266. See also *ibid.*, p. 608; Bannatyne, *Memoriales*, pp. 239-240; *Diurnal of Occurrents*, pp. 169-170; RPCS, XIV, 64-65.

[34] CSP SCOT, III, 171. Lethington's protest to Sussex about this was ignored. *Ibid.*, pp. 217-218.

[35] *Maitland Quarto*, pp. 20b-21.

[36] Thomas was soon released; after various adventures he died in Italy in 1572. See the article on him by W. S. McKechnie, SHR, IV (1906-1907), 274-293.

of the outlawed brothers, but to their father, against whom nothing had been alleged. The commendator of Dunfermline was appointed secretary; the privy seal was bestowed upon George Buchanan. Protests were unavailing—even those of Sussex, who felt that Lennox was behaving dishonorably. Lennox's reply was to detail the charges against his opponents. As for John Maitland, "he had the office of the keeping of the privy seal, and was promoted to be one of the senators of the college of justice; from which charges he withdrew himself, and untruly assisted and accompanied the adversaries, against his promised allegiances, he was worthily called, processed, and his living of Coldingham restrained, and chamberlains appointed thereto."[37]

Naturally the civil war resumed, and became much grimmer in character. Dumbarton castle was captured by Lennox's men in April 1571; archbishop Hamilton of St. Andrews was found therein and promptly hanged without trial. Perhaps the news of the fall of Dumbarton caused Lethington to enter the castle at Edinburgh. This he did on April 11, accompanied by his brother. He was so sick that he had to be carried in, "Mr. Robert Maitland holding up his head."[38] A month later, on May 16, 1571, the Maitland brothers were officially forfeited by Lennox's Parliament, held in the Canongate, and called the "Creeping Parliament" from the undignified posture its members occasionally had to assume to avoid the artillery fire of the castle.[39] John Maitland was forfeited for "intercommuning with rebels and traitors" at Linlithgow in May of 1570, for "assieging of Glasgow"—taking part in an unsuccessful raid on the city after the Linlithgow meeting—for dealing with France and Spain, and generally for making war on the king.[40] The lists of those forfeited in this and subsequent Parliaments held by the king's faction are very interesting;

[37] Bannatyne, *Memoriales*, pp. 347-350. October 13, 1570, Lethington to Sussex, CSP SCOT, III, 392-394. A. Lang, *A History of Scotland from the Roman Occupation*, II, 232. Alexander Hume of Manderston was put in possession of Coldingham, of which he held a good deal of the land in feu. NLS MSS 2949. RMS, III, 571-572.

[38] Bannatyne, *Memoriales*, p. 110.

[39] *Ibid.*, p. 123.

[40] NLS MSS 22.1.14, p. 166b. See also RPCS, XIV, 64-65, 96-97.

they include the names of a good many men, like Robert Melville and David Seton of Parbroath, who later became John Maitland's colleagues in James's government.

Edinburgh castle was now the chief stronghold of the queen's party; its defenders frequently rode out to harry their opponents. John Maitland took part in two skirmishes, neither of them very successful;[41] he does not seem to have been present at the most famous of these raids, the one which resulted in the death of Lennox at Stirling in September of 1571. The Maitlands received the news of the death of Lennox with relief; he had been pursuing a personal feud with Lethington on account of the murder of Darnley. They were even more encouraged by the choice of Mar rather than Morton as regent. John Maitland, who had inherited some of his father's poetical ambitions, addressed "Ane Admonitioun to my lord of Mar Regent." The gist of it is that if Mar should invite the English to send forces into Scotland, disaster would inevitably result. Mar's first concern should be his country's freedom— the sentiment one would expect from one of the Maitlands.[42] But Mar disappointed them. The real ruler of Scotland during his brief tenure of office was Morton, who succeeded him as regent late in 1572. The war dragged on in desultory fashion during Mar's regency, and members of the queen's party began to desert and make their peace with the government. By early 1573, only Edinburgh castle still held out for Mary. Morton resolved to finish matters quickly. In April 1573 he obtained active help from Elizabeth; a force of 1,500 men under Sir William Drury, the provost marshal of Berwick, amply equipped with artillery, soon arrived in Edinburgh. In the formal contract signed between Drury and Morton it was agreed that the leaders of the castle garrison, including both Maitlands, would be "reserved to be justified by the laws of Scotland, wherein her majesty's advice shall be used."[43]

The end came quickly. The castle garrison was small and demoralized, and Drury's artillery completed its discomfiture. On May 28, 1573, the castle surrendered. The two Maitlands,

[41] *Diurnal of Occurrents*, pp. 210, 224-225.
[42] *Maitland Quarto*, pp. 66b-68.
[43] CSP SCOT, IV, 548.

Kirkcaldy, Lord Hume, and Robert Melville were put in Drury's custody. On the following day Lethington and Kirkcaldy wrote to Lord Burghley, asking that they all be allowed to live in England.[44] It was as well for the secretary that he did not live to hear the answer. Drury removed his prisoners to Leith in order to superintend the embarkation of his military equipment; there, on June 11 or 12, Lethington was found dead in his bed. It was rumored that he had committed suicide, but there is no evidence of this.[45]

So ended the dazzling career of "the flower of the wits of Scotland," as Burghley once called him. The secretary really fell victim to the increasing inflexibility of his political preconceptions as he grew older. His ideal of the union of the crowns became such an obsession with him that he came to believe that if Elizabeth would not yield to persuasion in this matter, she must be made to yield to force. Furthermore, Lethington was so much of a *politique* that he failed to see that the surest guarantee of the English succession in a religious age was a common religious interest. Hence his persistent support of the rightful heir, in spite of her Catholicism. This was the worst of the secretary's blunders, and it brought about his ruin, although not the ruin of his cause. Scotland would give a king to England yet—but a Protestant king; and that made all the difference.

ii

A seventeenth-century account of the fall of Edinburgh castle, in listing the prisoners, describes John Maitland thus: ". . . who afterwards was chancellor, whose youth was decked with singular virtue and excellency in arts, especially with the imitation of his brother."[46] John had indeed imitated his brother, and the result was captivity and disaster. But John learned from his brother's mistakes. For one thing, he realized that Lethington had seriously underestimated the power of the

---

[44] *Ibid.*, p. 573.

[45] Russell, *Maitland of Lethington*, pp. 501-502. I have depended heavily on this excellent biography of the secretary for my account of his policy.

[46] Robert Johnston, "The Historie of Scotland during the Minority of King James," in *Tracts Illustrative of the Traditionary and Historical Antiquities of Scotland* (Edinburgh 1836), p. 385.

kirk. No Scottish statesman could disregard the ministers, as Lethington had done, and achieve any measure of success. It was necessary either to cooperate with the kirk or to bring it under royal administrative control and thus render it innocuous.

If Lethington had underestimated the power of the kirk, he had also overestimated the power of the nobility, as John Maitland realized. The noblemen upon whom Lethington had depended had proved to be broken reeds. They could not win Scotland over to Mary's cause, and, in steadily increasing numbers, they betrayed that cause until of all the earls and lords who had supported Mary at the beginning only Lord Hume remained in the castle with the Maitlands and Kirkcaldy. John Maitland entered his captivity convinced of the treachery and worthlessness of the upper aristocracy, and of the pernicious effect their extensive power had on the state. He shared the opinion of King James, expressed in *Basilicon Doron*, that the nobles believed "that their honor stood in committing three points of iniquity: to thrall by oppression the meaner sort that dwelleth near them to their service and following . . . to maintain their servants and dependers in any wrong . . . and for any displeasure that they apprehend to be done unto them by their neighbor, to take up a plain feud against him; and without respect to God, king, or commonweal, to bang it out bravely, he and all his kin against him and all his."[47] Maitland was convinced that the power of the upper aristocracy must be reduced, that their loyalty could not be depended on since they invariably put their own interests before those of the state.

In that dismal summer of 1573, however, it seemed most unlikely that Maitland would ever be in a position to put any of this hard-earned knowledge to use. A few days after his brother's death he was handed over to Morton by Drury, and kept for a time in the regent's house in Edinburgh and in his grim fortress at Tantallon.[48] Eventually, in February 1574, the regent permitted Maitland to go and live with his cousin Lord Somerville at Cowthally, at the western end of the Pentland hills. Surety was found in the amount of ten thousand

[47] Quoted in A. Cunningham, *The Loyal Clans* (Cambridge 1932), p. 103.
[48] CSP SCOT, IV, 588, 590, 602-603.

pounds for his "abiding at Cowthally until relieved, conducting himself as a good subject, and neither sending letters abroad nor receiving any from strangers."[49]

Maitland got on well with the Somervilles, for whom he had once performed a signal service in showing them how to recover an estate which was in dispute with a cadet branch of the family.[50] But he cannot have enjoyed the years of Morton's rule. Morton had disliked the secretary, and as long as Morton remained in power there was no hope of a political career, or even of the end of his confinement to Cowthally— and Maitland badly wanted a political career. Furthermore, Morton was treating Sir Richard most unfairly. The old man had been expelled from his house at Lethington, and the property had been turned over to one of Morton's henchmen, on the ground that Lethington had really belonged to the secretary. Since Morton would not rectify this patent injustice, Sir Richard wrote a piteous letter to Elizabeth asking for her help on behalf of himself and his sole surviving son. The English representatives in Scotland agreed that the old man had been badly treated, but the matter did not seem important to Elizabeth, and nothing was done.[51]

Morton's rule, however unpleasant it may have been to him personally, nevertheless taught Maitland several useful political lessons. Abroad, the regent's policy was to remain friendly with England, but not to truckle to her. At home he was bent on controlling both the self-seeking aristocracy and the fractious kirk, and he succeeded. He insisted that the nobility observe the rights of the crown and that they disgorge any property that was not rightfully theirs. Like Henry VII in England in a similar situation, he levied large fines for disobedience whenever he could. His policy toward the kirk was equally forceful. He attempted to control it, in the English fashion, through its bishops. This policy, coupled with his attempt to turn the episcopate into a source of revenue for

[49] RPCS, II, 334.

[50] For this story see James, Lord Somerville, *Memorie of the Somervilles*, I (Edinburgh 1815), 429-438.

[51] Sir Richard's letter is dated August 24, 1574. CSP SCOT, V, 46-47. See also *ibid.*, pp. 47-48, 57, 182.

his own relatives, led to the discrediting of the institution of episcopacy in the eyes of the faithful, and the attacks of Andrew Melvill on bishops as such gained widespread support. Morton steadfastly refused to pay any attention to clerical remonstrances; when Melvill attempted to read him a lecture on the error of his ways, he replied, "There will never be quietness in this country, till half a dozen of you be hanged or banished the country."[52] The regent, not unnaturally, became very unpopular with nobility and clergy alike, and acquired a reputation for pride and avarice which was not wholly deserved.[53]

The most serious weakness in Morton's position, however, was the fact that he was disliked, not only by the nobility and clergy, but also by the young king—a common enough situation for Scottish regents to find themselves in. A *coup d'état* early in 1578, carried out by the earls of Argyll and Athol, with the connivance of the king's guardian, the master of Erskine, put an end to the regency; the twelve-year-old James was now, technically, responsible for his own government. Morton was able to deliver an effective counterblow after about six weeks and recover his prominent position in the government, but not his title as regent.

The weakening of Morton meant better days for the Maitlands. The ex-regent was still powerful enough to protect his henchman, Hume of Fishwick, from the consequences of his unjustified occupation of the lands of Lethington, but on September 15, 1578, John Maitland was relieved from his ward.[54] He was now a free man, but not until Morton's power was destroyed could he hope for a political career. This was shortly accomplished, by one of the more enigmatic figures of this period, Esmé Stewart, duke of Lennox.

Lennox—or the sieur d'Aubigny, as he then was—came to Scotland from France in September 1579, ostensibly to congratulate his cousin the young king on his assumption of the

[52] R. Pitcairn, ed., *The Autobiography and Diary of Mr. James Melvill*, p. 68.
[53] For an able defense of Morton's policy while regent, see the *Dictionary of National Biography* article by T. F. Henderson.
[54] RPCS, III, 29. For the case of Hume of Fishwick, whom Sir Richard had been pursuing at law, see R. S. Rait, *The Parliaments of Scotland*, pp. 471-472.

government. Esmé quickly established a personal ascendancy over James; he was the first of a long line of favorites, of whom the last and most famous was George Villiers. It is easy to see why James should have been attracted to his cousin. Esmé was friendly and amusing and deferential, a complete contrast to the grim Morton and the irascible and pedantic Buchanan, who had been the king's chief tutor. James was a precocious and very sensitive adolescent, full of self-importance, and yet quite unsure of himself. Esmé was kind to the boy, flattered him and built up his confidence. James, who was starved for affection, gave it to Esmé, with an abnormal violence. He showered his cousin with favors—the abbey of Arbroath and the earldom of Lennox, later erected into a dukedom. "The king [is] so much affected to him that he delights only in his company, and thereby Lennox carries the sway," wrote the treasurer of Berwick, Robert Bowes, to his government.[55]

One important consequence of Lennox's influence over the king might be pointed out here. It was evidently on account of this situation that there developed, among the Scottish Jesuits and the continental Catholics generally, the persistent belief that James was a Catholic at heart and could be converted.[56] This curious delusion flew in the face of all the facts, but it was carefully nurtured by James in later years and proved invaluable to him on more than one occasion.

At this early stage of James's career there were more grounds for such a belief than later. Observers far removed from Scotland could not be expected to understand the nature of Lennox's hold over the king, and many of them did know that Lennox had not come to Scotland simply to make his fortune. He was an agent of the Guises. His ultimate purposes have remained somewhat obscure; if the confused plotting of 1582 may be taken as an indication, he evidently planned to recatholicize England and Scotland by force, with the aid of

[55] Quoted in D. H. Willson, *King James VI and I* (London 1956), p. 33. Bowes, a man with long experience in Scottish affairs, was frequently employed as resident ambassador in Edinburgh.

[56] See Rev. W. J. Anderson, "Narratives of the Scottish Reformation. 1. Report of Father Robert Abercrombie, S.J., in the year 1580," *Innes Review*, VII (1956), 36.

Spain and the Jesuits. In order to do this, it was necessary, first of all, to weaken the Protestant faction in Scotland and at the same time to build up a party for himself. Lennox brilliantly accomplished the first of these objectives, by bringing down Morton and eventually having him executed for his foreknowledge of the plot against Darnley. This was done with the indispensable assistance of Captain James Stewart, an able and ambitious soldier who was a cousin of the king's. He was created earl of Arran, and became a close associate of both Lennox and the king.

The fall of Morton in 1580 ushered in a five-year period of instability in Scottish domestic affairs, an instability chiefly due to the effect of that event on English policy. Elizabeth was made most unhappy by Morton's ruin. But she felt that she could not take any overt action to save him, on account of the complicated situation on the continent, which, in Elizabeth's view, made the friendship of France indispensable to England. Since Elizabeth assumed that Lennox was the agent of the French government, she reluctantly sacrificed Morton to the French alliance.[57] But she did all she could to destroy Lennox covertly, and this meant an abrupt reversion to the time-honored English policy of subsidizing an aristocratic faction—the Protestant faction, headed by Morton's two chief allies, the earls of Angus and Mar. Scottish politics during the next five years therefore resembled in many ways the turbulent years of Mary's personal rule.

Morton had made so many enemies that it was a fairly simple matter for Lennox to encompass his fall. It turned out to be much harder to build up a political faction to achieve his further goals, however, partly because he could not openly reveal his objectives, partly because his chief associate, the new earl of Arran, was balky, ambitious, and Protestant. Lennox's effort to create such a faction proved abortive in the long run, but it did open the door to Maitland.

[57] For an analysis of the situation that led to Morton's fall see M. Lee, Jr., "The Fall of the Regent Morton: a Problem in Satellite Diplomacy," *Journal of Modern History*, xxviii (1956), 111-129.

It was natural that Lennox, in casting about for support for himself, should turn to the followers of the fallen queen. They would join eagerly in the attack upon Morton, and, in Lennox's opinion, they should be willing at least to acquiesce in his further political schemes. So, in September 1580, we find Bowes reporting that Maitland and his fellow Castilian Robert Melville "are lately entertained and grow great in counsel and credit about Lennox."[58] It seems likely that it was at this time that Maitland became acquainted with the young king, and that their friendship began. Perhaps it was their common interest in poetry that formed the first bond between them. James was not a good poet—neither was Maitland, for that matter—but he was very much interested in poetry and in poetic theory, and he was a generous patron to a circle of court poets who would have had difficulty in finding patronage elsewhere in Scotland.[59] For whatever reason, the king became Maitland's friend, and the friendship proved enduring. This friendship was the indispensable prerequisite to Maitland's political career. Only through royal support could a man in Maitland's social position hope to achieve political power, and James turned out to be the sort of man who took political advice from his personal friends. James's relationship with Maitland was not like that with Lennox or with Villiers. It had no sexual overtones. But the king came to trust Maitland, whose steadfast loyalty to Mary recommended him to James in this respect. The foundations of Maitland's future greatness were laid.

It would be some time, however, before James would be either able or willing to take political advice from Maitland. In the meantime the latter made use of his new place in the sun to begin the process of restoring the family's position. His charter of restoration, granted in February 1581, gave him back

[58] CSP SCOT, v, 513.

[59] For the great importance of James's encouragement and example in the literary history of Scotland see J. Craigie, ed., *The Poems of James VI of Scotland*, Scottish Text Society publication, i (Edinburgh 1955), introduction, pp. xxiv-xxv. Maitland's poetry may be found in the collection of his father's work published by the Maitland Club and edited by Joseph Bain, *The Poems of Sir Richard Maitland of Lethington* (Glasgow 1830), and in A. Johnston, ed., *Delitiae Poetarum Scotorum*, ii (Amsterdam 1637), 138-143.

everything he had previously possessed save Coldingham and the privy seal. He was forced to renounce his claims to Coldingham to Hume of Manderston; as for the privy seal, Lennox had no intention of raising unnecessary suspicions as to the genuineness of his recent "conversion" to Protestantism by prematurely despoiling the aged Buchanan.[60] Two months later Maitland's seat on the bench was also restored: he took the place of Morton's fugitive cousin Archibald Douglas. The manner of his appointment was unusual. In 1579 the senators of the college of justice had complained of the poor quality of recent appointments, and Parliament had enacted that in future the college could conduct an examination of any royal nominee for a vacancy and reject him if he were found wanting. Therefore, in 1581, three men were nominated for the vacancy. A royal letter made it plain that the king favored Maitland, and the other two gracefully stepped down.[61] This examination could hardly be termed rigorous. Maitland approved of the principle of examining nominees for judicial positions, however, and some years later attempted to apply it in earnest.

We do not know what Maitland thought about Lennox's political schemes, or even if he knew about them at all. His seat on the bench was his only official position; he was not a member of the privy council, and there is no evidence that he was ever intimate with Lennox.[62] Morton's Scottish friends, and Robert Bowes, included him in the lists of those who were

60 SRO, *Register of Deeds*, XIX, 186b. SRO, *Privy Seal Register*, XLVII, 76. RMS, IV, 33-34. In June 1581 he had a gift of the lands of Lethington; SRO, *Privy Seal Register*, XLVIII, 26. The privy seal never was restored to him. When Buchanan died in 1582, Lennox had fallen and the Ruthven raiders were in power. The seal was given to Walter Stewart, commendator of Blantyre. Manderston's tenure of Coldingham was ratified by Parliament in October 1581; APS, III, 270, 277-278.

61 *Ibid.*, p. 153; R. K. Hannay, *The College of Justice* (Edinburgh 1933), pp. 112-113. One of the two disappointed candidates, John Lindsay of Menmuir, filled the next vacancy, in July 1581. James's letter is in Brunton and Haig, *Senators of the College of Justice*, p. 142.

62 There is mention in the correspondence of Sir Patrick Vans of Barnbarroch of some business or other in which Maitland was engaged in Lennox's behalf in August 1582, but the nature of the business was not disclosed. R. V. Agnew, ed., *Correspondence of Sir Patrick Waus of Barnbarroch*, Ayr and Galloway Archaeological Association publication, I (Edinburgh 1887), 254-257.

among "the duke's rulers and counsellors." Bowes put it this way, in September 1581: Maitland and Sir James Balfour "live yet in some darkness, and are not very openly seen in court, yet their advices and counsels do most prevail."[63] But this is mere speculation, of no more validity than the charge that Maitland was a Papist, or than Calderwood's ridiculous assertion that Maitland and Robert Melville had been responsible for Lennox's coming to Scotland.[64] It was assumed by all those who had led the fight against Mary—that is, the English government, the Scottish kirk and the remnants of the Morton faction among the lords—that all of Mary's erstwhile supporters were Papists and Guisans. Doubtless Lennox thought so too, and rehabilitated them for that reason. When he discovered that in Maitland's case, and in Robert Melville's too, he had erred, he apparently ceased—or never started— to take them into his confidence. But Maitland was convicted, in the minds of Lennox's opponents, of being one of the duke's supporters. As the proclamation of the Ruthven raiders put it, he was one of those "who have remained obstinate Papists . . . [and] who were his majesty's ancient and most notable enemies, who never would obey nor acknowledge his authority royal."[65]

Maitland himself was cured of his Marian sympathies, as his future policy was to show. But to the world at large he was still secretary Lethington's brother. It would be some time before he was able to live down his brother's reputation and his Marian past.

[63] *Border Papers*, I, 75-76. Balfour, also a lawyer, was now nearing the end of a career which, even for sixteenth-century Scotland, was remarkable for its double-dealing. See also May 18, 1582, John Colville to Thomas Randolph, CSP SCOT, VI, 121.

[64] June 1, 1582, the laird of Carmichael to Walsingham, in P. F. Tytler, *History of Scotland*, 3rd ed., VI (Edinburgh 1845), 311; Calderwood, III, 456-457.

[65] CSP SCOT, VI, 171-174.

CHAPTER 3

THE HEGEMONY OF ARRAN

IN THE SUMMER of 1582 Lennox's ambitious designs crumbled
into dust. England had always been hostile to him; he had
aroused the suspicious enmity of the preachers by a simoniacal
appointment to the archbishopric of Glasgow; and those Protestant lords who had rejoiced to see Morton fall were now
thoroughly alarmed. Most notable of these was Lord Ruthven,
now earl of Gowrie; and it was at Ruthven castle, in August
of 1582, that King James was seized and held, by a coalition
led by Gowrie, the master of Glamis, and Morton's allies the
earls of Angus and Mar.

This forcible removal of the king's support ruined Lennox,
who turned out to be nowhere near so resourceful in adversity
as he had been when the tide was running in his direction. The
Ruthven raiders, as the lords of the Protestant coalition were
called, insisted that he leave the country if he did not want
a worse fate to befall him, and finally he did so, at the end
of 1582. He returned to France, and died there in the spring
of 1583. Arran, his chief ally, was imprisoned. The pro-English party, supported by the kirk, was back in the saddle.

The new masters of Scotland did not pursue a vengeful
policy. Arran was soon released from durance and politely
consigned to political oblivion.[1] There were no forfeitures, not
even any deprivations of office. Maitland, like the rest of Lennox's associates, retired from court, but he retained his place
on the college of justice. We know very little of how he occupied his time during the rule of the Ruthven raiders, save in
one very important particular. On January 16, 1583, at the
advanced age of thirty-nine, he got married. The lady was

[1] D. Moysie, *Memoirs of the Affairs of Scotland*, ed. J. Dennistoun for the
Bannatyne Club (Edinburgh 1830), p. 41.

Janet Fleming, the only child of James, fourth Lord Fleming, eleven years her husband's junior.[2] It does not require too much imagination to suppose that Maitland spent his enforced political idleness in courting Lady Janet, and then in setting up housekeeping with her.

This was an important match. In one sense it was a family affair: Janet Fleming's aunt was Lady Mary Fleming, the widow of secretary Lethington. Even more significant, in some ways, was the fact that her mother was a sister of Lords John and Claude Hamilton. Maitland's subsequent alliance with the Hamiltons, and particularly his friendship with Lord John, the head of the family, can be attributed to the fact that he was now John Hamilton's nephew by marriage.

Maitland did not have long to contemplate his domestic felicity. Like many another victorious coalition, that of the Ruthven raiders was soon riven by mutual suspicion and hatred, and in less than eleven months it collapsed. In June of 1583 the king made good his escape from his captors, quite possibly with the connivance of Gowrie himself.[3] The chief contriver of the escape was Colonel William Stewart, one of Lennox's followers, and the king was immediately surrounded by most of the prominent members of Lennox's faction, such as the earls of Huntly and Montrose. But Colonel Stewart, and Huntly, and even the king himself, soon paled into insignificance before the man who, for the next two years, was to be the real ruler of Scotland.

The earl of Arran returned to court in August 1583. He soon established an almost absolute ascendancy over the mind of King James, who was virtually his only true friend at court. Almost every other prominent figure in Scotland disliked Arran in varying degree, and disliked his wife still more. Lady Arran was a sister of the earl of Athol; she had been married to the elderly earl of March, the king's uncle, whom she divorced

---

[2] J. Balfour Paul, ed., *The Scots Peerage* (Edinburgh 1904-1914), VIII, 542-543. The marriage contract is in SRO, *Register of Deeds*, xx, pt. 2, 379b.

[3] Sir James Melville of Halhill, *Memoirs of his own Life*, ed. T. Thomson for the Bannatyne Club (Edinburgh 1827), pp. 283-284. Sir James Melville was the brother of Maitland's friend and colleague Robert Melville. His memoirs were written at an advanced age, and are not always reliable.

for impotency at a time when she was big with Arran's child. The pair had other things in common. They were both inordinately greedy; the correspondence of the English ambassadors and agents in Scotland in this period is full of reference to their immoderate passion for other men's goods.[4] Now of course Arran and his wife were not unique in being greedy; most Scottish nobles were. But they had unrivaled opportunities for assuaging that greed, and their avarice was not colored by any political justification. Other men in high places in Scotland had been greedy—Morton, for instance—but Morton had a consistent line of policy; and so, men who believed in Morton's policy could look through their fingers at his more violent acts. Arran's only policy, however, was what was good for Arran. The result was that he had no party except those whom he rewarded with some share of his ill-gotten gains, and such supporters as these were hardly reliable since there were repeated quarrels over the available spoils.[5]

For the time being, however, this "profane mocker of all religion, more fit to be the executioner of some Nero nor (than) counsellor to a Christian prince"[6] carried all before him. The first result was a stiffening in the king's attitude toward the leaders of the Ruthven raid. Immediately after his escape James had declared his intention of being lenient to his erstwhile captors; but now a series of proclamations described the raid in increasingly severe terms. Finally, in December 1583, the convention of estates declared the raid to be treason, and "such as had been guilty in fact or assent were appointed to seek remissions."[7] Pressure had already been put on the raiders to this end. Gowrie, who had already admitted the illegality of the raid, now agreed to "do so much as should well please the king."[8] At the end of August the master of Glamis had departed for Ireland to avoid being placed in ward; he was

---

4 As one example among many, see August 16, 1584, William Davison to Walsingham, CSP SCOT, VII, 276-279.

5 See, e.g., August 22, and October 1, 1583, Bowes to Walsingham, CSP SCOT, VI, 589-591, 628-629.

6 Calderwood, IV, 47.

7 Calderwood, III, 761. See also RPCS, III, 613-614.

8 July 27, August 17, 1583, Bowes to Walsingham, CSP SCOT, VI, 558-559, 587-588.

followed, after some months, by Mar. Ireland was still too close
to Scotland for comfort; Glamis and Mar were repeatedly ordered to leave the British isles altogether. Angus, the most
powerful of the raiders, both because of his position as head
of the house of Douglas and his influence with the kirk, was
not forced into exile, but he was warded in the highlands where
his enemy Huntly could keep an eye on him.[9] The property
of these three was not disturbed, but the lesser men did not
escape so easily. Morton's cousin William Douglas of Lochleven was also warded in the north; he saved his estates only
by a prompt submission and departure for France. Others were
not so prudent; the Erskine commendators of Cambuskenneth
and Paisley, who "profanely disobeyed" an order to ward themselves, lost their abbeys.[10]

The return to power of Arran and the rest of the Lennox
faction, and the subsequent attack on the Ruthven raiders,
naturally worsened Scottish relations with England. Elizabeth
brushed aside James's disingenuous explanations of his motives in overturning the Ruthven raiders' government, and instructed Robert Bowes, her resident ambassador, to take a
firm line with the young king. James gave Bowes very little
satisfaction; his replies to Bowes's protests were long-winded
and evasive. Elizabeth therefore resolved to send Sir Francis
Walsingham himself to Scotland to see what could be done.
Walsingham, who foresaw failure, was very reluctant to go.
The Spanish ambassador in London reported that he "went so
far as to throw himself at the queen's feet and pronounce the
following terrible blasphemy. He swore by the soul, body, and
blood of God that he would not go to Scotland even if she
ordered him to be hanged for it, as he would rather be hanged

[9] August 29, December 6, 23, 1583, January 31, February 13, 1584, Bowes to
Walsingham, *ibid.*, pp. 595, 668-670, 682-683, csp scot, vii, 18-19, 26-27. rpcs,
iii, 626. Calderwood, iii, 749-750.

[10] September 10, 1583, Bowes to Beale, csp scot, vi, 602-603; September 19, 28,
1583, January 31, 1584, Bowes to Walsingham, *ibid.*, pp. 616, 622-623, csp scot,
vii, 18-19. nls mss 77, fol. 66. rpcs, iii, 620-621. sro, *Treasurer's Accounts,
1583-1585.* For the disposition of Lochleven's property see C. Innes, ed., *Registrum Honoris de Morton*, Bannatyne Club publication (Edinburgh 1853), i,
141-142. The increasing severity of the government toward the Ruthven raiders
can be traced in Calderwood, iii, 719ff.

in England than elsewhere."[11] Walsingham went, nevertheless; but, as he had anticipated, he got nowhere with James. This was partly his own fault; he adopted a hectoring, schoolmasterish tone with the self-assured young man, and he refused to cultivate the all-powerful favorite. The latter retaliated by hiring a common scold named Kate the Witch to "sit in the entry of the king's palace, to revile her majesty's ambassador."[12] Walsingham came to the conclusion that England should revert to her traditional policy and organize a plot against the new government.[13]

Queen Elizabeth was not convinced. She did not trust Arran, but organizing plots cost money, and in view of her rapidly worsening relations with Spain, which culminated in the expulsion of the Spanish ambassador in January 1584, it seemed best to take Arran's and James's professions of friendship at face value for the moment. This pleased the latter well enough. Their only possible alternative policy, that of friendship with France, proved unfeasible,[14] and Arran, while confident of his ability to cope with his Scottish foes, did not want to have them abetted by England. So, for the time being, relations between England and Scotland, while not friendly, as in Morton's day, remained officially correct.[15]

A major cause of English suspicion of the new Scottish government was the fact that the court was now swarming with former supporters of the captive Queen Mary. Among them was Maitland, who, wrote Bowes on August 17, 1583, was "lately called to court as an especial servant of the king's

[11] August 19, 1583, Mendoza to Philip II, CSP SPANISH, III, 499-501.
[12] Calderwood, IV, 442.
[13] September 12, 15, 1583, Walsingham to Elizabeth, CSP SCOT, VI, 611, 612-613. For Walsingham's mission see the detailed account in C. Read, *Mr Secretary Walsingham and the Policy of Queen Elizabeth* (Cambridge 1925), II, 205-222.
[14] For Arran's abortive negotiations with France see A. Teulet, ed., *Papiers d'état ... inedits ... relatifs à l'histoire de l'Ecosse au XVIe siècle*, Bannatyne Club publication (Paris 1852-1860), II, 635-645. Throughout the period of Arran's ascendancy sporadic attempts to negotiate with the continental Catholics were made by James and Arran. James even went so far as to write a letter to the Pope, on February 19, 1584, CSP SPANISH, III, 518-519. None of these negotiations had any results.
[15] For a convenient summary of these relations see Read, *Walsingham*, II, 222-226.

mother."[16] Less than two weeks later, on August 29, came a crucial turning-point in Maitland's career: he was made a member of the privy council.[17]

Maitland himself was well aware of the importance of this advancement. He knew that political power, for a man of his position in Scottish society, could come only through the council. He soon learned, if he did not know it already, that the council had to be the principal instrument for the increase in the power of the crown. So Maitland became, like Burghley in England, a privy councilor *par excellence*. As the editor of the council's *Register* points out, Maitland almost never missed a meeting.[18] His diligence, his willingness to tackle any kind of job, his grasp of the day-to-day business of government, commended him highly to King James, who was basically lazy and worked only in fits and starts. In fact Maitland eventually became the king's indispensable man.

But in August 1583 all this was far in the future. At the time of his appointment Maitland had very little influence with anybody; in fact, it is difficult to see any very good reason for the appointment at all. To be sure, the king liked him: he could discuss poetry, he was amusing, like all the Maitlands, and he shared James's enthusiasm for the chase.[19] The most probable reason for his elevation, however, seems to be that he, along with Colonel Stewart and Robert Melville, were appointed at this time to prevent the possibility of complete dominance by Arran, who was not yet firmly in the saddle.[20]

[16] CSP SCOT, VI, 587-588.

[17] RPCS, III, 594. He does not appear in the *sederunt*, however, until October 19. *Ibid.*, pp. 600-601.

[18] He was equally regular in his attendance as one of the auditors of the exchequer, as the pages of the *Book of Lords Auditors of Exchequer*, in the SRO, indicate.

[19] See James's note of February 3, 1594, addressing Maitland as "one of the number of us hunters," CSP SCOT, XI, 276-277. Maitland took advantage of his favor with James to get a complete restoration of all the family property on terms most favorable to himself, as well as legal recognition of his possession of the property brought to him by his wife. The record of these various complicated transactions may be found in RMS, IV, 49, 193, 209; RPCS, III, 632-633; APS, III, 318-319, 321-323; SRO, *Register of Deeds*, XX, pt. 2, 382; SRO, *Privy Seal Register*, L, 151; SRO, *Treasurer's Accounts, 1583-1585*.

[20] This inference is borne out to some extent by James Melville's statement

Maitland's attitude to Arran at this juncture is extremely difficult to determine. He certainly evinced no enthusiasm for Arran's policies. In fact, Maitland's only political proposal in his first months as a councilor would, if successful, have resulted in a diminution of Arran's power. He wanted to recall his new relatives, Lords John and Claude Hamilton, both still in exile after their forfeiture during Morton's regime; Maitland had evidently been in communication with them before he was summoned to court.[21] Wanting to restore the Hamiltons was a serious offense in Arran's eyes. Arran, after all, held the Hamilton earldom, and no Stewart, on principle, took very kindly to the Hamiltons, who had the best claim to the throne if James should die childless. Cunningham of Drumquhassel, a minor figure among the Ruthven raiders, was "straitly examined" for, among other things, "the bringing in of the Hamiltons, to the extreme danger of the king."[22] Yet Maitland did not suffer for his presumptuousness. He was able to pursue this policy safely by enlisting the aid of the earl of Huntly. Huntly was also a nephew of Lords John and Claude, and Huntly was too powerful a man, and too instrumental in James's escape from the Ruthven raiders, to be summarily accused of disloyalty. Furthermore, by acting with Huntly, Maitland made it appear that he was favoring the Hamiltons only for family reasons, something every Scot could understand. Arran did not much like this; he attempted to buy off Huntly by giving him the abbey of Paisley, of which Claude Hamilton had once been commendator. This did not work: in January 1584 Maitland and Huntly were again urging Arran to pardon the Hamiltons, and also to exchange the earldom of Arran for that of Ross.[23] This proposal was designed to

in his *Memoirs*, p. 374, that Arran prevented his appointment to the council. Bowes's letter mentioning Maitland's return to court associated him with Colonel Stewart, the Melvilles, and Sir Lewis Bellenden, the justice clerk. In this letter Bowes remarked that Colonel Stewart seemed to have more influence with the king than Arran. CSP SCOT, VI, 587-588. On the other hand, if we believe the vitriolic author of *The Staggering State of Scottish Statesmen*—not a contemporary work—Lady Arran referred to him as "her man Maitland." *Transactions of the Royal Historical Society*, I (1875), 310-311.

21 August 27, 1583, John Hamilton to Walsingham, CSP SCOT, VI, 594.
22 August 25, 1583, Bowes to Walsingham, *ibid*., pp. 591-592.
23 September 19, 1583, February 1, 1584, Bowes to Walsingham, *ibid*., p. 616; CSP SCOT, VII, 23.

tickle Arran's vanity, and quite possibly contained a trap. The last holder of the earldom of Ross had been the unfortunate Darnley. If Arran had made himself earl of Ross, many Scottish noblemen, and particularly many of the Stewarts, would have bitterly resented it.[24] But, for whatever reason, Arran did not take the bait. The Hamiltons remained in exile.

ii

Maitland rejoiced in his appointment to the privy council, but he realized that an unimportant man like himself could exercise very little influence without a permanent official position. From the beginning he had his eye on the office of secretary, which his brother had held for so long. The post was virtually vacant, since its incumbent, the commendator of Dunfermline, had been a partisan of the Ruthven raiders. There was much speculation as to the identity of Dumfermline's successor; Maitland soon appeared to be the leading candidate. Even before his appointment to the privy council Maitland had been carrying out some of the functions of the office; and, during Walsingham's embassy to Scotland he was consulted by James and Arran as to the best way of dealing with the English secretary.[25] "John Maitland," wrote Bowes on September 19, 1583, "has obtained the king's signature for the office of secretary." Then, four days later, Bowes wrote, without giving any reasons, that the grant of the office was "stayed."[26] Possibly Arran was annoyed by Maitland's support of the Hamiltons. In any case, we hear no more about the secretaryship until after the crisis of April 1584. Maitland was then in high favor; he was knighted, and the coveted office was his at last, and later was formally confirmed to him by Parliament.[27]

The crisis of April 1584 was precipitated by the chiefs of

[24] Arran's supposed ambitions were not forgotten. During the coup of 1585, when he was overthrown, he was charged with having said, referring to himself, "Here standeth the person of King James the Seventh!" Calderwood, IV, 384.

[25] August 22, 1583, Bowes to Walsingham, csp scot, vi, 589-591. September 10, Bowes to Beale, ibid., pp. 602-603.

[26] Ibid., pp. 616, 619-620.

[27] May 8, 1584, Bowes to Walsingham, csp scot, vii, 118-119. aps, iii, 300-301.

the Ruthven raiders, who were trying to get back into power in the usual Scottish fashion, by means of a *coup d'état*. It was a miserable failure, mainly because Arran knew all about it beforehand, and was well prepared when the blow fell. This was probably because the negotiations for the plot had to be carried on over a long distance and involved too many people. Two of the leaders, Mar and the master of Glamis, were in Ireland; Angus was warded in the north; Gowrie moved around a good bit, but was generally in the neighborhood of Perth. Furthermore, Gowrie was not fully trusted by the other three; they thought him indispensable, however, because he had so many powerful friends and relations. The conspirators had hopes that a show of strength would bring a flock of malcontents over to their side: aristocrats alienated by Arran's greed, the burghs, whose rights Arran and his friends had violated, the ministers, who loathed the all-powerful favorite.[28] And finally, there was England. Bowes and Walsingham were certainly aware of the plot as early as January 1584; they did all they could to help it along. They doubtless concealed from the conspirators the fact that English counsels were divided over Scottish policy; they made no promises, but Bowes urged the plotters to solicit Elizabeth's aid, and led them to expect that they would receive it, at least after they had a party in the field.[29]

Bowes, instead of encouraging the plot, should have done all he could to stop it. It is clear, from Bowes's own dispatches, that by mid-March at the latest James and Arran knew what was going on,[30] and, just as the conspiracy was about to break out, Arran wrecked it by seizing Gowrie. The other plotters' first reaction was that Gowrie had betrayed them, but they had gone too far to draw back. Mar and Glamis returned from

[28] Calderwood, IV, 21. For the attitude of the burghs see September 28, December 23, 1583, Bowes to Walsingham, CSP SCOT, VI, 622-623, 682-683. The violation of rights in the case of Dundee, of which Arran's ally Crawford was now provost, was particularly flagrant.

[29] January 24, April 10, 1584, Bowes to Walsingham, CSP SCOT, VII, 17-18, 58-59. April 16, John Colville to the laird of Cleish, *ibid.*, pp. 63-65. Read, *Walsingham*, II, 226.

[30] See his letters of March 15, 1584, *ibid.*, pp. 39-42. Sir James Melville apparently was one of the king's sources of information; *Memoirs*, pp. 322-323.

Ireland and, together with Angus, seized Stirling and issued a proclamation declaring their loyalty to the king: it was his evil advisers they disliked. James was not impressed; he and Arran set out for Stirling with a large army. The lords, who had collected only a few hundred men, made no attempt at resistance and fled to England. Their potential allies, who had not committed themselves, drew back. Arran had triumphed.[31]

Angus, Mar, and the master of Glamis were safe, but Gowrie was in the hands of the victors, and they were determined to make an example of him. He was, accordingly, executed as a traitor early in May. There is an ugly story connected with this—that Gowrie was trapped by Arran into making a confession of treason in return for a promise of pardon, which Arran later denied having given. The confession was deemed necessary because Gowrie had not actually been caught in the act of treason. Maitland was allegedly involved, as he was one of those who questioned Gowrie before his trial, along with Montrose, Robert Melville, and others. And yet, Robert Melville accompanied Gowrie to the scaffold, which he hardly would have done if the earl felt that Melville had betrayed him. About all that can be said is that the story is not improbable, and that all those who had to do with the death of Gowrie were in high favor with James and Arran afterwards.[32] Whatever Maitland's role in this affair, he can have felt no sympathy for Gowrie, who was the type of aristocratic politician he most disliked, greedy, selfish, and fickle. Maitland's future career was to be devoted primarily to minimizing the amount of political damage that men like Gowrie could cause.

After Gowrie it was the turn of the kirk. The kirk had supported the government of the Ruthven raiders, and most of

[31] The course of the plot may be followed in the letters of Bowes and others in CSP SCOT, VII, 35ff. It is mentioned in all contemporary accounts. On the crucial significance of the arrest of Gowrie, see the account in Calderwood, IV, 20-35, especially pp. 24-25, and Melville, *Memoirs*, pp. 326-327.

[32] The story of the entrapment of Gowrie is in a contemporary account of the earl's death, CSP SCOT, VII, 103-107. P. F. Tytler (*History of Scotland*, VI, 380-383) accepts the story; A. Lang (*A History of Scotland since the Roman Occupation*, II, 297), is suspicious of it. If the story is true, the fact that Gowrie was accused of dealing with sorcerers may have been the charge that persuaded James to permit the violation of the promise made in his name.

the leading ministers were extremely suspicious of the regime established by James after he had shaken them off. As early as mid-July 1583 the presbytery of Edinburgh sent a delegation to James to bemoan the fact that the "best affected [are] removed from his presence"; it was on this occasion that the king was warned to beware, "for there was never one yet in this realm, in chief authority, that ever prospered after the ministers began to threaten them. (Here the king smiled . . . .)"[33] After Arran obtained control of the government, relations became much worse. The ministers distrusted Arran, and he, in turn, disliked them. Their efforts to reconcile the king with the Ruthven raiders failed; their own cause was not helped by the sermons of men such as John Durie, who openly expressed approval of the Ruthven raid, or by the attitude of the General Assembly, which in October 1583 complained that "open renegades, and blasphemers of the truth, and maintainers of idolatry . . . oppressors of God's people . . . are received in court . . . and . . . are become familiar with your majesty."[34] A climax was reached in February 1584 when Andrew Melvill was summoned before the privy council to answer for a plainly seditious sermon in which he implied that the present king was going the way of James III, who had been ruined by favorites and ultimately victimized by a successful revolt. Melvill denied that his sermon was seditious; much more important, he denied that the council had any right to punish him for it. His position was that if a minister was accused on the basis of something he said in the pulpit, he must be tried in the first instance by an ecclesiastical court. The council was not impressed by this argument, and, after further wrangling, in which Maitland played an undistinguished part, Melvill fled to England to escape imprisonment. A proclamation issued by the government after his flight attempted to reassure the "best affected" by pointing out that Melvill's crime was sedition, not religious enthusiasm.[35]

[33] July 16, 1583, Bowes to Walsingham, CSP SCOT, VI, 540-543. Calderwood, III, 718.

[34] Calderwood, III, 735, 762.

[35] February 20, 1584, Forster to Walsingham, *Border Papers*, I, 128-129. February 24, Bowes to Walsingham, CSP SCOT, VII, 33-35. RPCS, III, 631-632. Cal-

The significance of this affair is far greater than the temporary exile of a prominent minister. Melvill's claim went to the heart of the problem of relations between king and kirk. If it were allowed, it would mean that no effective check could be placed on an organization which aimed at complete domination of the state. James was not disposed to allow this, and who can blame him? On the other hand, James's own views as to the proper relation between church and state went just as far in the opposite direction. In the words of his latest biographer, James regarded "the Scottish Reformation as an antimonarchical revolt against constituted authority."[36] The proper remedy, in James's view, was that contained in the doctrine taught by Patrick Adamson, archbishop of St. Andrews: "That a Christian king should be the chief governor of the kirk, and . . . have bishops under him, to hold all in order."[37] Melvill's attacks on episcopacy, and his extreme claim of February 1584, were met by the extreme Erastianism of the so-called Black Acts.

The revolt of 1584 gave James and Arran their chance to reduce the kirk to what they considered to be its proper place. They suspected the kirk of sympathy with the rebels; this suspicion was seemingly borne out by the flight of three prominent ministers when the revolt collapsed.[38] The upshot was the passage in the Parliament of May 1584 of the statutes known as the Black Acts. This Parliament was very short, even for Scottish Parliaments, lasting only four days, and its business was conducted in great secrecy. No one suspected that any legislation respecting the kirk was planned, according to Calderwood, since such proposals had always been discussed first in the General Assembly. When rumors began to circulate, a minister who went to the king to inquire was hustled off to ward in Blackness. After the Acts became known, more minis-

derwood, IV, 3-18. For a succinct summary of the whole affair see W. L. Mathieson, *Politics and Religion: a Study in Scottish History from the Reformation to the Revolution*, I, 231-236.

[36] D. H. Willson, *James VI and I*, p. 37.

[37] R. Pitcairn, ed., *The Autobiography and Diary of Mr. James Melvill*, p. 120.

[38] Calderwood, IV, 38, denies that the ministers knew anything about the revolt.

ters fled to England, after a Parthian volley against them. Among the fugitives was James Melvill, nephew of the redoubtable Andrew.[39]

By the terms of the Black Acts, episcopacy was explicitly approved. In a clause drafted by Maitland[40] it was declared that king and privy council had jurisdiction over all cases and all persons; anyone who denied that jurisdiction thereby committed treason. No assembly was to be held unless it was authorized by Parliament or had the king's license to meet, and no one, in the pulpit or anywhere else, was to "utter any false, untrue or slanderous speeches to the disdain, reproach and contempt of his majesty, his council and proceedings . . . or to meddle in the affairs of his highness and his estate." The kirk also suffered financially; it was to be made to pay for the upkeep of a royal bodyguard. For this purpose the government was to receive the first fruits of all vacant benefices. In addition, all beneficed men were to contribute annually: benefices worth more than one thousand pounds a year must pay two hundred pounds, and lesser benefices proportionately. Finally, all monks' portions which had lapsed owing to the death of the recipient were to go to the king.[41]

These measures naturally caused a tremendous uproar, for James and Arran were determined to see them enforced. A pamphlet war broke out between the ministers now in England and archbishop Adamson, in which very violent language was used against the archbishop.[42] This vehemence probably did more harm than good; it may well have been prompted by the exiles' knowledge that their extreme point of view was beginning to lose ground.

James at first attempted to force the ministers to hold a General Assembly to register their submission to the Black

[39] *Ibid.*, pp. 62-65, 73-78.

[40] Archbishop Adamson so stated in 1591; Calderwood, v, 121.

[41] APS, III, 292-296, 298-299, 303. Monks' portions were the pensions paid to monks and nuns after the monasteries' religious function was ended by the triumph of the Reformation. In July 1584 orders went out for all beneficed persons to appear by August 10 with information respecting their rents. SRO, *Treasurer's Accounts, 1583-1585.*

[42] Calderwood, IV, 73-122, gives some of the important documents from both sides.

Acts; when this failed, owing to the refusal of the ministers to meet, he tried to make them sign, as individuals, a form of submission drawn up by Adamson, on pain of being deprived of their livings by the archbishop.[43] This did not break the opposition; on September 4 there was a fiery scene between John Craig, one of the Edinburgh ministers, and Adamson and Arran in the king's presence at Falkland. But before the end of the year a compromise was arranged, which split the kirk party. On November 16 the ministers of southern Scotland came to Edinburgh on summons, and were met by Maitland, who made them a conciliatory speech and led them to the royal presence. Here, for the first time, there appeared the formula which was eventually to be agreed upon: the clergy would obey the law in so far as it agreed with the word of God. Very few ministers signed immediately; but by the end of December many had, including Craig. The latter wrote a letter to his brethren in explanation of his action: he and his colleague John Duncanson, he said, had had a private conference with James, Arran, and Maitland, in which it was agreed "First, that our subscription was neither sought to be allowance, either of the Acts of Parliament, nor of the state of the bishops, but to be a testimony of our obedience to his majesty. Next, it was not craved, but according to the word of God, and therefore our obligation containeth nothing but our obedience to the king's majesty, his laws and commissioners, according to the word of God. Which two heads are so reasonable, that no man can refuse the same, who loveth God, or the quietness of the kirk or commonweal."[44]

Craig and his fellow subscribers doubtless felt that this formula committed them to very little; but in practice it meant a great deal, since it separated the moderates among the clergy from their more violent brethren, and created a kind of uneasy truce between the moderates and the government. On the other hand, it meant that the government would be conciliatory to those ministers who subscribed; there was a certain amount of face-saving on both sides. Gradually the government made

43 *Ibid.*, pp. 144-146. APS, III, 347. RPCS, III, 701-704.
44 Calderwood, IV, 198-199, 209-211, 246-247.

headway. In the decree of January 2, 1585, which set up the machinery by which subscriptions were to be obtained, there was created a commission, of which Arran, Montrose, and Maitland were the key members, to adjust ministers' stipends.[45] This was the carrot for the clerical donkey: those ministers who subscribed might expect a sympathetic hearing with respect to their salaries. Conversely, pressure was applied by withholding the shares of the thirds of nonsubscribing ministers, and by depriving them of the right to plead in the royal courts.[46] To make the government's position perfectly clear, Maitland drew up a set of articles in February 1585 which spelled out in detail what the ministers were promising: there was to be no more declinature of jurisdiction, no public preaching against the king, no alleging of inspiration, "except so far as it agreeth with the Holy Scripture"—a substantial exception. Yet the subscriptions rolled in, despite this forbidding *explication de texte*, thanks in large part to the venerable and respected Erskine of Dun, the only signer of the first band of the Lords of the Congregation still alive, who was especially zealous in obtaining signatures.[47]

This settlement with the kirk has been described in detail because it was Maitland's first important venture into the making and execution of state policy, and shows him at his best. He was tactful, patient, and conciliatory; he kept a tight rein on his naturally sharp tongue. He had to overcome not only the suspicion and hostility of many ministers, but also the obstacles thrown in his way by his superiors. The bad-tempered Arran was contemptuous of the clergy, and was hated by them; as for James, his attitude is best expressed by the story Calderwood tells of his toast to his dog: "Tell-True, I drink to thee above all the rest of my hounds; for I will give thee more

[45] *Ibid.*, pp. 339-343. This had been authorized by Parliament in May 1584; APS, III, 303-304.

[46] R. S. Brydon, *The Finances of James VI 1567-1603* (unpublished Ph.D. dissertation, University of Edinburgh), pp. 124-125. RPCS, III, 712-713.

[47] Calderwood, IV, 349-351. For Erskine of Dun's role, see J. Stuart, ed., *Miscellany of the Spalding Club*, 1st series (Aberdeen 1841-1852), IV, 69-74. For evidence as to the proportion of signers to nonsigners, see the letters to the exiled minister John Carmichael in March and April 1585, in D. Laing, ed., *Miscellany of the Wodrow Society* (Edinburgh 1844), pp. 432-437.

credence nor (than) either the bishop or Craig."[48] Adamson, who was highly unpopular anyway, was not helpful; in one of his numerous defences of the Black Acts he denounced Andrew Melvill's declinature of jurisdiction as a "preposterous imitation of the pretended jurisdiction of the Pope of Rome."[49] Such statements were not likely to win over many waverers. Perhaps the most eloquent testimony to the effectiveness of Maitland's work was the hatred he engendered among the clerical extremists, who attacked him in a libel "wherein Justice is brought in lamenting, that one of Cameleon's clan, one of the disciples of Matchiavell, had so great place in the commonwealth, to the ruin of justice." He was also attacked as one of those who "had wearied their wits and pens trafficking with France and Spain, to pluck the crown off his [James's] head."[50]

The settlement with the kirk doubtless occupied most of Maitland's time in the months following the abortive revolt of the Ruthven party, but it was not his only task. In one of the acts of the Parliament of May 1584 it was decreed that all copies of George Buchanan's *De Jure Regni apud Scotos* should be brought to the secretary for revision and correction, which was rather ironic in view of the fact that the form of the book was that of a dialogue between Buchanan and Maitland's younger brother Thomas. King James did not care for this book, which maintained the position, widely held by the clerical extremists, that the king was below the law, and was an administrator rather than a legislator. Buchanan had also used the example of James III, who, in Buchanan's view, was a tyrant, and therefore properly dealt with by his subjects. James VI had heard far too much of James III in recent months.[51]

In that same May Parliament Maitland was also given a

[48] Calderwood, IV, 351.

[49] *Ibid.*, p. 258. Adamson's popularity may be gauged by the fact that in September 1584 the council had to order the citizens of Edinburgh to stop insulting him. RPCS, III, 690-691.

[50] Calderwood, IV, 349, 408.

[51] APS, III, 296. For a good brief analysis of the *De Jure Regni*, see P. Hume Brown, *George Buchanan, Humanist and Reformer* (Edinburgh 1890), pp. 283-292. That Buchanan's view was also that of the kirk is indicated by the "dialogue" between Hume of Godescroft and the earl of Angus in Calderwood, IV, 466-483.

commission, along with Arran and Montrose, to reform the college of justice.[52] What this meant, in practice, was the replacement of politically unreliable members. The nature of the replacements may be gauged by a letter of John Colville, one of the fugitives in England, in which he remarks that John Bartane, "a man that has kept himself obscure these twenty years past for papistry and necromancy" was now a lord of session.[53] Among others replaced was Maitland's father, Sir Richard, who was full of years, and had certainly earned his retirement. He resigned in favor of the justice clerk, Sir Lewis Bellenden, a close ally of Maitland's in the complicated political broil that was about to ensue.

Overshadowing these administrative matters in the minds of most men was the question of the spoils. In the Parliaments of May and August 1584 the rebels of April were forfeited, and their lands, and those of any others on whom Arran's wrath might fall, were available to the victorious party to divide, and quarrel over. They did both. Arran himself profited immoderately; he was made donator of the escheat of the earl of Gowrie. His popularity was not increased by this, nor by his public brutality to the widowed countess.[54] Maitland, on the other hand, was neither vengeful nor excessively greedy. His chief reward was the office of secretary. He also acquired the escheat of the minister of Haddington, who had been denounced rebel, the office of baillie of Musselburgh, various tacks out of the bishopric of Dunkeld, and the estate of Boncle, which had belonged to Angus.[55]

There was another piece of property in which Maitland had an interest: his old possession, the priory of Coldingham. At one point it was rumored that he would get it back. This report turned out to be false; Maitland never did get it back,

---

[52] APS, III, 310.

[53] The letter was written in February 1585; D. Laing, ed., *Original Letters of Mr. John Colville 1582-1603*, Bannatyne Club publication (Edinburgh 1858), pp. 83-84. William Davison, currently the English resident in Scotland, was equally critical; CSP SCOT, VII, 182-184.

[54] RPCS, III, 673-674, 684. For Arran's brutality to Lady Gowrie see Calderwood, IV, 197-198.

[55] June 10, 1584, Davison to Walsingham, CSP SCOT, VII, 184-186. SRO, *Treasurer's Accounts 1583-1585*. SRO, *Privy Seal Register*, L, 148-151.

in spite of sporadic attempts to reassert his rights. But it caused him trouble all the same, because the other claimant to Coldingham, which was currently in the possession of the eldest son of Hume of Manderston, was the earl of Bothwell; and it seems very likely that Bothwell's later violent hatred of Maitland had its origin in their competition for possession of Coldingham.[56]

In 1584 the feud between the earl and the secretary lay far in the future, however. Bothwell was much more concerned now with the actual possessors of what he regarded as his property. In September of 1584 he waylaid the younger son of Manderston and two companions, and "killed all the three, but hewed Davy Hume, who was the earl of Arran's man, all to pieces."[57] From this time forward Arran and Bothwell were at daggers drawn. As a result the future antagonists, Bothwell and Maitland, entered into a temporary alliance. For in this same month of September came the first overt break between Maitland and Arran,[58] and from this time forward Maitland began steadily to work against the all-powerful favorite.

iii

Maitland had never liked the dictatorial and grasping Arran. As early as September 1583 Walsingham, during his embassy to Scotland, had noted that Maitland did not care for Arran's violent courses.[59] Maitland could do little then; but a year later, entrenched in his office and secure in the king's favor, he began, obscurely and rather ineffectually, to maneuver against Arran. As Spottiswoode put it, "Mr. John Maitland, though he had followed him [Arran] still from Mor-

[56] May 11, 1584, Davison to Walsingham, CSP SCOT, VII, 123-125. Maitland had renounced his claims to Coldingham when he was restored, and this was explicitly stated in two separate enactments of Parliament, in 1581 and 1584. APS, III, 270, 277-278, 313. In April 1585, after Manderston had been accused of barratry and treason, one of Maitland's relatives was appointed factor of the priory, indicating that the secretary was prepared to revive his claims. SRO, *Privy Seal Register*, LII, 110.

[57] September 11, 1584, Hunsdon to Burghley, CSP SCOT, VII, pp. 328-330.

[58] Maitland and Robert Melville were accused of mishandling a supposed conspiracy against Arran. September 6, 1584, Davison to Burghley, *ibid.*, pp. 318-320.

[59] CSP SCOT, VI, 598-600.

ton's execution to that time, began to fall away and work his own credit."[60] He resumed his policy of pleading for the Hamiltons in association with Huntly, and failed as resoundingly as he had before. "Arran carried away the prize, because of Huntly's folly," says Calderwood, without telling us what Huntly's folly was.[61]

Behind this intrigue with respect to the Hamiltons lay something deeper and far more dangerous. Maitland was in touch with the deposed queen. This was not owing to any great sympathy for Mary's cause, but simply to the circumstances of the moment. At this time Arran was making a great parade of his pro-English sentiments; in August 1584 he had met Lord Hunsdon on the border and had a long private conversation with him.[62] Maitland accompanied Arran on this occasion, but was not allowed to participate; during the meeting he and others "kept scout watch in the open churchyard"—which must have been galling to a man who, by virtue of his office, should have been the king's chief agent in foreign affairs.[63] Maitland was evidently prepared to become temporarily anti-English if this was the only way to weaken Arran.

The evidence of Maitland's intrigue with Mary is puzzling and obscure. In the summer of 1584 an agent of the deposed queen, Fontenay, was in Scotland, whence he sent her a long report, dated August 15. Fontenay bears witness to Maitland's friendliness and his influence in the following terms: Maitland "professes to be very much your servant. I desire him as such, as being a man of importance, whom they esteem to be discreet and clever. He is of the triumvirate with Arran and Montrose,

[60] Archbishop John Spottiswoode, *History of the Church of Scotland*, ed. Bishop M. Russell and M. Napier for the Spottiswoode Society, II (Edinburgh 1851), 323.

[61] Calderwood, IV, 208-209.

[62] August 14, 1584, Hunsdon to Walsingham, *ibid.*, pp. 171-175. Hunsdon was the leading English advocate of a policy of friendliness to Arran.

[63] August 17, 1584, Davison to Walsingham, CSP SCOT, VII, 280-281. At this time Maitland's only function with respect to foreign affairs, aside from one general discussion with Davison in June (for which see *ibid.*, pp. 200-203), seems to have been to receive Davison's complaints with respect to border violations. See, for instance, August 26, 1584, Hunsdon to Davison, *ibid.*, pp. 297-298. Maitland's irritation over being left out is remarked upon by Mary's agent Fontenay in a dispatch written late in 1584, CSP SCOT, VI, 278 (where it is misdated January 1583).

I understand, for the affairs of the estate and of the council."[64] Davison, the English resident ambassador, also believed that Maitland was "wholly [the] Scottish queen's, body and soul."[65] Mary evidently thought so too. In January 1585, on Fontenay's expulsion from Scotland, she sent Maitland a cipher for correspondence with her, and left Fontenay's unfinished business in his hands.[66]

I have been unable to find any evidence of direct communication between Maitland and Mary. This does not mean, of course, that they did not correspond; in fact, it seems likely that they did, or Mary would not have entrusted him with her affairs in preference to, say, Huntly, who did write effusively to the queen during this period.[67] But by the time Mary sent Maitland the cipher, the secretary was no longer prepared to use it.

For early in 1585—the exact date is uncertain—Maitland discovered what he felt to be a much surer way of undermining Arran than by plotting with the captive queen. The secretary knew that the principal source of Arran's strength lay in his favor with the king. If he could be displaced, or even rivaled, in James's affections, he might be overturned. And now, for the first time since Arran obtained his sway over the young king, a potential rival had appeared at court, a man in whom the king was showing a marked interest; Patrick, master of Gray.

Gray was an ambitious and attractive young man who had spent a good many years in France, and who had recently returned to Scotland with the young duke of Lennox, son of the late favorite. Gray had been high in the councils of Mary's party, and was vehemently disliked by the kirk; he was generally regarded as a Papist.[68] But Gray's religion, and his past political associations, sat lightly on him. Fontenay, in his report to Mary in August 1584, expressed grave suspicion of Gray, and events were to prove him right. For what Gray

---

[64] CSP SCOT, VII, 269.

[65] *Ibid.*, p. 249.

[66] A. Labanoff, ed., *Receuil des lettres de Marie Stuart*, VI (London 1844), 80-81. CSP SCOT, VII, 684-685. See also September 28, 1584, Mary to Fontenay, *ibid.*, pp. 341-342.

[67] E.g., August 31, 1584, Huntly to Mary, *ibid.*, p. 305.

[68] March 15, 1584, Bowes to Walsingham, *ibid.*, pp. 39-40.

wanted was political influence, and, like Maitland, he saw how to get it, by winning the king's favor and overturning Arran. The favorite could not be eliminated by alliance with the Marians, however; of this, Gray, who had had considerable experience of their ineffectual conspiracies, was convinced. There had to be another way—and, at the end of 1584, Gray found it.

Gray had been among those who accompanied Arran to his meeting with Hunsdon in August of 1584; at that time he was presented to the Englishman as the representative whom James would shortly send to London to declare his mind to Elizabeth. What was on James's mind was Elizabeth's kindness to his fugitive rebels, and possibly an Anglo-Scottish league. If Elizabeth was obliging on the first point, Gray was instructed to reveal all he knew of Mary's conspiracies.[69]

With respect to these ostensible objects of his mission Gray achieved considerable success. Elizabeth was willing to negotiate a league. She did not learn much about Mary's plotting from Gray, and expressed a certain amount of annoyance,[70] but the recent capture at sea of the Jesuit Crichton doubtless told her all she wanted to know on that point. She was even willing to order the fugitive lords to move away from the Scottish frontiers; as Gray derisively put it, they were to be sent to Oxford to school.

Gray was an able negotiator, but the real cause of his success was not his diplomatic skill, but rather his underhand agreement with the English government on the subject of Arran. Elizabeth and Walsingham neither liked nor trusted Arran, but the only alternative to dealing with him, especially after the fiasco of the Protestant lords in April 1584, seemed to be the even less palatable course of dealing with Mary, who was wrongly believed to be calling the tune in Scotland.[71] Gray reassured the English with respect to Mary's influence, which was, in fact, almost nonexistent. In his turn he was him-

[69] Gray's instructions are in *Letters and Papers Relating to Patrick, Master of Gray,* Bannatyne Club publication (Edinburgh 1835), p. 11, and in A. I. Cameron and R. S. Rait, eds., *The Warrender Papers,* SHS, 3rd series, vols. XVIII-XIX (Edinburgh 1931-1932), I, 164-167.

[70] November 1584, Walsingham to Hunsdon, CSP SCOT, VII, 425.

[71] See, for example, Davison's letters of May 28 and June 10, 1584, *ibid.,* pp. 164-165, 182-184.

self reassured as to the real English attitude toward Arran; his informant was the devious and perjured, but very shrewd, Archibald Douglas, who had been a hanger-on at the English court since his flight from Scotland at the time of the fall of his cousin the regent Morton.[72] At once Gray saw the possibilities of this state of affairs. If the English could be induced to support him rather than Arran, the latter could be overthrown in collaboration with England. The English were only too willing.

Gray returned to Scotland from London at the end of January 1585, and, as an earnest of his good intentions toward England he obtained a formal vote of the privy council against any "association" with Mary; Fontenay, her agent, was told to leave the country.[73] At the same time Gray quietly began to build a party among those who were hostile to Arran. Just how this was done is hard to say; it is possible that Gray worked through the Melvilles, whose dislike of Arran was public knowledge.[74] At any rate it is clear that among Gray's earliest recruits, and the two on whom he relied most heavily in the months to come, were Bellenden, the justice clerk, and Maitland.

The four months between the return of Gray and the coming of the English ambassador Edward Wotton to Scotland were spent by Gray and Arran in an uneasy jockeying for position, particularly with respect to James. Arran was beginning to distrust Gray, whose influence with the king was obviously increasing. He thought to solidify his own influence by discovering various "plots" against James; in February 1585 Bellenden was sent to England to tell Elizabeth about one of them.[75] For Arran's purposes Bellenden was an unfortu-

[72] The evidence for this is a letter from Walsingham to Edward Wotton, dated June 18, 1585, in which Walsingham says that Gray "was only by his [Douglas'] persuasion wrought to take the course that he doth." J. Bain, ed., *The Hamilton Papers*, II (Edinburgh 1892), 654-655.

[73] January 22, 1585, Gray to Elizabeth, CSP SCOT, VII, 540-541. January 24, Gray to Walsingham, *Gray Papers*, pp. 41-43.

[74] A passage in Melville's *Memoirs*, p. 331, suggests this.

[75] His instructions are in CSP SCOT, VII, 569-570. See also HMC, *Report on the Laing Manuscripts in the University of Edinburgh*, ed. Rev. H. Paton, I (London 1914), 40-44, and February 15, 1585, Gray to Burghley, CSP SCOT, VII, 560.

nate choice, since he was Gray's man. Elizabeth's reply was that she did not believe in the plot, and that she was sending an ambassador—Wotton—to Scotland to discuss the various questions at issue between England and Scotland, including the possibility of an alliance.[76]

Maitland took advantage of Bellenden's embassy to England to strengthen his personal standing with Elizabeth's government. On April 12 he wrote Bellenden a letter, very Protestant in tone, explaining carefully to Bellenden that he favored the league, as did James, because it would safeguard the true religion.[77] This letter was obviously designed to be shown to the English, in order to reassure them as to his reliability, and it evidently served its purpose—at least to the extent of inducing Walsingham to open a friendly correspondence with him. Toward the end of the letter Maitland remarked that nothing much was going on in Scotland except for the uproar on the western marches. This outbreak was the current installment in the long feud between the Maxwells and the Johnstones; it had broken out in February of 1585, when Maxwell, who objected to the favor shown to his enemy by the government, refused to obey an order to ward himself in Blackness. By April the disturbance had grown to such an extent that James asked the convention of estates for a tax of twenty thousand pounds and planned to summon the lieges of the south to march against Maxwell.[78]

"It is believed," Maitland wrote, in describing this affair to Bellenden, "the lord Maxwell is agreed with the rebels [i.e., the fugitive lords] and would fain open them a door if they had force to enter." This was, in fact, true. Maxwell had written to his cousin John Hamilton, who passed the letter on to the English government.[79] It was normal for Scottish rebels

---

[76] CSP SCOT, VII, 641, 644.

[77] The letter is printed in *Warrender Papers*, I, 180-182.

[78] March 10, 1585, Scrope to Walsingham, *Border Papers*, I, 174-175. RPCS, III, 725, 735, 737, 739, 741-742.

[79] March 26, 1585, Forster to Walsingham, *Border Papers*, I, 176. Maxwell's letter, dated March 18, is in CSP SCOT, VII, 596. The mothers of Maxwell and John Hamilton were sisters. There was a further connection between Maxwell and Maitland. Lady Maitland had obtained the wardship and marriage of Maxwell, who was her first cousin, once removed. Maxwell bought up these

to ask for English aid, and Maxwell, though a Catholic, was no exception. But it did bring into sharper focus the whole problem of the fugitive lords. Elizabeth was most anxious for their restoration; James was exceedingly hostile to them. Gray was thus caught in a nasty dilemma. His goal was to replace Arran as the king's favorite; but how could he become the king's favorite if, in the process of overturning Arran, he compelled James to swallow the unpalatable pill of restoration of the lords? Furthermore, while Gray himself might not object to this restoration—his mother was a Ruthven—his chief collaborators, especially Maitland, did not relish the prospect.[80] As late as August 30 Wotton was writing that Maitland "is a great favorer of the Hamiltons, and as yet no earnest friend to the lords."[81] It seems likely that the fact that the return of the lords meant also the return of Lord John Hamilton ultimately reconciled Maitland to a distasteful necessity.[82]

All of these conflicting strands were drawn together during the embassy of Edward Wotton to Scotland in the summer and fall of 1585. Wotton, a cousin of Walsingham's, was sent to Scotland for two purposes: to negotiate a league, and to conspire with Gray against Arran.[83] He arrived in Scotland on May 29, and at once got in touch with Gray. Gray's immediate worry was the size of the pension Elizabeth was preparing to offer James in the event of an alliance; he had mentioned the sum of twenty thousand crowns to James, and he was afraid that he would suffer in James's esteem if the pension were smaller. He also did not want Wotton to deliver any message

---

rights from her, and on August 26, 1584, obligated himself to pay the last installment of the purchase price by Martinmas. SRO, *Register of Deeds*, XXII, 340-341.

80 May 28, 1585, Walsingham to Wotton, *Hamilton Papers*, II, 645-646. On the other hand, there was the awkward fact that in May 1585 Gray was divorced by his wife, a relative of the master of Glamis, for adultery. *Scots Peerage*, IV, 285.

81 *Hamilton Papers*, II, 686-687. The lords were not overfond of Maitland either. In a letter to Elizabeth of August 1584 they lumped him together with Arran, Montrose, and Colonel Stewart, as those "that utterly hate and mislike your majesty." *Colville Letters*, p. 69.

82 Lord John himself had recently patched up his long-standing quarrel with Angus and Mar at Elizabeth's behest; this may also have helped Maitland make up his mind. CSP SCOT, VII, 386-387.

83 Wotton's instructions are in *ibid.*, pp. 611-614.

to Arran; this would allow Arran to boast that "he is suited by England," and also would upset Maitland.[84] Throughout the ensuing months Maitland was to betray repeated signs of tension and fear.[85] He was by no means a coward; he had stood up manfully to danger before, and would do so again; but for some reason he was always very nervous of Arran.

There was considerable discussion of the possibility of assassinating Arran. Gray, Maitland, and Bellenden all favored this, once the league was signed and James formally committed to England, as the only sure way of disposing of Arran, who, they assured Wotton, was the great obstacle to the "amity."[86] This was reported to Walsingham, who replied that such a step would be most unwise. James would hold England responsible, and the only people who would benefit would be the pro-French party in Scotland. It would be better, said Walsingham, even to try to reconcile Gray and Arran than to do this.[87] Walsingham seems to have come to this decision partly out of suspicion of the motives of some of Gray's friends, including Maitland;[88] he was also afraid that Mary's friends would use any act of violence against Arran to turn James decisively against England. Wotton did not share Walsingham's fears with respect to Maitland. On June 30 he wrote, "Gray and I think the latter [Maitland] is sound, and the wisest man in Scotland, well affected in religion and worth winning."[89] He continued to send similar assurances throughout his stay in Scotland.

After considerable discussion Wotton and the confederates agreed on a policy: they would get the league signed first; then they would tackle the problem of the fugitive lords, and

[84] May 31, 1585, Gray to Walsingham, ibid., pp. 651-652.

[85] See, for instance, Wotton's letters of June 5 and 9, 1585, ibid., 659-660, 662-664.

[86] June 1, 9, 1585, Wotton to Walsingham, ibid., pp. 654-655, 662-664. From certain phrases in the letters of June 1, and May 31, Wotton to Walsingham, ibid., pp. 652-653, it seems that the question of assassinating Arran had arisen before, and that a letter from Elizabeth had stopped it.

[87] June 6, 1585, Walsingham to Wotton, Hamilton Papers, II, 648-649.

[88] See, for instance, his letter of August 21, 1585 to Wotton, ibid., p. 681.

[89] CSP SCOT, VII, 681-682. On the same day he wrote Archibald Douglas that an attempt by Arran to win Maitland over had failed. Salisbury Papers, XIII, 269-270.

finally they would dispose of Arran, either by putting pressure on James for "justice" against the favorite, or by force. The second step would clearly be the crucial one, since James favored the league, and so, nominally, did Arran. But James was still very hostile to the fugitive lords, and "Arran fears the return of the lords above everything"—as well he might.[90]

So the negotiations for the league went forward, Wotton the while ingratiating himself with James by showing himself to be as enthusiastic a huntsman as the king.[91] At the end of June an English draft was sent to Scotland to serve as a basis for discussion. The league was to be both offensive and defensive; its purpose was to defend the religion, and other Protestant princes would be allowed to join. Neither side could make a treaty with a third party without the consent of the other. James would take Elizabeth's advice with respect to his marriage, and in return nothing would be done to prejudice his "pretended title of succession in England."[92] When he received the draft, Wotton showed it to Maitland; on Maitland's advice he then took it privately to James, who thought it satisfactory and promised to submit it to the convention of estates, which in turn would empower James to negotiate over the details. The convention of estates duly acted, on July 31; Maitland had meanwhile promised Wotton that the Scottish commissioners for the league would be "fit persons," and James had vowed to Maitland and Gray that if there was any opposition to the league at the meeting of the estates, he would hold Arran and Montrose responsible, and would banish them.[93]

90 June 5, 9, 27, 30, 1585, Wotton to Walsingham, csp scot, vii, 659, 661-662, 680-681, 682-683.

91 Melville, *Memoirs*, p. 335. There was a good deal of anguished correspondence about a gift of some hounds which had been promised the king; they had not yet come, and James was fretful. Wotton feared that Arran might use the incident as a talking-point against England. The final arrival of some horses instead delighted James, much to Wotton's relief. On such trivia the destinies of nations sometimes hang. The course of this "crisis" may be followed in csp scot, vii, 649ff. A similar situation arose in 1586, during the final negotiations for the league; see Willson, *James VI and I*, pp. 71-72.

92 csp scot, vii, 661. See also the fuller draft, csp scot, viii, 43-45.

93 July 8, 23, August 2, 1585, Wotton to Walsingham, *ibid.*, pp. 8, 36, 54-55.

Gray evidently was succeeding in his plan of undermining Arran in the king's estimation.

After Maitland had had a chance to study the text of the proposed treaty, however, he began to have some reservations about it. He proposed a number of changes. The treaty was to be defensive only. James was to be declared Elizabeth's successor in Parliament. All Scots were to become citizens of England, and vice versa. The king of France was to be comprehended in the treaty if he wished. Other changes were proposed too—whether by Maitland or not is not clear. The most important of these provided for a mutual exchange—or expulsion—of rebels, a clause which Elizabeth accepted with the additional proviso that they should "first be lawfully proved to be rebels," a convenient loophole. Otherwise she would have no part of the Scottish proposals, especially that on the succession. The most that she would do was to write a private letter to James, promising that as long as he behaved himself, she would do nothing to prejudice his "pretended" title—and she insisted on the word. James accepted this, probably at Gray's urging. Gray may well have feared that if he could not get James's consent to the alliance on England's terms, Elizabeth would abandon him. So Maitland's proposals were rejected.[94]

Maitland's "coldness" on the league did not proceed from any desire to wreck the alliance, as Wotton temporarily feared, nor was it a reflection of the attitude of James, as Walsingham, doubtless with the clause on the succession uppermost in his mind, seemed to think.[95] Maitland simply believed that Scotland was getting the worst of the bargain. Like his brother, he did not believe that Scotland should be treated as a client state. He knew that Elizabeth was virtually committed to war with Spain, and that under such circumstances Scottish friendship was vital to her. He saw no reason for closing immediately with England when more favorable terms could almost cer-

94 *Warrender Papers*, I, 200-202. CSP SCOT, VIII, 43-46. August 19, September 13, 1585, Wotton to Walsingham, *ibid.*, pp. 70-71, 103-104.

95 September 15, 1585, Wotton to Walsingham, *ibid.*, p. 104. September 24, Walsingham to Wotton, *ibid.*, pp. 112-113.

tainly be obtained with a little patience. For the moment, however, his advice was ignored.

While these negotiations were going on, the plot against Arran was proceeding. Here the main problem was to attract as many important people as possible, and Gray went about this by allowing his hostility to Arran to become more and more open; by the beginning of July things had reached such a pass that James himself intervened and ordered Gray to be civil to Arran. Arran was universally unpopular; more and more people began to drift over to Gray's side. The rebellious Maxwell was Gray's ally, and his rebellion continued to prosper: he even captured his enemy Johnstone. Other Catholic nobles had been alienated by Arran's negotiations with Elizabeth. Bothwell was openly and contemptuously hostile to Arran. Huntly and Athol were Gray's friends; he even had hopes of Colonel Stewart. The kirk, although it did not trust Gray and his friends,[96] hated Arran; the ministers blamed him for the plague currently raging in Scotland, and even for the bad summer weather. Since all the followers of the fugitive lords could be counted on too, this gave Gray a great preponderance of strength. Arran's efforts to break up the combination against him were unavailing, although they were alarming enough to cause Gray, Maitland, and Bellenden to pledge to have no secrets from each other, so that no suspicion could arise owing to Arran's spreading of rumors. When the end came, Arran's only wholehearted supporters, aside from his immediate family, were Colonel Stewart, Crawford, and Montrose.[97]

The chain of events that led to the favorite's overthrow started by accident. On July 27, 1585, the English and Scottish wardens of the middle march, Sir John Forster and Thomas Ker of Ferniehirst, met to deal with border affairs, which had been getting more and more chaotic in recent years, thanks to the usual feuds and the frequent changes in the office of

96 Calderwood, iv, 372, 377-378, reports a rumor that the hostility between Gray and Arran was collusive, and was devised by Maitland and Robert Melville to discover how popular the government really was.

97 CSP SCOT, vii, 671-672, 674-675, 691-692. June 9, July 2, 8, 1585, Wotton to Walsingham, ibid., pp. 661-662; ibid., viii, 2-3, 6-8. Willson, James VI and I, p. 55.

warden on the Scottish side.[98] There was a scuffle at the meeting, and Lord Russell, the son of the earl of Bedford, was
killed. The affair was unpremeditated, as Forster's first reports made clear; the slain man was present purely by chance.
But everybody concerned, including Forster, saw very quickly
that this accident could be used as a political lever against
Arran. Ferniehirst was a Catholic, and was Arran's appointee.
Arran, seeing how the wind was blowing from England, had
begun to traffic with France and the Catholics. Thus the broil
could be made to look like a plot devised by Arran to wreck
Anglo-Scottish friendship and break up the league, and carried out by Ferniehirst out of personal dislike of Russell.[99]

Wotton saw this at once. He took a very strong line with
James, who tearfully protested his innocence and had Arran
warded in St. Andrews. In this matter it seems that Wotton
was taking Maitland's advice. He passed on to Walsingham
Maitland's suggestion that England should act as if the whole
business had been plotted beforehand by Arran and Ferniehirst. James should be pressed, but not allowed to despair;
if this were done, James could be persuaded to send Arran
to England for trial, or at the very least Arran and Montrose
could be sent to England as hostages for the observance of
the treaty of alliance. All this will be difficult to manage, Wotton concluded, but Maitland "con questo re puo fare tutto
quello che volle."[100]

It is the heightened influence of Maitland at this juncture,
both with Wotton and with the king, that offers the most reasonable explanation of Gray's astonishing about-face. Gray at
first expressed his pleasure at the turn events had taken, in
a letter to Archibald Douglas dated July 31.[101] But then he
must suddenly have realized that his personal position had be-

[98] For the situation on the borders at this time see D. L. W. Tough, *The
Last Years of a Frontier* (Oxford 1928), pp. 232-238.

[99] The changing tone of Forster's reports is very revealing. See *Border Papers*, I, 188ff, CSP SCOT, VIII, 47. The feelings of Russell and Ferniehirst for
each other may be gauged by the former's comment to Walsingham, in a letter
of May 16, 1585, that Ferniehirst was half mad. PRO, *Border Calendar*, Ind.
6887.

[100] CSP SCOT, VIII, 42-43, 47-48. The whole affair is well summarized by W. C.
Dickinson, "The Death of Lord Russell, 1585," SHR, XX (1922-1923), 181-186.

[101] CSP SCOT, VIII, 49-50.

come very much weaker. The negotiations for the alliance were going forward. Arran was ruined, through no doing of his. He was no longer indispensable—and it was Maitland who, seemingly, was becoming so. It was Maitland who was receiving friendly letters from England, from Elizabeth, Walsingham, and Leicester.[102] It was Maitland who was thick as thieves with Wotton. It was Maitland whose advice the English were following.[103] Gray knew that the English had some doubts about Maitland because he had been a Marian; but Gray was tarred with the same brush.[104] He had to move, and move quickly, to demonstrate his own indispensability to the English.

So Gray took an incredibly dangerous gamble. He persuaded James to release Arran from ward. The king, who was genuinely fond of Arran, needed little convincing. In announcing his decision to Elizabeth, on August 6, James explained that he was not convinced of Arran's guilt, and besides, Lady Arran was ill. Arran in any case was not to be permitted to come to court until the whole business was cleared up.[105] Elizabeth was furious at the news; but everyone else's reactions were most satisfactory to Gray. Wotton was desperate, and talked of trying to deal with Arran. He knew very well that Maitland and Bellenden by themselves could not destroy Arran, since "they are not men to carry any great influence with the nobility."[106] Maitland and Belenden were panicky; they went to Wotton and begged him to persuade Walsingham to overlook Gray's fault, since they believed they could win him over once again. The universal opinion was that if Gray and Arran really had come together, only force could overturn them.[107]

Gray then suddenly veered round. On August 9 Wotton

[102] *Warrender Papers*, I, 182-183, 187-189.

[103] Gray, of course, could not be certain of this. But it happened to be true. August 5, 1585, Walsingham to Wotton, *Hamilton Papers*, II, 667-668.

[104] For an example of the English suspicions of Gray, see Elizabeth's letters to King James early in 1585, in J. Bruce, ed., *Letters of Queen Elizabeth and James VI*, Camden Society publication (London 1849), pp. 10-13.

[105] CSP SCOT, VIII, 58. Melville (*Memoirs*, pp. 344-345) says that Arran bribed Gray to get his release by promising to obtain the vacant abbey of Dunfermline for Gray. Gray did, in fact, acquire Dunfermline shortly thereafter.

[106] August 19, 1585, Wotton to Walsingham, CSP SCOT, VIII, 70-71.

[107] August 6, 7, 13, 19, 1585, Wotton to Walsingham, *ibid.*, pp. 59, 60, 70-71; *Hamilton Papers*, II, 673-675.

reported a conversation with Gray, who, said Wotton, now repented of his move on Arran's behalf, but left Wotton with the impression that England would do well to support him, or he really would side with Arran. At the same time Gray wrote a letter to Archibald Douglas which revealed what his new tack really was. He accused his chief co-conspirators, Maitland and Bellenden, of being secret Marians; at the same time he attempted to commit the English firmly to his support by proposing that the fugitive lords be restored at once, as the first order of business, before the conclusion of the league, a timetable which he knew Elizabeth much preferred.[108]

This brilliant stroke worked out almost entirely as Gray had planned. By adopting the English view with respect to the timing of the restoration of the lords, Gray convinced the English that he was the most suitable instrument for their purposes in Scotland, and his peccadillo with respect to Arran was overlooked. Only in one particular did he fail: he could not persuade England to abandon Maitland and Bellenden. So he dropped that tack, and proceeded to work with them again; but he continued to try to undermine them, by pointing out, truly enough, that they were not at all enthusiastic for the return of the lords.[109]

The plot now went forward with considerable speed. On September 10 Walsingham informed Wotton that the lords would be "let slip," to use Gray's own phrase, at the proper time.[110] The time came in the middle of October. By October 16 the lords were at Kelso, collecting their forces; there they were joined by some of their border allies. Colonel Stewart's effort to break up their concentration before it was completed was checked at Jedburgh, possibly through information sent to the lords by their allies at court.[111] By the end of the month the lords were ready to move on Stirling, where the king was in residence.

Arran tried desperately to save the situation. He rushed to

[108] August 21, 1585, Walsingham to Wotton, *ibid.*, p. 681. August 9, 25, Wotton to Walsingham, CSP SCOT, VIII, 62, 79-80.

[109] On these points see Wotton's letters of August 30, September 1 and 11, 1585, CSP SCOT, VIII, 84, 88-89, 101; *Hamilton Papers*, II, 688-689.

[110] *Hamilton Papers*, II, 697.   [111] Melville, *Memoirs*, p. 348.

Stirling and denounced Gray to James as the author of this treasonable business. James ordered Gray to come to court and explain himself. Gray, who was gathering soldiers in Fife, nominally for use in a proposed levy against Maxwell, decided, after some hesitation, to brazen it out. He came to Stirling and persuaded the king that he was innocent, doubtless with the aid of Maitland and Bellenden, who were also there. Arran then apparently thought of murdering Gray, but at that moment word came that the army of lords was within a mile of Stirling. Arran, after a night spent on the battlements with Montrose, fled from Stirling on November 2, the day the lords entered the town. The following day James, after a futile attempt to escape, accepted the lords' terms, Maitland and Bellenden acting as intermediaries. The coup was a brilliant success.[112]

The overthrow of Arran marks off an important epoch in the reign of James VI. Until that time the king had not been the most important person in the government; after Arran's fall, he undoubtedly was. No one, after 1585, ever dominated James quite so completely as Lennox and Arran had, with the possible exception of Buckingham at the end of his life; and never again was James to be subjected to the sort of treatment he received at the hands of the Ruthven raiders. Before 1585 James had been king in name; now he began to be king in fact.

For Maitland this state of affairs was ideal for both his personal and his political ambitions. If he was to achieve real political power, it could only be as the king's servant, not as the minion of some favorite. The strengthening of the crown was his major political objective, and this would not be accomplished by a man like Arran, whose purposes were, at bottom, the same as those of Gowrie: the satisfaction of his ego and his greed. Arran had, in fact, brought the crown into dis-

---

[112] Maitland, in conducting the negotiations, adopted a rather lofty tone to the lords, if Spottiswoode's account is correct, *History*, ii, 332. If so, it was for the king's benefit only, since the interview was collusive. The best contemporary account of the coup is Gray's own, csp scot, viii, 158-160. See also Calderwood, iv, 381-393, and the correspondence in csp scot, viii, 131ff, and in *Border Papers*, i, 207-210. Andrew Lang's account of the affair is succinct: *History*, ii, 315-316.

repute, since his selfish actions were carried out under color of its authority. The power and prestige of the Scottish crown was at a low ebb in 1585, when King James assumed the active management of his inheritance. The measure of Maitland's achievement was its vastly enhanced authority in 1595, the year of his death.

CHAPTER 4

THE LEAGUE WITH ENGLAND

WITH the king a virtual prisoner in their hands, and the once-dreaded favorite a fugitive, the leaders of the victorious coalition were in a position to do whatever they chose with the government. They chose, naturally enough, to entrench themselves in power. The various strong places of the realm were taken over. Lord John Hamilton became captain of Dumbarton, Mar, of Stirling, Bellenden, of Blackness, and the old Douglas keep at Tantallon was returned to the earl of Angus. Edinburgh castle, the most important in the land, was given over to Sir James Hume of Cowdenknowes, whom Maitland had once been instrumental in saving from the wrath of Arran.[1] Parliament was promptly summoned, and met at Linlithgow in December 1585. The fugitive lords were legally restored to their estates, and the composition of the new privy council was formally approved. Beyond this, the chief task of the Parliament was to remedy some of the confusion caused by Arran's irregular and grasping methods of administration.[2] No effort was made to wreak vengeance on Arran and his followers. The fallen favorite lost his earldom and the office of chancellor, which he had held since 1584, and he had to disgorge the property he had accumulated during his years of power.[3] His principal allies, Montrose, Crawford, and Colonel Stewart, were warded for a few months and then released. This

---

[1] June 23, 1584, Davison to Burghley, csp scot, vii, 203-206.

[2] See, e.g., aps, iii, 376, 377, 380.

[3] *Ibid.*, pp. 378, 380. I will continue to refer to the former favorite as "Arran" although he was stripped of his title with the restoration of the Hamiltons and should properly be called "Captain Stewart." The genuine earl of Arran, the older brother of Lord John Hamilton, was insane. One of the acts of this Parliament, *ibid.*, p. 396, gave him into the custody of Lord John.

leniency was designed to reconcile the young king to the removal of his favorite, and was brilliantly successful.

Power in the new regime lay in the hands of four men: Angus, Gray, the master of Glamis, and Maitland. Angus' strength lay in the fact that he was the darling of the kirk as well as the head of the house of Douglas. Gray, now commendator of Dunfermline, had great personal influence with the king. The master of Glamis was captain of the guard and treasurer of the kingdom. Maitland was rewarded by a pension of a thousand pounds a year,[4] and in his hands lay the day-to-day administration of the government. Of the four it was Maitland who possessed the greatest share of the king's confidence—at least the master of Glamis seemed to think so.[5] There were others who might have played a great role: Lord John Hamilton, the earls of Huntly and Mar. For the moment, none of them so desired. They supported the government, but they did so from a distance, and intervened only when their own interests were directly involved.

Two members of the victorious coalition were disgruntled. Lord Maxwell, as his share of the spoil, was made warden of the west march. He celebrated his triumph by having Mass said in Dumfries, and by brazenly claiming that the king had given him permission to "use his own conscience in religion."[6] He was consequently clapped into Edinburgh castle for a short time. More serious for Maxwell was James's award of the lordship of Dalkeith to the earl of Angus.[7] Dalkeith was part of the estates of the late regent Morton. Angus and Maxwell each had a claim to Morton's earldom; Angus's acquisition of Dalkeith boded ill for Maxwell's future prospects.

The other malcontent was the earl of Bothwell. He was angered by his failure to obtain the captaincy of Edinburgh castle.[8] There was also the eternal question of Coldingham, newly ratified to Hume of Manderston by the Linlithgow

---

[4] SRO, *Privy Seal Register*, LIII, 61. Apparently he was also compensated for the loss of Boncle, which was returned to Angus; *ibid.*, p. 154.

[5] December 20, 1585, Glamis to Walsingham, CSP SCOT, VIII, 172.

[6] January 16, 1586, Woddrington to Walsingham, *Border Papers*, I, 217-218.

[7] January 24, 1586, Sir John Selby to Walsingham, *ibid.*, p. 218.

[8] November 11, 1585, Woddrington to Walsingham, *ibid.*, p. 211.

Parliament, at which time Maitland, too, made it clear that he was not abandoning his claims.[9] "Every day once at least the earl Bothwell troubles this court," wrote Logan of Restalrig to Archibald Douglas on December 6. "The earl Bothwell, my Lord Hume, and the secretary is [sic] not like to agree."[10]

One other member of the new government remains to be considered: King James himself. For various reasons the four leaders of the coalition were agreed that they must win the confidence of the king: Gray and Maitland because their political future depended on him, Angus and Glamis because they saw that the king's hostility was the chief cause of the failure of the government of the Ruthven raiders, of which they had been prominent members. So they set out to conciliate the king, and to take him into partnership. On the whole they met with notable success.[11]

It was a most unusual young man with whom they had to deal. It has been the custom among historians to underestimate, and to sneer at, King James VI and I. His foibles, his weaknesses, the many rather unpleasant aspects of his character have been played up to the point where there is little doubt that the description of James in *1066 and All That* does represent what is "memorable" about him: "King James I slobbered at the mouth and had favorites: he was thus a Bad King." This remark reflects the prevailing view of James as a failure —a failure as king of England. This is not the place to argue the merits of James's English rule; but it is worth remembering that the man who was such a "failure" as king of England was unquestionably the most successful king of Scotland since Robert Bruce.

We have a description of James about this time, written in August 1584 by Fontenay, Mary's agent in Scotland, to his brother. It is worth quoting at length:

9 APS, III, 387. See also November 19, 1585, Woddrington to Walsingham, *Border Papers*, I, 212-213.

10 *Salisbury Papers*, XIII, 287.

11 For James's feelings at this time see Sir James Melville, *Memoirs of His Own Life*, pp. 351-352. Melville, by his own account at least, was a close confidant of the king at this period.

"To tell you freely what I have known of him . . . he is for his age, the first prince who has ever been in the world. . . . He grasps and understands quickly; he judges carefully and with reasonable discourses; he restrains himself well and for long. In his demands he is quick and piercing, and determined in his replies. . . . He is learned in many languages, sciences, and affairs of state—I daresay more than all those of his kingdom. In short he has marvelous spirit—for the rest, full of virtuous glory and good opinion of himself. Having been nourished in fear, he has still this fault, that he often dare not contradict the great lords, and nevertheless he likes very much to be considered brave and to be feared. He has such a good heart that there is nothing so laborious that, for the sake of virtue, he would not wish to try. . . . But if once he saw himself surpassed in such exercises he abhors them ever after. He hates dancing and music in general, as likewise all wantonness at court, be it in discourses of love or in curiosity of habits. . . . His ways for want of being well instructed are very rude and uncivil in speaking, eating, manners, games, and entertainment in the company of women. He never stops in one place, taking a singular pleasure in walking, but his gait is bad, composed of erratic steps, and he tramps about even in his room. He has a loud voice, and is very grave in his words. He likes hunting above all the pleasures of this world, remaining there at least six hours together chasing all over the place with loosened rein. He has a weak body, but is in no wise delicate. In short, to tell you in one word, he is an old young man resembling the sirens of Socrates. I have only noticed in him three things very bad for the preservation of his state. . . . The first is his ignorance and lack of knowledge of his poverty and his little strength, promising too much of himself and despising other princes. The second, that he loves indiscreetly and inadvisedly in spite of his subjects.

"The third is that he is too lazy and too thoughtless over his affairs, too . . . devoted to his pleasure, especially hunting, leaving all his affairs to be managed by the earl of Arran, Montrose, and the secretary. I know well that this is excusable at his young age, but it is to be feared that continuance will confirm him in this habit.

"For this purpose having lately mentioned to him some word of how it appeared to me . . . he replied . . . that he would guard well against such misfortune, because no affair of importance ever happened of which he did not know, although he did not seem to. And although he spent much of his time hunting, he could do as much business in one hour as others would in a day, because simultaneously he listened and spoke, watched, and sometimes did five things at once . . . adding that sometimes he has wished to force and keep himself six days continually at accounts, but that immediately after he never fails to be ill."[12]

In this remarkable report most of the characteristics of the mature king are seen in the youth of eighteen: intelligence, love of learning, suspicion, dissimulation, timidity, conceit, lack of assurance, bad judgment of men. The one major trait in James's character which Fontenay failed to notice, which, indeed, had hardly showed itself as yet, was James's tenacity in pursuit of a goal which he had set for himself, such as the English succession.[13] But if James's character was formed, his political views were not, save in the broadest outline, and as yet he had received no serious political education. James wished to be an absolute king, but he had no idea of how to go about becoming one. The men who had dominated his youth, Morton, Lennox, and Arran, had governed, not by collaborating with and attempting to teach James, but by distracting him. Gray might well have attempted the same thing; but James was older now, and Gray lacked the force of character to dominate James which the other three men had possessed. In any case, Gray's influence was quickly challenged and eclipsed by Maitland, and from the fall of Gray until his own death Maitland was to be the king's chief adviser. It was Maitland who gave James his political education, who, with

12 August 15, 1584, Fontenay to Nau, csp scot, vii, 273-276.
13 James's persistence and tenacity of purpose are brought out well by Helen G. Stafford in her excellent study of the succession question, *James VI of Scotland and the Throne of England* (New York 1940).

James, worked out the policies by which James governed Scotland and, in so doing, helped to formulate the ideas with which James was to attempt to govern England. Maitland's contribution to King James's mental development has been generally overlooked; it can hardly be overestimated.

ii

The new government faced two problems to which immediate solutions had to be found: it had to decide on its attitude toward the kirk, and toward England. With respect to the kirk the young king had definite opinions which Maitland and his colleagues had to take into account. The principles of the kirk, James felt, led straight to the political doctrines of Buchanan's *De Jure Regni*. Furthermore, the kirk was even more radical now than it had been in Knox's day, owing to the widespread acceptance by the ministers of Andrew Melvill's anti-episcopal views. James's policy was the policy of the Black Acts; the kirk must be kept in its place.

Maitland, on whom the burden of working out the government's ecclesiastical policy chiefly fell, shared his master's Erastian opinions and his dislike of clerical extremists. But the secretary's experience in working out the compromise of 1584-1585 led him to believe that the kirk could not be compelled by force to accept the Black Acts. Some sort of agreement with the moderate elements in the kirk would be necessary for a workable and permanent solution. For the moment, however, in order to induce a reasonable frame of mind in the clerical moderates, and in order to give himself time to persuade the king of the wisdom of a policy of compromise with these moderates, Maitland bowed to the king's wishes. To convince the king of his sincerity—and to make negotiation with the moderates easier—Maitland went so far as to oppose the immediate return of the ministers who had fled during Arran's regime, most of whom were extremists. On this point he was unable to carry his colleagues with him, but in all other respects the other members of the coalition, with the single exception of Angus, were willing to go along.[14] The result was that the kirk

14 See Glamis' comment, quoted in Calderwood, IV, 449. See also Melville, *Memoirs*, p. 353.

obtained very little immediate satisfaction from the overthrow of Arran, save in the matter of the restoration of the fugitive ministers. On the other hand, the hated archbishop Adamson, who had been seized by some enthusiastic supporters of Andrew Melvill at St. Andrews at the time of Arran's fall, was appointed to the privy council and was given a pension from the thirds of his archbishopric, which had previously been paid to Arran's brother.[15] Furthermore, there was no repeal of the legislation of 1584. The Black Acts remained the law of the land.

The extremist ministers were naturally furious, the more so as their hopes had been so high. One of their members, James Gibson of Pencaitland, preached a most intemperate sermon accusing the king of persecution and comparing him to Jeroboam. Gibson was called to account; he naturally alleged that the spirit of God was responsible for his preaching. There was an explosive scene between him and the king in council, which James ended with the inelegant remark, "I will not give a turd for thy preaching!" Gibson was sent to Edinburgh castle to reflect upon his intransigence.[16]

The folly of men like Gibson undoubtedly strengthened the hand of the moderates among the clergy. At the same time, the secretary's wish for compromise made headway at court, backed as it was by such influential nobles as John Hamilton and Mar, who were sincere Protestants and favored a *modus vivendi* with the kirk. So, negotiations for a compromise began, on the basis that the Black Acts were not to be repealed, but were to be "interpreted," particularly with reference to the place of bishops in the kirk and the kirk's jurisdiction. The bishop was declared to be simply another minister with certain important administrative functions, which he was to exercise in collaboration with a "senate or presbytery of the most learned and godly ministers within his bounds," appointed by the General Assembly. The General Assembly was to have a good deal of supervisory authority over the bishop. Nothing was said about the bishops' place in Parliament. The kirk

---

15 NLS MSS 6.1.13. APS, III, 378, 395-396, 420.

16 Calderwood, IV, 485-488. A proclamation of December 23, 1585, carefully explained that Gibson's offence was sedition, not religious zeal. RPCS, IV, 40.

thus obtained acknowledgment of the preeminence of the General Assembly, and of the legality of the recently established system of presbyteries. In return, the ministers accepted the office of bishop and agreed to a fairly narrow definition of the kirk's jurisdictional authority. "Jurisdiction of the kirk consisteth in doctrine, ministration of the sacraments, exercise of discipline, and correction of manners. . . . There are some offences which properly pertain to the kirk to inquire upon, as heresy, apostasy, witchcraft, idolatry, and all frailty in the flesh, blasphemy, perjury, usury, abusing of the sacraments, breaking of the Sabbath." The implication was that all other matters, notably politics, were outside its ken.[17]

The extremists were frantic. Their state of mind is illustrated by a letter of James Melvill describing the Linlithgow Parliament and its aftermath. The king was "triumphing over the ministers, calling them loons . . . seditious knaves, and so forth. . . . What could we do? We ran to the lords, every one after [the] other, and sometimes all together . . . we threatened them, waried them, and cursed them."[18] All in vain. So the extremists decided to strike back at archbishop Adamson, the symbol of all they detested. In April of 1586 the provincial synod of Fife, led by James Melvill, excommunicated the archbishop, who replied by excommunicating James Melvill and his uncle Andrew. All of this was accompanied by a good deal of turmoil, and by considerable bad language on both sides, especially on the part of James Melvill.[19]

The king could not allow the action of the synod to pass unchallenged. It struck not only at archbishop Adamson personally, but at episcopacy as such, and violated the agreement with respect to the position of bishops, which had stated that bishops were subject to the jurisdiction of the General Assembly only. The issue was dealt with at the General Assembly of May 1586. James appeared in person at the second session, which was summoned to Holyrood for the purpose, made a

[17] The agreement, dated February 17, 1586, is in Calderwood, IV, 491-494. See also D. H. Willson, *James VI and I*, pp. 70-71.

[18] Calderwood, IV, 489-491. The letter is dated January 2, 1586.

[19] Calderwood, IV, 494-547, gives a full account of the synod, and of the charges and countercharges on both sides.

little speech assuring the assembled divines of his "perseverance and soundness in religion," and presided over the election as moderator of his hand-picked choice, David Lindsay, with whom he was on good terms.[20] The king then retired, after appointing a commission headed by Maitland to deal with the Assembly.

The crucial issue was the acceptance by the Assembly of the terms of the recently negotiated compromise, and this was finally obtained, although with some difficulty. The Assembly attempted to justify the actions of the synod of Fife by declaring that bishops could be tried and censured by presbyteries or synods like other ministers, but the royal commissioners would not accept this. Finally a formula was worked out which gave the substance of victory to the king.[21] As for the archbishop himself, he assured the Assembly in writing that he was innocent of the offenses of which he was accused, and the whole affair was smoothed over.[22] Even so, a good deal of pressure had to be exerted. Maitland had to make a public statement that if the Assembly supported the synod of Fife, "not only the whole discipline of the church should be discharged, but also the ministers' stipends; and the [arch]bishop should be set up to preach in Edinburgh, speak in the contrary who would."[23]

The king was dissuaded from wholesale reprisals against the enemies of Adamson by the efforts of Maitland, the master of Glamis, and the newly-appointed English ambassador, Thomas Randolph, who realized how unpopular Adamson was;[24] but Andrew Melvill, at least, James was determined to

[20] BUK, II, 646. If we can trust the report of Richard Fletcher, an agent of the archbishop of Canterbury, Adamson feared the General Assembly and hoped that it would be provoked into refusing to go to Holyrood, which would have infuriated the king and probably caused the breakup of the Assembly. NLS MSS 6.1.13.

[21] BUK, II, 652-655. This negotiation was probably the occasion of an angry letter from James to Maitland; the king felt that Maitland was being much too conciliatory. CSP SCOT, VII, 171 (where the letter is wrongly assigned to the year 1584).

[22] BUK, II, 657-658, 662-663.

[23] Calderwood, IV, 583-584.

[24] On this point see April 22, 25, 1586, Randolph to Walsingham, CSP SCOT, VIII, 328-330, 336-338. Wotton, the last ambassador, had fled at the time of the coup against Arran, and Elizabeth was tactful enough not to send him back.

punish. So on May 25, after the General Assembly had dispersed, the privy council ordered the redoubtable preacher into the north country to seek out Jesuits, "confer with them and travail, so far as in him lies, to reduce them to the true and Christian religion"—a chastening task for the irascible Andrew. Only if his persuasive powers failed was he to report the Jesuits to the authorities. And, lest the teaching of theology at St. Andrews suffer during his absence, the council thoughtfully instructed the archbishop to hold two theology classes weekly, on Tuesday and Thursday, at St. Salvator's college.[25] One cannot help wondering whether the Maitland family wit was asserting itself here. At all events, Melvill's mission to the followers of St. Ignatius did not last long. He was restored in August, on the earnest supplication of his nephew, "the dean of faculty, and a master of every college," coupled with the intervention of the master of Gray and the renewal on favorable terms of a lease held of his college by the king's master falconer![26]

Thus a rather uneasy truce was established between the government and the kirk, a truce dependent on the extent to which the excitable partisans of both sides restrained themselves in the ensuing months. That no one showed much enthusiasm for the existing arrangement is by no means an argument against it. The compromise was mainly Maitland's work. The secretary now believed that the government should be conciliatory to the kirk and should cooperate with it in matters, such as certain administrative actions of the recent General Assembly, which did not affect the substance of the royal power. As yet Maitland was rather fearful of the power and influence of the kirk. It would not be long before he concluded that the crown could turn that power and influence to its own advantage.[27]

[25] RPCS, IV, 74-75. Calderwood, IV, 584-585, dates this act May 26, 1586.

[26] Calderwood, IV, 585-586.

[27] For the administrative actions of the Assembly see BUK, II, 648-651, 656-657, 658-662, 664-668. Archbishop John Spottiswoode (*History of the Church of Scotland*, II, 343) claims that Maitland was motivated by hostility to the ministers, a view which is not supported by the evidence.

iii

The second great problem which faced the new Scottish government was the negotiation of the alliance with England, which all the members of the ruling coalition believed to be desirable. Four days after Arran's flight from Stirling, Gray wrote to Walsingham announcing that all was well in Scotland and urging the speedy conclusion of the league. A formal letter to the same end from the king to Walsingham's mistress followed in due course.[28] The English secretary was in no mood for delay. He was fearful of the possible revival of French influence in Scotland, a possibility which loomed much larger in January 1586 with the arrival in Scotland of a French resident ambassador, the first in almost twenty years.[29] His fears were increased by Archibald Douglas.

Douglas was the one important member of the anti-Arran coalition who had not gone back to Scotland, who dared not go back, owing to the steady and unremitting hostility of Maitland. "The secretary," wrote Logan of Restalrig to him on December 6, 1585, "is the only evil willer ye have here."[30] Maitland's dislike of the house of Douglas had not abated with the years, and, in Archibald's case, never did abate. It was doubtless fed by the fact that Maitland occupied Douglas' seat on the court of session. Naturally Douglas did all he could to poison the minds of Burghley and Walsingham against Maitland, and to some extent he succeeded, at least with Burghley. Maitland and Robert Melville, in the lord treasurer's view, were "devoted to the king's mother and to France."[31] Maitland's past support of Mary had by no means been forgotten.

Walsingham also paid some heed to Douglas, but in view of Maitland's great influence with the king, he resolved to take

<hr/>

28 CSP SCOT, VIII, 151, 157-158.

29 His instructions, dated October 7 and December 15, 1585, are in A. Teulet, ed., *Papiers d'état . . . inedits . . . relatifs à l'histoire de l'Ecosse au XVIe siècle*, II, 727-735, 739-741.

30 *Salisbury Papers*, XIII, 287.

31 January 12, 1586, Burghley to Leicester, J. Bruce, ed., *Correspondence of Robert Dudley, Earl of Leycester, during his Government of the Low Countries*, Camden Society publication (London 1844), pp. 52-53.

at face value the secretary's assurances that he favored the league.[32] At the same time he resolved to appoint an ambassador who would not be taken in by the wiles of the Scots, and his choice fell on old Thomas Randolph, a veteran of over twenty-five years' experience in Scottish politics. Randolph had been present at the beginnings of the Anglo-Scottish alliance during the Wars of the Congregation; perhaps Elizabeth, who had a sense of the fitness of things, insisted that he should negotiate the ultimate treaty, as a climax to his long career of faithful service.

The appointment was not popular in Scotland. James disliked Randolph because of his efforts in 1581 in behalf of the regent Morton, whose memory still rankled.[33] Walsingham found it necessary to write a curiously defensive letter to Maitland, stressing the advantage to the negotiations of Randolph's age and experience, assuring Maitland of Randolph's goodwill, and adding, "because he is one whom I have always . . . accounted . . . as my inward, good friend, I shall think myself particularly very much beholding unto you for any favor he may receive at your hands."[34] Ultimately the Scots withdrew their objections to Randolph, who arrived in Scotland in late February 1586, and the negotiations got under way.[35]

Even before Randolph arrived, the underhand struggle between Maitland and Gray, fed as it was by the mutual suspicion and dislike which had developed during their alliance against Arran, broke into the open. The fate of Archibald Douglas, whom Gray earnestly supported, was only the ostensible cause of the disagreement. The real prize at stake was the king's confidence, and the power which went with it. As soon as Maitland felt himself securely enough entrenched, he began to attempt to undermine Gray. He and the master of Glamis told James all about Gray's dealings with the fugitive lords in 1585; they also claimed that Gray had illegally pos-

[32] December 20, 1585, Maitland to Walsingham, csp scot, viii, 171-172.
[33] January 9, 1586, Burghley to Walsingham, *ibid.*, pp. 183-184.
[34] February 11, 1586, Walsingham to Maitland, csp scot, ix, 678 (where the letter is misdated 1589).
[35] Randolph's instructions are in csp scot, viii, 207-209.

sessed himself of some of the king's jewels.[36] "There is great dislike conceived between the secretary and the master of Gray, who is not so great a courtier as he was," wrote Walsingham's agent, Roger Ashton, on February 4, 1586. "The secretary and the master of Glamis are now the chief guiders."[37] A few days later Gray struck back. Capitalizing on the annoyance of Lord John Hamilton, Angus, and Mar at the king's refusal to drive Arran and Colonel Stewart from the country, he persuaded this trio and Hume to go to the king and demand the removal of all "suspected persons" from his presence. This was aimed at Maitland and Robert Melville chiefly; James would have none of it.[38] It is surprising to find John Hamilton acting against Maitland in this way; perhaps he was annoyed by Maitland's ostentatious favor to his brother Claude, whom he never liked very well.

When this failed, Gray tried a different tack. Walsingham had sent an agent of Edward Wotton's named Thomas Mills to Scotland, to serve as a liaison man between himself and Maitland.[39] Gray sought out Mills and complained bitterly of the secretary and the master of Glamis. Maitland was not really in favor of the league, Gray said, but he had covered his tracks so cleverly that no direct accusation could be made. Glamis was even worse: at Maitland's prompting he had told James about the money Gray had gotten from England. Furthermore, Maitland was throwing obstacles in the way of Gray's plan to recruit an army and join Leicester in the Netherlands, because the secretary was afraid that Gray would turn the army against him before he went off to do battle with Parma.[40] Unfortunately for Gray, his assertions on the only matter that

[36] January 1586, Logan of Restalrig to Archibald Douglas, *Salisbury Papers*, IV, 6 (where the letter is misdated 1590).

[37] CSP SCOT, VIII, 215-216.

[38] February 12, 15, 1586, Ashton to Walsingham, *ibid.*, pp. 223-224. February 17, an unknown correspondent to Burghley, *ibid.*, pp. 224-225. One of the causes of "suspicion" doubtless was the fact that Maitland, Robert Melville, and Arran were the only people who had conferred with the newly-arrived French ambassador. January 31, Woddrington to Walsingham, *Border Papers*, I, 219.

[39] February 11, 1586, Walsingham to Maitland, A. I. Cameron, ed., *The Warrender Papers*, I, 208.

[40] March 2, 1586, Mills to Walsingham, CSP SCOT, VIII, 237-239.

really interested the English, Maitland's attitude to the league, were not believed. One of Randolph's assistants wrote to Walsingham on March 13 that, in his first interviews with the ambassador, Maitland had been most cooperative.[41]

The negotiations for the league went very smoothly at first. Randolph arrived in Edinburgh on February 26 and had formal audience with James two days later. He met the secretary: "Much good time was spent between us, who could exceed [the] others [sic] in compliments and cunning speeches." They talked of secretary Lethington, whom Randolph had known very well, and Maitland promised to further the league "to the uttermost of his power."[42] And indeed, he was all complaisance at first, apparently accepting the text of the league as it stood, and circumventing all French efforts to delay matters.[43] But then Maitland began to reiterate some of the objections he had made in the summer of 1585. There was the problem of the succession; Maitland wanted a statement written into the league to the effect that Elizabeth would do nothing to prejudice James's claim without just cause. He wanted Elizabeth to bestow a title on James. Scot and Englishman each should have the commercial privileges of a native in the other's country, as Scot and Frenchman did. Finally there was the question of the date from which cognizance of border grievances was to be taken.[44] These were important points, but they might well have been smoothed over gracefully, since there was so much good will on both sides, and since there was no disagreement on the main objectives of the proposed alliance, namely, the maintenance of the reformed religion and the mutual promise of assistance in the event of invasion. Randolph was not seriously worried by Maitland's objections, and

[41] Ibid., pp. 242-243.

[42] March 2, 1586, Randolph to Walsingham, Letters and Papers Relating to Patrick, Master of Gray, pp. 66-70.

[43] March 13, 1586, Fletcher to Walsingham, csp scot, viii, 242-243.

[44] March 14, 1586, Randolph to Walsingham, ibid., pp. 244-247. On the matter of this date, the English wanted 1573; the Scots held out for 1567, since this would include the devastating invasion of Scotland by the earl of Sussex in 1570. On this point see June 29, 1586, the English commissioners to Walsingham, ibid., pp. 482-483; June 1, Walsingham to an unknown correspondent, Salisbury Papers, iii, 143; June 5, Walsingham to Randolph, Gray Papers, pp. 86-87; June 30, Gray to Walsingham, ibid., pp. 100-102.

he prepared to take up some of the secondary purposes of his mission, such as the questions of the delivery of the murderers of Lord Russell and the expulsion from Scotland of the Jesuits Holt and Brereton, and of Courcelles, the French ambassador's aide, a man who was looked upon as a dangerous Guisan. Then Elizabeth made a blunder. She reduced the amount promised as a pension to James by a thousand pounds sterling.[45]

Instantly Maitland's suspicion of English intentions revived. He had always thought that James could charge a higher price for his alliance, and here was Elizabeth brazenly lowering the price before the agreement was even concluded. Randolph persuaded James to agree to the text of the league, but not before Maitland had added two conditions: the queen must give satisfaction on the pension, and she must promise to do nothing to impair James's claim to the succession without just cause. It was not necessary to include this in the league; a private letter would do—a form was suggested for Elizabeth to sign. Maitland in fact wished to go further; he proposed that the whole question be turned over to a convention of nobility, a proposal which if realized would open the door to infinite further demands. James would not consent to this; but it was always possible that he might change his mind.[46] And in a memorandum which accompanied Randolph's letter dealing with these matters, Maitland made it clear that he had not given up on the matter of reciprocal privileges for merchants.[47]

Maitland was aware that he was personally running a grave political risk by his attitude on these questions. But he was willing to do so because he believed that Gray, in his eagerness to solidify his position with the king, who really wanted the league, was far too willing to settle on England's terms. He excused himself as best he could to Walsingham by blandly thanking his English counterpart for defending him against those who ac-

[45] March 17, 1586, Randolph to Walsingham, CSP SCOT, VIII, 249-253. March 19, Walsingham to Randolph, *ibid.*, pp. 253-254. The queen, to Walsingham's annoyance, also refused to pension anyone else in Scotland.

[46] April 2, 1586, Randolph to Walsingham, *ibid.*, 300-302. *Warrender Papers*, I, 209-211. Maitland later claimed that he had suggested the convention of nobles merely in order to give legal sanction to the league. April 25, Randolph to Walsingham, CSP SCOT, VIII, 336-338.

[47] *Ibid.*, pp. 303-304.

cused him of trying to delay matters, and at the same time by pointing out that there was considerable opposition within Scotland to the league.[48] Gray naturally pressed his advantage. He had picked up rumors of a Catholic plot, in which he tried to involve Maitland, who, according to Gray's information, was in receipt of a French bribe.[49] Maitland did his best to protect himself by spreading rumors against Gray, with little success.[50]

Then, suddenly, the whole aspect of things changed. On April 19 Gray wrote to Douglas, "The secretary and I are agreed; he promises in all respects to be your friend."[51] Randolph's letter of April 22 supplies the explanation of this rapid about-face; Arran was plotting to recover power and to murder Maitland, Gray, Angus, and Glamis. When Maitland discovered this he quickly warned the others, and they agreed to stand together against Arran.[52] Maitland, as the price of the alliance, sent a friendly message to Douglas, and got one in return from Walsingham, who evidently thought that fear of Arran would weaken the secretary's stand on the points at issue between the two countries.[53]

So, at the end of April, Archibald Douglas returned to Scotland; immediately upon his return he had a long conversation with Gray, to decide whether their position was strong enough to attempt Maitland's immediate overthrow. Gray thought not: "the secretary his greatness with the king did consist in this, that he had set down certain platts (plans) unto the king, how he might preserve his state in obedience and be in estimation and credit with foreign princes. And because the end of these platts carried with them certain protraction of time, he thought it would be hard to move the king . . . [against Maitland until] such time as he might know the[ir] final success."[54] It is evident from this that Maitland and the

48 April 3, 1586, Maitland to Walsingham, *ibid.*, p. 306. Even Gray was shaken by Elizabeth's action on the pension, and urged Walsingham to get the cut restored. March 31, May 17, Gray to Walsingham, *ibid.*, pp. 294, 381.
49 *Ibid.*, pp. 309-310.
50 April 13, 1586, Walsingham to Gray, *ibid.*, p. 315.
51 *Ibid.*, pp. 326-327.
52 *Ibid.*, pp. 328-330.
53 *Ibid.*, pp. 339-340, 344.
54 April 29, 1586, Douglas to Walsingham, *ibid.*, pp. 346-347.

king were already at work on the program which was to emerge in the legislation of 1587.

Douglas and Gray therefore resolved to concentrate on solidifying their position by bringing the negotiations with England to a successful conclusion. But first Douglas had to clear away the stain on his good name with respect to his part in the murder of Darnley; and so the usual collusive trial was duly arranged. James was perfectly amiable about this: Douglas' only guilt was "in foreknowledge and concealing a fault, so common in those days, that no man could misknow, but so perilous to reveal, in respect of the actors of the tragedy, that no man could utter any speech thereof, without extreme danger."[55] Thus what was a capital crime in the master was harmless in the man; but times had changed since the regent Morton had been executed for *his* foreknowledge.

This matter out of the way, Douglas plunged into a long series of conversations with James and Maitland over the league; in fact he virtually usurped Randolph's position as chief English negotiator. The king and the secretary dodged one trap set by Elizabeth: they refused to sanction any Scottish expedition to the Low Countries unless Elizabeth declared war on Spain. Maitland pointed out that those Scottish merchants who were trading with Spain would oppose such a move.[56] But fundamentally the Scottish reservations with respect to the league remained the same: the succession, the pension, and the privileges of the merchants. In these matters it was clearly Maitland who was insisting, and who kept James from yielding.[57] Walsingham, who believed that Maitland's recalcitrance could be ended by an English bribe, steadily refused to make any real concessions, and Maitland became increasingly irritable.[58] By the end of May he was attempting to put the whole responsibility for the negotiations on Douglas' shoulders, and,

---

[55] May 6, 1586, Douglas to Walsingham, *ibid.*, p. 358.
[56] *Ibid.*, pp. 362-363.
[57] See Maitland's letter of May 16, 1586 to Walsingham, *ibid.*, pp. 380-381.
[58] June 3, 1586, Walsingham to Burghley, *ibid.*, p. 417. June 28, Walsingham to Randolph, *ibid.*, pp. 476-477. Walsingham was very unhappy about Elizabeth's parsimony, which he considered very dangerous. May 20, Walsingham to Leicester, *Leycester Correspondence*, pp. 275-276. See also Walsingham's memorandum of April 29, *Warrender Papers*, I, 212-213.

according to Douglas, was considering the opening of serious negotiations with France.[59] By this time there was not even a pretense of friendship between the two men. Maitland tried at the last minute to wreck Douglas' collusive judicial clearance— or so Douglas reported to Walsingham, adding that "the secretary has been, is, and like to continue, the cause of all the ill that is passed in that land these five years." He suggested that, if England turned against Maitland, he could easily be overthrown.[60]

The final stages of the negotiations were virtually taken out of Maitland's hands. His attempt to cause delay by insisting that the whole question be put to a convention of nobility was unsuccessful. He was instructed by the king to deal with the secondary issue of border problems; he attempted to turn this into a means of putting off the completion of the league by alleging that it would take time to prepare a complete list of border complaints. He opposed the delivery to England of those accused in the death of Lord Russell, telling James that if they were unfairly treated in England, he would be driven from his kingdom like Edward Balliol—hardly a tactful thing to say to the self-centered king. Almost to the very day of the signing, Maitland continued to work for postponement and delay.[61]

Yet the secretary did not lose the king's confidence and favor —just the reverse. On May 31 James promoted Maitland to the office of vice-chancellor and made him keeper of the great seal for life.[62] James knew that Maitland was, in fact, the spokesman of a very considerable opposition to the league. Many

[59] May 27, 1586, Douglas to Walsingham, csp scot, viii, 399-400.

[60] Ibid., pp. 424-425.

[61] This paragraph is based on the letters written by Douglas, Randolph, and Mills in June 1586; ibid., pp. 414-477. Some of those involved in the Russell affair were Maitland's personal friends; May 28, 1586, Randolph to Walsingham, ibid., p. 407.

[62] rpcs, iv, intro., p. xiii. Six weeks earlier, James had given to Maitland and the master of Glamis the immensely valuable wardship and marriage of the new earl of Eglinton, aged two. sro, Privy Seal Register, liii, 164. Randolph estimated the value of this gift at ten thousand pounds sterling. csp scot, viii, 364-365. This estimate is borne out by the fact that they had to pay the sizeable sum of five hundred pounds for official confirmation of the grant. sro, Treasurer's Accounts 1585-1586.

nobles were alarmed by the prospect of losing "all the benefits they might look for in France" if the league took effect.[63] The Scottish merchant class, although Protestant, was not happy. Randolph reported on June 10 that "the merchants have lately made an offer to him [the king], either that they have the like liberty granted to them that they have in France, or that the league take no place."[64] The borderers generally were unhappy too, a fact of which Maitland, with his extensive border connections, was well aware.[65] And, of course, apart from all this, there were the members of the still-potent Catholic faction, whose dissatisfaction had grown so great that they were beginning to plot with Spain.[66]

James respected Maitland's opposition. He simply refused to pay any attention to it because, as Elizabeth undoubtedly guessed, he was prepared to sign the league at virtually any cost. In the past eight years, ever since he had been old enough to take any interest in politics, the king had been the victim of three aristocratic *coups d'état*, all engineered from England or with English connivance, in accordance with the time-honored English policy of subsidizing aristocratic faction, and of keeping Scotland disorderly and weak. James was determined to put a stop to this, by means of the alliance. So James, in spite of occasional moments of hesitation, was, of all those involved on the Scottish side, by far the warmest supporter of the league.

Maitland was perfectly aware of the immense desirability of the league, but he deplored his master's tactics. He was in no hurry; he was willing, after the manner of his brother, to try the effect on Elizabeth of delay and negotiation with other powers. On the whole, this was a mistaken attitude; there was so much to be gained from the alliance that it was unwise to endanger it by haggling over terms. The king's instinct was right; the actual terms of the treaty were much less important

---

[63] May 18, 1586, Douglas to Walsingham, csp scot, viii, 382-385.

[64] *Ibid.*, p. 433.

[65] For the whole problem of the impact of the league and the eventual union of the crowns on the border, see the interesting, although occasionally exaggerated article by J. J. Bell, "The Armstrongs and the Border, 1585-1603," *History Today*, ii (1952), 101-107.

[66] See below, pp. 181ff.

than the fact of its conclusion. James, by signing the league, became in effect the head of the English faction in Scotland, in the place of the Protestant magnates; and this meant an enormous potential increase in the power of the crown. To be sure, the consummation of the alliance did not automatically reduce Scotland to peace and order. But the government could now set about this crucial task with some prospect of success.

The king's acceptance of the league was made easier by some last-minute English concessions. Elizabeth wrote that she would do nothing in derogation of James's claim to the succession without just cause. She held out hope that the cut she had made in the proposed pension might be restored in the future. Finally, Walsingham promised that, if necessary, the queen would write again, promising fair treatment for those involved in the Russell affair.[67] So, at the end of June, the commissioners of both sides met in Berwick. The Scots raised a whole series of objections, including the question of privileges for the merchants. Elizabeth refused to yield on any of them, and the Scots gave in. One clause was dropped from the original draft: that dealing with border questions. It was obvious that a long and possibly acrimonious discussion would be necessary before this could be settled; so, in order to avoid delays, it was decided to turn the whole matter over to the commissioners for the treaty, who would sit as a special commission for the purpose. They did so, and accomplished nothing. On July 5 the league was formally concluded.[68] Gray had triumphed, and Maitland had apparently suffered a stunning defeat.

Maitland was not at his best during the negotiations for the league. There were extenuating circumstances: his father had died in March 1586, at the patriarchal age of ninety, and Maitland was further distracted by having to take charge of the arrangements for the marriage of his sister Mary, who had sacrificed herself for many years to the requirements of the blind Sir Richard and was at last free to live her own life. But

[67] June 2, 1586, Elizabeth to James, CSP SCOT, VIII, 414-415. June 28, Walsingham to Douglas, *ibid.*, p. 476.

[68] The treaty is in *ibid.*, pp. 43-45, 491. There is a convenient summary of the whole course of the negotiations written by Randolph after his return; *ibid.*, pp. 533-537.

the fact of the matter is, that Maitland, unlike his brother Lethington, was never particularly successful in his negotiations with foreign powers, possibly because they never really interested him. Certainly his opposition to the swift conclusion of the English alliance was short-sighted, and it was well for the solution of the domestic problems that really concerned him that his opposition was overridden. The English alliance, by assuring the Scottish government of the support of the only foreign state which was in a position to cause it serious trouble, was an indispensable prerequisite to the strengthening of the Scottish crown. But before that process could get fairly under way, the league was to be shaken to its very foundations.

THE END OF MARY

IN THE SUMMER of 1586, with the two major problems of the kirk and the league apparently settled, Maitland plunged vigorously into the details of administration. The government instructed various sheriffs and their deputies to appear before the privy council with lists of all those at the horn and of those relaxed. All feuars of church lands who had not had their grants confirmed were ordered to do so by December 10. A muster of the lieges was planned for the highlands—an unusual step. Since a good many royal castles and dwellings were in disrepair, it was decided to spend the income from any prelacy that should fall vacant in the next three years on repairs and provision of munitions. Finally, a round-up of Jesuits was ordered, because they were felt to be seditious—also, no doubt, because the ministers would be pleased.[1]

The border presented a series of problems of its own, problems which required prompt handling as an earnest of the government's enthusiasm for the English alliance. The turbulent Maxwell had been restored to his wardenry in the west, but was most unreliable, and old Ker of Cesford, the warden in the middle march, was inefficient: "the thieves are his masters," Randolph had written.[2] Maitland and James decided to appoint the earl of Angus lieutenant over all the borders, and to levy a small tax to pay for two hundred soldiers for him.[3] This was done, but

[1] SRO, *Treasurer's Accounts 1586-1587*. RPCS, IV, 89, 91-92, 107-108. On November 25, as a result of a case involving the earl Marischal, it was decided that a man, once horned, could not be relaxed by the king alone, without the advice of the council. *Ibid.*, pp. 118-119.

[2] June 6, 1586, Randolph to Walsingham, CSP SCOT, VIII, 420-421.

[3] RPCS, IV, 101. September 26, 1586, Lincluden to Douglas, *Salisbury Papers*, III, 175-176. Douglas' claim, in his letter of September 14, to Walsingham, CSP SCOT, IX, 18, that Maitland devised this plan to wreck the league in Scot-

it did not help matters much. The regular border musters were
frequently postponed, and the money collected to pay for them
went for the back wages of the royal guard. Angus quarreled
with Maxwell and accomplished virtually nothing; to avoid an
actual outbreak he was replaced, in December 1586, by Lord
John Hamilton as lieutenant in the west march, since the latter
was on good terms with Maxwell. Maitland concluded from this
experience that the border problem was not to be solved by giving a commission of lieutenancy to a great noble, no matter
how dependable he personally might be: such an appointment
aroused too many jealousies.[4]

As for the league itself, even Archibald Douglas, with whom
Maitland continued to feud,[5] was forced to admit that the secretary was "true."[6] Maitland was still recalcitrant only on the
matter of those accused in the murder of Lord Russell. He
genuinely feared that they would not be treated fairly if they
were turned over to England as the treaty required, and he had
some cause for alarm.[7] So he took matters into his own hands.
He notified the Kers that they would be executed if they set foot
in England, innocent or guilty. They at once went into hiding.[8]
James promised that he would see them delivered, but nothing
was done, and this matter, and the uncertain state of the borders
generally, were almost immediately forgotten in the much more
serious crisis which now began.

In August of 1586 the English government revealed to the
world, and to the queen of Scots, that it knew all about the
conspiracy in which she was involved with Anthony Babington
and his hare-brained companions, and that it proposed to put
her on trial. The question immediately arose: what would James
do? Would he stand by his mother, or would he not?

At first the matter hardly seemed very pressing to the king.
He told Gray to write to Archibald Douglas, who had just ar-

---

land by making it seem expensive, was simply another attempt by that worthy
to ruin the secretary's reputation in England.

[4] Border policy at this time may be conveniently traced in RPCS, IV, 101ff.
[5] July 17, 1586, Forster to Walsingham, *Border Papers*, I, 229.
[6] August 5, 1586, Randolph to Walsingham, CSP SCOT, VIII, 590.
[7] August 1, 1586, Mills to Douglas, *Salisbury Papers*, III, 155-156.
[8] July 30, 1586, Douglas to Walsingham, CSP SCOT, VIII, 567-569.

rived in England as Scottish ambassador, and instruct him to congratulate Elizabeth on her escape. "It cannot stand with his [James's] honor that he be a consenter to take his mother's life," Gray wrote, "but he is content how[ever] strictly she be kept, and all her old knavish servants hanged." Walsingham did his best to keep the king in this frame of mind by sending him extracts from Mary's intercepted correspondence, dealing with her plan for disinheriting him and having him carried off to Spain. Gray was prepared to go further than his master. The "necessity of all honest men's affairs," he wrote, "requires . . . [that] she were out of the way."[9]

When Gray wrote these letters, neither he nor James nor anyone else in Scotland believed that matters were likely to be carried to extremes. But by October it began to be apparent that Mary was in serious danger. The French agent, Courcelles, was doing his best to arouse the king.[10] On October 1 Gray wrote Douglas that James was "very instant for his mother."[11] In the middle of the month the king resolved to send one of his favorite courtiers, William Keith, on a special mission to England.

Thus began the series of negotiations which concluded only with the execution of the unfortunate Mary on February 8, 1587.[12] From the beginning it was Maitland's steadfast and unheroic objective to involve himself in this affair as little as possible. He was anxious to save Mary's life, but he was aware very early that there was only one way to do this, if it could be done at all, and that was to threaten to end the league if she were executed. But Maitland knew that saving Mary's life was not the primary objective of his royal master. What James

[9] September 8, 10, 1586, Gray to Douglas, *Salisbury Papers*, III, 171-173. September 10, Walsingham to Phelippes, CSP SCOT, VIII, 705. See also CSP SCOT, IX, 9, and September 24, Courcelles to Henry III, R. Bell, ed., *Extract from the Despatches of M. Courcelles, French Ambassador at the Court of Scotland*, Bannatyne Club publication (Edinburgh 1828), pp. 3-9.

[10] October 5, 1586, Courcelles to Chateauneuf, CSP SCOT, IX, 80-81. The strategy that the French finally adopted was to frighten James by assuring him that if Mary died he would be assassinated on behalf of some English claimant to the succession. November 21, Henry III to Courcelles, *ibid.*, p. 161.

[11] *Salisbury Papers*, III, 178.

[12] A detailed and accurate account of the entire business may be found in R. S. Rait and A. I. Cameron, *King James's Secret* (London, 1927. Henceforth abbreviated KJS).

wanted was reassurance as to the succession. If the English assured him that Mary's crime in no way touched his rights, he would be prepared to look through his fingers at whatever Elizabeth might do to his mother. This was apparent in his instructions to Keith—at which time, to be sure, James probably still believed that Elizabeth would not proceed to extremities. Maitland did not care for this policy. He criticized Douglas' advice to concentrate exclusively on the succession question, and gave "plain advice to the king, that if England stand strict at this time, that they are no more to be trusted, and foreigners to be sought."[13]

Having spoken his piece, Maitland retired into the background. He refused to take part in any embassy to England; he foresaw failure, and wanted no connection with such a failure as this would be. Gray was equally reluctant, and thoughtfully proposed that Maitland be sent to England. So did Douglas. But here two factors came to the secretary's rescue. He was indispensable at home: if he went, "the king has no man to do his hourly affairs."[14] Secondly, there was his former opposition to the league. Gray had been boasting of himself as the Scotsman who had most influence with Elizabeth: very well, let Gray go to England and see what he could do.

Gray's triumph over Maitland in the negotiation of the English alliance now recoiled on his head. He foresaw the disaster which would overtake him: no matter what the result, whether he accepted the commission or refused, he would be ruined. His only hope, he confided to Douglas in a long and gloomy letter on October 25, was to revive his discarded plan of going to fight the Spaniards in Flanders.[15] But after he heard of his friend Philip Sidney's death, he did not even want to do that.[16]

[13] October 21, 1586, Gray to Douglas, *Salisbury Papers*, III, 183-184. KJS, p. 36. This advice may have led to a temporary coolness between James and the secretary. On November 6 Scrope passed on to Walsingham the intelligence that "The secretary is suspected by the king and not consulted in secret affairs." *Border Papers*, I, 238-239.

[14] October 21, 1586, Gray to Douglas, *Salisbury Papers*, III, 183-184.

[15] *Ibid.*, pp. 185-188.

[16] November 6, 1586, Gray to Douglas, *ibid.*, pp. 190-192. On the same date Gray wrote to Walsingham indicating that he still favored Mary's death. CSP SCOT, IX, 149.

THE END OF MARY

He saw no way out of his dilemma, and in fact there was none. He had to accept the commission, and it led directly to his ruin.

Keith had not gotten very far in London. He was able to satisfy James with respect to the succession: he was informed officially that James's claim was in no way touched by Mary's condemnation.[17] But he could get nowhere on the question of Mary's life. By November James began to get really alarmed. Scottish opinion was becoming excited. Many people believed that the sending of such a minor figure as Keith meant that James had already consented to Mary's death.[18] "All men drive at him [James], first for his mother, next for . . . his title," wrote Gray on November 10.[19] The Catholic party was beginning to stir hopefully. Conferences were being held here and there, among people like Huntly, Crawford, Montrose, Graham of Fentry, Athol, and—most sinister of all—Arran.[20] "They that hated most her prosperity regret her adversity," wrote Gray.[21] Maitland summed it up this way: "The people and all estates here are so far moved by the rigorous proceeding against the queen that his majesty and all that have credit are importuned and may not go abroad for exclamations against them and imprecations against the queen of England."

Maitland wrote this in the postscript of a letter to Keith on November 27.[22] This letter marked his one important intervention in the negotiations. Maitland had temporarily convinced his master that a firmer policy must be followed. James had at last "screwed up his courage to the point of suggesting to his representatives that they might threaten to break the league with England if Mary's life was taken."[23] A convention of estates was summoned, at which the nobility declared their

17 November 12, 1586, Burghley to Shrewsbury, csp scot, ix, 152.

18 November 20, 1586, Courcelles to Henry III, *Courcelles' Despatches*, pp. 17-21.

19 *Letters and Papers relating to Patrick, Master of Gray*, pp. 114-116. See also October 21, 1586, Courcelles to Henry III, *Courcelles' Despatches*, pp. 9-12.

20 csp scot, ix, 147-148. October 25, 1586, Gray to Douglas, *Salisbury Papers*, iii, 185-188.

21 On November 23, *Salisbury Papers*, iii, 196.

22 kjs, pp. 56-57.

23 *Ibid.*, p. 55. See also December 25, 1586, Gray to Walsingham, csp scot, ix, 201-202.

readiness to fight if Mary was executed.[24] But James's courage rapidly drained out of him. Elizabeth, when she learned of James's changed attitude, exploded with rage. Douglas' letter to the king reporting the queen's anger also reported a conversation with Leicester with respect to the league and the title.[25] On December 15 James wrote to Leicester and remarked, "How fond and inconstant I were if I should prefer my mother to the title let all men judge."[26] James, faced with the choice, had made his decision. He chose the English alliance, and the English crown. Under such circumstances the mission to England of Gray and Robert Melville on Mary's behalf was a hollow sham. No one knew this better than Gray, who asked Walsingham to do him the favor of refusing to receive him when he came, so that he might preserve his reputation.[27]

Maitland now decided to return to his inconspicuous role. His resolve was strengthened by Keith's disclosure that from the beginning Douglas had been working hand in glove with the English and systematically betraying the king. Maitland must have been pleased to learn from Keith that the English now tended to blame Gray more than him for the momentary stiffening of James's attitude.[28] He answered Walsingham's blankly polite memorandum of December 8 with a document equally platitudinous and meaningless.[29] He did draft the instructions for Gray and Melville—they were a powerful plea on Mary's behalf—but his advice that they be kept secret from Douglas was ignored by James.[30] This was unfortunate, since James

[24] December 7, 1586, Woddrington to Walsingham, *ibid.*, pp. 185-186. RPCS, IV, 129. The convention was asked to vote a tax; it refused, and the nobility offered a voluntary gift. The commissioners of burghs were not prepared to contribute funds in case war resulted from Mary's death. See R. S. Rait, *The Parliaments of Scotland*, pp. 153-154. In January 1587 Maitland led the barons of Lothian in raising their share of the voluntary gift; RPCS, IV, 135-137. Calderwood, IV, 605, states that one proposed use of the funds was to send embassies to Spain, France, and Denmark in Mary's behalf.

[25] December 8, 1586, Douglas to James, KJS, pp. 72-82.

[26] *Ibid.*, pp. 101-102.

[27] December 13, 1586, Gray to Walsingham, CSP SCOT, IX, 191.

[28] December 9, 1586, Keith to Maitland, KJS, pp. 89-92. As an example of Douglas' treachery, see his letter of November 20 to Walsingham, CSP SCOT, IX, 160.

[29] CSP SCOT, IX, 186-188, 231-232.

[30] January 10, 1587, George Young to Maitland, KJS, pp. 139-144. Young,

deliberately omitted from the instructions any threat of what he might do if his wishes were not met.[31] This fact lent credence to the assurances repeatedly given to the English government by Douglas that the king would "digest" Mary's death.[32] James's equivocal letter of January 26, 1587, to Elizabeth added a finishing touch of proof to Douglas' assertions.[33] Despite Gray's best efforts—and the master, whatever his private views, did conduct himself, as he said he would, as a "Scottis man"[34]—the English were convinced that James would limit himself to verbal protest if Mary were executed. And so, indeed, it turned out.

At the end of January 1587, Gray, Melville, and Keith left London; they were back in Edinburgh on February 7, and were duly thanked by the privy council for their services.[35] The treacherous Douglas thought it well to remain in England. There ensued a period of hideous suspense. James was very much on edge; he was hunting less than usual.[36] The tension was reflected by the council's decree of February 1 that anyone found guilty of infamous libel was to receive the punishment befitting the crime of which he accused the injured party. This measure was frankly designed for the protection of king and council. The council also ordered the clergy to pray for Queen Mary, and carefully prescribed the form of prayer.[37] Two days later James attended a service in Edinburgh at which archbishop Adamson was to officiate. The ministers forestalled this by installing one of their own number, John Cowper, in the pulpit. James told him he could remain if he would carry out the order to pray for the queen. Cowper replied that he

---

the secretary of the privy council, accompanied Gray and Melville as an unofficial agent of Maitland's.

[31] December 21, 1586, Courcelles to Henry III, *Courcelles' Despatches*, pp. 22-25.

[32] Gray repeatedly warned James about this. See, e.g., his letter of January 21, 1587, KJS, pp. 169-172.

[33] CSP SCOT, IX, 247-248.

[34] The phrase appears in his letter of October 25, 1586 to Douglas, *Salisbury Papers*, III, 185-188.

[35] RPCS, IV, 144.

[36] February 8, 1587, Hudson to Walsingham, CSP SCOT, IX, 278.

[37] RPCS, IV, 140-141.

would act as the spirit of God directed him. James knew very well what that meant; he ordered Cowper to vacate, and had him clapped into Blackness for some undutiful remarks he made while doing so. Five days later the council decreed that any member of the ministry who spoke irreverently or slanderously of king, council, or laws, or uttered "any speeches which may entertain factions or move uproar or sedition among his highness's subjects" was to be warded until he repented.[38]

Rumors of Mary's death began to be heard. Early in February a Scottish agent of Burghley's, Poury Ogilvie, informed his employer that James was "desperate of his mother's life," and that the Hamiltons had offered, if James would match their proposed levy of five thousand men, to burn Newcastle.[39] The Catholic faction was urging James to join them.[40] James affected not to believe the rumors at first, but the arrival of Robert Carey in Berwick with Queen Elizabeth's hypocritical letter of apology made it all plain enough.[41]

Accounts vary as to how James received the news of his mother's death. Poury Ogilvie reported that he was unmoved. Calderwood says that he could hardly contain his joy, and that Maitland had to turn the courtiers out of the room, so that they would not witness the unseemly spectacle. On the other hand, Scrope's informants reported that James took the news "very grievously and offensively," and was planning on revenge.[42] It seems reasonable to acquit James of the charge of gloating, but there is no reason to suppose that he particularly regretted the death of a woman he could not remember, who had killed his father and who, at the end, was planning to disinherit him and send him off to Spain as a prisoner.[43]

[38] For this whole affair see *ibid.*, pp. 142-144, and D. Moysie, *Memoirs of the Affairs of Scotland*, p. 59.

[39] CSP SCOT, IX, 275-276.

[40] February 7, 1587, Cranston to Douglas, *ibid.*, p. 266.

[41] Elizabeth's letter, dated February 14, 1587, is in *ibid.*, p. 285. For a spirited, but not entirely convincing, defense of Elizabeth's behavior in the matter of Mary's death see J. E. Neale, *Elizabeth I and her Parliaments, 1584-1601* (London 1957), pp. 137-143.

[42] March 2, 1587, Ogilvie to Douglas, *Salisbury Papers*, XIII, 332-334. Calderwood, IV, 611. February 21, 1587, Scrope to Walsingham, CSP SCOT, IX, 300-301.

[43] Mary frequently mentioned her plan to disinherit James, but no testament to that effect was ever found, and there is good reason to believe that no such

James has been widely and unjustly criticized for his behavior in this whole affair by those who forget that he was brought up to fear and distrust his mother. James did not desire Mary's death; but he would not risk breaking with Elizabeth in order to save her. Suppose he had succeeded in saving Mary's life by a policy of threats, as Maitland and others had suggested— what would the result have been? He would have lost all hope of peacefully succeeding to Elizabeth; the English crown would be his only if he became the tool and puppet of Spain. In the words of his latest biographer, James, if he saved his mother's life by this means, "would merely have succeeded at great risk in doing himself much harm."[44] James's choice was not only the natural one under the circumstances; it was also the wisest, however unheroic it may seem.

Mary's execution was not a matter in which James could consult his personal feelings, however. Scottish opinion was deeply stirred, and there was a great clamor for war, especially from excitable people like Bothwell. Walsingham was informed that "There is [sic] nightly . . . pasquils affixed against the king and the . . . council, provoking him to a revenge of his mother's death."[45] James had to deal with this situation somehow. He refused to admit Robert Carey to Scotland, though he did send to learn Carey's message. All formal communication with England was cut off, and the borderers were given quietly to understand that the government would wink at their depredations. Negotiations were opened with France, by means of the renewal of the ambassadorial commission of the aged Roman Catholic archbishop of Glasgow, who had been Mary's representative in France. At the same time, as a further sop to the Catholics, there were restored two more of Mary's old and faithful servants, the bishops of Ross and Dunblane.[46] All this was

---

document ever existed. See J. D. Mackie, "The Will of Mary Stuart," SHR, XI (1914), 338-344. The Spanish explained the absence of the document by stating that Elizabeth had personally burnt it. January 28, 1587, Mendoza to Philip II, CSP SPANISH, IV, 13-15.

[44] D. H. Willson, James VI and I, p. 76.

[45] CSP SCOT, IX, 327-328. See also March 6, 1587, Carvell to Walsingham, ibid., pp. 330-331.

[46] Moysie, Memoirs, p. 61. March 10, 1587, Woddrington to Walsingham, CSP

done to give public opinion time to cool down; James's real policy was revealed by a letter Gray sent to Archibald Douglas on February 28. Gray apologized to Douglas for a previous letter in which he had forbidden Douglas to write: he had done this by James's order, because Douglas was widely regarded in Scotland as having some responsibility in Mary's death. The king wanted Douglas to continue to report. Gray told Douglas to advise Elizabeth to take a bold line with James, and to insist that *necesse est unum mori pro populo*; if she did so, James would acquiesce.[47] That this was true became clear as March wore on. By the middle of the month Douglas' nephew Richard informed him that the king was waiting to see what sort of compensatory offer Elizabeth would make. By this time Walsingham was confident that James would not fight; if he did, he would lose all chance of the English succession.[48]

Walsingham himself had contributed to this Scottish acquiescence, perhaps even more than he knew. In late February and early March, when matters still looked to be very much in the balance, he composed a memorial for Maitland which was a powerful argument against a breach with England, a document which Conyers Read describes as "one of the ablest state papers which survive from Walsingham's pen."[49] The gist of Walsingham's argument was that if James fought, he would irreparably destroy his chances for the succession, and that there was absolutely nothing to be gained by fighting anyhow. It was obvious that Scotland by herself could not conquer England. Therefore outside help would have to be obtained, and that meant France or Spain. It was unlikely that either of these powers would be

---

SCOT, IX, 333. March 18, Forster to Walsingham, *Border Papers*, I, 252. A summary of James's instructions to the archbishop of Glasgow is in CSP SCOT, IX, 340-341. See also March 24, Courcelles to Henry III, *Courcelles' Despatches*, pp. 49-59.

[47] *Salisbury Papers*, III, 230-231. See also March 2, 1587, Poury Ogilvie to Douglas, *Salisbury Papers*, XIII, 332-334.

[48] March 12, 1587, Richard Douglas to Archibald Douglas, *ibid.*, pp. 335-339. March 22, Walsingham to Stafford, S. C. Lomas, ed., *Calendar of State Papers, Foreign Series, of the Reign of Elizabeth*, XXI, pt. 1 (London 1927), 246-247. Stafford was the English ambassador in France.

[49] C. Read, *Mr Secretary Walsingham and the Policy of Queen Elizabeth*, III, 181. The document is given at length by Read, *ibid.*, pp. 182-186.

able or willing to help James; but even if they were, they would do so, not for his benefit but for theirs; and their interests, both religious and dynastic, were widely different from those of James. Even if James turned Catholic, he would gain nothing from France or Spain: consider the case of Don Antonio, the Portuguese pretender, a Catholic prince despoiled by a Catholic.

This document evidently made a deep impression on Maitland, who during these months was rethinking his whole approach to Scottish foreign policy. During the crisis which led to Mary's death he had advocated the old policy of balancing between England and France, after the manner of his brother William. It was put this way in an English memorandum, probably written by Randolph, in November 1586: "Some, like the secretary, persuade a middle course—not to join with France, nor yet to follow England, or depend on favour thence, but to join with some Protestant prince of good power in sure league, viz., by marriage, as well to relieve the king's present want by dowry as to strengthen him hereafter in the action of his claim to England, and so to hold afar off, that England may rather seek to follow them, than they England."[50] The policy of balance was beginning to seem bankrupt by 1587, however, chiefly because of the growing evidence of governmental paralysis in France. There was nothing Henry III could do, even if he had wanted to;[51] and Maitland knew that the Guises were hand in glove with Spain. Under these circumstances the policy of balance made no sense unless Spain were substituted for France in the equation, and this Maitland would not do. Maitland was always very suspicious of Spain, possibly because at bottom he was a fairly good Protestant.

There was another consideration here as well. Maitland's only rival for King James's favor, the master of Gray, was rapidly losing influence,[52] and it seemed likely that if the secre-

50 CSP SCOT, IX, 166-169.

51 It is clear that the chief French objective in this crisis was the same as that of James: to save Mary if possible, but above all, to remain friendly with Elizabeth. See A. Teulet, ed., *Papiers d'état ... inedits ... relatifs à l'histoire de l'Ecosse au XVIe siècle*, II, 856-872, 885-890; CSP SCOT, IX, 202-218.

52 An indication of Gray's weakness was his attempt to ingratiate himself with Maitland by confirming the latter in his position as baillie of Musselburgh. As commendator of Dunfermline Gray was lord of Musselburgh. Mait-

tary played his cards right, he would soon be the king's chief political adviser. He would then be able to put into effect his ideas on domestic policy, most of which were directed at weakening the power of the aristocracy. Many noblemen would be disgruntled; but if they could not obtain support in England —if, on the other hand, England supported the Scottish government—the nobles' capacity for resistance would be enormously reduced. Both the foreign and the domestic situation, therefore, dictated adherence to the English alliance. Maitland adopted this policy and never wavered from it thereafter.

Maitland probably received Walsingham's memorial sometime around March 10, although there is no way of determining the exact date. Even before this date there was evidence of the change in his views. To be sure, he had been responsible for the renewed negotiations with France; but on March 6 Walsingham's agent Carvell reported that Maitland was "very well-inclined towards her Majesty, and a favorer to the maintenance of peace and amity."[53] Furthermore, in the weeks that had passed since the news of Mary's death had arrived, no action had been taken, even though everyone agreed that Maitland alone now had the king's ear.[54] The best evidence as to his change of opinion, though, comes in a letter of Richard Douglas to his uncle Archibald on March 14, in which Richard reported that he had had a long conversation with Maitland, in which Maitland stated that he agreed, with Archibald, that James should come to terms with England.[55] The secretary evidently repented

---

land's original grant of the office of baillie had been made when Dunfermline was in the hands of the crown. SRO, *Privy Seal Register*, LV, 17. SRO, *Treasurer's Accounts, 1586-1587.*

[53] CSP SCOT, IX, 330-331. In the same letter, as evidence of Scottish feeling, Carvell enclosed this quatrain:

To Jesabell that Englishe heure
receyve this Scottish cheyne
As presagies of her gret malhoeur
for murthering of oure quene.

The chain was a little cord of hemp, tied halter-wise.

[54] For instance, Carvell, *ibid.*, pp. 330-331; Archibald Douglas, *ibid.*, pp. 305-306; Gray, *ibid.*, p. 324; Poury Ogilvie, *ibid.*, pp. 326-327; Richard Douglas, *Salisbury Papers*, III, 134-135.

[55] *Ibid.*, p. 235.

that he had taken Richard so fully into his confidence. About ten days later the latter sought Maitland out at Lauder, where he was "busily occupied with his masons and workmen at the building of his house in the Forth of Lauder"—Thirlestane castle, still the seat of the Maitland family. On this occasion Maitland reverted to his old position and coupled this with a violent personal attack upon Archibald, who, he said, had called him a passionate fool in front of the privy council and attempted to ruin him by a forgery.[56] Richard was bewildered by Maitland's shifts: on March 28 he reported that Maitland was planning to send a private agent to Walsingham and at the same time he was "the only cause of the restitution of the bishop of Glasgow. . . . How the secretary can allow these so contrary courses I leave you to judge."[57]

What baffled the inexperienced Richard Douglas was simple diplomatic strategy. Maitland and his master fully intended to come to terms with Elizabeth, but they wanted to sell their acquiescence in Mary's death as dearly as possible. Maitland undoubtedly meant every word he said about Archibald, and it must have given him pleasure to be able to unburden himself so completely, and thus spur the treacherous Douglas into using all his influence to get concessions from England. With respect to these concessions James would not descend to particulars: England should make him an offer.[58] He still maintained a public posture of aloofness from England. But the best indication that he intended to come to terms was the fact that on April 2 he suddenly moved against Lord Maxwell. Maxwell, although forewarned, was unprepared to resist, and agreed to go into exile, and not to return without the king's permission, provided that his estates were not confiscated. He had played into Maitland's hands by getting involved in an intrigue with Arran, and Maitland was evidently largely responsible for James's move. The expulsion of one of the most important Catholic lords in southern Scotland was a clear indication that James was not going to adopt a pro-Catholic foreign policy.[59]

[56] March 23, 1587, Richard Douglas to Archibald Douglas, *ibid.*, pp. 236-239.
[57] *Ibid.*, pp. 134-135 (where the letter is misdated 1586).
[58] March 31, 1587, Richard Douglas to Archibald Douglas, *ibid.*, pp. 239-240.
[59] For the Maxwell business see April 2, 1587, Forster to Walsingham, *Border*

So, at least, the English assumed. Despite Archibald Douglas' efforts, they would make no offer to James, and Elizabeth began to complain that James did not believe in her innocence. After some months of useless fencing, James in July was re- duced to telling Archibald what he wanted: public acknowledg- ment of the succession, an English dukedom and lands, and a promise that his cousin Arabella Stewart would not be married without his consent.[60] As the queen showed no disposition to meet James's demands, relations between the two countries con- tinued strained. Consequently, the summer of 1587 was a very lively and lawless one on the borders, despite the officially correct attitude of the Scottish government and an occasional appar- ently genuine effort to keep some of the worst malefactors in hand.[61] But the significant fact is, that, thanks in some measure, at least, to Maitland's shift of view, the Anglo-Scottish alliance, though seriously shaken, survived the strain put on it by Mary's death. This was impressive testimony to the strength of the revolution in sentiment effected by the Scottish Reformation, as well as to the usefulness of the alliance to both countries. It was also the best possible guarantee of its permanence: if the alliance could survive the execution of a queen in a dynastic age, it could survive any shock.

The survival of the alliance involved the ruin of one of its

Papers, I, 253-254; April 11, Woddrington to Walsingham, *ibid.*, p. 254; April 15, Richard Douglas to Archibald Douglas, *Salisbury Papers*, III, 244-246; RPCS, IV, 158-159; Moysie, *Memoirs*, p. 62; T. Thomson, ed., *The Historie and Life of King James the Sext*, pp. 223-224.

60 *Salisbury Papers*, III, 267-268. The request for the English title and lands should be explained. English common law held that no alien could hold or in- herit land in England. If James could acquire English land, either in this way or by Elizabeth's acknowledgment of his rights as heir to his grandmother, Darnley's mother, he would no longer be considered an alien in English law, and his claim to the succession would be greatly strengthened. See H. G. Stafford, *James VI of Scotland and the Throne of England*, pp. 39-40.

61 For a good brief summary of the Anglo-Scottish negotiations in 1587 see Read, *Walsingham*, III, 187-193. For the borders see *Border Papers*, I, 258ff, esp. pp. 262-263, 267-268. SRO, *Treasurer's Accounts, 1587-1588* indicate that the government was more anxious to keep order during this summer than has hitherto been supposed. So does Maitland's letter to Forster of July 16, 1587, informing him that James had ordered the wardens of the middle and west marches and the keeper of Liddesdale to keep the peace and cooperate with the English wardens. PRO, *Border Calendar*, Ind. 6887.

principal architects. The master of Gray was now, by every political test, a thoroughly superfluous man; by the beginning of March 1587, he had lost every vestige of the king's confidence. This was mainly the doing of the earl of Leicester, who betrayed Gray by revealing to James Gray's confidential letters to him in which Gray had advocated the execution of Mary.[62] Gray consequently became very anti-English, and got involved in the plots of the northern Catholics led by Huntly, a fact which was soon revealed to Walsingham and Maitland.[63] But it was not his association with Huntly that was to ruin Gray; it was, rather, a chain of intrigue which was begun by his old enemy Arran.

In March of 1587 Arran, hopeful of regaining his power, wrote to the king and accused all his enemies, Maitland as well as Gray, of being accessory to Mary's death and of planning to seize James and deliver him into the hands of Elizabeth. Those accused were properly indignant, and insisted on a formal hearing, which was set for April 10. Arran refused to enter himself in ward, as demanded by the council, however, and his charges thus collapsed.[64] The agent of Gray's ruin was not to be Arran, but his brother, Sir William Stewart. On March 26 James had decided to send Stewart to France, probably to communicate with the archbishop of Glasgow. According to Stewart, Gray became very friendly and attempted to draw him into a plot, similar to that of 1585, against the present government. Stewart betrayed Gray's confidences and, hoping to ruin as many of his brother's enemies as possible, went into detail as to what Gray had told him about 1585. James refused to go into the question of the coup of 1585, but he was quite prepared now to ruin his onetime favorite. On May 15, as the climax to a series of accusations, Stewart charged Gray before

62 March 3, 1587, Poury Ogilvie to Walsingham, CSP SCOT, IX, 327-328.

63 April 26, 1587, Poury Ogilvie to Walsingham, *ibid.*, pp. 405-407. See also *Salisbury Papers*, XIII, 340-342. Maitland's informant was Graham of Fentry, an honest and rather stupid Catholic whom Maitland had cajoled into believing that he was pro-French. One reason for the attack on the Catholic Lord Maxwell was to break up these conspiracies.

64 March 31, 1587, Richard Douglas to Archibald Douglas, *Salisbury Papers*, III, 239-240. RPCS, IV, 157-158. Archbishop John Spottiswoode, *History of the Church of Scotland*, II, 374.

the convention of estates with trafficking in France with agents
of Spain and the Pope, with being in favor of liberty of conscience in Scotland, with plotting, in alliance with Maxwell, the
murder of Maitland, Cowdenknowes, and Douglas of Lincluden,
the collector-general, and with consenting to Mary's death in
return for an English bribe. Gray made a general confession
of guilt, and admitted writing to Queen Elizabeth in August
of 1586 to the effect that if it was necessary to kill Mary for
her own security, she should do so, *quia mortui non mordent.*
Gray's life was spared, but he was banished, and he was forced
to surrender the recently acquired lands of the abbey of Dunfermline, which were given to Huntly.[65]

Thus the brief day in the sun of the master of Gray came
to an end. Like so many Scottish aristocratic politicians of this
period, he had a considerable talent for intrigue and no notion
of consistent policy. He is often credited with a sincere belief
in the English alliance, and it is true that he was as responsible
for the successful conclusion of the pact of 1586 as anyone
else in Scotland. But his desperate intrigues in the last months
before his ruin, when he knew that he was slipping from power
and favor, and was willing to join the Catholic party to save
himself, indicate that his belief in the policy of the English
alliance was less strong than his desire for personal aggrandize-
ment. Furthermore, even in an age of notoriously treacherous
politicians, Gray was preeminent among them. James did well
not to trust him again. Gray lingered on for some years on the
fringes of Scottish politics; like Arran, he made an occasional
effort to recover favor, but he never became an important political figure again.

[65] RPCS, IV, 164-168, 173. April 29, 1587, Woddrington to Walsingham, *Border
Papers*, I, 255-256. Calderwood (IV, 612-613) says that Gray's life was saved by
the intercession of Lord John Hamilton. Gray expressed his gratitude in a letter
of May 19 to Lord John, Hamilton MSS, Box 1. Maitland may have had more
to do with Gray's downfall than appears on the surface. On February 26
Courcelles reported an outburst of James against Gray: he "prayed the secretary to find some mean to have him out of his presence. . . . The secretary
thought it not convenient, that the king should declare himself so suddenly,
but to attend the assembly of the nobility." *Courcelles' Despatches*, pp. 38-47.
This certainly sounds as though Maitland was planning something similar to
what actually happened.

The gift of Gray's property of Dunfermline[66] to Huntly is a matter of some importance. This was the first sign of favor that James had shown to the leader of the Scottish Catholics since Arran's fall, and it reflects a significant change in circumstances. Now that Mary was dead, the Scottish Catholic party, and those English Catholics who were not partisans of Spain, had no leader. James determined to become their leader, not by turning Catholic, but by holding out some hopes to them from time to time, so that they would support his claim to the succession. This was a policy which would pay enormous dividends if successful, but it was also an extremely difficult one to follow, since concessions to the Catholics would obviously annoy both the English and the kirk. All three of these conflicting forces must be somehow kept in balance, must not be allowed to turn against the king. That James was able to manage this successfully, to be simultaneously the chief hope of both the pro-English faction and the Catholics, is evidence of political skill of no common variety.

Maitland favored this policy; indeed, he may have been the author of it: Richard Douglas reported that the gift of Dunfermline to Huntly was made on Maitland's initiative.[67] As time went on, however, there began to be apparent a difference between Maitland and James as to the proper means of implementation. Basically the difference was one of emphasis as between kirk and Catholics. James, who disliked the kirk and was personally fond of Huntly, favored greater friendliness to the Catholics; Maitland, while believing that the Catholics should be kept in hand, came to feel that James should place his chief trust in the kirk.

Maitland's acceptance of the policy of the English alliance necessarily altered his view as to the proper relationship between government and kirk. Good relations with England required at least tolerable relations with the kirk. The alliance with England was based on the common Protestantism of the two coun-

[66] Huntly did not get quite all the lands of Dunfermline. The lordship of Musselburgh was given to Maitland. J. Paterson, *History of the Regality of Musselburgh* (Musselburgh 1857), p. 24. C. Innes, ed., *Registrum de Dunfermelyn*, Bannatyne Club publication (Edinburgh 1842), p. 484. RMS, IV, 441-442.
[67] *Salisbury Papers*, III, 254-255.

tries in the face of the rising power of reformed Catholicism on the continent. If the recent crisis proved anything at all, it proved that the English ruling class would not tolerate a Catholic successor to Elizabeth, but was prepared to accept James, provided he were impeccably Protestant. If, however, James proved not to be impeccably Protestant, if he flirted too openly with Catholics, he would become utterly dependent on the great Catholic nobles such as Huntly; furthermore, England would speedily revert to her old policy of support of an aristocratic Protestant faction which would be backed by the kirk—the combination which had ruined Mary and secretary Lethington and, very nearly, himself, as Maitland well remembered.

Fortunately for Maitland, the circumstances of 1587 were very favorable to his new policy. For the one important group in Scotland which did not in the least regret Mary's death was the ministers, and, in the difficult months that followed her execution they made matters as easy for the government as possible by remaining silent on political subjects. The tone of the General Assembly of June 1587, at which Maitland and Bellenden represented the king, was on the whole polite and friendly to the government in spite of the fact that Andrew Melvill was the moderator.[68] The ministers did not even raise the question of the restoration of the archbishop of Glasgow. In adopting this conciliatory attitude Melvill had another end in view than simply supporting the government in the crisis over Mary's death. Time was to demonstrate that he and his fellow extremists in the ministry had not receded from their theocratic opinions, but their experiences of the last few years had revealed to them that they were not as powerful either in the kirk or in the country at large as they had thought. They were considerably chastened by their failure to obtain the repeal of the Black Acts, and by the country's apathetic response to their passionate denunciations of this legislation. So they decided to bide their time, to cooperate with the government as long as it showed no signs of softness toward Catholicism, and to try to

[68] For example, see the courteous exchange between the Assembly and James over his proposal that Robert Pont be appointed bishop of Caithness. Calderwood, IV, 624-626.

recover their lost leadership and control in their own organization. In this respect Maitland's policy of conciliation was happily timed.

On only one point did Melvill and his cohorts refuse to change their views. This was with respect to their old enemy archbishop Adamson, at whom they continued to snipe throughout the Assembly. Just after its adjournment there occurred a significant incident. There was in Scotland at this time a Huguenot poet named du Bartas, who had come to James on an informal mission from Henry of Navarre to inquire about military aid and a possible marriage between James and his master's sister Catherine.[69] James made much of du Bartas, whose poetry he greatly admired, and at the end of June 1587 journeyed with him to St. Andrews. There he ordered Melvill to deliver them a lesson on church government. Melvill did so, in terms which kept the king "in anger all that night." The next day Adamson gave a prepared lesson to the two visitors, which Melvill attended, and to which he promptly delivered an impromptu reply, accusing Adamson of popery; "the bishop was dashed and stricken dumb." Both James and du Bartas agreed that Melvill had had the better of the exchange. "The bishop . . . after that day began to be weary of preaching, and to fall more and more in disgrace," writes Calderwood, accurately enough.[70] The fact was, that James and Maitland had decided that Adamson must be sacrificed to the policy of conciliation with the kirk.

In fact James's policy throughout the spring and early summer of 1587 was to be as friendly as possible to as many people as possible at home, in view of the difficult situation Mary's death had caused, and, more than that, to persuade people to be friendly to each other—to put an end to the numberless aristocratic feuds. The king was particularly anxious to accomplish this in time for his twenty-first birthday, which was approaching. So, on the last day of the convention of estates at which Gray was condemned, the people of Edinburgh were treated to a remarkable spectacle: "Upon Monday the 15th of May, after supper, the king came from the palace of Holyrood-

69 June 14, 1587, Courcelles to Henry III, *Courcelles' Despatches*, pp. 71-72.
70 Calderwood, IV, 638-639.

house to the castle of Edinburgh; from that to the Tolbooth . . . from thence came to the Market Cross, where a long table was set, furnished with bread, wine, and sweetmeats. The Cross was covered with tapestry, and upon it the trumpeters blowing, and the musicians singing. The king, in presence of the multitude, drank to the nobility, and every lord drank to another. The gibbets at the Cross were broken down with fire-balls and fire-spears; the glasses, with wine, sweetmeats, were cast abroad in the streets. . . . They went back to the palace in the same order as they came up. The king, with my Lord Hamilton on the right hand, and the secretary on the left; the duke [Lennox] and Lord Claude in other's hands before the king; Angus and Montrose in hands; Huntly and Marischal; Crawford and the master of Glamis likewise. In the meantime the cannons of the castle thundered."[71]

The lords who marched in this astonishing procession holding hands like brothers were men who were at feud with each other. It need hardly be added that they were not reconciled by the king's gesture or by walking down the High Street; but nothing was lost by it; it made a momentary impression, and it is an indication of the increasing solidity of the government that it could persuade the lords to participate in this spectacle.

So matters stood in midsummer of 1587, on the eve of the most important Parliament of James's reign. The kingdom was quiet and relatively orderly; the government was fairly firm, and was on friendly terms with all the important elements in Scottish society. And the central figure in the government was the indefatigable Maitland. Now that Gray was gone, he stood forth as the king's only adviser, and in the Parliament to come he was to be raised to the highest office in the kingdom, the chancellorship.

Yet there were serious weaknesses in his position, weaknesses which the chancellor-to-be did not fully appreciate. The greatest of these was just this dangerous and isolated preeminence, which was about to be underlined by his new appointment. "All the noble men envy the secretary's credit," Poury Ogilvie had

[71] *Ibid.*, pp. 613-614.

written in March;[72] they were to become still more envious
when Maitland as chancellor became the first subject of the
kingdom. Maitland was the first chancellor of Scotland in the
sixteenth century who was neither a bishop nor a great lord. He
was also the first chancellor to be granted precedence over all
other officers of state.[73] The chancellorship tickled Maitland's
vanity, no doubt; but it did not add to his power, which depended on the king's favor. It was an unnecessary office to him,
and his acceptance of it was a political mistake of the first order,
a blunder whose seriousness was compounded by the fact that
Maitland was preparing to use his newly acquired authority to
launch an attack on the overblown power of the aristocracy in
the Scottish state. The nobles hated him for this; his exalted
official position simply made them hate him still more. Maitland
would have made his task easier for himself if he had eschewed
the trappings of authority and contented himself with its substance.

Maitland was evidently dazzled by his success, so dazzled that
he failed to notice that his friends among the nobility were
slipping away from him. The warning signal that he should
have heeded was the behavior of his hitherto steadfast ally,
the master of Glamis. Glamis had ambitions for the chancellorship,[74] which had been held by his brother, and as he became
aware that he would not acquire it, his friendliness to Maitland
waned. In February 1587 he made a significant marriage, to
one of the beautiful daughters of Douglas of Lochleven. This
marriage naturally estranged him from Maitland, who regarded
the Douglases as the enemies of his house. "The master of
Glamis is not so great with the secretary as he was," wrote
Logan of Restalrig in comment on this event.[75]

The gradual estrangement from Glamis, and the latter's alliance with the house of Douglas, an alliance cemented by An-

[72] CSP SCOT, IX, 326-327. There was also a flare-up at the May convention of
estates; *James the Sext*, p. 228.
[73] G. Brunton and D. Haig, *An Historical Account of the Senators of the
College of Justice*, intro., p. xxxiii.
[74] November 8, 1586, Restalrig to Archibald Douglas, *Salisbury Papers*, III,
192-193.
[75] *Ibid.*, pp. 228-229. Douglas had seven daughters, all beautiful, known as the
"seven pearls of Lochleven."

gus' marriage with Glamis' niece in the same year, was to cause endless trouble for Maitland. It cost him his only really dependable supporter in the politically active upper aristocracy. His natural family allies, the Hamiltons, were riven with dissension, and even when the dissension was ended by the madness of Lord Claude, the lack of interest in politics shown by the phlegmatic Lord John, the head of the family, helped Maitland not at all. Furthermore, the hostility of Glamis spelt difficulty in the government itself, for Glamis was treasurer of the kingdom.

All these troubles were as the cloud no bigger than a man's hand, however, in mid-1587. Maitland was now firmly in control. The crisis over Mary had strengthened his hands, by ridding him of his only serious rival for the king's favor and by permanently settling the future direction of Scottish foreign policy. The new chancellor could now devote his attention to his real political interest, the strengthening of the power of the Scottish crown.

CHAPTER 6

THE PARLIAMENT OF 1587

THE PARLIAMENT of 1587 was the most important Parliament held in Scotland during the reign of James VI; if we except that of 1560, perhaps the most important of the century. This fact has not been sufficiently recognized by historians, probably because the two most striking enactments of this Parliament, the annexation of the temporalities of benefices, and the admission of representatives of the lesser landholders to Parliament, seemed to have very little immediate effect on the course of Scottish life. In actual fact, however, they were part of a much larger plan of reform, a plan which was never implemented in its entirety, but which ultimately succeeded in adding considerably to the power of the crown.

Maitland and the king were chiefly responsible for this plan. It is impossible exactly to apportion responsibility, since they were absolutely agreed on the central purpose of the plan as a whole, which was the weakening of the upper aristocracy. As early as 1584 Mary's agent Fontenay had noted James's aversion to, and fear of, the aristocracy; James had told him that their swollen power "arose from the fact that for forty years or more they had only had for governors in this kingdom women, little children, and traitorous and avaricious regents . . . it is not possible to subdue and reduce them all at once to their duty, but . . . little by little he would have them in good order."[1] Ever since his bitter experiences in his brother's time, Maitland had felt the same way. He had kept his opinions pretty much to himself, but they were beginning to be bruited around. While in England on his vain mission on behalf of Mary, the master of Gray wrote to Maitland, "They say here . . . that you de-

[1] August 15, 1584, Fontenay to Mary, CSP SCOT, VII, 271.

sired not the king and England to agree, because it would wrack the noble men, and gave an example of it by King James the fourth."[2] This was a misconception. Maitland wanted no second Flodden: quite the contrary. The long period of peace with England had put an end to the military indispensability of the aristocracy; the alliance of 1586, by making the king virtually the sole recipient of English favor and English funds, had simultaneously increased the king's resources and cut the nobility off from what had been for centuries one of the chief sources of its own strength. Maitland and James hoped and expected that English goodwill would be even more effective than the levies of Henry VIII in leveling the Scottish aristocracy.

James and Maitland were agreed as to the chief purpose of their policy, then; and the king, as was now his habit, left the details of the plan to Maitland. The latter's influence over James was now at its peak—great enough to secure the chancellorship, great enough to cause a rumor that he was about to be created earl of March,[3] great enough, indeed, to persuade James of the distasteful necessity of securing the active cooperation of the kirk. James accepted intellectually the necessity of such collaboration, but he was still entirely out of sympathy with even the moderate faction among the ministers. He was nevertheless persuaded to adopt Maitland's policy, and to hold to it for eight years and more. This was by no means the least of Maitland's accomplishments.

The aristocracy was so powerful and so firmly entrenched that Maitland dared not attempt a frontal attack on their privileges; his plan was rather to undermine them by increasing the efficiency of the central administration. This was not the sort of change which could be brought about by legislation alone, or even primarily by legislation; but Maitland was resolved to accomplish whatever he could by law. A recent decree of the privy council against the surreptitious acquisition of letters of relaxation from horning was confirmed.[4] Letters of horning—that is, of outlawry—were issued in cases of debt,

2 January 12, 1587, Gray to Maitland, KJS, p. 151.
3 July 18, 1587, Carvell to Archibald Douglas, *Salisbury Papers*, III, 268.
4 RPCS, IV, 118-119. APS, III, 450.

and were obtained by creditors in order to bring defaulting debtors to book, on the legal fiction that failure to pay a debt, as directed by a court, was an act of rebellion. In the past, many debtors, by favor or fraud, had persuaded the king to suspend such letters; this was now declared illegal. The sessions of the lords auditors of the exchequer were regularized: they were to sit from July 1 to August 31 every year, and besides their regular duties they were to see to the upkeep of the royal castles and houses and cope with the fact that "costly, superfluous, and unnecessary merchandise are [sic] commonly brought within this realm and . . . profitable wares . . . are carried forth of the same that . . . should pay custom to our sovereign lord," by altering the tariffs accordingly.[5] A law of 1540 requiring an annual report of sasines (feudal tenures) of crown lands was reenacted, but it remained virtually a dead letter for thirty years more.[6] More important was the enactment that all collectors of royal revenue must find surety among the merchants of Edinburgh that they would settle their accounts at the annual sitting of the lords auditors of the exchequer, and make their payments within twenty days of the end of each term.[7] Maitland and the king were to make considerable use of this system of sureties, or cautioners. It was not a particularly fair or efficient system, but it was about the only device available to combat the most pernicious weakness of the Scottish administrative system, the large number of hereditary office-holders. James and Maitland were very anxious to destroy these heritable jurisdictions, but here, too, they dared not attempt so direct a blow at the power of the aristocracy. As James put it ten years later in the *Basilicon Doron*, "The greatest hindrance to the execution of our laws in this country are these heritable sheriffdoms and regalities,[8] which being in the

---

[5] *Ibid.*, p. 455.

[6] *Ibid.* See also M. Livingstone, *Guide to the Public Records of Scotland* (Edinburgh 1905), pp. 166-169. The council had previously decreed that gifts of royal property could be made only with the approval of the treasurer, the secretary, the comptroller, and the collector-general. RPCS, IV, 138.

[7] APS, III, 456. See also G. P. McNeill, ed., *The Exchequer Rolls of Scotland*, XXI (Edinburgh 1901), preface, liv-lv.

[8] For grants of regality, see above, p. 6. The possessor of a grant of regality even had the right to repledge, or reclaim from the king's court, and try

hands of the great men, do wrack the whole country: for which I know no present remedy, but by taking the sharper account of them in their offices . . . and ever as they vaike [become vacant], for any offenses committed by them, dispose them never heritably again."[9] Yet James, despite his recognition of the evils of the system, despite the legislation against such grants, continued to make them.[10] One of Maitland's major difficulties throughout his career was the fact that his master, while quite willing to be convinced of the theoretical desirability of some reform, was always making exceptions on behalf of his favorites.

The heritable jurisdictions, among their many other faults, seriously handicapped the administration of justice, and particularly of criminal justice. Maitland, who was a lawyer and a judge, was painfully aware of this; so was the king, who had been showing a personal interest in the problem in recent months.[11] They therefore undertook the long-overdue reorganization of the system of criminal justice. This was a propitious time for such an undertaking, since in 1587 the hereditary justiciar, the earl of Argyll, was a boy of eleven, and his guardians were quarreling among themselves.

The root of the problem of criminal justice lay in the fact that the aristocracy, the holders of the heritable jurisdictions, had a basic contempt for the law. To cite but one example among many: in 1584 the earl of Bothwell urged Sir Patrick Vans of Barnbarroch, one of the members of the college of justice, to accompany him to his trial for the murder of David Hume, in order to overawe the court. As Bothwell put it, "we will most earnestly crave your presence the said day, accompanied [by] your friends and servants, to the defense of our

himself, any inhabitant of the regality accused of any crime save treason. On the right of repledging, see W. C. Dickinson, ed., *The Sheriff Court Book of Fife 1515-1522*, pp. 344-346, and J. Stuart, ed., *Miscellany of the Spalding Club*, 1st series, II, preface, xlvi-xlvii.

[9] C. H. McIlwain, ed., *The Political Works of James I* (Cambridge 1918), p. 26.

[10] C. A. Malcolm, "The Office of Sheriff in Scotland," SHR, XX (1922-1923), 299-300. J. Stuart, *Miscellany*, II, xlviii.

[11] CSP SCOT, IX, 183-184.

lives."[12] The cavalier attitude of these men could not be altered by legislation, of course; but their power for mischief might be checked, even though the heritable jurisdictions could not be directly attacked.

Possibly the most significant enactment for the future of Scottish justice was contained in a revenue measure. It reads as follows: "that the treasurer and advocate pursue slaughters and other crimes although the parties be silent or would otherwise privily agree."[13] This gave the government the right to interest itself in, and to insist on the prosecution of, any criminal case, whether or not the aggrieved party wished to prosecute. The government had previously possessed this right only with respect to pleas of the crown; as recently as 1583, in a forgery case which had been settled between the parties involved, it was held that the government could not bring the case into court since the injured party declined to appear.[14] But now all that was changed, and the king's advocate became virtually a public prosecutor. The royal power was further extended by the astonishing enactment that theft or assistance to thieves on the part of a landholder was an act of treason.[15] This meant that landed men accused of such crimes were reserved for the king's justice. This act was aimed principally at highland and border magnates; if it could be enforced, a long stride toward the elimination of lawlessness would have been made.

Along with these important measures went an elaborate plan for revision of the machinery of criminal justice. The old custom of justice eyres had fallen into almost complete disuse; virtually all criminal cases were now tried in Edinburgh, which made royal justice both costly and time-consuming. To remedy this situation, it was resolved to resume the holding of eyres, twice yearly, in April and October. The country was divided into quarters, each of which was to be visited by two justices, to be appointed by the justiciar, or, in his default, by the crown,

[12] R. V. Agnew, ed., *Correspondence of Sir Patrick Waus of Barnbarroch*, II, 307, 311-312.

[13] APS, III, 457.

[14] G. W. T. Omond, *The Lord Advocates of Scotland*, I (Edinburgh 1883), 48-49.

[15] APS, III, 451.

from the personnel of the college of justice or from the ranks of the advocates. The responsibility for preparing indictments for these eyres was taken out of the hands of the sheriffs and put in the hands of the local landed gentry, who were to co-operate, where necessary, with members of the burgh councils, and who were, themselves, to hold quarter-sessions to deal with minor crimes. The appointment of these gentry rested with the crown. This part of the enactment was an attempt to undermine the power of the heritable jurisdictions by creating something like the English justice of the peace; it was not notably successful.[16] Various regulations dealing with juries were laid down, including the rather drastic requirement that, once the jury had retired to consider its verdict, it was to be locked up and sealed off from the outside world until it had arrived at one.[17]

There remained the question of enforcement. How was the government to see to it that malefactors were produced at court, in the absence of anything resembling a police force or a standing army, and given the normal Scottish attitude toward the law? The usual system, one which was extensively used during James's minority, was to rely upon commissions entrusted to the magnates. This ran directly counter to Maitland's whole policy. The magnates could not be ignored or by-passed, however; so Maitland and James fell back on the idea of the "general band." This idea was feudal in origin; it was based on the custom that the feudal superior of the land was responsible for the conduct of his vassals. Thus, in the general band, the king's feudal underlings bound themselves, according to the copy of 1590, to "keep and cause to be kept good rule within our lands." They were responsible for the production at court of any accused resident of their lands, and they were liable to fine and punishment if they failed to produce the wanted man. This fixing of responsibility on the landlord, whose own property was liable to seizure if he failed to meet his obligations, undoubtedly

16 Indeed, James found it difficult to impose such a system even after he became king of England. See the comments in W. C. Dickinson and G. Donaldson, eds., *A Source Book of Scottish History*, III (Edinburgh 1954), 278-282.
17 APS, III, 458-461.

increased the authority of the royal courts; unless their own interests were nearly touched, most landlords would cooperate, simply in order to avoid trouble.[18]

With respect to civil justice the problem was similar. Like the justiciar's court, the court of session was overloaded. It was enacted, therefore, that all cases of violence arising out of property questions—though not, be it noted, the determination of the property questions themselves—be settled in the sheriff's court. To minimize the evil consequences of this decision, the procedure to be followed was carefully stipulated in the act. To reduce still further the burden of the court of session, which was being increased by "willful, obstinate, and malicious pleaders," it was enacted that the losing party in all cases involving sums of money must pay one shilling in the pound of the amount involved to the court; in cases where money was not involved, a flat rate of five pounds was assessed. This system of "sentence silver" lasted until 1641.[19]

The members of the court of session were not only overburdened, they were underpaid. Their fees, which amounted to about one hundred and ten pounds a year if they attended regularly, were supposed to come from quot silver, or legacy dues, which before the Reformation had been owing to, and collected by, the Catholic church. In 1564, a sum of one thousand six hundred pounds, annually was assigned from this source to the court. But quot silver was hard to collect, since the old consistorial courts had vanished, and the fee of one hundred and ten pounds, hardly adequate in the 1530's, was even less so by the 1580's, in view of the inflation and the debasement of the Scottish coinage. This situation clearly carried a threat to the quality of the Scottish judiciary, and to their independence, since it left them open to the temptation of bribes. No serious

---

18 I. F. Grant, *The Social and Economic Development of Scotland before 1603*, pp. 182-184. See RPCS, IV, 787-789, for the general band. Those landlords who did not wish to cooperate often made use of the ingenious legal device of making over their property to some member of their families, or to a reliable friend, frequently by means of a pre-dated deed. It was necessary to legislate against this practice in 1592; APS, III, 574-575. For a typical case of this kind see RPCS, IV, 670.

19 APS, III, 445-447. R. K. Hannay, *The College of Justice*, p. 87.

effort was made to cope with this problem by legislation at this time, but the privileges of the senators, including their right to the quot silver, were reaffirmed.[20] Maitland was aware of the problem, but he felt that, in view of the exiguous state of the crown's income, the solution would have to be other than financial. For the moment he put the question aside.

A weakness even more fundamental than this ineffective judicial system was the fact that over large areas of the kingdom —the highlands and borders—the crown's authority was often little more than nominal. This had been brought home to James and Maitland by the eruptions on the border after Mary's execution and by the extremely violent turn recently taken by the ancient feud between the MacDonalds and the MacLeans, which the privy council had been unable to stop.[21]

To the lowland Scot the highlands were a wild and far-off area, inhabited by savages. A contemporary account of the MacDonald-MacLean feud begins as follows: "these Island men are of nature very proud, suspicious, avaricious, full of deceit, and evil invention against his [sic] neighbor . . . they are so cruel in taking of revenge, that neither have they regard to person, age, time, or cause . . . in all respects they exceed in cruelty the most barbarous people that ever has been since the beginning of the world."[22] The basic trouble was that the chronically impoverished central government simply did not have the resources to impose its will in such an inaccessible area. Furthermore, the highlands were so poor that reducing them to order would not add materially to the king's revenues; the chief problem was to prevent the highlanders from despoiling the king's more settled and prosperous lowland subjects by their raids.[23] In the reign of James IV the government, evidently despairing of its own ability to reduce the highlands to order, entrusted

[20] APS, III, 444-445. Hannay, *College of Justice*, pp. 63-67, 77-78, 81-82. See also D. Laing, ed., *The Miscellany of the Bannatyne Club*, II (Edinburgh 1836), 51-64.

[21] RPCS, IV, 159-160.

[22] T. Thomson, ed., *The Historie and Life of King James the Sext*, p. 217.

[23] It must be said that James did not believe this. He was convinced that the highlands could be turned into a profitable source of revenue for the crown. On this point see Grant, *Social and Economic Development*, pp. 525, 535ff. Miss Grant's chapter on the highlands, pp. 472-550, is a very able analysis.

the task to the heads of certain great clans, notably the earls of Huntly and Argyll. These men, whose strength lay partly in the lowlands, received power and privilege from the crown in return for the prevention of anarchy and the protection of the lowlands from the depredations of the wild clansmen living in the more inaccessible parts of the highlands. This policy was, on the whole, dangerous and unwise. The crown thereby erected a series of petty kings in the north, who were powerful enough to defy the government with impunity when they wished, and whose interest frequently lay, not in keeping peace in the highlands, but in fomenting trouble so that they might aggrandize themselves under the pretext of restoring order.

The situation on the border was less difficult and at the same time more pressing, since good relations with England were partially dependent on a solution. Since the destruction of the earls of Douglas in the fifteenth century no border chieftain had the power of a Huntly or an Argyll; but the heads of the great border families commanded a good many followers, and, like their highland counterparts, they were greatly aided by the inaccessibility of many of the border glens.[24] The "border problem" was of fairly recent origin. During the centuries of Anglo-Scottish hostility the borderers' lawless incursions into England were winked at, and often encouraged, by the government. But with the development of friendly relations between England and Scotland in the 1560's, it was necessary to put a stop to the raids and establish law and order. After twenty-five years the goal had not been reached, because the government had no resources to maintain a standing force to keep order, and because it had to rely on the heads of the great border families as its chief officials. A Hume was almost always warden of the east march, a Ker of the middle march, a Johnstone or Maxwell of the west march, where the problem was complicated by the Catholicism of the majority of the inhabitants, including most of the Maxwells; and the earl of Bothwell was hereditary keeper of Liddesdale,

24 There is an excellent and detailed description of border geography in D. L. W. Tough, *The Last Years of a Frontier*, pp. 1-24.

the most desolate and lawless area of all.[25] In the absence of a standing force, the government's chief reliance had been in sporadic acts of violence, such as the famous "raids" of the regent Moray—sudden descents on a border town such as Hawick or Jedburgh, and the wholesale execution of malefactors after trial by a kangaroo court. The whole system of border administration—if system it could be called—was highly unsatisfactory.

The problem presented by the highlands and borders obviously could not be solved by legislation, but a legislative foundation for administrative action was necessary, and was found in the device of the general band. Highland and border landlords, and also highland and border clan chiefs, were ordered to find surety that they would produce malefactors on demand. It was necessary to include both landlords and clan chiefs because the two were not always the same. In the highlands, especially, there were a good many "broken men," that is, members of a clan who dwelt on the property of someone other than the clan chief; there were in fact, "broken" clans, entirely landless, the most famous of which was the Clan Gregor. The landlords of broken men—virtually all the important highland, middle-march and west-march landlords—were ordered to find the necessary sureties by October 1, 1587, or within fifteen days on demand. The clan chiefs of such men were required to supply hostages, whose lives were forfeit if no redress for future transgressions was forthcoming. If a clan failed to supply these hostages, it was automatically outlawed. An annual survey of clan manpower was to be made, so that the government would have an up-to-date list of potential malefactors. The landlords of borderers and highlanders living in the lowlands had to find sureties also; if they were unwilling to do so, the tenant in question could be returned to his birthplace. The justice clerk was entrusted with the chief responsibility for the enforcement of this act; twice a year he was

[25] These border wardenships were not regarded as particularly desirable jobs, but since they represented legal authority, it was important to, say, Lord Maxwell that he fill the post rather than his enemy Johnstone. See *ibid.*, pp. 84-85.

empowered to summon the landlords and chiefs "of all notable lymmers and thieves . . . to underlie the law conforming to the laws and general band." On the first day each month the privy council was to devote its meeting to highland and border business. In addition, a special committee was created, consisting of borderers whom Maitland regarded as reliable, to deliberate on the best methods of "quieting the border in time of peace."[26]

How was this enactment to be enforced? The government did not have the resources to pacify these areas by force, and it suffered from a shortage of competent and loyal officials. Until such time as these deficiencies could be remedied, the government was compelled to depend on the great landowners, who must either be coaxed into cooperation or coerced by the threat of the general band.[27] What in fact happened was that the great landowners refused to cooperate because they saw very clearly that the ultimate result of the implementation of this policy would be the strengthening of the crown. The steady and persistent opposition of the greatest highland leader, the earl of Huntly (Argyll was a minor), and the greatest border chief, the earl of Bothwell, to the government from this time forward, and their bitter personal animosity toward Maitland, are in large measure explained by their well-founded fear of what would happen to their power if James's and Maitland's policy was ever fully effectuated.

Underlying all of the government's administrative problems, and, indeed, the cause of most of them, was its chronic poverty. The crown's ordinary income was small. Crown land brought in only fifty thousand pounds a year, or something under five thousand pounds sterling.[28] Taxation was becoming more frequent, but it was still regarded as an unusual, emergency measure rather than as a normal way for the government to add to its income, and the increasing number of tax levies was

26 APS, III, 461-467, 517.

27 For example, in the MacDonald-MacLean feud mentioned above, the king, in addition to acting through the council, also wrote to Huntly, instructing him to take steps to stop the fighting. J. Stuart, ed., *Miscellany of the Spalding Club*, 1st series, III, 214-215.

28 CSP SCOT, IX, 664.

regarded with much suspicion.[29] The long royal minority had resulted in considerable drain, in the form of pensions and gifts to those in favor at various times, and James himself was both extravagant and constantly in debt, continually making gifts to his friends and favorites without the advice of his council, without even keeping the proper officials informed, while his servants' wages remained in arrears.[30] The council issued a number of decrees of revocation of these gifts, evidently without very much success, as the very frequency of the decrees attests.[31] Matters were made still worse by the inflation, which, combined with the debasement of the currency, drove prices up very rapidly in the last three decades of the sixteenth century.[32] The consequence was that the government was always close to bankruptcy.

James and Maitland tried, without much success, to do something about this. As in the matter of the hereditary jurisdictions, James could easily enough be brought to admit that the financial situation was serious, but he could not withstand the importunities of his friends. Maitland was handicapped by the fact that neither he nor his friend Robert Melville, the treasurer-depute, had very much understanding of financial matters. Both were honest and self-sacrificing in their financial administration,[33] but they were not particularly imaginative. Their main idea was to make the old system work more efficiently, rather than to devise new measures for raising money, and where they did try a new departure, as in the case of the annexation of the temporalities of benefices, they miscalculated

[29] R. S. Brydon, *The Finances of James VI 1567-1603*, p. 36, citing a memorandum of 1587 directed to the estates, urging them to assert their authority in tax questions, since otherwise James would tax "so oft as he pleases upon cullorit (colored) causes."

[30] *Ibid.*, pp. 27-28. D. H. Willson, *James VI and I*, p. 54.

[31] In the year and a half that had elapsed since Arran's fall there were five separate decrees of revocation, in addition to that of the Parliament of December 1585. APS, III, 382. RPCS, IV, 58-59, 109-110, 134, 180-181, 185-186.

[32] Brydon, *Finances of James VI*, p. 90. J. H. Romanes, "The Kindly Tenants of the Abbey of Melrose," *Juridical Review*, LI (1939), 214-215. I. H. Stewart, *The Scottish Coinage* (London 1955), pp. 95-96.

[33] Maitland seems not to have collected his official salary as secretary after 1585. In the *Treasurer's Accounts* for 1586 his name is scored through in the semiannual salary lists; after that year it simply does not appear.

the financial benefits that would accrue. Yet in fairness to Maitland it should be emphasized again that the fundamental cause of the poverty of the crown was the poverty of the country, and this was not alleviated until the eighteenth century.

Maitland tried to save money by improved administration. The enactments with respect to the exchequer and the judicial system mentioned above were designed in part to bring more money into the treasury. It was recognized that the tax system was unfair as well as unproductive; a committee was appointed to look into the possibility of reform and to determine how the newly annexed temporalities of the church were to be taxed. There is no record that this committee ever accomplished anything. The Scottish tax structure remained essentially the same.[34]

Another committee of which Maitland was a member was created to study the question of recoinage.[35] During the last decades of the sixteenth century it was the regular policy of the government continually to debase the coinage in the expectation of profit for itself. The debasement proceeded at a rapid rate. A pound of silver made 640 shillings in 1582; in 1601 it made 960. A pound of gold made the equivalent of 7,200 shillings in 1584; in 1601 it made 11,520. Comparisons with England are enlightening. In 1565 the pound sterling was worth 6 pounds Scots; in 1601 it was worth 12 pounds.[36] The government profited from the debasement to the extent of some 100,000 pounds between 1583 and 1596.[37] But in the long run currency debasement does not pay; the result was a rapid rise in prices and great popular distress. The policy was always extremely unpopular;[38] nevertheless it was continued.

The government's outlook on economic questions in general

---

[34] APS, III, 517. R. S. Rait, *The Parliaments of Scotland*, pp. 492-493.

[35] APS, III, 437.

[36] Brydon, *Finances of James VI*, p. 90.

[37] *Ibid.*, p. 91.

[38] One of the charges against the government of Lennox and Arran was that "for their own particular commodity they so tossed and raised the money . . . that that which was coined and current the first year was cried down, and commanded to be brought again to the coining-house the next year, to the common loss of the whole country, and to make the king to suck the blood of the poor." Calderwood, IV, 411.

was as conservative and unimaginative as its fiscal policy. By nature Scotland was a poor country, lacking resources and capital; in the face of this situation the chief objective of the government was to avoid war—James thoroughly understood the economic advantages of peace—and to assure abundant supplies of the necessities of life for the people rather than to encourage the export trade, to protect the consumer rather than the producer.[39] In spite of the government's poverty, no general tax on imports was levied until 1597.[40] The export of a great many commodities was forbidden, and the prohibition was strictly enforced in times of dearth; at other times permission to export one or another of the items on the prohibited list could be obtained by purchase of a special license. Export duties were charged; in 1582 the royal burghs obtained a lease of the customs for four years, for four thousand pounds a year plus thirty tuns of wine; the contract was renewed in 1586, but it was unprofitable to the burghs, and was allowed to lapse in 1589.[41]

The enactments of the Parliament of 1587 followed traditional lines in these matters. Scottish fishing ships were required to land at least one third of their catch in Scotland, in order to prevent dearth; the lords auditors of the exchequer were ordered to enforce this law and also the various enactments banning the export of various necessities. They were also ordered to review the current customs rates, to determine whether any changes were necessary. Usury was defined as charging more than ten percent interest, and was prohibited; so, too, were the ancient crimes of forestalling and regrating.[42]

In one respect the government's economic policy was, if

[39] T. Keith, *Commercial Relations of England and Scotland, 1603-1707* (Cambridge 1910), preface, p. xix. Grant, *Social and Economic Development*, p. 355.

[40] *Ibid.*, p. 358. An occasional attempt was made before 1597 to levy import duties—e.g., the levy on English cloth in 1590, RPCS, IV, 461-462—but the enactment of 1597 was the first general tariff.

[41] *Ibid.*, p. 416. Grant, *Social and Economic Development*, p. 451. T. Pagan, *The Convention of the Royal Burghs of Scotland* (Glasgow 1926), p. 56. G. P. McNeill, ed., *The Exchequer Rolls of Scotland*, XXII (Edinburgh 1903), preface, p. xxxi.

[42] APS, III, 451-453, 455.

not exactly progressive, at least abreast of the times. In typical mercantilist fashion, monopolies were created, particularly for the benefit of foreign craftsmen, in order to stimulate industrial development. This was not a new policy in 1587; in 1583, for example, a twenty-one year monopoly of the mining of gold, silver, tin, and lead was granted to Eustace Roche, a Fleming.[43] Roche was not very successful, and ultimately, in 1592, his monopoly was upset in the courts, but in the meantime he had acquired a monopoly of the manufacture of salt.[44] Maitland was interested in Roche's operations, sufficiently so to cause a rumor that he and David MacGill, the king's advocate, were going to buy up Roche's mining monopoly.[45] The real fruit of Maitland's interest appears in the lengthy statute of 1587 granting considerable privileges to certain Flemish craftsmen, with the intention of founding a Scottish textile industry. The three craftsmen mentioned in the statute were to agree to stay in Scotland five years and bring thirty skilled workers with them. They were to take only Scottish apprentices. In return they were presented with a gift of one thousand marks, became naturalized citizens of Scotland and burgesses of Edinburgh, and were exempted from all taxation and burgh duties. A few years later a nine-year monopoly of papermaking was granted to a German entrepreneur and his partners on similar terms.[46]

These measures did not have any appreciable effect on Scottish industry. A detailed breakdown of Scottish exports for the year 1614 shows that the country's principal exports were still food and rural raw materials.[47] The government's chief

[43] RPCS, III, 601-602. R. W. Cochran-Patrick, *Early Records relating to Mining in Scotland* (Edinburgh 1878), pp. xvii-xviii.

[44] *Ibid.*, pp. lxi-lxiii, 53-73. RPCS, IV, 319-320. See also Roche's letter of September 25, 1588 to Geoffrey LeBroman, CSP SCOT, IX, 618-619. A detailed study of Roche's career would furnish a great deal of information with respect to Scottish industry in the later sixteenth century.

[45] June 1, 1587, Richard Douglas to Archibald Douglas, *Salisbury Papers*, III, 259-261.

[46] APS, III, 507-509. RPCS, IV, 452-453. A few years later the entry of a hundred Flemish clothmaking families was authorized. Pagan, *Convention of Royal Burghs*, pp. 208-209.

[47] Grant, *Social and Economic Development*, pp. 309-311. Keith, *Commercial Relations*, pp. 1-2.

concern was still to protect the consumer. A shrill decree against the hoarding of food in times of scarcity was issued in 1586, and in June 1587 James wrote to his ambassadors in Denmark ordering them to see to it that certain Scottish merchants who had been buying food in Danzig for resale in continental Europe returned home with their cargoes, in order to relieve the dearth that currently existed.[48] James clearly indicated that the merchants should be punished for their callous devotion to moneymaking while their countrymen starved. In brief, the economy of Scotland continued to lag behind that of the rest of western Europe, and grew at a considerably slower rate than that of her southern neighbor. The unimaginative policy of the government, dominated as it was by fiscal considerations, contributed little or nothing to economic growth. Such prosperity as Scotland enjoyed under James VI was owing almost entirely to the long period of peace, which permitted for the first time the accumulation of a certain amount of capital.[49]

The land was still the chief source of wealth in Scotland, and it was from the land that James and Maitland expected to obtain the greatest increase of their meager resources. The usual sweeping revocation of all gifts and grants made during the king's minority was enacted—James had just turned twenty-one.[50] The status of certain lands annexed to the crown, such as the earldoms of Ross and Orkney, was changed so that the lands could be feued to increase the crown's income.[51] But these measures, while they might prove helpful, would not substantially augment the crown's resources, chiefly because it was politically impossible to implement the act of revocation. Such an implementation would have affected adversely every major landholder in Scotland and a good many of the lesser ones, and they would not have stood for it, as James and Mait-

---

[48] RPCS, IV, 84. *Barnbarroch Correspondence*, II, 401-402.

[49] Grant, *Social and Economic Development*, p. 423, calls James "one of the most thoroughgoing innovators and reformers in economic affairs that Scotland had ever known." It appears to me that this judgment is not borne out by the facts.

[50] APS, III, 439-442.

[51] *Ibid.*, p. 439.

land very well knew. There remained one other major source of income—the lands of the church.

For a long time now the king and the chancellor had been dissatisfied with the amount of money accruing to the crown from the property of the church. In theory the crown was supposed to get whatever surplus remained from the thirds of benefices after the salaries of the clergy had been paid; it was also supposed to acquire the so-called "monks' portions" as the old Roman Catholic monks died off.[52] Furthermore, of course, as benefices fell vacant owing to the death of the holder, their income reverted to the crown. But all these advantages proved to be more theoretical than real. In practice, vacant benefices seldom remained vacant for very long. Pensions and gifts were granted from the thirds, and often the holder was exempted from paying the thirds at all, upon his undertaking to provide for the ministers of those churches annexed to his benefice. The revenue from the monks' portions was supposed to support the royal bodyguard; but in August 1585 the bodyguard had to be reduced to forty men because of lack of funds, and in January 1587 it was necessary for the council to revoke once again all gifts made out of the monks' portions by the king in consequence of the "inopportune and unreasonable suit of sundry persons."[53] The king's misplaced generosity was again proving costly to his government.

There was, Maitland felt, but one solution to this problem, a radical but perfectly logical solution, which would have the tremendous additional merit of pleasing the kirk. This was to follow the English example of the 1530's, but to go even further, and to annex the temporalities of all the benefices in Scotland to the crown.

The preamble to the statute of annexation explains the government's action almost exclusively in financial terms.[54] Past kings have given away to the church so much of the crown's property that the king now finds it impossible to live off his own. Since the king does not want to burden his subjects with

[52] For the thirds of benefices and monks' portions see above pp. 15, 56.
[53] RPCS, IV, 5-7, 134.
[54] The act is in APS, III, 431-437.

excessive taxation, and since the motivation behind the original gifts has ceased to operate (the only reference to the religious revolution), the king has decided to repossess himself of his rightful patrimony, that is to say, all of the temporalities of benefices—they are enumerated in the act in careful detail. This property henceforth was to be treated like any other: its possessors were to pay taxes on it, and the king, as landlord, could set in feu any property not already feued. Compensation, as determined by a heavily official committee, would be paid to the dispossessed.[55] Existing feus were not upset, nor were existing pensions from the revenues of church property. The rights of lay patrons on these lands were not disturbed, nor were the hereditary baillies and stewards; but the latter lost their power to repledge a man already summoned to the king's court.[56] Burghs of regality and barony which had held of an ecclesiastical superior now held of the king, but their status was otherwise unchanged; thus the monopolistic position of the existing royal burghs was left undamaged.

Specifically exempted from the annexation were several sorts of property destined for the support of the ministers of the kirk. The houses and castles of the prelates were not annexed, nor were the manses of the ministers in the rural parishes nor any burghal property which formed the sole support of the minister in the burgh. Also exempted were four acres of land "most ewest (nearest) to the kirk and commodious for the minister serving the cure thereof," all property which was used to support education, or for the benefit of the poor and the sick, and, finally, the teinds.

The teinds, or tithes, were the most important of the church's spiritualities, and had been recognized by Parliament as the rightful property of the kirk as long ago as 1567.[57] That recognition was repeated in the present act. But putting the kirk in possession of the teinds was another matter. Even before the Reformation the problem of the teinds had become complicated, owing to the practice of annexing parishes to the mon-

55 *Ibid.*, pp. 438-439.
56 On this point see Livingstone, *Guide to the Public Records*, p. 130.
57 APS, III, 24.

137

asteries and bishoprics, which "exercised the patronage, drew the teinds, and made their own arrangements for the performance of the spiritual offices of the parish by a vicar or curate."[58] About three-fourths of the parishes of Scotland had been thus annexed before 1560. The practice of leasing out the collection of the teinds to tacksmen had become very common, too, owing in part to the annexations, in part to the confusion attendant on the Reformation, when teind-holders often found difficulty in collecting what was owing to them, and were generally pleased enough to rent out their rights to people who were physically able to enforce payment. The teinds, in short, had become a negotiable commodity, and had become inextricably interwoven with other types of property. The consequences are described by a leading authority as follows:

"Underneath the titulars of the teinds, and intermediate between them and the rest of the population, there was a large class of persons known as tacksmen of the teinds, and under these again . . . sub-tacksmen, all interested in the teinds, and often so conflictingly, that the business of the annual levying of the teinds of the kingdom had become in many places and parishes a periodically repeated scramble and uproar. The records of the privy council and of the court of session are full of actions for the settlement of disputes as to the proprietorship of the teinds of this estate or that . . . and of actions by one claimant against another for wrongful spoliation of the teinds of previous years . . . of all the causes of illegal convocations in arms, with resulting raids and bloodshed . . . none was so constant or so beyond control as the annual leading of the teinds."[59]

The government was perfectly aware of the complexities involved in separating the teinds from the other forms of church property, but the act of annexation dealt with only one of them. The teinds of church lands set in feu with the teinds attached were not annexed; instead, the king agreed to pay ten

58 Grant, *Social and Economic Development*, p. 242.
59 D. Masson, RPCS, 2nd series, I, intro., clxiii.

percent of the rental of such feus to the "ecclesiastical persons to whom the teinds are reserved." Aside from this, however, no method was proposed, or machinery erected, whereby the teinds might be placed in the hands of their rightful owners. The ministry continued to be paid out of the thirds, as before; no serious effort was made to enforce the kirk's right to the teinds until 1617.

This was no oversight on the part of the government, nor was it a matter of administrative difficulty only. The truth of the matter was, that the king did not want the kirk to have the teinds.[60] Maitland's colleague on the bench, Lindsay of Menmuir, whose later career was to reveal his great talent for finance, was at work on a scheme, a "constant platt," as such things were called, for the support of the clergy. The plan was not completed until a year after Maitland's death; it would have been eminently satisfactory to the kirk; but James, and Lindsay's colleagues among the Octavians, who then governed Scotland, would have none of it.[61] Not until after the turn of the century, when James had succeeded in erecting the sort of church in Scotland that was satisfactory to him, was he willing to provide for its endowment, and to enforce its right to the teinds.[62]

In addition to these exemptions from the act of annexation on behalf of the kirk, there were also a good many exemptions which favored various individuals. Those church lands which had been previously erected into temporal lordships were not annexed; among them was Maitland's lordship of Musselburgh. Certain other abbey lands were also exempted, and the revenues of still others were promised to their present holders for life.

---

[60] Brydon, *Finances of James VI*, p. 111. See also the kirk's complaint in 1593; CSP SCOT, XI, 85.

[61] Masson, *op.cit.*, pp. clxiii-clxiv.

[62] The complexities of the problem of the teinds have been barely suggested in the above account. For further information see Masson, *op. cit.*, pp. cxlvii-clxxvi; A. Birnie, *A Short History of the Scottish Teinds* (London 1928), pp. 37-40; A. A. Cormack, *Teinds and Agriculture* (London 1930), pp. 81-93; T. Burns, *Church Property* (Edinburgh 1905), pp. 63ff. The chancellor's own attitude on the matter of the teinds was doubtless influenced by the fact that the Maitlands themselves held tacks of them. SRO, *Register of Deeds*, XL, 266-268.

The possibility of still further exemptions was not foreclosed; it was declared that any lands the king and the chancellor chose to exempt before August 15 (the effective date of the act was July 29) would also be excluded from the operation of the act. These exemptions, and the governmental policy they implied, were the most significant part of the act.

The real importance of the act of annexation, and Maitland's purpose in pushing it through, have been generally overlooked. The chancellor was naturally accused of seeking his own gain, and of hypocritically persuading the king that the crown would profit, in order to overcome James's reluctance.[63] This accusation need not be taken seriously. There is every reason to suppose that Maitland was sincere in his belief that the crown would profit. As it happened, he was mistaken: the crown did not profit to any marked degree. But as it turned out, this miscalculation did not greatly disturb Maitland. The original purpose of the act may have been financial, but this objective faded into the background even before the act became law.

The real significance of the act of annexation is revealed, not by tables of rents, but by the government's handling of the property it now had at its disposal. Some church property had been erected into temporal lordships before July 1587; this was not annexed. Other specified properties were exempted also, with the clear implication that they, too, would be erected into lordships. The holders of annexed property were not dispossessed; they too might hope for, or expect, an erection on their behalf. Such an erection was the ambition of every lay holder of a benefice of whatever sort. It would give him what he most desired: hereditary and permanent possession of the land. It would also have the additional advantage, in a period when taxation was becoming more frequent, of having the land considered as baronial land for tax purposes, as was actually done for the tax of 1588.[64] Thus, by the act of annexation, the

63 *James the Sext*, pp. 230-232. The author of this work, probably John Colville, is consistently hostile to Maitland.

64 McNeill, *Exchequer Rolls*, XXII, intro., p. xxxix. Only tenants-in-chief were liable for taxation; one half of any tax voted was paid by the church, one

crown had obtained an asset of enormous potential value in its struggle to increase its power and control over the kingdom.

James and Maitland suddenly became aware of this. The order in which the exemptions from the general annexation are listed in the text of the act suggests that this possible use of the act had not occurred to them when the proposal was first made, that, in fact, it dawned on them as the final text was being drafted. The first exemptions listed are of those properties which had already been erected into temporal lordships. There follow three further individual exemptions: those of the abbey lands of Dunfermline, Paisley, and Pluscardine. Dunfermline was presently held by the earl of Huntly; Pluscardine, by Alexander Seton, Lord Urquhart, the future president of the court of session and lord chancellor; Paisley, by Lord Claude Hamilton. It was clearly the king's intention to erect all three of these in favor of their present holders. As for Lord John Hamilton, there followed the specific promise that he could continue to enjoy the revenues of the abbey of Arbroath, the richest in Scotland, as he had before—a necessary promise in view of the recent restoration of the archbishop of Glasgow, which evidently made Lord John nervous for his abbey lands.[65] One more commitment was made in this section of the act: John Bothwell, the son of the bishop of Orkney, was permitted to retain the revenues of the abbey of Holyroodhouse, which had been promised him by a written agreement of 1582, in consequence of the earlier bargain by which the bishop had exchanged the temporalities of his see with Robert Stewart, then commendator of Holyroodhouse, who became earl of Orkney.

---

third by the barons, one sixth by the burghs. As the process of erection of church lands into temporal lordships continued, the tax structure began to be seriously affected. In 1597 the holders of these lordships were ordered to pay at the clerical rate, on this occasion only; at the same time liability to taxation was extended to feuars of crown lands and of those annexed lands still in the hands of the crown. APS, IV, 142-146; Rait, *Parliaments of Scotland*, p. 493. The problem was not solved. In 1621 a sort of income tax was introduced; this was regarded as extortionate, and was a factor in the rebellion against Charles I. *Ibid.*, pp. 494-495. On the whole question of taxation see also J. D. Mackie, ed., *Thomas Thomson's Memorial on Old Extent*, Stair Society Publication, x (Edinburgh 1946), 83-86, 120-122.

65 *Salisbury Papers*, xiii, 296-297.

There then follow, in the act, all those general exemptions with respect to the teinds, and so forth, which we have already noted.

It was at this point that the king and Maitland must have realized the tremendous political possibilities latent in the matter of erections. It was evidently too late to incorporate their discovery in the text of the act as approved by the committee of the articles; the necessary additions had to be tacked on to the end of the act, as a sort of appendix, at the full session of Parliament which met to approve the royal legislative program. This is proved by the language with which the additions are introduced: "The which day our sovereign lord sitting in judgment in plane (full) parliament by his declaration made in [the] presence of his three estates . . ."[66] There follows the clause reserving the right to add to the list of exemptions up to August 15; then come five additional exemptions: the temporalities of Kelso, Coldingham, and Lesmahago, and part of those of the collegiate church of Lincluden and of the nunnery of Northberwick.

These five exemptions indicate how James and Maitland planned to use the political power which had so suddenly been revealed to them. Kelso, Coldingham,[67] and Lesmahago were currently held by Bothwell; the lands of Lincluden and Northberwick were held by two important members of the official class, Robert Douglas and Alexander Hume respectively. The power of erection was thus to be used in two different ways: first, to bribe, neutralize, or reward certain members of the aristocracy, to try to reduce them to tractability, by holding out to them the promise of an erection on their behalf in re-

[66] APS, III, 436.

[67] Hume of Manderston continued to hold Coldingham until May 1587, when Bothwell obtained possession. May 29, 1587, Carvell to Walsingham, *Border Papers*, I, 259-260. By that time Maitland seems finally to have yielded up his claims, quite possibly in return for a bribe from Bothwell: on March 20, 1587, Bothwell resigned the office of baillie of Lauderdale in Maitland's favor. A. Thomson, *Lauder and Lauderdale* (Galashiels 1905), p. 371. SRO, *Privy Seal Register*, LV, 199-200. SRO, *Register of Deeds*, XXVI, 306. SRO, *Treasurer's Accounts, 1586-1587*. See also the oblique reference to the bargain between Maitland and Bothwell in Restalrig's letter of February 25, 1587, *Salisbury Papers*, III, 228-229.

turn for good behavior. That this was clearly contemplated is shown by the short list of additional exemptions made before August 15; most prominent on the list of those favored were the young duke of Lennox and the earls of Huntly and Marischal.[68] Secondly, the power of erection was to be used to promote an official class, to develop a sort of *noblesse de robe* out of the lesser gentry. In this way the government could both attract able and devoted servants and reward them for their service. Maitland's own fortune was based on government service; he would now proceed to elevate and reward his colleagues. Most of these men were lairds or cadets of great houses; in this way the loyalty of these classes to the government would be fostered and encouraged.

In both respects the policy of the king and Maitland was remarkably successful. It is true that they were unable to neutralize or control either Bothwell or Huntly, but a large number of nobles, like John Hamilton and Marischal, did become loyal supporters of the crown, and their loyalty, inactive though it often was, was a major factor in the ultimate isolation and ruin of both Huntly and Bothwell. The development of an official class also proceeded apace. From 1587 on, very few great nobles held high office in Scotland. There were some exceptions: the master of Glamis remained as treasurer; Arran's old ally Montrose was to become chancellor in 1598; Mar became treasurer in 1616. But most of James's officials were "new" men; this was particularly true after 1603, and it was through this official class, nurtured by the king and Maitland on the spoils of the church, that James later governed Scotland by his pen.[69]

Maitland had a further purpose in the act of annexation. He wished to please the kirk, whose ministers may have been the originators of the plan.[70] The kirk looked upon the act as the death-knell of episcopacy; "it was the bane of episcopal power and jurisdiction," wrote Calderwood[71]—and so, in the

[68] RMS, IV, 445ff.
[69] For a survey of the erections out of the abbey lands annexed in 1587 see Appendix I.
[70] So says the author of *James the Sext*, p. 231.
[71] Calderwood, IV, 640.

short run, it proved to be. Maitland's compromise of 1586 on the position of bishops had broken down, and so the government decided to sacrifice the bishops in fact. Beginning late in 1586, the crown began to direct its presentations to benefices to the presbyteries rather than to the bishops, and presbyteries were allowed to exercise powers of deprivation.[72] But the bishops were not sacrificed in name, in spite of the annexation of their temporalities. "Her [i.e., the kirk's] eye," wrote James Melvill, was "bleared with . . . fair promises,"[73] but it soon became clear enough again. By February 1588 the General Assembly was calling for the repeal of the act of annexation, on the ground that only "profane persons" and Papists were profiting from it, and that the kirk itself was being despoiled.[74] Indeed, there is no doubt that, like the government, the kirk did not profit financially from the act of annexation. In 1596 four hundred churches still had no pastors or readers; one minister was so poor that, for lack of a manse, he had to live in the steeple of his church; the clergy were even lacking in that indispensable tool of their profession, books, which they often had to borrow from their more prosperous parishioners.[75] The kirk derived little satisfaction from the works of this Parliament. "Except the ratification of the Acts made . . . before for establishing of the true religion and abolishing of Papistry, no good was done for the kirk": thus James Melvill.[76] But even so, the kirk was convinced of the government's good intentions, thanks to Maitland, and relations remained friendly, to the chancellor's great satisfaction.

Another factor leading to the passage of the act of annexa-

---

[72] The proportion of presentations so directed rose from one quarter in 1588 to over half in 1590 to almost all in 1592. G. Donaldson, "The Polity of the Scottish Church 1560-1600," *Records of the Scottish Church History Society,* XI (1955), 224-225.

[73] R. Pitcairn, ed., *The Autobiography and Diary of Mr. James Melvill,* p. 260.

[74] Calderwood, IV, 665.

[75] J. K. Hewison, *The Covenanters: a History of the Church in Scotland from the Reformation to the Revolution,* I (Glasgow 1908), 155, 157-158. For the borrowing of books see A. H. Millar, ed., *The Compt Buik of David Wedderburne, Merchant of Dundee,* SHS, 1st series, XXVIII (Edinburgh 1898), xxiv-xxv.

[76] *Autobiography of James Melvill,* pp. 259-260. The other acts on behalf of the kirk, largely routine, are in APS, III, 429-431.

tion was the kirk's long-standing complaint, voiced in this Parliament by the highly respected moderate minister David Lindsay, that bishops and lay commendators of monastic houses undertook to speak for the clerical estate in Parliament, and that they had no right to do so. The kirk held that, as one of the estates of the realm, their representatives, designated by the General Assembly, should sit in the place of the bishops and abbots. No one denied that these latter did not speak for the kirk; but the government was utterly opposed to the idea that the nominees of the General Assembly should have a voice in Parliament. The lawyer Edward Bruce, commendator of Kinloss, therefore met the kirk's argument by denying the validity of the kirk's conception of Parliament as representing the estates of the realm. What Parliament represented, Kinloss said, was land; bishops and abbots sat, therefore, not as lords spiritual, but as tenants-in-chief.[77] The act of annexation, by indirectly abolishing episcopacy, appeased the kirk somewhat; but it helped to intensify an entirely different problem, that of parliamentary representation as such, which the other famous enactment of this Parliament was designed to solve.

Whether the members of the Scottish Parliament represented land or estates, there was one immense gap in their ranks: the lairds were not represented. In Maitland's opinion it was essential that they should be, for they, as a group, represented the keystone of the combination he was seeking to create. It was from these men that the proposed official class would come; it was this group which, in the words of a leading authority, "seem(s) to have been particularly susceptible to the exhortations of the protestant preachers."[78] Maitland knew that the aristocracy would resent the introduction of the lairds into Parliament, but their resentment would be comparatively ineffective at the present time, owing to the relative youth and inexperience of many of the leading nobles, and to the growing strength of many of the lairds—as a report of February 1585 put it, "there is a great number of them of larger means than

[77] Rait, *Parliaments of Scotland*, p. 175. See also *James the Sext*, p. 232.
[78] G. Donaldson, ed., *Accounts of the Collectors of Thirds of Benefices, 1561-1572*, intro., p. x.

many of the nobility."[79] This, though exaggerated, was nearer the truth than the sneering remark of Archibald Douglas that the Protestant party consisted of a few nobles, the merchant class, and the "meanest sort of gentlemen called lairds, whose second sons and brethren are for the most part merchants and travellers by sea."[80] Whatever the relative strength of lairds and aristocrats, the former were essential to Maitland's plans; they must be brought into closer connection with the government, and one way of doing this was to bring them into Parliament.

By the middle of the sixteenth century those entitled to sit in Parliament consisted of four groups: prelates, lords of Parliament, representatives of royal burghs, and royal officials. Parliament was an outgrowth of the medieval *curia regis*, as in England, and therefore, technically, as Kinloss said, represented all tenants-in-chief. By the fifteenth century the lesser landowners had ceased to attend. James I, after his return from his English captivity, attempted to rectify this situation by imitating the English parliamentary structure. By the act of 1528 James created the dignity of lords of Parliament, men who were individually summoned—a group which numbered fifty in 1583.[81] All other tenants-in-chief were released from the obligation of personal attendance, provided they elected representatives at the head court of each shire. This attempt to imitate the English system of knights of the shire gradually withered. In the reign of James III the greatest number of lairds to attend a Parliament was thirty; in that of James IV, twelve; in that of James V, two or three.[82]

The Reformation revived the issue of the lairds in Parliament. At the great Parliament of 1560 over a hundred lairds appeared and petitioned for the right to take part; since they were supporters of the dominant faction, their petition was granted, though, as Rait has shown, the constitutional problem was completely misunderstood by all concerned.[83] In 1567, in

[79] CSP SCOT, VII, 577. There follows a list of forty lairds, some of them, like Cesford and Lochleven, very important people indeed.
[80] *Salisbury Papers*, III, 295.   [81] Rait, *Parliaments of Scotland*, p. 199.
[82] Omond, *Lord Advocates*, I, 22.
[83] Rait, *Parliaments of Scotland*, pp. 199-203.

the first Parliament of the regent Moray, another attempt was made to create a representative system, which again proved abortive. In Rait's words, "The smaller barons did not wish to be bound to elect, and pay the expenses of, representatives in every Parliament; they wanted to be able to appear in person when, and only when, they were interested in the questions under discussion."[84] This was clearly impracticable, and was finally recognized as such.

In 1585, at the Linlithgow Parliament, a petition was presented asking for a revival of the representative system. We do not know about the auspices under which the petition was presented, but Maitland and Douglas of Glenbervie, later earl of Angus, "for themselves and in name and behalf of the rest of the barons took instruments of the foresaid act," and the matter was referred to the king for further deliberation.[85] The subject was much on Maitland's mind for the next year and a half. His colleague on the bench, Lindsay of Menmuir, was set to work drawing up drafts of possible statutes. Lindsay suggested, among other things, that two thirds of each estate constitute a quorum, that a two-thirds vote of each estate be necessary for the passage of any proposal, that at least two days elapse between the report of the committee of the articles and the vote on the report, that each estate choose its own representatives on that all-important committee, that members of the court of session sit *ex officio* with the committee and in full Parliament, to give their advice in questions of law, and, most interesting of all, that the "spiritual" lords of session[86] become members of the spiritual estate in Parliament, since "the estate of the clergy is like to decay by the dissolution of all benefices and annexation of the temporality thereof to the crown."[87]

In the end, Maitland rejected all these proposals. The stat-

[84] *Ibid.*, pp. 203-204.

[85] APS, III, 422.

[86] When the court of session was established in the 1530's, it was stipulated that half the members should be clerics. This provision was still adhered to, technically, by the appointment of commendators, lay parsons, etc.

[87] These drafts are printed in Lord Lindsay, *Lives of the Lindsays*, I (London 1858), 485-489.

147

ute, as it finally emerged, hewed very closely to the lines of the petition of 1585. The act of James I was specifically revived. Chancery was to send down a commission to a baron of each shire to convene the freeholders and elect the requisite commissioners, who must be residents of the shire. This election was to be an annual affair, whether Parliament was summoned or not; after the first election, it was the responsibility of the outgoing commissioners to arrange for the election of their successors. Chancery was to be notified of the names of those elected; when Parliament was called, they would be summoned individually, as were lords of Parliament. Their representation on the committee of the articles was to be the same in number as that of the burgesses. The expenses of these commissioners were to be paid by their constituents. Prelates and lords of Parliament could not vote; nor could any freeholder whose estate was worth less than forty shillings a year. This was an obvious imitation of the famous English requirement, yet, because the freehold had to be worth forty shillings by the Old Extent, a medieval assessment of unknown origin which was still used as the basis for taxation, this requirement had the effect of limiting the franchise. In the sixteenth century, and still more in the seventeenth, an estate of forty shillings of Old Extent was worth far more than forty shillings. The franchise was further restricted by the barring of feuars, no matter how vast their holdings, unless they were also tenants-in-chief. Even after 1597, when they were compelled to pay taxes, the feuars of crown lands did not claim the rights of freeholders, and in fact they did not obtain the vote until 1661.[88]

The preamble of the act states that its purpose is to provide the king with more adequate information as to the state of the realm. This was no more than a diplomatic phrase. The king and Maitland had plenty of information about the state of the realm, and whatever gaps there might be in their knowledge were not likely to be filled by this device. The real purpose of the act must be sought elsewhere.

[88] APS, III, 509-510. Mackie, *Old Extent*, pp. 215-226. A. V. Dicey and R. S. Rait, *Thoughts on the Union between England and Scotland* (London 1920), pp. 53-56. See also Rait, *Parliaments of Scotland*, pp. 206-208.

It is my opinion that Maitland's motives have been generally misunderstood. The two greatest authorities on the Scottish Parliament, Professors R. K. Hannay and R. S. Rait, have said that the chancellor, by this act, was attempting to re-vivify the moribund Parliament, in order to build it up as a rival to the General Assembly, "a much more representative body than the existing Parliament," in Rait's words.[89] There is no evidence for this; the evidence, in fact, all points the other way. In 1587 Maitland was anxious to conciliate the kirk; he was not interested in weakening the influence of the General Assembly, but rather in allying himself with it. Furthermore, the chancellor had no desire to revivify Parliament. He rejected Lindsay's various proposals for strengthening its personnel and machinery. During the five years of Maitland's greatest power, from 1587 to 1592, Parliament was not called at all.[90] When it finally did meet, in 1592, the purpose of the meeting was to condemn Bothwell for treason, an act of such political significance that the most solemn form of condemnation possi-ble was thought to be necessary. Maitland preferred to govern through the convention of estates, which could do virtually everything a Parliament could do and was more easily con-trolled because the government could determine the personnel, could keep the body small and manageable. There was no inno-vation in Maitland's use of the convention. From the date of James's accession until his departure for England in 1603, "conventions were held almost every year, and frequently of-tener than once a year."[91] In the five years after 1587 during which no Parliament was held, there are six conventions re-corded in the *Register* of the privy council, and it is possible that there were others of which the record has not survived.

If Maitland's purpose was not to revivify Parliament or offer a challenge to the General Assembly, then what was it? One of

---

[89] *Ibid.*, p. 206. R. K. Hannay, "General Council and Convention of Estates," SHR, XX (1922-1923), 113-114; R. K. Hannay and G. P. H. Watson, "The Build-ing of the Parliament House," *The Book of the Old Edinburgh Club*, XIII (1924), 9-12.

[90] A Parliament was apparently planned for October 1589, but it was not held owing to the king's voyage to Denmark. RPCS, IV, 384-385.

[91] R. S. Rait, "Parliamentary Representation in Scotland," SHR, XII (1914-1915), 253-254. See also Rait, *Parliaments of Scotland*, pp. 144-146, 151-154.

his motives was certainly financial. The lairds could be required
to pay for their new privilege, and pay they did, to the extent
of forty thousand pounds. The lairds regarded their representation as having been purchased; one of them remarked in
1600, "we have bought our seats."[92] Maitland and the king
also assumed that the lairds would be less reluctant to pay
their share of regular taxation if their position as a separate
order in the state were recognized.[93] The forty thousand pounds
was collected, though with difficulty, and there is no evidence
that the lairds paid up any more joyfully after 1587 than
before. Like the other financial enactments of the Parliament,
this plan showed meager results at best.

More important to Maitland was the opportunity afforded
by the act to bring the lairds into contact with the government
and hence into alliance with it. Like the act for the reorganization of criminal justice, this act was designed to create that
body of supporters which was essential to Maitland's policy.
This explains the enormously cumbersome machinery of election provided by the act. Lindsay had proposed, in one of
his drafts, that the English model be followed in the election
of commissioners—that is, that the sheriff be empowered to
hold elections, either annually or whenever Parliament should
be summoned. Maitland rejected this suggestion; the sheriff
was either an aristocrat or a dependent of the aristocracy, and
should be by-passed. Hence the plan, foreshadowed by the
petition of 1585, of royal nomination of a laird to conduct
the election in the first instance, and the placing of subsequent
responsibility on the commissioners themselves.[94] Hence, too,
the plan for annual elections, which would serve the purpose
of reminding the lairds of their privileges and obligations, and
of making available a group of potential representatives for
the frequently held conventions of estates.

The machinery of the act was far too complicated, and did

[92] Brydon, *Finances of James VI*, p. 88.

[93] Rait, *Parliaments of Scotland*, pp. 208-209. RPCS, IV, 246-247. Hannay, "General Council and Convention of Estates," SHR, XX (1922-1923), 113-114.

[94] In the seventeenth century, after the union of the crowns, when the loyalty
of the sheriffs was no longer in doubt, the chancery writs to hold elections
were directed to them. Rait, *Parliaments of Scotland*, pp. 223-225.

not function well. The majority of the lairds were apathetic, and disliked having to pay so heavily for their new privileges.[95] Furthermore, there was no penalty for noncompliance with the act; the fines for nonattendance which were levied against all other estates by this Parliament were not extended to the lairds till 1617.[96] Then too, in a country unused to the English system of "self-government at the king's command," and where disobedience to orders often went unpunished, the tendency was to be careless or casual about the king's instructions. The lack of a large and dependable official class was an obstacle to efficient enforcement in this case, as in so many others. The act of 1587 undoubtedly contributed to the political education of the lairds as a class. It also helped to emancipate them from the magnates, a fact which the earl of Crawford was clever enough to realize or snobbish enough to resent; he made a public protest against the act which was written into the record.[97] But neither education nor emancipation can be achieved overnight. Maitland's act did not automatically create a phalanx of government supporters among the lairds. It did create resentment among the magnates.

The direction of Maitland's policy was apparent. In October 1588 the English ambassador William Ashby wrote, "The greatest strength of Scotland consisteth in the gentlemen which they here call lairds, and the boroughs which are almost all well affected in religion; therefore the king with these may easily bridle the earls."[98] Maitland was aware, if Ashby was not, that bridling the earls would not be easy. He needed the wholehearted support of the burghs as well as the lairds. His new willingness to cooperate with the kirk was the key step in winning the burghs, but their other interests had to be taken into account—subject, always to the consideration that the government's economic policy was dictated by its own fiscal necessities and the welfare of the consumer rather than the prosperity of the commercial classes. So, nothing was done about the continuous de-

95 *Ibid.*, pp. 209-210, 230-231.
96 APS, III, 443. C. S. Terry, *The Scottish Parliament, its Constitution and Procedure 1603-1707* (Glasgow 1905), p. 86.
97 APS, III, 510.
98 CSP SCOT, IX, 623-624.

basement of the coinage. But a committee headed by MacGill, the king's advocate, to establish a uniform system of weights and measures eventually accomplished its task. Less effective was a very badly drawn statute creating a series of commissions to determine wine and timber prices. The burghs were promised that their obligation to pay one sixth of any tax would not be increased by the annexation of the temporalities of benefices. The complaint of some burghs that others of their number elected lairds as their parliamentary representatives was met by the provision that no one could be a member of more than one estate.[99] The burghs would have liked more. They were anxious for a veto over the erection of new royal burghs to share their jealously guarded monopoly, but this they did not get, although in fact there were only seven such erections between 1572 and 1603.[100]

The enactments of this Parliament, taken together, constituted a comprehensive and skillful attack on the four major sources of aristocratic strength. By means of the general band the aristocratic landlord was required to assume considerable responsibility for his subordinates or suffer severe financial consequences; hostages were demanded of the clan chief to the same end. At the same time the government attempted to cripple a major source of the landlord's power and increase its own powers of enforcement by its judicial reforms. Other legislation was designed to improve the fiscal situation of the government, strengthen the economy of the country, and thereby improve the position of the Scottish middle class. Above all, Maitland desired to increase the administrative efficiency of the central government.

In all this Maitland was a reformer in the strict sense of the word, rather than an innovator. His program was designed not only to undermine the power of the aristocracy, but also to appeal to those elements in Scottish society whose alliance with the government was indispensable if this plan were to succeed,

[99] APS, III, 437-438, 443, 451-452, 498-499, 521-522. This last enactment could not be enforced; see Rait, *Parliaments of Scotland*, pp. 294-296.
[100] *Ibid.*, pp. 258-259. Grant, *Social and Economic Development*, pp. 375, 445-446, 454-455.

namely, the kirk, the lairds, and the burgesses. No radical reform program would be able to attract all three of these groups simultaneously. The only act which could be called at all unprecedented was the annexation of church lands. In all other respects Maitland who, like most lawyers, was a cautious man, not given to improvisation, simply wanted to make existing laws and institutions work.

The work of this Parliament was most impressive on paper; but, as Maitland well knew, the pages of the Scottish parliamentary record were filled with laudable enactments which turned out to be dead letters for lack of enforcement. Here the key institution was the privy council. In Scotland, as in western Europe generally in the sixteenth century, conciliar government was the solution to the problem of how best to increase the power of the crown. Maitland therefore seized upon the present occasion to legalize his control over the council, by obtaining the customary parliamentary approval of its personnel. As Maitland designed it, the council consisted of two groups, the "ordinary and daily" council, and the occasional members. The latter group consisted of fourteen magnates and two bishops, including Adamson. The "ordinary and daily" council, the real governing body of the kingdom, consisted entirely of officials or members of the court of session, Maitland's colleagues, who sympathized with his program.[101] Its only aristocratic member was the treasurer, the master of Glamis.

In addition to a reliable council, Maitland did all he could to assure himself of a dependable administration by filling all possible government posts with his supporters. One example may be cited here. In the years of Maitland's greatest power, from 1587 to 1592, there were nine appointments to the court of session. Four of these were Maitland's relatives, his nephews Cockburn of Clerkington and Douglas of Whittingham, and his distant cousins the Setons, John Seton of Barnes, a member of the royal household, and his younger brother Alexander Seton, Lord Urquhart, the future lord chancellor.[102] The

101 APS, III, 444.
102 Maitland's grandmother was a Seton. This relationship may seem rather tenuous, but the closeness of the families is demonstrated by the fact that

fifth, William Melville, was the younger brother of Maitland's long-time colleague, Robert Melville. The sixth, Sir John Cockburn of Ormiston, succeeded Bellenden as justice clerk. The seventh, James Elphinstone, was the third son of Lord Elphinstone; he went on to the secretaryship and undeserved disgrace as Lord Balmerino. The eighth was the obscure Andrew Wemyss of Myrecarnie. Only one, the earl of Montrose, was a great lord, and Montrose, at the time of his appointment in November 1591, was just emerging as a supporter of Maitland's, after years of political eclipse.

In addition to the public business just described, this Parliament also passed a good many private acts, ratifying the property holdings of several magnates and of a number of lesser men—a necessary formality, since the king had just reached his majority. Among them were several in favor of Maitland. He became chancellor for life, in recognition of his "singular qualities and dexterity." Various property rights were ratified to him: the lordship of Thirlestane, with privileges of regality, the lordship of Musselburgh, the superiority of Leith, his hereditary position as baillie of Lauderdale. He was also given the right to set the tacks of the abbey of Kelso. Soon afterwards his grateful sovereign gave him the barony of Stobo and the lordship of Dunbar.[103]

By the end of the Parliament Maitland was becoming aware of the hostility that his program and his personal preeminence were creating among the aristocracy. As Burghley's agent Roger Ashton remarked in one of his reports, "This country cannot abide one man to guide all."[104] Maitland was clearly "guiding all," and his political intentions were now manifest. It remained to be seen whether he and his master could achieve their goal, or whether, before the necessary support could be built up, the magnates would rise up and overwhelm this program of reform, as they had done so often in the past.

Maitland's daughter married the seventh Lord Seton, a nephew of Urquhart and Barnes, and the chancellor's son, the first earl of Lauderdale, married Urquhart's daughter.

[103] APS, III, 454, 489-491. RMS, IV, 441-443, 465-466, 479. SRO, *Privy Seal Register*, LV, 110-112. For Leith see *Juridical Review*, XXV (1913), 313-332.
[104] CSP SCOT, X, 127-129.

CHAPTER 7

THE ARMADA CRISIS

THE twenty-seven months which elapsed between the dissolution of Parliament in July 1587 and the king's departure for Denmark in October 1589 mark what might be called, in twentieth-century terminology, the first half of Maitland's administration. As Richard Douglas wrote to his uncle Archibald, "The state of this country and all matters whatsoever, both domestic and foreign, rests only upon the chancellor's shoulders."[1] It was a time of alarums and excursions, in which the domestic problems that most interested Maitland were frequently pushed into the background by the challenge of armed and resurgent Catholicism. The great crisis of Elizabethan England, and of European Protestantism, was rapidly approaching. The destiny of Scotland as well as England was at stake in the Channel in the summer of 1588; like his good sister of England, King James had to face the Catholic menace in the double form of foreign invasion and domestic conspiracy. The latter threat was made all the sharper by the mounting hostility of the Scottish aristocracy to the king's chief minister. Maitland was now the object of the hatred of all the many malcontents in Scotland; not merely his power, but his very life, was often in question. "If the chancellor had not been secretly warned the 13th of this month," wrote Hunsdon on November 25, 1587, "Bothwell had slain him in the court."[2]

Since Maitland had constantly to work under the double harassment of problems of foreign policy and of having to maintain his personal position against the malice of his enemies, it is not surprising that his administrative achievements in these months were not as great as he and his master would

[1] *Salisbury Papers*, III, 282-283. The letter is dated September 22, 1587.
[2] CSP SCOT, IX, 507-508.

have wished. Indeed, his greatest accomplishment was political rather than administrative: he succeeded in making a firm ally of the kirk. He "entered in special friendship with him [Robert Bruce, the minister], Mr. Andrew [Melvill] and me," wrote James Melvill under date of February 1589, "and kept true and honest till the day of his death. He held the king upon two grounds sure, neither to cast out with the kirk nor with England."[3] As a consequence, not only his own reputation, but also that of the king, began to rise among the godly. Many Protestants were becoming annoyed at the ministers for their public rebukes to the king, wrote one of Walsingham's correspondents on January 1, 1588, "he being so well inclined to religion as any prince in Europe. . . . If ever he is towards religion otherwise than well, it will be the ministers' sharp threatening [that] will be the cause of it."[4]

These golden opinions were not unearned. King James spent the winter of 1587-1588 "in commenting of the Apocalypse, and in setting out of sermons thereupon against the Papists and Spaniards."[5] More important, the king agreed to overlook the extra-legal summoning of a General Assembly in February 1588, and consented to most of its requests. This Assembly met amid rumors of the coming of the Armada; "great was the fear, fervent were the prayers of the godly, not without abundance of tears, sighs and sobs," wrote Calderwood.[6] It asked that James and his court and administration resubscribe the confession of faith of 1581. The king agreed to this; he also consented to pursue Papists and Jesuits, a detailed list of whom was handed to him, and to use his authority to plant kirks in the north and the southwest and protect the ministers sent to those dangerous areas. Only in the realm of finance was the king unwilling seriously to exert himself. The General Assembly condemned the act of annexation as profiting only "profane persons"; and it made the usual requests with respect to the ministers' salaries. James promised to see what he could do; in the end, nothing was done, beyond an elaborate enactment against

3 R. Pitcairn, ed., *The Autobiography and Diary of Mr. James Melvill,* p. 271.
4 CSP SCOT, IX, 532.   5 *Autobiography of James Melvill,* p. 260.
6 Calderwood, IV, 647.

dilapidation of the thirds. The increased revenue resulting from this measure seems to have gone to the government rather than to the ministers, however. But James was otherwise most accommodating. In return the Assembly finally acceded to the government's long-standing request that it censure the minister James Gibson for comparing the king to Jeroboam.[7] As the year wore on, and the threat of the Armada loomed larger and larger, the kirk grew more and more nervous, and correspondingly more grateful for the ever-increasing indications of James's staunchness in the faith. In May of 1588 the officials and ministers of Edinburgh formally thanked James "for his pains taken for the peace of the church and the realm. . . . The king, well pleased therewith, promised to give them greater cause to rejoice."[8] He lived up to his promise by ordering six prominent Jesuits to surrender for deportation within ten days or suffer outlawry, and by promising to bar all Papists from the bench and from the privilege of suing in court.[9] But most of all, the ministers rejoiced in the king's attack on Lord Maxwell at the end of May, 1588,[10] for they rightly regarded this action as definite proof that the government was committed to the Protestant cause.

The winning of the kirk was undoubtedly the chancellor's greatest achievement in this period. Some of his other efforts fell short of the mark, notably the attempt to implement the enactments of the recent Parliament with respect to the administration of criminal justice. The elaborate system of eyres planned in the legislation of 1587 could not be put into effect immediately. There was no money to pay a group of full-time justices; even if funds had been available, there was no one to send out. James and Maitland simply could not run the risk of a breakdown of the central administration by permitting their small group of loyal and efficient subordinate officials to go out into the countryside for weeks, perhaps months, at a

[7] R. S. Brydon, *The Finances of James VI, 1567-1603*, p. 125. APS, III, 545-547. RPCS, IV, 254. NLS, *Balcarres Papers* 29.2.8. For this Assembly see Calderwood, IV, 649-676; Archbishop J. Spottiswoode, *History of the Church of Scotland*, II, 379-382.

[8] May 8, 1588, Bowes to Walsingham, CSP SCOT, IX, 558-559.

[9] May 26, 1588, Bowes to Walsingham, *ibid.*, pp. 559-561. RPCS, IV, 284-285.

[10] See below, pp. 163-164.

time. So, in October 1587, it was proclaimed that criminal cases would be handled in Edinburgh as usual, on dates ranging from the end of November to the end of February. James announced his intention of presiding in person; he therefore banned any repledging by regality courts for a long list of crimes until after March 15, 1588. To protect the king against himself, it was declared that James would make no gifts out of the escheats of those convicted, "and the treasurer is discharged from passing of the said escheats even although the gifts thereof should be subscribed by his highness."[11] At the same time Maitland tried to make eyres possible for the future by putting an end to the shortage of competent officials trained in the law. He and Lindsay of Menmuir set about obtaining funds for the endowment of a chair of civil and canon law at the newly-founded University of Edinburgh. The funds were finally raised by 1589, and the first appointment was made in 1590.[12]

Maitland's effort to implement the policy of the general band was more successful. The privy council prodded those landlords and clan chiefs who were supposed to find sureties for the good behavior of their tenants and clansmen;[13] there was sufficient compliance with the law to cause the government some embarrassment. On October 25, 1587, the king wrote to Douglas of Lochleven asking him to take charge of a border malefactor, since "our own houses are not able to keep such a multitude."[14] At the same time pressure was applied to the magnates to bring their private feuds to the council for settlement. Some of them readily agreed. Others, like the earl of Caithness, were recalcitrant; Caithness and two of his brothers had to be denounced as rebels before they found surety that they would appear to answer the charges of Lord Oliphant.[15]

The government thus made some headway in its campaign

---

[11] RPCS, IV, 217-220.

[12] R. K. Hannay, *The College of Justice*, pp. 85-86. Sir A. Grant, *The Story of the University of Edinburgh during its First Three Hundred Years*, I (London 1884), 184-189.

[13] E.g., on March 8, 1588, Angus, Bothwell, and Mar were ordered to find surety for their men on pain of rebellion. RPCS, IV, 819. SRO, *Treasurer's Accounts*, April 1588.

[14] C. Innes, ed., *Registrum Honoris de Morton*, I, 154.

[15] RPCS, IV, 210, 229-230, 241, 261.

for law and order; but Scotland remained a lawless country. "Cruelty and murder increased as a popular sickness," wrote the author of a contemporary *Life* of King James;[16] and the writer's bias against Maitland's government must not be allowed to obscure the essential truth of this observation. To these years belong such acts of violence as the killing of Sir William Stewart, Arran's brother, by the earl of Bothwell and the assault by two lesser members of the Hamilton family on a writer to the signet who had the improbable name of Habbakuk Bisset; these are but two of the many cases noted in the council's *Register* and elsewhere.[17] Progress was being made, but the customs of generations cannot be altered in an afternoon. It would be many years yet before the Scot, and particularly the Scottish noble, would come to obey the law as a matter of course.

Maitland next turned to the problem of implementing the legislation which admitted the lairds' representatives to Parliament. In November 1587 instructions went out to hold elections of commissioners to Parliament, as provided in the act. These instructions were received very apathetically. A conference of various interested lairds was held late in January 1588; the result was a new set of orders to hold these elections, issued on February 1. This order seems not to have been obeyed very well either. In May 1589 a third set of instructions had to be issued, in preparation for the Parliament planned for October of that year and never held. There is no evidence that this order was any better obeyed than its predecessors; the government finally let the matter drop, and summoned its own nominees as lairds' representatives to the various conventions of estates held during these years. No further attempt to make the electoral machinery work seems to have been made till 1594.[18] The king and Maitland were much more pertinacious about collecting the forty thousand pounds which the lairds had agreed to pay for their seats in Parliament. The money was, in fact, desperately needed, to pay the royal bodyguard, for the upkeep of Edinburgh castle, and for the embassies connected with the king's

16 T. Thomson, ed., *The Historie and Life of King James the Sext*, p. 237.
17 RPCS, IV, 204-205, 239.
18 *Ibid.*, pp. 227-228, 245-246, 384-385. SRO, *Treasurer's Accounts*, December 1587. R. S. Rait, *The Parliaments of Scotland*, pp. 209-210.

marriage, for which special purpose an additional tax of one hundred thousand pounds was voted in April 1588.[19] But the government's financial difficulties continued. In 1589 the king was so heavily in debt to Sir Robert Melville, the treasurer-depute, that the profits of the mint were assigned to him until the debt should be recovered. In 1596, when Melville left office, the government still owed him five thousand marks.[20]

Lack of money was at the bottom of most of Maitland's administrative difficulties. This was certainly the chief obstacle to a successful highland policy, and consequently the government's progress in this area was very limited. The chancellor had some success in requiring conformity to the terms of the general band; but his major experiment in the highlands was a fiasco. In August 1587 the king, as landlord, set all of Orkney and Shetland in feu to Maitland and Bellenden, at a rental of four thousand pounds a year, almost twice the previous figure.[21] James was anxious to demonstrate the truth of his theory that the highlands could be turned into a source of revenue for the crown; it was also intended to penalize the earl of Orkney, Lord Robert Stewart, the king's bastard uncle, for his oppressive rule in the islands.[22] The plan was a total failure. The earl could not be displaced; he enlisted the aid of his nephew Bothwell, who added this to the long list of grievances he had against the chancellor. Bellenden, who was far more active in the scheme than Maitland, also fell out with his colleague. Eventually, in April 1589, in return for a consideration to Maitland, the islands were returned to the earl at a rental of £2,075.[23]

---

[19] RPCS, IV, 231, 245-246, 251, 269-270, 296-297, 344-345. Brydon, *Finances of James VI*, p. 30.

[20] *Ibid.*, pp. 50-51. R. W. Cochran-Patrick, *Records of the Coinage of Scotland*, I, intro., clvi.

[21] D. Balfour, ed., *Oppressions of the 16th Century in the Islands of Orkney and Zetland*, Maitland Club publication (Edinburgh 1859), intro., pp. liii-liv. RMS, IV, 467-468.

[22] Balfour, *Oppressions*, pp. 95-98.

[23] Lord Robert rewarded Bothwell by making him his heir, in default of his own legitimate sons. As he had at least four, and possibly five, living at the time, this was little enough. *Ibid.*, pp. liii-liv. RMS, IV, 565. SRO, *Register of Deeds*, XXXII, 330b. The progress of this affair may be followed in the letters of the various English correspondents in Scotland, and of Richard Douglas; CSP SCOT, IX, 485-486, 531-533; *Salisbury Papers*, III, 282-283, 299-301, 317-319. See also R. V. Agnew, ed., *Correspondence of Sir Patrick Waus of Barnbarroch*, II, 410-412.

No such calamity awaited the government's border policy. On August 12, 1587, shortly after the end of Parliament, the council issued a stern proclamation to the denizens of the east and middle marches, ordering them to cease raiding in England. This was followed by an order that certain border landlords, including Bothwell and Ferniehirst, produce certain of their tenants before the council in connection with recent raids; Ferniehirst was warded for disobedience.[24] In August, also, there occurred a meeting between the wardens of the middle march, Cesford and Forster, on Scottish initiative, the first such meeting in some time.[25] The English border officials were suspicious and unfriendly, particularly Lord Hunsdon, who became excited in September over a rumor that the Scots were planning to seize Berwick by a *coup de main*. Hunsdon was very suspicious of James, who, he reported in November, was expecting Spanish aid by February.[26]

Curiously enough, the last and largest of the border raids of 1587 served to clear the air. Early in December, in reprisal for a recent English raid, some two thousand Scots swept over the border, led by Buccleuch, Johnstone, and the young laird of Cesford.[27] James and Maitland were greatly annoyed and reacted promptly. Buccleuch and young Cesford were warded, in spite of the fact that the latter was about to marry Maitland's niece, and Buccleuch had to find surety to the extent of ten thousand pounds that he would behave in future before obtaining his release.[28] This raid came as a considerable shock to the chancellor, particularly in view of the part played by his nephew-to-be. Perhaps because of his preoccupation with his disastrous highland adventure, Maitland had not given much

24 RPCS, IV, 209, 211-213. D. L. W. Tough, *The Last Years of a Frontier*, pp. 244-245, suggests that these raids were not exclusively political in character; the borderers were short of corn.

25 *Border Papers*, I, 266-267. See also August 14, 1587, James to Cesford, CSP SCOT, IX, 477.

26 *Border Papers*, I, 286-288. Hunsdon suggested at one point that the best way to bring the Scots to heel was to seize all their merchant shipping, a proposal which the English government properly disregarded. Such a move would have enraged the most pro-English section of Scottish society. October 26, 1587, Hunsdon to Burghley, *Salisbury Papers*, III, 292-293.

27 *Border Papers*, I, 289-291.

28 December 8, 1587, Hunsdon to Burghley, *ibid.*, pp. 294-295. RPCS, IV, 234.

personal attention to border affairs; he had not even accompanied the king when the latter visited Peebles in November of 1587. But now the chancellor began to act. On January 3, 1588, the release of all English prisoners taken in the various raids was ordered. On the 6th all those with grievances with respect to the borders were instructed to file their complaints with the clerk register in ten days, and on the 18th a commission, consisting of three of Maitland's official colleagues, was appointed to negotiate with the English on such complaints. It did its work rapidly and efficiently, to the surprise and pleasure of the English officials, who had expected very few results from the meetings.[29]

In spite of this raid, the Scottish government was not much worried about the state of the east and middle marches. It was from the west march that trouble was likely to come, since the dominant family there, the Maxwells, were Catholics and resented the religious as well as the administrative policy of the government. The recent exile of Lord Maxwell had not seriously weakened the family, since the government had thought it politic to replace him as warden by his cousin Lord Herries. Maitland now decided to move against Herries. On the last day of January 1588, Herries was denounced rebel for not appearing to answer a complaint against him. Early in February he was also denounced as a Papist, and the lieges were summoned for the first of March, to move against him. Herries thought it the better part of valor to submit. He appeared before the council on March 5 and promised that he himself would attend kirk, and that he would permit no Papistry in his wardenry. On March 3, when it was apparent that Herries would submit, a private meeting of some of the council was held at Maitland's house to plan out future policy. It was decided to carry out the proposed forceful visitation of the west march, and to tighten up the system of cautioners, which was very loosely administered. From now on, sureties would be required to find three times the amount taken by those for whom they stood pledge, and in criminal cases would be put on trial within fifteen days.

[29] PRO, *Border Calendar*, Ind. 6887. *Border Papers*, I, 308-310. CSP SCOT, IX, 541-542. For the work of the commission see Tough, *Last Years*, pp. 123-124.

On March 4 Bothwell and others were summoned to answer for the conduct of certain borderers for whom they had given surety. On March 9 it was announced that a justiciary court would be held in Dumfries on April 1 to settle the affairs of the west march. The holding of this court was postponed, but the king did visit Jedburgh in April to do justice in the middle march. This time Maitland went with him; the expedition was very successful.[30]

The English border officials were delighted by the Scottish government's administrative vigor. To show their gratitude they put on a show for the king when he passed by Berwick on his return from Jedburgh: "a volley of all the great ordnance, which he liked well, and at his departure sent the master gunner and his people 100 French crowns in reward."[31] Even more pleasing to England was James's prompt reaction to the return of Lord Maxwell. Maxwell had gone into exile in April 1587 under pledge not to return without the king's license. He had broken that pledge by returning in late April 1588, after a sojourn in Spain. Everyone assumed that Maxwell was acting as a Spanish agent,[32] and he was, in fact, an important cog in a Catholic plot of whose full ramifications the government was as yet unaware. James was very angry at Maxwell's return, and proclaimed that no one should have any dealings with him. The impeccably Protestant Angus was temporarily reappointed lieutenant of all the marches; his animosity to Maxwell was well known. On May 8 Maxwell was denounced rebel. The lieges were summoned, and on May 25 the king set out for Dumfries. It was all over very quickly. Maxwell had not had time to rally his followers, and the northern Catholic lords held back, possibly because of the swiftness of James's action. Maxwell's strongholds were seized, and he himself, after a vain attempt at flight, was captured, by Sir William Stewart, Arran's

---

[30] RPCS, IV, 240-241, 244, 247-248, 258-259. RPCS, XIV, 367-369. CSP SCOT, IX, 534-535. D. Moysie, *Memoirs of the Affairs of Scotland*, pp. 65-66. Tough, *Last Years*, pp. 246-247. April 28, 1588, Richard Douglas to Archibald Douglas, *Salisbury Papers*, III, 322.

[31] April 30, 1588, Woddrington to Walsingham, CSP SCOT, IX, 557-558.

[32] See, for instance, November 15, 1587, Scrope to Walsingham, CSP SCOT, IX, 505-506.

brother, and brought back to Edinburgh.[33] James remained for about a month in Dumfries, receiving pledges for the good behavior of various Maxwells.[34] When he finally left the border, at the end of June, he announced his intention of returning in the autumn.[35]

Maitland, who had accompanied the king to Dumfries, was hopeful of using the opportunity presented by Maxwell's ruin to bring the borders, and particularly the west march, under greater administrative control. A convention of estates in July 1588 ordered all those who had suffered from the lawless behavior of any highlander or borderer since the Linlithgow Parliament—that is, since December 1585—to present their complaints and something of their proofs to the government, which would then act against those complained of, and also against their landlords and clan chiefs, in accordance with the general band.[36] Perhaps more important was the appointment in September 1588, after the death of the earl of Angus, of Maitland's friend and relative the laird of Carmichael as warden of the west march and steward of Annandale, one of Maxwell's hereditary offices.[37] Carmichael held the post for four years, and did much useful work. He was forced out in July 1592, as a consequence of his patron's fall from power, and Maxwell was restored; but the pernicious consequences of this restoration were mitigated by the death of Maxwell at the hands of his old enemy Johnstone in a pitched battle at Lockerby in 1593. And, indeed, Carmichael's tenure of office marks a turning-point in the his-

[33] For the proclamations against Maxwell see RPCS, IV, 274ff. See also May 7, 1588, Richard Douglas to Archibald Douglas, *Salisbury Papers*, XIII, 370-372. For the expedition itself, see Moysie, *Memoirs*, pp. 67-69, and Calderwood, IV, 678-679. Stewart did not live long to enjoy his triumph. He was killed by Bothwell in July in a street brawl in Edinburgh, after an unseemly quarrel in the king's presence, in the course of which "Sir William disdainfully bade Bothwell kiss his arse." *Ibid.*, pp. 679-680.

[34] Lord Herries and the laird of Lochinvar, Maxwell's sureties for his remaining in exile, had to pay the amount of their pledge; the third surety, Lord John Hamilton, was not required to pay, since the government was anxious for his support at the time. RPCS, IV, 286-287, 289-290.

[35] *Ibid.*, p. 292.

[36] *Ibid.*, pp. 298-300.

[37] *Ibid.*, p. 322. Carmichael was the grandson of Janet Maitland, the sister of old Sir Richard, through her daughter by the fourth Lord Somerville. James, Lord Somerville, *Memorie of the Somervilles*, I, 404.

tory of the west march. The area continued to be turbulent and lawless after 1588, but the palmy days when a Maxwell or a Johnstone could defy the central government with impunity were over.

Clearly the government's greatest administrative success in the months that followed the dissolution of the Parliament was scored on the border. One cause of that success was the cooperation afforded by England. Although it was scarcely necessary, James borrowed some guns, and a few soldiers to work them, from Lord Scrope at Carlisle to help reduce one of Maxwell's castles. The English were happy to lend James the ordnance, and the king was pleased "that her majesty would send the cannon unto him without pledge."[38]

The cause of this unusual generosity on Elizabeth's part was the great naval crisis that was now at hand. The coming of the Armada could not be long delayed, and with each passing day the friendship of James seemed more and more important. The English regarded the ruin of the Catholic Maxwell as an indication that James would stand by them, but they wanted the king to commit himself publicly. This he had not done. The only official notice the Scottish government had taken of the impending struggle was a rather ambiguous proclamation by the council on May 7, ordering the lieges to be prepared to resist invasion from abroad, without stating who the invaders might be.[39] This was hardly very reassuring.

Maitland was prepared to give the assurances the English wanted, but only at a price. Once he and his master had decided not to break with England over Mary's execution, the only realistic alternative was to strike a bargain on the most advantageous possible terms. Nothing could be done too hastily, however, owing to the intensity of anti-English feeling in Scotland, which must be given time to cool down. As a sop to Scottish opinion, and to make himself personally a little less odious to the nobility, Maitland had made a theatrical gesture at the last Parliament. "This day, being the last of the Parliament . . . the chancellor made a long oration in the name of the three estates, offering their lives, lands, and goods in the revenge of

[38] CSP SCOT, IX, 573.   [39] RPCS, IV, 277.

the king's mother's murder, which was confirmed by a general voice of all the whole house."[40]

This speech was intended to impress the English with the gravity of the situation. They had already been told, unofficially, what they should offer King James in order to mollify him.[41] Until they saw fit to do so, the king planned to remain cold and aloof, and to flirt with the Catholic party. Maitland, in the meantime, was to assure the English that he could guarantee Scottish friendship if the price was paid, and at the same time to hold the Protestant party together.

The chancellor had by far the more difficult task. It was made no easier by his speech in Parliament, which turned out to be a mistake. It simply enraged the English and revived their suspicions of his Marian proclivities, and it did not make the Scottish aristocracy feel any more kindly toward him.[42] Even James felt it necessary to disavow the speech, calling it "unknown and unlooked-for."[43] The English were informed that Maitland had not really meant what he had said: he "spoke nothing but that which he was earnestly pressed to do by the nobility and estates there convened."[44] The chancellor became noticeably cooler to the Catholics and reverted to a policy of ostentatious friendship with the great Protestant magnates, Angus, Mar, and Glamis.[45] By the end of 1587 even the suspicious Hunsdon was convinced of Maitland's good will toward England, thanks in some measure to the assurances of Angus and to the fact that Maitland was reportedly the victim of an abortive Catholic assassination plot.[46] "The chancellor finds that there is no standing for him but by her majesty, and therefore if he were a little heartened

[40] July 31, 1587, Ashton to Burghley, CSP SCOT, x, 127-129.
[41] See above, pp. 110-111.
[42] August 18, 1587, Archibald Douglas to James, HMC, *Laing Manuscripts Preserved in the University of Edinburgh*, I (London 1914), 62-64.
[43] September 22, 1587, Richard Douglas to Archibald Douglas, C. Read, ed., *The Bardon Papers*, Camden Society publication (London 1909), pp. 99-102.
[44] October 24, 1587, Bellenden to Archibald Douglas, CSP SCOT, IX, 491-494.
[45] August 19, 1587, Ashton to Walsingham, *ibid.*, pp. 478-479. September 22, Richard Douglas to Archibald Douglas, *Salisbury Papers*, III, 282-283.
[46] November 6, 1587, Richard Douglas to Archibald Douglas, E. Lodge, ed., *Illustrations of British History*, 2nd ed., II (London 1838), 323-329. December 9, Angus to Hunsdon, *Border Papers*, I, 295-296. Hunsdon's account of this plot, CSP SCOT, IX, 507-508, is garbled.

and might be sure of her majesty's favor . . . he would wholly run that course, which if he be once brought to do, all is well, and there will be no doubt or fear of the king," Hunsdon informed Burghley on December 28.[47]

As Maitland was holding out this carrot to the English donkey, the king was beating it by flirting with both domestic and foreign Catholics. The chief Spanish agent in Scotland, Robert Bruce, sensed that James was not serious in these negotiations,[48] and in fact he was not. James well knew what fate lay in store for him at the hands of a victorious Spain. As he later remarked to Sir Robert Sidney, "he looked for no other benefit of the Spanish . . . than that which Polyphemus promised to Ulysses, namely, to devour him after all his fellows were devoured."[49] But the king's attitude encouraged Huntly and the other leaders of the Scottish Catholic party to think that they might now be able to get rid of Maitland, whom they detested both as aristocrats and as Catholics. Huntly and his friends well knew, however, that they could not attack Maitland on the religious issue, or the overwhelming majority of Protestants would rally to his support. Their most promising policy was to persuade some Protestant lords to join them in seeking Maitland's dismissal on the grounds of misgovernment and hostility to the nobility as a class.

Huntly found the material ready to hand, in Bothwell and Lord John Hamilton. Bothwell was enraged by Maitland's proEnglish attitude—he had been the most vociferous of those who demanded an attack on England after Mary's death—and also by the chancellor's proceedings in Orkney and on the border.[50] More surprising was the attitude of Lord John Hamilton, who hitherto had been one of the chancellor's steadiest supporters. Maitland, after all, was his nephew. But so was Huntly, and the Maxwells were his close kin. Huntly was evidently able to persuade Lord John that Maitland was planning to destroy

47 *Border Papers*, I, 298-300.
48 This Robert Bruce must not be confused with the minister of the same name. See his letter of October 2, 1587 to Mendoza, CSP SPANISH, IV, 144-146.
49 Quoted in D. H. Willson, *James VI and I*, p. 80.
50 September 22, 1587, extracts of letter of Robert Carvill, CSP SCOT, IX, 485-486. See also Hunsdon's report of November 25, *ibid.*, pp. 507-508; December 27, Richard Douglas to Archibald Douglas, *Salisbury Papers*, III, 299-301.

the power of the Maxwells at the behest of England, and that to achieve this, the government would favor the claims of the earl of Angus, whom Lord John disliked, to power and office in the west.[51] So Lord John, an earnest Protestant, was persuaded to join in calling for the chancellor's dismissal.

The crisis came early in 1588. On January 27 the Catholic party and the Hamiltons came together at Dunfermline and Linlithgow. Their ostensible purpose was to accompany Huntly's kinsman, the laird of Gicht, to his trial for the slaying of a relative of the earl Marischal; their real purpose was to seize the king and eliminate Maitland and the other Protestant ministers. The king was warned of the attack in time, however, and the citizens of Edinburgh rose in his defense.[52] James was very angry. He cooled noticeably to the Catholics, and was very obliging to the General Assembly that met in February of 1588. Maitland, meanwhile, set about breaking up the aristocratic coalition by detaching its Protestant members. He attempted, without much success, to pacify the hot-tempered Bothwell by abandoning the Orkney adventure, by coming to an agreement over some lands that had been in dispute between them, and also, apparently, by hinting to the earl that he would some day resign the chancellorship in his favor.[53] He had better fortune with Lord John Hamilton, thanks to the intervention of Lady Maitland, and possibly owing to the good offices of the kirk, and to the promise that the lands of Lord John's abbey of Arbroath would be erected into a temporal lordship.[54]

Owing to the English refusal to make James a sufficient offer, however, the king gradually became friendly with the Catholic

51 CSP SCOT, IX, 531-533. February 28, 1588, Robert Bruce to Mendoza, CSP SPANISH, IV, 224-225.

52 February 2, 1588, Richard Douglas to Archibald Douglas, *Salisbury Papers*, III, 306-308. February 2, Hunsdon to Walsingham, *Border Papers*, I, 308-310. See also CSP SCOT, IX, 535-536, CSP SPANISH, IV, 227-228, and *Salisbury Papers*, XIII, 374-375.

53 April 11, 1588, Richard Douglas to Archibald Douglas, *Salisbury Papers*, III, 317-319.

54 April 11, 1588, Richard Douglas to Archibald Douglas, *Salisbury Papers*, III, 317-319. May 5, John Selby to Walsingham, CSP SCOT, IX, 558. May 8, Bowes to Walsingham, *ibid.*, pp. 558-559. See also May 12, occurrents out of Scotland, HMC, *Report on the Manuscripts of the Earl of Ancaster* (London 1907), pp. 142-143. The promise respecting Arbroath is contained in a royal order dated February 14, 1589, Hamilton MSS, box 1.

party once again. Via Lord Hunsdon the king intimated that Elizabeth had not satisfied him of her innocence in his mother's death.[55] By the end of March 1588 Hunsdon reported that the anti-English group was in the ascendant again at court, "to whom the chancellor fearing his own life hath joined himself."[56] Thus emboldened, Huntly tried once more to bring about Maitland's fall. He gave a banquet for the king at Dunfermline, "where the alteration of the officers of state was craved of the king"—specifically, that Maitland be replaced as chancellor by Claude Hamilton, and that he himself be made captain of Edinburgh castle—"and liberty of conscience." According to Sir James Melville, they also wanted the king to send an ambassador to Spain. Once again James refused, and quickly returned to Edinburgh, lest Huntly be tempted to repeat his abortive coup of January.[57]

At the end of April 1588 the King and Maitland decided to change their tactics. Flirting with the Catholics had not frightened Elizabeth, and had only led to internal difficulties. So they decided to try the effect of an ostentatiously pro-Protestant gesture. The illicit return of Lord Maxwell gave them the opportunity they sought. The result they had been seeking quickly followed. Elizabeth wrote James a friendly letter, and in June she sent him two thousand pounds sterling. She also agreed to send a statement signed by all the English judges to the effect that Mary's condemnation did not affect James's claim to the succession, and she offered to renew the ratification of the league if James wished.[58]

This was by no means as much, either financially or otherwise, as James and Maitland wanted, but they knew now how anxious England was for their friendship. So they changed

[55] March 16, 1588, Hunsdon to Burghley, CSP SCOT, IX, 547-550. March 30, de Vega to Mendoza, CSP SPANISH, IV, 241-243.

[56] Border Papers, I, 320-322. See also March 25, 1588, Richard Douglas to Archibald Douglas, Salisbury Papers, XIII, 365-366.

[57] Calderwood, IV, 676-677. April 10, 1588, Bowes to Walsingham, Border Papers, I, 322-323. Sir James Melville of Halhill, Memoirs of His Own Life, p. 361. The quotation is from Moysie, Memoirs, p. 66.

[58] J. Bruce, ed., Letters of Queen Elizabeth and King James VI of Scotland, pp. 47-49. May 26, 1588, Richard Douglas to Archibald Douglas, Salisbury Papers, XIII, 372-374. June 22, Carey to Carmichael, CSP SCOT, IX, 575-576.

their tactics once again, and reverted to their attitude of aloofness, convinced now that they had the whip hand. Early in July, as the Armada was about to sail, Archibald Douglas, still the king's unofficial agent in London despite Maitland's extreme dislike of him, was instructed to tell the English that James would "take the best course for his own surety and state of his country that he may."[59] Huntly was restored to favor; he was about to marry the sister of the young duke of Lennox, and had turned Protestant for the occasion. A convention of estates, held on the occasion of the gathering of dignitaries for Huntly's wedding, besides dealing with problems connected with the king's own marriage, voted to put off the trial of Lord Maxwell until October, and agreed to follow a policy of armed neutrality against Spain, as outlined by Maitland.[60]

This failure of the Scots to pledge open support to England in this, her darkest hour in the sixteenth century, was most alarming to the new English ambassador, the inexperienced William Ashby. James made it clear that he had been led to expect a solid offer from England; therefore Ashby's first interview, which abounded in generalities, was most unsatisfactory. A mere statement that Mary's condemnation did not affect James's claim to the English throne, even if accompanied by a certified copy of Elizabeth's public declaration of her innocence and of the unfortunate Davison's guilt in Mary's death, was no longer enough. Ashby was nervous, and at the same time convinced that the Scots could be won by the solid offer they were expecting. So, on the evening of July 31, in an interview with James in the chancellor's garden, at a time when rumors were flying of a Spanish landing in England,[61] Ashby gave the Scots what they wanted. He promised James an English dukedom, a pension of five thousand pounds sterling a year, and, in addition, enough money to pay for a royal bodyguard of fifty men and a border force of a hundred horse and a hundred foot. James at once closed with the offer. He wrote to Elizabeth the

59 *Salisbury Papers*, III, 332-335.
60 July 21, 30, 1588, Ashby to Walsingham, CSP SCOT, IX, 583, 585-586. August 1, Richard Douglas to Archibald Douglas, *Salisbury Papers*, III, 341-342. Spottiswoode, *History*, II, 384-386. Huntly's wedding took place on July 21; Moysie, *Memoirs*, p. 69.
61 CSP SCOT, IX, 588.

next day, pledging full support, and at the same time issued a proclamation declaring Scottish solidarity with England.[62] Colonel Sempill, a Spanish agent who had come to Scotland with Maxwell, was flung into prison.[63] The year-long diplomatic struggle had ended in a brilliant victory.

So Scotland girded itself to face the menace of the Armada. The suspense was tremendous. A subdued General Assembly which met on August 6 humbly thanked the king for his "good mind and earnest affection to the defence of the true religion," and was even rather half-hearted in the pursuit of its old quarry, archbishop Adamson. The archbishop's latest peccadillo was his having married Huntly in defiance of the instructions of the Edinburgh presbytery. Adamson pleaded illness and sought a postponement; the Assembly granted it, "although they found the testimonial [as to his health] not altogether sufficient."[64] The Assembly's most important act was to empower the Edinburgh presbytery "to call before them Papists and apostates which shall happen to resort to court"; this was directed particularly at Huntly, of whose recent "conversion" to Protestantism the Assembly was rightly suspicious.[65]

Then, suddenly, the menace of the armed and triumphant Counterreformation vanished like the mists of the morning. The end came on the beach at Anstruther in Fife, where a battered ship and its hungry crew of Spaniards were greeted by James Melvill with food and a lecture on the errors of the Popish religion. "The Lord of Armies," wrote Melvill, "was . . . directing their hulks . . . to the islands, rocks, and sands, whereupon he had destined their wrack and destruction."[66]

The Scottish Protestants rejoiced, but the pleasure of the

[62] August 1, 1588, James to Elizabeth, *ibid.*, pp. 588-589. August 1, Richard Douglas to Archibald Douglas, *Salisbury Papers*, III, 341-342. August 3, Ashby to Walsingham, CSP SCOT, IX, 589-590. RPCS, IV, 307-309.

[63] August 11, 1588, Woddrington to Walsingham, CSP SCOT, IX, 595-596. Spottiswoode, *History*, II, 386-387, says that Maitland was largely responsible for Sempill's arrest, and that Sempill was protected by Huntly. He was subsequently allowed to escape lest he embarrass James by revealing the latter's negotiations with Spain. J. D. Mackie, "Scotland and the Spanish Armada," SHR, XII (1914-1915), 21-22.

[64] Calderwood, IV, 684-687.

[65] *Ibid.*, p. 691.

[66] *Autobiography of James Melvill*, pp. 261-264.

government was soon mixed with gall. Its great diplomatic victory over England disintegrated as rapidly as had the Spanish fleet. As soon as the peril was past, Elizabeth promptly disavowed her ambassador. Ashby, it seemed, had exceeded his instructions. Elizabeth would not grant James a dukedom, or any lands, nor would she pay for a bodyguard or a border patrol. She did hold out some hope with respect to the pension, however, and she sent three thousand pounds sterling to the king at once, to soften the blow.[67] Since Ashby was neither recalled nor punished, it seems reasonable to assume that his disobedience was pleasing to the queen. As the exiled master of Gray commented to Archibald Douglas, "I am sorry to know from Scotland that the king our master has of all the golden mountains offered, received a fiddler's wages."[68]

The king and Maitland by this time were accustomed to the ways of Elizabeth's diplomacy. They did not break off relations with England. Sir Robert Sidney, who was sent north to perform the unpleasant task of notifying James that he would not get what he had been promised, that he would in fact get nothing right now but the three thousand pounds and fine phrases, was politely received. On August 31 he had an uncomfortable interview with Maitland, in which the latter insisted that Ashby's promises be kept.[69] Two days later, Maitland informed Sidney that if Ashby's promises were carried out, the king would do anything Elizabeth wanted. On the other hand, if these promises were not performed, the king would be forced to other shifts, and the chancellor would probably be assassinated.[70] Sidney knew that this last was not merely idle chatter; he had himself reported a recent plot against Maitland's life. Huntly, Crawford, and Colonel Stewart had planned to murder the chancellor on the night of August 23, as he went from the king's rooms to his own, but Maitland had been warned in time.[71]

While the chancellor worked on Sidney with promises, the

[67] August 18, 1588, Ashby to Walsingham, csp scot, ix, 578. August 22, Walsingham to Ashby, *ibid.*, pp. 599-600.

[68] *Ibid.*, pp. 648-649.

[69] September 1, 1588, Sidney to Walsingham, *ibid.*, pp. 607-608.

[70] September 2, 1588, Sidney to Walsingham, *ibid.*, pp. 608-610.

[71] August 27, 1588, Sidney to Walsingham, *ibid.*, pp. 601-602.

other side of the medal was displayed before Ashby. Spain, Maitland told him, had made the king very great offers. They would help him avenge his mother and obtain the English crown for himself; they would put an army at his disposal and make no stipulations on religion. This they had been willing to grant before the Armada disaster; now, the offers were apt to be much greater. Again and again, in the next few months, Maitland harped on the same string—that Spain could most easily strike at England through Scotland, unless England took steps to prevent it.[72] He threatened England with Scottish help for Elizabeth's rebels in Ireland. He suggested that James might send an ambassador to England to harangue the House of Commons and complain of how badly he had been treated.[73] Scottish public opinion, Maitland told Ashby, was extremely hostile to England. Only the king's religious zeal and natural fondness for Englishmen had restrained him thus far, but something would have to be done soon.[74]

The English were not unduly perturbed. They doubtless realized that these Spanish offers were largely imaginary, and they were reassured as to Maitland's personal position by the friendly letters he wrote to Walsingham and Burghley in mid-September. Walsingham counted on the soothing effects of the three thousand pounds; he also thought that James might be awarded the Garter.[75] But the secretary and his mistress were sure that since James had "digested" the execution of his mother, he would not break with them over the disavowal of Ashby. They were quite right.

James himself, in the latter half of 1588, was beginning to understand the implications of Mary's death for the future of Anglo-Scottish relations. These implications were made quite clear by the recent negotiations; the result was a major shift in the tactics employed by the Scots to achieve what James regarded as the principal Scottish objective in the alliance with

[72] See, for instance, the English agent Fowler's report of his conversation with Maitland on the occasion of the murder of the duke of Guise, *ibid.*, pp. 665-666.

[73] December 29, 1588, Fowler to Walsingham, *ibid.*, pp. 654-655.

[74] *Bardon Papers*, pp. 103-107.

[75] CSP SCOT, IX, 615-618. September 7, 1588, Walsingham to Sidney, *ibid.*, pp. 611-612.

England: his peaceful succession to the English throne. Hitherto he and Maitland had striven, like Mary and Lethington in the early 1560's, to get a firm promise on this point from Elizabeth, in public if possible. Now, like Mary and Lethington, James and his minister came to the conclusion that Elizabeth would never make such a commitment. If she would not make it when the Spanish fleet was approaching her shores, she would not make it at all. On the other hand, the king and Maitland were convinced that Elizabeth would not do anything to prevent the Stewart succession, either, as long as they remained friendly. The queen's willingness to certify that Mary's execution did not damage James's claim was proof of that. So, too, was the remark she let drop in her letter to James announcing the great naval victory: "if, by leaving them [the Spanish] unhelped, you may increase the English hearts unto you, you shall not do the worst deed for your behalf."[76] The king could afford to wait. He was but twenty-two; Elizabeth was fifty-five.

So James resolved to cease pressing Elizabeth for formal guarantees. He would be friendly and cooperative and as patient as possible. But James knew—none better—how kaleidoscopic sixteenth-century politics were. No one could tell precisely what the situation would be when the queen finally did die. Therefore James decided to continue to stay on good terms with the Scottish Catholic party. This policy was much safer and more attractive now than it had been before, since the defeat of the Armada made it impossible for Spain to harm him, for the time being at least. Since the Scottish Catholic leaders were in touch with Continental informants, friendliness to those leaders had the additional advantage of keeping the king partly informed as to Spanish activities and intentions.

Maitland was not entirely pleased with the king's attitude toward the Catholics. The strengthening of the power of the crown was a more important immediate objective to him than was the English succession. The crown would not be strengthened by encouraging the Scottish Catholic party, which was led by just those elements which Maitland wished to repress: lawless highland and border magnates like Huntly and Max-

[76] Bruce, *Letters*, pp. 52-54.

well. Furthermore, encouraging the Catholics would alienate the kirk, whose cooperation was becoming more and more indispensable to the chancellor. There was no open disagreement between Maitland and the king, of course; James continued to depend entirely on him. "The chancellor guides all" wrote the English agent Roger Ashton on November 8, 1588.[77] Each man agreed on the desirability of the other's objective and on the tactics to be employed. They differed as to the relative importance of these objectives, no more.

Thus passed the year of the Armada. In the history of England the year 1588 was an *annus mirabilis*, like 1940. For Scotland the destruction of the Spanish fleet was important, not because it changed things greatly there, but because it did not. Scotland was at peace with Spain, and remained so. Her tactics with respect to the English succession changed somewhat, but that was all. The real significance of the failure of the Armada was that the pattern of Scottish life was undisturbed. King James would not be disinherited by his mother's supposititious will; Andrew Melvill would not be burned as a heretic; Edinburgh would not suffer the fate of Antwerp; there would be no Inquisitors. These results, though negative, were nevertheless of vast importance.

Now that the danger was past, Maitland hoped to be able to get back to his administrative tasks. But in 1589 his hopes were to be frustrated by two complications. The first was the exposure of a Catholic and aristocratic plot directed in part against himself. The second was the king's marriage.

[77] CSP SCOT, IX, 628-629.

CHAPTER 8

HUNTLY'S REBELLION

IN THE MIDST of the excitement of the Armada crisis the earl of Angus, who had been in failing health for some time, died at the comparatively early age of thirty-three. He left his wife pregnant; when she gave birth to a daughter, a scramble for the inheritance followed. The earldom of Angus was finally awarded to William Douglas of Glenbervie, who had to make good his claims in court against the king himself.[1] Glenbervie was an old friend of Maitland's—they had collaborated over the lairds' petition to the Linlithgow Parliament which led to the admission of the lairds to Parliament—and after his claim to the earldom was recognized, he awarded Maitland the barony of Braidwood.[2] The new earl died in 1591, however; his son was a Catholic, and hostile to Maitland. Angus' other earldom, that of Morton, passed to Douglas of Lochleven, who had been the closest friend of the regent Morton and the half-brother of the regent Moray. Lochleven was an ancient enemy of the house of Lethington; his dislike was reinforced in Maitland's case by his bitter hatred of the whole Hamilton connection. The death of Angus was thus most unfortunate for Maitland. Ever since his decision to ally himself with the kirk, the chancellor had been on good terms with the pious earl—the "minis-

[1] James's great-grandfather was Archibald Douglas, sixth earl of Angus, the second husband of Margaret Tudor. James lost his case, but got thirty-five thousand marks as compensation from the new earl.

[2] SRO, *Privy Seal Register*, LIX, 55. SRO, *Treasurer's Accounts, 1588-1590*. Braidwood was an old possession of Glenbervie's; it was not part of the earldom of Angus. The official explanation of Maitland's acquisition of Braidwood was that Glenbervie had surrendered it to the king, who gave it to Maitland in lieu of money owed him. Maitland paid rental of one penny a year. SRO, *Register of Deeds*, XXXII, 373-374, XXXVII, 236-237b. The gift nevertheless looked suspiciously like a bribe, since Maitland had sat on the court which decided in Glenbervie's favor.

176

ters' king," as James called him.[3] Angus' passing deprived Maitland of the support of one of the few great nobles on whom he could depend, and ultimately led to the elevation of two of his enemies.

The chancellor's personal position was further weakened in the latter half of 1588 by James's recent acquisition of two new personal favorites. One of these was Alexander Lindsay, younger brother of the earl of Crawford, "the king's only minion and conceit . . . his nightly bed-fellow," according to Lord Hume.[4] Lindsay was a commonplace man who represented no particular problem in himself; but his family was at feud with that of the master of Glamis, and as Lindsay's influence grew, Glamis became more and more disaffected, particularly when it began to be bruited about that Glamis was about to be replaced by Lindsay as captain of the guard.[5] But when Glamis finally was replaced, the king's choice was, from Maitland's point of view, infinitely worse. The man thus honored was the king's other new favorite, none other than the earl of Huntly himself.

George Gordon, sixth earl of Huntly, was a gay and attractive young man whose marriage to the sister of the duke of Lennox had admitted him to the king's inner circle. He was an ardent Catholic, who became a "convert" to Protestantism for the sake of this marriage; only the king, who, where his favorites were concerned, believed what he wanted to believe, appeared to think it genuine. Huntly, according to James's latest biographer, was "both treacherous and cruel. . . . On his native heath he could be as barbarous as the most savage of his clansmen. . . . He . . . captured two cooks from an enemy clan and roasted them alive, and adorned the turrets of his castle of Strathbogie with the severed limbs of his foes."[6] His immense power stretched all through the highlands, as the large number of bands of manrent made to him in the

3 Calderwood, IV, 680.
4 April 30, 1588, Woddrington to Walsingham, CSP SCOT, IX, 557-558.
5 October 1588, Hudson to Walsingham, *ibid.*, p. 627. November 22, Richard Douglas to Poury Ogilvie, *Salisbury Papers*, III, 374. See also D. Moysie, *Memoirs of the Affairs of Scotland*, pp. 70-71.
6 D. H. Willson, *James VI and I*, p. 99.

years after 1585 makes clear.[7] In the days of Maitland's rise
to power, Huntly had been friendly enough with him; they
were both nephews of Lord John Hamilton, and both had disliked the earl of Arran. But with the unfolding of Maitland's
real political objectives, Huntly's condescending friendship
had turned to bitter dislike. To Maitland, on the other hand,
Huntly embodied everything in Scottish society that he was
trying to destroy. For the next seven years there was to be
continued hostility between them, broken only by occasional
truces.

One of these truces was in effect in the latter part of 1588.
The Catholic party had met in September, and had planned
to ambush the chancellor in Fife early in October as he tra-
veled to the king—or so Maitland was told. The chancellor
threatened to strike back by advising the restoration of the
master of Gray, which might cost Huntly his possession of
Dunfermline.[8] Huntly thereupon decided to alter his tactics.
While awaiting the fruition of his plots with Spain, he resolved to act the Protestant, play up to the king, ingratiate
himself with Maitland, and accumulate what power he could.
He was most submissive to the kirk. He informed the king of
the plot to "take away the chancellor." He was formally
reconciled to Maitland, and played host to him and the king
at Dunfermline. He even sought the favor of Elizabeth.[9] He
received his reward in the captaincy of the guard.

Maitland himself appears to have been partially deceived.
He evidently believed that the Catholic party had been entirely
disheartened by the defeat of the Armada. At the same time,
the English were behaving very badly. Not only had they

[7] These bands are given in J. Stuart, ed., *Miscellany of the Spalding Club*,
1st series, IV, 230ff. A band of manrent was a device commonly used by powerful highland magnates to build up a following among lesser men not otherwise
attached to them. It was essentially a promise of mutual support and protection, "roughly the Celtic equivalent to the practice of commendation." A. Cunningham, *The Loyal Clans*, p. 76.

[8] September 10, 1588, Bowes to Burghley, *Border Papers*, I, 332-333. October 9, Selby to Walsingham, CSP SCOT, IX, 622.

[9] November 6, 26, 1588, Ashby to Walsingham, *ibid.*, pp. 627-628, 637-638.
December 1, Ashton to Hunsdon, *ibid.*, pp. 642-643. December 13, Ashton to
Walsingham, *ibid.*, pp. 646-648. November 22, Richard Douglas to Poury Ogil-
vie, *Salisbury Papers*, III, 374.

done nothing for James since the three thousand pounds sterling arrived in September 1588; they were also trying to prevent the Estates-General of the Netherlands from negotiating
directly with James on the matter of Colonel Stewart's financial claims against the Estates. They clearly seemed to be
trying to control Scotland's foreign relations.[10] The king was
annoyed, and even Maitland was discouraged. "The chancellor," wrote Ashby on November 26, 1588, "groweth weary of
the course he hath held, finding so cold correspondence from
England and his king so lightly regarded."[11] Maitland believed that he could control Huntly and his friends, a view
that Huntly and the Catholics sedulously fostered: "They all
go to church, and flatter the chancellor and his party" wrote
Walsingham's agent Thomas Fowler.[12] As for England, "he
[Maitland] is of mind, that the king shall seek no more, because it is great dishonor to him to crave and be said nay so
often."[13] The English representatives were very discouraged.
"I fear here will be a very evil starred country," wrote Ashton
on December 13. "Great blame is laid on the king. . . . It is
plainly spoken here [that] he is running to his own destruction, as his mother did before."[14]

Walsingham's reactions to the disquieting situation in Scotland are interesting. "God send that young prince . . . faithful
counsellors" who will help him to uphold religion and establish justice, "the lack whereof doth greatly weaken the regal
authority," he wrote. "Every great personage in that realm
pretendeth to be a king, and thereby taketh liberty to commit
strange and great insolencies and oppressions on the weaker
sort. The use of a Star Chamber might work a great redress
therein. . . . The only way to work true redress of that diseased state is for the king to bend himself altogether for a
time to matters of government, calling about him such as are
not limed with faction, but inclined to justice. . . . The ex-

---

[10] On this point see J. Ferguson, ed., *Papers Illustrating the History of the
Scots Brigade in the Service of the United Netherlands 1572-1782*, I, SHS, 1st
series, XXXII (Edinburgh 1899), 115ff, especially Elizabeth's letter of November 10, 1588 to James, p. 129.

[11] CSP SCOT, IX, 637-638.   [12] *Ibid.*, p. 650.

[13] December 22, 1588, Fowler to Burghley, *ibid.*, pp. 651-652.

[14] *Ibid.*, pp. 646-648.

traordinary regalities the nobility of that realm do challenge . . . [must] be kept within such limits as the law may have her just and due course without respect of persons. It is likely that the barons and burgesses . . . will be forward enough in this action, and so many of the noblemen as are wise and truly religious."[15]

Maitland would have subscribed wholeheartedly to these sentiments. In the midst of the ceaseless diplomatic negotiation and intrigue of these months he continued to work at the pressing problems of administration. On July 27, 1588, at the height of the tension over the Armada, a convention of estates met and appointed a series of commissions, consisting of officials of the burghs for the towns and of magnates and lairds in the shires.[16] These commissions were assigned a number of administrative tasks, including the enforcement of the laws against Jesuits and Papists. In November 1588 an extensive reorganization of the system of criminal justice was put into effect. The system of eyres planned in 1587 was temporarily abandoned. Instead, the shires were divided into twelve groups, and courts were to be held twice yearly in Edinburgh for each group, on the theory that if the king's officials could not be spared to go on circuit, they might accomplish virtually the same result by handling in Edinburgh the cases they would have judged in the country. Each official was responsible for presiding over the court held for one group of shires; to Maitland fell the sheriffdoms of Lanark, Renfrew, and Ayr, and the bailleries of Kyle, Carrick and Cunningham. At the same time, proclamations were issued against various methods of obstructing justice, particularly the pernicious practice of attempting to overawe the courts by a show of force.[17] The attempt to enforce the general band went on.[18] At the same time, possibly as a precaution against the growing influence of Huntly, Maitland had three members of the official class added to the privy council; the most important

15 December 22, 1588, Walsingham to Fowler, C. Read, *Mr Secretary Walsingham and the Policy of Queen Elizabeth*, III, 343-344.

16 RPCS, IV, 300-303.

17 CSP SCOT, IX, 629-634. SRO, *Treasurer's Accounts*, November 1588.

18 See, e.g., RPCS, IV, 346.

was the new warden of the west march, the laird of Carmichael.[19]
A new recoinage was ordered, which in the next two years
brought in a profit of some twenty-six thousand pounds.[20]

Maitland also endeavored to improve his already very
friendly relations with the kirk. The latter had naturally rejoiced at the defeat of the Armada; they took further comfort
from events in France. These were, in their view, "the most
remarkable work of God's justice . . . making, first, King
Henry to cause his guard stick the duke of Guise under trust
. . . and [later] a Jacobin friar . . . most treasonably to stick
the king. . . . Thus God glorified his name most remarkably."[21]
But the ministers were alarmed by the favor James showed
to the Catholic faction. In January 1589 they petitioned the
king to pursue Jesuits more earnestly, to drive Papists from
court, and to allow a mixed commission of ministers and "well
affected barons . . . to pass to every quarter of this realm"
and find out who "profess the religion and will join . . . in
the defense thereof, and who will not."[22] The king consented
to all this, but the alarm of the kirk did not subside. At the
General Assembly in February 1589 it was declared that "the
land was defiled all throughout . . . with Popery, superstition,
bloodshed, and all kind of villainy."[23]

Suddenly, and most spectacularly, the fears of the preachers
were confirmed. There really was a Catholic plot. On February
27, 1589, Ashby presented James with a packet of letters
which had been intercepted on their way to Parma in the
Low Countries. Those chiefly implicated were Huntly, Errol,
Crawford, Maxwell, and Claude Hamilton, all Catholics, and
Bothwell, whose hatred of England and of Maitland led him to
promise support to the Catholics if they would guarantee him
his abbey lands. The burden of these documents was that the
Catholic lords regretted that King Philip had not planned to
land his forces in Scotland rather than England in 1588; they

---

19 *Ibid.*, p. 326.

20 *Ibid.*, pp. 317-318, 322, 326. J. Brydon, *The Finances of James VI, 1567-1603*, p. 91.

21 R. Pitcairn, ed., *The Autobiography and Diary of Mr. James Melvill*, p. 264.

22 Calderwood, v, 1-3.   23 *Ibid.*, p. 5.

asked him to send six thousand men and some money. If he did so, an invasion of England would be launched within six weeks of their arrival. Huntly assured the Spanish that his "conversion" to Protestantism was forced and bogus, and that he repented it; Errol wrote with the fulsome enthusiasm of a recent convert. All of this explosive and highly treasonable material was sent on to James accompanied by a covering letter from Elizabeth. "Good Lord! methink I do but dream," she wrote, "no king a week would bear this!" Pluck up the treason by the roots, the queen urged, "take speedy order lest you linger too long. . . . They must be clapped up in safer custody than some others have been."[24]

The Catholic trafficking with Spain was nothing new. Huntly, Maxwell, and Claude Hamilton had been so engaged ever since 1586, using the much-traveled Robert Bruce as their messenger; at one point, early in 1587, Bruce and Parma had worked out a detailed plan to smuggle Spanish soldiers into Scotland in thirty empty grain ships.[25] Rumors of these dealings had been circulating for some time; it was inevitable that sooner or later something would leak out. This was more than a leak, however; it was a positive flood. Nevertheless the king chose to treat the disclosures as relatively unimportant. They were certainly no very great surprise to him; he himself had been in touch with Spain, and had written Parma a friendly letter as recently as December 1588.[26] What did upset James was the extent of the Catholic lords' commitment to Spain, and the baseness of Huntly's personal treachery toward himself. "What further trust can I have in your promise, confidence in your constancy, or estimation of your honest meaning?" he wrote to the earl in the first flush of his discomfiture.

[24] *Ibid.*, pp. 7-8. The captured letters are printed in *ibid.*, pp. 8-35, along with a covering letter from the English council to Ashby.

[25] The plotting may be followed in detail by a reading of CSP SPANISH, III, 580ff, and IV, *passim*. See also J. D. Mackie, "Scotland and the Spanish Armada," SHR, XII (1914-1915), 1-23, and T. G. Law, "Robert Bruce, Conspirator and Spy," in P. Hume Brown, ed., *Collected Essays and Reviews of Thomas Graves Law* (Edinburgh 1904), pp. 313-319. Law's biographical sketches of Colonel Sempill and the Jesuit Crichton in this volume are also worth reading in connection with the various Catholic plots.

[26] A. I. Cameron, ed., *The Warrender Papers*, II, 93-94.

"I, whom to, particularly as a man . . . and generally as a Christian king, you have so inexcusably broken unto. . . . Are these the fruits of your new conversion?"

James expected Huntly to repent, and like "the forlorn son . . . say, 'Peccavi in coelum et contra te,' "[27] but he did not plan to punish the sinner very severely. The earl was warded in Edinburgh castle, but "the next day the king went to the castle to dinner, where he entertained Huntly as well and kindly as ever, yea he kissed him at times to the amazement of many . . . and hath given his wife, servants and friends free access to him."[28] Errol, who was also in Edinburgh, was permitted to escape. The king was deaf to the importunities of Ashby and the others who favored severe punishment. He visited Huntly every day. The rumor began to circulate, assiduously spread by Bothwell, that the letters were forged in England "or else contrived here by the chancellor."[29] On March 7 Huntly was released from his mild captivity, his place in the castle being taken by Claude Hamilton; the next day the king "rode a-hunting, which he forbore all the time of his [Huntly's] imprisonment."[30] A few days later he accepted Huntly's invitation to hunt with him, and to dine afterwards. During the hunt they were joined by Errol, who, with Huntly, attempted to persuade James to ride north with them. The king refused; he "offered rather to die there than to go." At the same time a report reached the hunting party of a tumult in Edinburgh. Huntly and Errol promptly fled to the north, leaving James to return to his capital alone.[31]

James's leniency to Huntly was most disquieting to Maitland. The chancellor regarded the exposure of the earl's treach-

[27] CSP SCOT, IX, 699-700.
[28] March 1, 1589, Fowler to Walsingham, *ibid.*, pp. 700-701.
[29] March 5, 1589, Ashby to Walsingham, *ibid.*, p. 703. March 6, Fowler to Walsingham, *ibid.*, pp. 703-704.
[30] March 10, 1589, Ashby to Burghley, *ibid.*, pp. 709-710.
[31] March 14, 1589, Ashby to Burghley, CSP SCOT, x, 1-3; March 14, Fowler to Walsingham, *ibid.*, pp. 4-5; March 15, Ashton to Hudson, *ibid.*, 7-8. The "tumult" in Edinburgh was variously explained as arranged by Huntly to unnerve the king, and as owing to Protestant outrage against Huntly. March 18, Fowler to Walsingham, *ibid.*, p. 10. March 18, Woddrington to Burghley, *Border Papers*, I, 335-336. Huntly's dinner was not wasted; James ate it anyway, despite the absence of his host.

ery as a heaven-sent opportunity to ruin him. Maitland's plan
was not to execute Huntly; that would simply lead to another
blood-feud. He wanted to compel Huntly to fly, and then
banish him.[32] From the very beginning he urged strong measures on James, who was the chancellor's guest at his town
house for about two weeks at the beginning of March. On the
day of the revelation of Huntly's treachery, it was Maitland
who roused the town of Edinburgh to prevent Huntly from
flying or attempting to seize the king.[33] He began to raise a
small troop of impeccably Protestant horse. "The chancellor
plays his part in these matters stoutly, wisely, and honestly,
else all had come to nothing," wrote Fowler on March 6.[34]

Maitland was careful to leave the king in no doubt as to
his motives. He accompanied James on his visits to Huntly;
he was civil to the earl, in order to persuade the king that he
had no personal animus against Huntly, that his hostility was
purely political.[35] The king was convinced, but he continued
to disregard Maitland's advice. So the chancellor resigned himself to making some concessions to the king's point of view.
But the limit was reached when he discovered that his master
was not only going to free Huntly, but to leave him in command of the guard as well. All of Maitland's accumulated
frustration and annoyance at James's policy toward the Catholics burst out. "I heard the chancellor tell the king," wrote
Fowler, "that if he would maintain Huntly in that sort he
would not have a Protestant in Scotland to follow or acknowledge him."[36] Maitland then delivered his ultimatum: either
Huntly was dismissed as captain of the guard, or he would
resign. "This put the king in a great brangle," wrote Ashton.[37] James yielded, and Huntly was dismissed. But the king
would do no more, despite all the urgings of Maitland and
the English. To Fowler he complained of his powerlessness:
"when it comes to execution of justice . . . he fears to deal,
at least with many of them at once, by the example of his

---

[32] March 14, 1589, Fowler to Burghley, CSP SCOT, x, 3-4.
[33] March 14, 1589, Ashby to Burghley, *ibid.*, pp. 1-3.
[34] CSP SCOT, IX, 704-705.
[35] March 18, 20, 1589, Ashby to Burghley, CSP SCOT, x, 8-10, 12-13.
[36] *Ibid.*, p. 4.   [37] *Ibid.*, p. 8.

forbears [those] that were the best and severest justices were always cut off untimely."[38] He affected not to believe in Huntly's guilt; not even an examination of the messenger who had been captured with the letters could convince him. Huntly, he said, was young, merry, and "no dealer in matters of state."[39]

In refusing to follow his chancellor's advice James was motivated by more than his affection for Huntly. In late March, the king sent the laird of Easter Wemyss on embassy to Elizabeth, with instructions to ask for the fulfillment of the promises made by Ashby in 1588.[40] The implication was clear: Elizabeth had to fulfill these promises before James would punish Huntly. Maitland, who wanted Huntly punished, urged the English to impress James with the depth of their concern by sending a special embassy to Edinburgh.[41] Before Elizabeth could act on the suggestion, however, Huntly made a mistake which played into the hands of his opponents. He attempted to recover his position by force.

The first step in Huntly's scheme was taken by Errol, who on March 22 wrote a disingenuous letter to Robert Bruce the minister. Maitland, he said, had falsely accused him of attempting to subvert both church and state. It is rather Maitland of whom the kirk should beware; he is "altogether irreligious" and is using the kirk to further his own ambitions.[42] The Catholic coup was planned for early April. The king was hunting a few miles from Edinburgh, which was empty of all persons of importance save Maitland. Huntly and the Catholics mustered their forces in the north, and their ally Bothwell did likewise in the south. Everything depended on speed

---

[38] March 20, 1589, Fowler to Burghley, *ibid.*, pp. 10-11.

[39] *Ibid.*, pp. 11-12. Fowler agreed that Huntly was not politically minded; he called the earl "shallow-witted," but possessed of able advisers. March 14, Fowler to Burghley, *ibid.*, pp. 3-4. There is some evidence that this judgment was accurate, and that the real brains behind Huntly was his cousin Sir Patrick Gordon of Auchindoun. Huntly's reliance on Auchindoun is evident in the brief account of the earl's examination before his trial in May, RPCS, IV, 821-822. After Auchindoun's death at the end of 1594 Huntly's behavior rapidly became much less politic, and also much less pronouncedly Catholic.

[40] March 18, 1589, James to Elizabeth, *Salisbury Papers*, XIII, 408. March 20, Ashby to Burghley, CSP SCOT, X, 12-13.

[41] March 23, 1589, Fowler to Burghley, *ibid.*, p. 15.

[42] Calderwood, V, 52-54. Errol had been denounced rebel the day before; RPCS, IV, 367.

and secrecy. But Bothwell, who never could resist a theatrical gesture, made a flamboyant speech in Kelso, to the effect that Maitland was forcing James to follow a pro-English course, that he was in English pay and was arranging for an English army to enter the country, overthrow the nobility, and reduce Scotland to slavery. The king was really opposed to all this, Bothwell said; he besought his hearers to join him in delivering both James and the country from "the tyranny of those who murdered the king's mother."[43] Carmichael went at once to the king with the report of this speech. He caught up with James on the afternoon of April 6. At midnight Carmichael's son arrived with the news that Bothwell was moving on the capital. At about the same time word came from the master of Glamis, who had just avoided capture outside Dundee, that Huntly, Crawford, and Errol were on the march. The king at once returned to the capital. He arrived at three o'clock in the morning, routed Maitland out of bed, and sent off messages in all directions to summon the Protestant magnates: Lord John Hamilton, Morton, Angus, Marischal. "The king," wrote Fowler, "is exceeding angry."[44]

Huntly's plan had completely misfired. He was unable to muster the full strength of the Catholic party, which was riven by internal feuds which he could not heal.[45] Bothwell could not raise the borders; the responsible elements remained loyal to the government, and Bothwell had to flee north with but thirty horse. James, prodded by his chancellor, showed considerable vigor. On April 10 he set out in pursuit of his rebels; Maitland went with him. "The chancellor keeps his watch nightly in turn, is daily in his armor, marches in the vanguard, and none more forward," reported Fowler two weeks later.[46] He also helped to keep the peace between the bickering Protestant lords, some of whom disliked each other quite as much as they did Huntly.[47] As the king advanced, the rebels began to dis-

[43] April 7, 1589, Fowler to Burghley, CSP SCOT, x, 24-25.
[44] Ibid. SRO, Treasurer's Accounts, April 1589. See also April 10, 1589, Fowler to Archibald Douglas, Salisbury Papers, III, 404.
[45] April 23, 1589, Fowler to Walsingham, CSP SCOT, x, 45-47.
[46] Ibid., p. 47.
[47] April 28, 1589, Fowler to Ashby, ibid., pp. 53-54.

perse. They had succeeded in capturing the master of Glamis; Crawford, who wanted to kill him, deserted Huntly in a rage when the latter refused.[48] Bothwell returned to the borders and began simultaneously to send humble messages to James and to try to recruit another army. He also produced a man named Lindsey, who offered to prove, among other things, that Maitland was in English pay and planned to deliver the king to English captivity and give the crown to the Hamiltons.[49] The king refused to be diverted by Bothwell's antics; he pressed on against Huntly. The climax came on the night of April 17, at the crossing of the Dee outside Aberdeen, where the two armies confronted each other. Huntly's forces promptly began to melt away. His men had been told that the king was the captive of the chancellor and his wicked cohorts; and here was the king himself leading his army against them. Huntly decided not to fight, and fled. By morning his forces had dispersed, and James entered Aberdeen. The rebellion was over.

Once again the question of the punishment to be meted out to the rebels had to be faced. Fowler, who had accompanied the expedition, pressed for Huntly's execution. None of the council favored this. Maitland hoped that the rebels' strongholds could be razed, but it was soon apparent that not even this could be done. The king's forces were none too strong, and they were clamoring for their pay. The master of Glamis, who had been released by Huntly, arrived in Aberdeen on April 22 and intimated that Huntly and the others would be willing to surrender if the penalties were not too severe. And so it was arranged. The earl surrendered; the king garrisoned Strathbogie and Errol's house at Slaines. A band was drawn up, to be signed by those whose loyalty was suspect, which pledged them to defend king and kirk and pursue Jesuits, under penalty of twenty thousand pounds for disobedience, for

[48] April 14, 1589, Fowler to Ashby, *ibid.*, pp. 38-39.
[49] April 21, 1589, Ashby to Burghley, *ibid.*, p. 44. Maitland procured a safe-conduct for Lindsey to come and accuse him before the king. Lindsey never appeared, which was wise in view of the fact that Parliament had enacted in 1587 that a man who falsely accused another of treason should suffer the penalty thereof himself. APS, III, 450.

which sum cautioners had to be found.[50] This done, James returned to Edinburgh early in May, bringing Huntly with him.[51]

The king's principal object in returning so promptly from the north was to deal with Bothwell, who was still in arms. Bothwell made no effort to resist; his men had begun to desert with the news of Huntly's surrender.[52] On May 11 he formally submitted to the king, in a little ceremony in Maitland's back garden.[53] Shortly thereafter he and Huntly were tried for treason, along with Crawford, who had also surrendered, and all three were condemned, although with difficulty. Bothwell insisted on his innocence; he had levied troops, he declared, only to attack the chancellor. Huntly said much the same thing in his preliminary examination, although he pleaded guilty. The assize nevertheless debated until two in the morning before it condemned the three earls, in spite of the presence of both Maitland and the king.[54] The Scottish aristocracy, it was clear, was reluctant to punish any of its members merely for making war on the king and an unpopular minister. The master of Glamis and Lord John Hamilton interceded for Huntly. Only the kirk favored extreme measures.[55] The upshot was that the earls were merely warded for the time being.

In spite of the enormity of Huntly's offense, Maitland was less inclined to press for severe penalties now than he had been on the original disclosure of Huntly's treason in February. For one thing, the preparations for the king's marriage were far advanced, and reconciliation between factions was clearly desirable at such a time. Of equal concern to the chancellor was the attitude of England. The mission of the laird of Easter Wemyss was an almost complete failure. Elizabeth's reply to James's demands was regarded as "general and somewhat

[50] RPCS, IV, 375-380.

[51] For James's expedition the chief source is Fowler's correspondence for April 1589, in CSP SCOT, X, 36ff.

[52] May 2, 1589, Ashby to Walsingham, *ibid.*, pp. 58-59.

[53] May 11, 1589, Fowler to Burghley, *ibid.*, pp. 69-70.

[54] *Ibid.*, pp. 83-84. RPCS, IV, 821-822. Calderwood, V, 57-58.

[55] April 27-28, 1589, Fowler to Walsingham, CSP SCOT, X, 51-53. May 10, Fowler to Burghley, *ibid.*, pp. 67-68. May 12, Hudson to Walsingham, *ibid.*, p. 72.

cold."[56] She did send three thousand pounds sterling, and she promised James the Garter, but she would not hear of honoring Ashby's promises, and she would not even give much satisfaction with respect to the numerous complaints of Scottish merchants against English pirates. Even worse, to Maitland, was Elizabeth's advocacy of the restoration of the master of Gray. Maitland attributed this to the machinations of his old enemy Archibald Douglas, and he remembered that English support of Gray four years before had led to the downfall of the then chief minister, Arran. He was upset by the report that the queen had given Douglas four thousand pounds sterling. He wrote rather waspishly to Walsingham that all his difficulties had stemmed from his pro-English policy, and that the slanders spread by "mercenaries who live there at your charges and sell you their intelligence dear enough" were not to be believed.[57] The English agents in Scotland unanimously recommended against the return of Gray, which would annoy the king as well as Maitland; they all advised that England support the latter. "Never man deserved so much nor could do more than the chancellor," wrote James Hudson to Walsingham, "yet you never seek him in any kind sort, and never cease to seek them that can do you no good but by his assistance."[58] The English nevertheless persisted, apparently because they knew that Gray was anxious to ruin Huntly in order to regain the abbey of Dunfermline.

So James and Maitland bowed to the wishes of the queen as gracefully as they could—if they were willing to forgive Huntly, they could hardly do less for a man who, whatever his faults, had never broken into open rebellion. Walsingham did assure the chancellor that Elizabeth would drop Gray if he did not behave himself.[59] Gray was received politely enough, and, in an attempt to ingratiate himself with Maitland, turned against Archibald Douglas. The mutual recriminations that resulted were a source of some amusement to the court.[60] What-

[56] May 6, 12, 1589, Hudson to Walsingham, *ibid.*, pp. 65-66, 72. See also *ibid.*, pp. 50-51, 58.
[57] *Ibid.*, p. 64.   [58] *Ibid.*, p. 65.
[59] *Ibid.*, pp. 74-75.
[60] June 8, 1589, Ashby to Burghley, *ibid.*, pp. 98-99.

ever hopes the English may have built upon Gray were quickly dissipated. His influence was gone, and in a few months he retired from court. Before his departure Gray performed an important political service for the chancellor, a service which may account for Maitland's acquiescence in his return. He helped to arrange a reconciliation between Maitland and Both-well.[61] This startling maneuver on the chancellor's part was caused by a new and dangerous political crisis which developed in the weeks after Huntly's surrender and which also helps to explain Maitland's reluctance to adopt extreme measures against the rebel earl.

The central figure in this latest threat to Maitland's position was the master of Glamis, whose dissatisfaction had been mounting since 1587. He wanted to be chancellor. He was so angry at his loss of command of the guard in November 1588 that he had to be warded briefly in Edinburgh castle.[62] Even before the collapse of Huntly's rebellion there were rumors that he was hostile to Maitland, and it was widely rumored afterwards that he had allowed himself to be captured by Huntly.[63] This is unlikely; he would hardly have deliberately put himself in the power of his enemy Crawford; but it is certain that he actively urged clemency for Huntly. By the middle of June 1589 the coolness between him and Maitland had gone so far that formal efforts at reconciliation were being made by their mutual friends.[64] Matters became still worse during July, when James returned to Aberdeen to supervise the process of collecting fines and pledges from those involved in the late rebellion.[65] Glamis accompanied the king and arranged for the surrender and pardon of Errol. In this he had the assistance of Bellenden, who had been cool to Maitland ever since the Orkney fiasco, and of Mar and Athol.[66] It seemed as though the great

61 July 17, 1589, Gray to Hudson, *ibid.*, pp. 120-121.
62 June 4, 1589, Gray to Burghley, *ibid.*, pp. 92-94. Moysie, *Memoirs*, p. 71.
63 E.g., June 14, 1589, Fowler to Walsingham, csp scot, x, 102-103.
64 June 16, 1589, Gray to Burghley, *ibid.*, pp. 106-107.
65 As usual, Maitland was accused of lining his own pockets; see W. Mackay, ed., *Chronicles of the Frasers*, shs, 1st series, xlvii (Edinburgh 1905), p. 211. Even Fowler thought the chancellor covetous; March 28, 1589, Fowler to Burghley, csp scot, x, 17-19.
66 July 17, 1589, Gray to Hudson, *ibid.*, pp. 120-121. August 11, Ashby to

Protestant magnates were about to join with their Catholic counterparts to bring down the man they all disliked, and whose popularity was not increased by the recent heavy taxation, which was even extended to crown lands.[67]

Maitland was very much alarmed, and strengthened his position as best he could. Once again, and for the last time, he won over the mercurial Bothwell, thanks to Gray. He attempted to reconcile Bothwell with Lord Hume. This almost turned out disastrously, since Hume took advantage of the occasion to attempt to ambush Bothwell. Maitland got word of this just in time to warn the earl, who barely made his escape.[68] The chancellor also secured the release from ward of Claude Hamilton, and planned to try to reconcile him with his brother Lord John.[69] But Maitland was rescued from his difficult situation less by his own exertions than by the steady favor of the king and by the great event which had been in train throughout the spring and summer of 1589, namely, the king's marriage. James was determined that domestic broils should not mar the arrival of his bride. To this end he exerted himself with some success to patch up the difficulties between Maitland and his opponents, both aristocrats and disaffected officials. He released from ward the leaders of the late revolt, and also Lord Maxwell, after the latter had found surety of one hundred thousand pounds for his future good behavior.[70] The kirk, whose opposition to the releases was voiced at the synod of Lothian in September, was partly mollified by a stringent decree on Sabbath observance.[71] A general political truce ensued, observed by all save Glamis, whose caballing continued to annoy James until his departure for Denmark.[72]

Thus ended the affair known as the Brig of Dee, after the

Burghley, *ibid.*, p. 137. Bellenden's hostility to Maitland was reported as early as November 1588; CSP SCOT, IX, 635-636.

[67] RPCS, IV, 344-345, 396-397, 410-411.

[68] August 26, 1589, Ashby to Walsingham, CSP SCOT, X, 148.

[69] August 23, 1589, Richard Douglas to Archibald Douglas, *Salisbury Papers*, III, 352-353 (where the letter is misdated 1588).

[70] August 22, 1589, Ashby to Burghley, CSP SCOT, X, 145-146. October 7, Fowler to Burghley, *Salisbury Papers*, III, 434-436. RPCS, IV, 412.

[71] Calderwood, V, 60. RPCS, IV, 419-420.

[72] October 19, 1589, James to Maitland, CSP SCOT, X, 174.

river crossing where James and Huntly confronted each other in April. In the following year the chancellor, looking back on these events, blamed the defection of the Protestant magnates for the failure to crush Huntly and his allies. "If my advice had been followed," he wrote to the minister Robert Bruce, "and our own fellowship had not countenanced and dealt for them . . . [they] should not have had the . . . power to have uttered their evil will. . . . As to me, although to cover their treasons they seem to take them particularly to my part, yet, I thank God, time and their behavior hath detected their designs."[73] Here Maitland was certainly in error; he never did realize how widely and deeply he was hated and resented by the Scottish aristocracy.

What Maitland did know, and failed to tell Bruce, was that the policy of leniency was not adopted by James simply for expediency's sake, but as a positive good. These months had clearly revealed the feebleness of the Scottish Catholics; they would be dangerous only if they received substantial outside support in men and money. Since they were not dangerous, the king resolved to continue his policy of showing a certain amount of favor to them. Maitland, on the other hand, deeply regretted the king's failure to crush Huntly and the others, not because they were Catholics, but because they were rebels. To him it seemed unwise to allow the hypothetical possibilities of the situation that might exist at Elizabeth's death to take precedence over the pressing need of the present moment. For the time being, however, these problems and differences of view were put aside. The king was about to take a wife.

[73] April 7, 1590, Maitland to Bruce, Calderwood, v, 92-93.

CHAPTER 9

THE KING'S MARRIAGE

ON May 28, 1589, shortly after the collapse of Huntly's rebellion, there occurred a riot in the streets of Edinburgh, led by the officials of the town, and directed against Maitland. The tumult had nothing to do with Huntly. The burghers believed that Maitland was opposed to James's proposed marriage with the daughter of the king of Denmark; they were vociferously in favor of it. James himself had to pacify his unruly subjects by promising to go through with the Danish marriage upon suitable conditions; and, in due course, he did.[1]

The idea of a Danish wife for James was nothing new in 1589. It had been suggested as early as 1582,[2] and had been intermittently under discussion between the two governments since 1585. In the summer of that year a Danish embassy came to Scotland; but James was not yet interested in marriage. The matter was not allowed to drop, however, largely owing to the influence and activity of Colonel Stewart, the most active Scottish proponent of the Danish match, and in 1587 the king, with his twenty-first birthday approaching, prepared to negotiate seriously. In May of that year a convention of estates authorized the sending of an embassy to Denmark. The ambassadors were Sir Patrick Vans of Barnbarroch and Peter Young, James's old tutor. They were instructed to say that James wanted to marry one of the Danish king's two daughters, but not to commit themselves to anything, especially on the subject of dowry. They were to be equally noncommittal on the question of the Orkneys, which had been under dis-

[1] May 28, 1589, Fowler to Burghley, csp scot, x, 87-88. "Here is a strange country," commented Fowler; "I should say a most vile people." Sir James Melville, *Memoirs of His Own Life*, p. 368, says that James himself instigated the riot against his own chancellor. This is most improbable.

[2] April 11, 1582, Woddrington to Walsingham, csp scot, vi, 112.

193

cussion for the past two years.[3] The Orkney and Shetland islands had been turned over to Scotland in the fifteenth century, at the time of the marriage of James III to a Danish princess, in pledge for a part of her dowry, which was never paid. Now the Danes were talking of redeeming the pledge and reoccupying the islands, something James would find difficult to prevent in view of Danish naval strength. The securing of the Scottish title to the islands would be one of the major objectives of a Danish marriage, and a powerful argument in its favor.

The embassy of Vans and Young was not very successful. They had difficulty in seeing King Frederick, who was ill; they suspected that the illness was diplomatic.[4] The Danes kept raising the matter of the Orkneys. Then there was the problem of which of King Frederick's daughters was in question. On their arrival the ambassadors were informed that the elder daughter, Elizabeth, was uncontracted; then, it developed, she was spoken for; but James might have her younger sister Anne if he liked. This thoroughly irritated Vans and Young; they were further annoyed by the fact that the Danes refused to imperil their good relations with England for the sake of this marriage, or to show any particular distress at the execution of James's mother.[5] In August 1587 the envoys returned home.[6]

James was not unduly perturbed by the failure. He was in no great hurry to be married; unlike most of the Stewarts, he showed little interest in the opposite sex. And in any case a new possibility had been opened up in the summer of 1587

[3] A. I. Cameron, ed., *The Warrender Papers*, II, 44-46.

[4] Since the king died early in 1588, it was probably genuine. The ambassadors evidently saw him only once; August 13, 1587, an anonymous correspondent to Walsingham, CSP SCOT, IX, 475-477.

[5] August 12, 1587, Courcelles to Henry III, R. Bell, ed., *Extract from the Despatches of M. Courcelles*, pp. 77-78. See also September 20, instructions for Daniel Rogers, S. C. Lomas, ed., *Calendar of State Papers, Foreign Series of the Reign of Elizabeth*, XXI, pt. i, 369-371. Rogers was the clerk of the English privy council; he was being sent on a special mission to Denmark.

[6] See their account of the embassy, *Warrender Papers*, II, 35-42. In R. V. Agnew, ed., *Correspondence of Sir Patrick Waus of Barnbarroch*, II, 381ff, there are some interesting sidelights with respect to the embassy, notably in regard to Barnbarroch's expenses. He never was fully reimbursed; as late as 1702 his descendants were still asking for payment. R. S. Brydon, *The Finances of James VI, 1567-1603*, p. 60.

with the visit to Scotland of the Huguenot poet du Bartas:
the prospect of the hand of the Princess Catherine, the sister
of Henry of Navarre. When du Bartas returned to France in
September 1587, the king sent William Melville, the brother
of James and Robert and a newly appointed senator of the
college of justice, along with him, to bring back a firsthand
report of the lady's charms.[7]

Negotiations for both marriages were pursued in a desultory and semi-official way throughout 1588, during the excitement attendant on the Armada. The Navarre match had
its attractions. There was, quite possibly, a great future in
store for Henry of Navarre. He was reputedly very wealthy;
he was also childless, and, as all the world knew, at odds with
his wife. His sister could not inherit his claim to the French
crown, but she could inherit his property. There was religious
affinity; there was the ancient Franco-Scottish alliance; there
was the possibility of help in case James had any difficulty in
making good his English claims when the time came—help
which Denmark evidently would not give.[8]

But there were three major obstacles to this marriage. The
first was financial. The glowing reports of the huge dowry of
Princess Catherine turned out to be, at best, promises for the
future. All the resources of brother and sister alike were committed to the civil war. It was this factor which was decisive
with Maitland. He had been rather favorable to the match;
but by the beginning of 1589 he had changed his mind, on
learning of the large dowry Denmark was willing to pay.[9] Because he was in no hurry to close with Denmark, however, he
was persistently accused, in the ensuing months, of continuing
to favor the Navarre match.

The second obstacle in the way of this latter marriage was
its political and commercial implications. An alliance with
Henry of Navarre would commit James openly to the Protes-

7 Melville, *Memoirs*, p. 364.
8 See the memorial outlining the advantages of the Navarre match, drawn
up, in all probability, by one of Henry of Navarre's agents, CSP SCOT, IX, 658-
661.
9 February 8, 1589, Ashby to Walsingham, *ibid.*, pp. 677-678; February 20,
Fowler to Walsingham, *ibid.*, pp. 680-682.

tant cause in Europe, and would lead him into war against Spain and the Guises. It would put an end to the attitude of cautious friendship and balance with respect to the Scottish Catholic party which Elizabeth's broken promises of 1588 had led him to adopt. The Danish match was open to none of these objections. The Danes were impeccably neutral. There would be no embroilment with Spain and the Guises. For this reason the Scottish merchant class was wholeheartedly in favor of the Danish marriage. The Scottish townsmen were zealous Protestants, but they much preferred the blessings and the profits of peace to religious war. They took advantage of the war between England and Spain to smuggle into Spain as many English goods as possible, at a tidy profit for themselves, and they did not want this trade stopped.[10] Nor did they want their dealings with those French ports controlled by Navarre's enemies interrupted. Furthermore, the Danish connection opened to them the vista of a vastly increased Baltic trade.[11] It was for these reasons that they rioted against Maitland, under the mistaken impression that he still favored the princess of Navarre.

But the major obstacle to the Navarre match was the attitude of the lady herself. She would have none of James, despite the urgings of her brother, who seemed really anxious to have her marry him. "Try cautiously to make her like him," wrote Henry to his mistress, the lady known as *la belle Corisande*, in November 1588, "tell her the condition we are in, how great a prince he is and how good. . . . Talk to her in rather a casual way about the matter; that it is time for her to marry, and that there is no other party but him. As for our relation [the comte de Soissons], he is no good."[12] But alas! it was Soissons whom Catherine loved, and she was determined to have him or nobody.

James naturally was not told about this; but throughout 1588 the king became more and more inclined to Denmark as the Danes' attitude to the marriage began to change. In Feb-

[10] For this trade see CSP SPANISH, IV, 186-187, 279-280, 470-471.

[11] On this point see H. G. Stafford, *James VI of Scotland and the Throne of England*, pp. 52-53.

[12] H. D. Sedgwick, *Henry of Navarre* (Indianapolis 1930), p. 173.

ruary of that year Colonel Stewart, just back from Denmark, was assuring James that he could have Anne.[13] In April, as evidence that James was serious about marrying someone, a convention of estates voted that a tax of one hundred thousand pounds should be collected over the next three years to help defray the expenses of the marriage.[14] By mid-November Colonel Stewart, who had returned to Denmark during the summer, was again back in Scotland, this time with assurances with respect to the size of the dowry.[15] The Danes now seemed much more anxious for the match than before; the death of King Frederick in April seems to have had something to do with this. The Danes' eagerness certainly had its effect on James, who early in 1589, according to Melville, "after fifteen days' advisement and devout prayer," announced to his council that he had decided in favor of Denmark.[16]

There was considerable delay in getting the final negotiations started. There was a good deal of uncertainty as to who would head the mission; finally the earl Marischal was named, partly, at least, because he was a wealthy man who was willing to bear some of the cost of the embassy himself.[17] Then, the exposure of the Catholic plot and the events that followed delayed matters still further. Rumors that the Navarre match was being reconsidered began to circulate, particularly after the return of the laird of Easter Wemyss early in May 1589 from London, where he had failed to induce Elizabeth to further James's marriage plans. Easter Wemyss, a long-standing friend of Henry of Navarre, was vehemently opposed to the Danish match. It was rumored that England did not want

13 CSP SCOT, IX, 540-541.
14 RPCS, IV, 269-270.
15 D. Moysie, *Memoirs of the Affairs of Scotland*, p. 70. November 26, 1588, Ashby to Walsingham, CSP SCOT, IX, 637-638. SRO, *Epistolae Regum Scotorum 1505-1607*, contains a good deal of correspondence with respect to Colonel Stewart's various missions in 1588. Colonel Stewart evidently undertook these journeys at his own expense; see *Barnbarroch Correspondence*, II, 378-379, 419, 421-422, 430-431.
16 Melville, *Memoirs*, p. 365. Another factor in James's choice may have been the respective ages of the two ladies. Anne was fifteen and good-looking; Catherine of Navarre was thirty-one, eight years older than James, and reputedly crook-backed. J. H. Willson, *James VI and I*, p. 86.
17 March 20, 1589, Fowler to Burghley, CSP SCOT, X, 10-11. RPCS, IV, 391.

James to marry at all; that Maitland was opposed to the Danish match, and that therefore James would put it off for a while.[18] It was in this atmosphere of uncertainty that the riot of May 28 took place. It was touched off by the rumor that Marischal's orders to sail for Denmark had been withdrawn.

The riot seems to have caught James and Maitland by surprise. They had every intention of pursuing the Danish match; to reassure the citizenry, they immediately earmarked half of Elizabeth's recent subsidy, that is, one thousand five hundred pounds sterling, to help pay Marischal's expenses.[19] Maitland was not happy about this, and made his feelings plain. He was angry about the riot; he held Peter Young responsible for it, and called him a seditious knave. The chancellor's pride was hurt, and salt was rubbed in the wound by the boast of the Edinburgh merchants that they had triumphed over him on this issue.[20] In private conversation with the English agent Thomas Fowler, Maitland was even more bitter. None but fools had been involved in the negotiations thus far, he remarked, "and even now go such like, but of a higher degree: for the [earl] Marischal and the lord of Dingwall . . . will not both make a wise man."[21]

Maitland was worried about more than his wounded feelings. He wanted to be sure that James's ability to make good his claim to the English succession would be strengthened as much as possible by the marriage. To this end he instructed Marischal to demand, as one of the conditions of the marriage, that Denmark furnish ten thousand men, at Danish expense, when the time came if James so demanded. Marischal was further to ask for a dowry of a million pounds, for surrender of Danish claims to the Orkneys, and that all Scots be regarded as citizens of Denmark for commercial purposes.[22] These were very extensive demands. Fowler was convinced that Maitland was

18 May 17, 23, 1589, Fowler to Walsingham, csp scot, x, 75-76, 82-83. May 18, Wigmore to Walsingham, *ibid.*, p. 77.

19 May 29, 1589, Ashby to Walsingham, *ibid.*, pp. 88-89.

20 June 4, 1589, Gray to Burghley, *ibid.*, pp. 92-94. June 7, Fowler to Walsingham, *ibid.*, pp. 96-98.

21 June 7, 1589, Fowler to Burghley, *ibid.*, pp. 95-96. Dingwall, a relative of Marischal's, was accompanying him to Denmark.

22 *Ibid.*, pp. 103-105.

trying to wreck the marriage by this means.[23] This was not so: Maitland was simply establishing a position from which he could bargain.

There was another matter which worried the chancellor, and that was the attitude of Elizabeth. For some time she had insisted that James marry only after asking her advice, and this James had not done. England much preferred the Navarre match, since it would embroil James with the continental Catholics.[24] Fortunately, however, the English had formerly advocated a Danish marriage for James;[25] so they could raise no serious objections now, especially since the Danes had refused to give any anti-English flavor to the alliance. So, as the Danish negotiations progressed, Elizabeth's attitude remained grimly unhelpful, but perfectly correct, much to Maitland's relief.[26]

Marischal left for Denmark in the middle of June 1589, after some delay owing to the opposition of the most earnest partisans of the match to the severity of the instructions drafted by Maitland.[27] The Scottish envoy received a tremendously enthusiastic reception on his arrival; much to his surprise, he discovered that the Danes fully expected the wedding to take place, and that their preparations for it were already far advanced. James was touched: he "grows in affection for the gentlewoman, and talks much of her virtues; she has taken great pains to learn French for his sake."[28] In the course of the next few weeks James worked himself up to the point where he believed himself to be pining with love for the lady; so that, when Dingwall and John Skene, the lawyer, arrived from Denmark with word that the Danes were balking on certain points of the negotiation, especially the dowry, James sent Dingwall back to Denmark with positive instructions to accept whatever

[23] June 24, 1589, Fowler to Burghley, *ibid.*, pp. 109-111.
[24] June 16, 1589, Burghley to Shrewsbury, E. Lodge, *Illustrations of British History*, II, 377. See also September 8, 1587, Courcelles to Henry III, *Courcelles' Despatches*, pp. 79-80.
[25] June 11, 1585, Walsingham to Wotton, CSP SCOT, VII, 669-670.
[26] August 18, 20, 1589, Walsingham to Ashby, CSP SCOT, X, 140-141, 144.
[27] June 7, 1589, Fowler to Walsingham, *ibid.*, pp. 96-98.
[28] July 6, 1589, Fowler to Walsingham, *ibid.*, pp. 115-116.

was offered and to bring the lady back with him.[29] The final obstacles to the marriage were thus cleared away. On August 28 Colonel Stewart arrived in Scotland with word that the ceremony had been performed, with Marischal standing proxy for his master.[30]

James suddenly realized that nothing was ready to receive his queen. He began a series of rather ineffectual preparations. As usual, he had no money; on August 30 the commissioners of the burghs agreed to supply him with twenty thousand pounds at once. This agreement was a triumph for Maitland, who had been negotiating with the burgh commissioners for over a month. It was doubtless the fact of the marriage, which they so vociferously favored, which induced the townsmen to pay.[31] James also wrote a series of extraordinary begging letters to his nobles and officials, asking them to lend him money, to give him horses, and gifts of beef, mutton, venison and fowl for the marriage feasts.[32] Recourse was also had to England. James sent John Colville to London to make some purchases. Elizabeth waxed generous for once, wrote the king a kindly, if not exactly enthusiastic, letter of congratulation, and arranged what amounted to a gift of plate of two thousand pounds sterling. James was grateful, though, apparently, not sufficiently so for the English taste.[33]

[29] August 5, 1589, Fowler to Walsingham, *ibid.*, pp. 131-132. Maitland was not consulted on this change of instructions. He was in Edinburgh at this time, trying to raise money to help pay the expenses of the negotiations, while the king was in Aberdeen dealing with some of the problems left over from Huntly's rebellion. Melville, *Memoirs*, pp. 368-369. See also CSP SCOT, x, 125-126.

[30] Moysie, *Memoirs*, p. 78. The marriage treaty is given in L. Laursen, *Traités du Danemark et de la Norvège*, III (Copenhagen 1916), 14-24. James obtained a dowry of seventy-five thousand thalers. It was also agreed that the question of the final disposition of the Orkneys was to remain in abeyance until King Christian IV came of age; this amounted to a tacit recognition that the *status quo* would not be disturbed. The other Scottish demands were not met.

[31] RPCS, IV, 410-411. Maitland's negotiations can be traced in Ashby's correspondence from July 31, 1589 on; CSP SCOT, x, 125ff.

[32] See, e.g., *Barnbarroch Correspondence*, II, 439; R. Chambers, *Domestic Annals of Scotland from the Reformation to the Revolution*, 2nd ed., I (Edinburgh 1859), 192-193; J. Stuart, ed., *Miscellany of the Spalding Club*, I, 3-4. James had done the same thing in 1588 when he provided the feast for Huntly's wedding. See July 11, 1588, James to the laird of Abercairny, Sir W. Fraser, *The Lennox*, II (Edinburgh 1824), 463.

[33] September 27, 1589, Ashby to Burghley, CSP SCOT, x, 159. October 30,

More disturbing to the king than his empty treasury and larder was the weather. It was a stormy September, and James, all impatience to see his new wife, became increasingly worried as the days went by. He lashed out at Maitland and others who "had delayed the dispatch of the ambassadors so long, until the season of sailing upon the seas was near past."[34] He sent Colonel Stewart off to see what he could discover, with a letter to Anne describing his nervous condition.[35] No news came. The weather continued bad. Then, on October 10, there arrived in Scotland a Dane who had been in attendance on Anne, with the news that the weather had driven her fleet to take refuge in Norway. The queen herself had been in danger of drowning. There was no hope of the Danish ships' putting to sea again for some time to come.

James was in agonies. He immediately decided to send Bothwell, the hereditary admiral of Scotland, with six ships to fetch his bride. Bothwell promptly presented the council with an estimate of the expenses—and the king had no money. No one knew what to do. The king flared out that he himself would go, alone, in a single ship, if need be. Whereupon "the chancellor, seeing the king in a great perplexity, he stands up and makes offer that, rather than the king's desire should be frustrate, he and his friends would fit out five or six ships well manned and furnished. He furnished himself a ship of 126 tons, and half another."[36] Maitland did this, according to the king's later statement, because he was afraid that otherwise James would carry out his threat, and because "he has been this long time slandered for over great slowness in the matter of my marriage."[37] This seems accurate enough. In spite of the events of the last few months, the rumors of Maitland's hostility to the marriage persisted. The chancellor was anxious to quash them once and for all.

Burghley to Ashby, *ibid.*, pp. 182-183. A list of the plate is in *ibid.*, pp. 160-162. See also J. Bruce, ed., *Letters of Queen Elizabeth and King James VI*, pp. 55-56.

[34] Melville, *Memoirs*, p. 369.

[35] October 2, 1589, Ashby to Burghley, CSP SCOT, x, 162-163. James's letter is in *Warrender Papers*, II, 109-110.

[36] October 20, 1589, Fowler to Burghley, *Salisbury Papers*, III, 438-439.

[37] RPCS, IV, 427-429.

The king accepted his chancellor's offer with alacrity, and immediately decided to go himself anyway, and to take Maitland with him. The administration of the country might suffer in the chancellor's absence, but this was preferable to having him assassinated while the king was not there to protect him. James tried to keep his decision a secret; Maitland steadily denied that the king had any intention of going to Denmark; but the story soon leaked out. It was noticed that the furnishings of the chancellor's ship were very elaborate, and that a number of James's officials and court favorites were preparing to go.[38] James's plan was rash, in view of the recent bad weather, and doubtless the cautious chancellor did not much care for it. But James wanted to play knight-errant; he was determined to go, and there was no way Maitland could stop him.

It was necessary to make arrangements for the administration of the country during the king's absence. Since James was taking several high officials with him, there was nothing else to do but to entrust the government to the nobility. This was accordingly done. The presidency of the council was bestowed upon the youthful Lennox, who was to be assisted by Bothwell, with whom Maitland was again "reconciled till the next opportunity."[39] All the officials left in the country were to attend the council regularly, and so were four nobles. Two groups of four were created; they were supposed to relieve each other at fifteen-day intervals. Certain groups of lairds were to do likewise. This council was not to have charge of the border, however. Border affairs were put in the hands of Lord John Hamilton, who was to be assisted by a special council of his own. A special great seal and signet were constructed, since Maitland would have the regular seals with him in Denmark. Sir Robert Melville was ordered to perform Maitland's routine administrative duties as chancellor, and Hay, the clerk-register, those of the secretaryship. None of

[38] Melville, *Memoirs*, pp. 371-372. October 18, 1589, Ashby to Burghley, csp scot, x, 173-174. October 20, Fowler to Burghley, *Salisbury Papers*, iii, 438-439. In this letter Fowler criticized Maitland severely for not taking any of the "ancient nobility" into the secret.

[39] August 11, 1589, Ashby to Burghley, csp scot, x, 137.

those involved in the recent rebellion, other than Bothwell, was entrusted with any part in the government.[40]

Maitland thus did all he could to assure a friendly administration while he was gone, by making Bothwell and Hamilton the two key men. Bothwell was further instructed not to pursue his feud with Hume during the king's absence.[41] In addition, a most important unofficial commission was given to the minister Robert Bruce, who stood high in the confidence of both James and Maitland.[42] James ordered that Bruce be kept informed of the activities of the government, knowing that he could be relied on to protest loudly against any sort of governmental misbehavior.[43] The kirk was on very good terms with the king and Maitland just now, thanks to Maitland's policy of conciliation, which was now expected to pay some dividends. Maitland and the king depended on the kirk to help keep Scotland peaceful during their absence.

In addition to his various sets of instructions with respect to the conduct of the government, James also left behind him that remarkable paper explaining that he, and he alone, was responsible for his decision to go to Denmark which is quoted in the opening chapter.[44] Maitland, James assured his subjects, knew nothing about the king's plan or he would have done his best to frustrate it. He himself was going, James explained, because it was an easy trip, and because he did not want anyone to think that he was not enthusiastic about his marriage. He was tired of the rumors that were going around; he knew that his delay in getting married "bred in the breasts of many a great jealousy of my inability, as if I were a barren stock." Therefore: "It is my pleasure that no man grudge or murmur at . . . my proceedings; but let every man live a peaceable and quiet life . . . until my return."[45] Having thus explained

[40] The documents setting forth these arrangements are given in RPCS, IV, 422-427, 429-430. See also C. Innes, ed., *Registrum Honoris de Morton*, I, 163.
[41] RPCS, IV, 423. SRO, *Treasurer's Accounts, 1588-1590.*
[42] Bruce was a connection-by-marriage of Maitland's. Lady Maitland's first cousin was married to William Bruce of Airth, and Maitland and Alexander Bruce of Airth, the minister's father, were curators to the young Lord Fleming. J. Balfour Paul, ed., *Scots Peerage*, VIII, 545; SRO, *Register of Deeds*, XXXV, 69.
[43] Calderwood, v, 67.   [44] See above, p. 3.   [45] RPCS, IV, 427-429.

himself to his people, and done what he could to absolve Maitland of responsibility for his trip, James and his chancellor
set sail, on the evening of October 22, 1589.[46]

The Scottish party arrived in Norway on October 28, after
a rough passage. The king made his way to his bride in rather
leisurely stages.[47] It was not until November 19 that James
arrived in Oslo. According to the story, he immediately went
"with boots and all to her highness. . . . His majesty minded
to give the queen a kiss after the Scots fashion at meeting,
which she refused as not being the form of her country." But
after the king explained matters "there passed familiarity and
kisses."[48] The Danish account of the meeting of James and
Anne unhappily says nothing of all this, and makes out James's
behavior to be perfectly conventional, as it doubtless was.[49]
On November 23 the pair were married by David Lindsay.[50]

Thus Anne of Denmark enters into the Scottish scene. She
was not an interesting woman. She had no particular distinction of mind or spirit. She showed occasional neurotic
tendencies, she enjoyed intrigue, she was stupid, and she bore
grudges—one of them against Maitland, whose task she made
much more difficult, as we shall see. James, once the first flush
of his self-induced amorous enthusiasm had cooled, showed no
particular interest in her. He was fond enough of her, but it
was never more than the affection bred by long familiarity, and
after their removal to England they drifted apart. Her political
role was confined to forwarding the careers of her favorites and
hampering those she disliked. She was not conspicuously successful in either direction.

James and his entourage remained in Oslo for a month after
the marriage, feasting, hunting, playing cards, and quarreling.
As archbishop Spottiswoode remarked, "It is hard for men in

[46] Moysie, *Memoirs*, p. 80. James's decision to go to Denmark in person was
almost certainly his own, as he said it was, but it is also certain that Maitland
knew about it from the beginning. The various measures for the disposition
of the government required considerable thought and discussion, and were
certainly Maitland's.
[47] A. H. Millar, "The Wedding-Tour of James VI in Norway," *Scottish
Review*, XXI (1893), 151-152.
[48] Moysie, *Memoirs*, pp. 80-81.
[49] Willson, *James VI and I*, pp. 90-91.
[50] Moysie, *Memoirs*, p. 81.

drink, at which they were continually kept, long to agree."[51] In fact the aura of alcohol hangs heavily over the whole sojourn in Denmark. The principal dispute was between Maitland and Marischal, over precedence and money. Marischal claimed precedence on the basis of his ambassadorial commission; Maitland held that the commission had expired with James's arrival in Norway. Marischal wanted to use part of Anne's dowry to defray his expenses as ambassador; Maitland objected, in the interest of keeping the dowry intact as long as possible. James backed the chancellor on both points.[52] The king did his best to put an end to this kind of bickering, and partially succeeded, only to vitiate his own efforts shortly before his return by dismissing Marischal's relative William Keith from his position in the wardrobe.[53] The ostensible reason for Keith's dismissal was the fact that he dressed better than the king; Maitland was immediately held responsible for it, and the quarrel with Marischal was reopened.[54]

This thoroughly unnecessary wrangle had unpleasant consequences. The nobility "all hated [Maitland] to the death for his proud arrogance used in Denmark against the earl Marischal," writes the unfriendly author of *The Historie and Life of King James the Sext*.[55] Maitland's foolish striving for personal preeminence, which had led him to take the chancellorship, had betrayed him again, and had gotten him into a dispute with one of the few great Scottish nobles who might have had some sympathy for his program. Fortunately for Maitland the earl did not bear grudges; but they were never particularly friendly afterwards. The worst feature of the whole thing was that the dispute was over things which were unimportant, except for the question of money. Here Maitland was undoubtedly right in wanting to spend as little as possible, although

[51] Archbishop J. Spottiswoode, *The History of the Church of Scotland*, II, 406.

[52] Melville, *Memoirs*, pp. 372-373. December 20, 1589, Hay to Ashby, CSP SCOT, x, 221-222. The writer of this letter, Hay of Easter Kennet, the clerk-register, obviously sympathized with his official chief.

[53] April 16, 1590, Bowes to Burghley, *ibid.*, pp. 272-276.

[54] April 21, 1590, Archibald Douglas to Burghley, *ibid.*, p. 278. April 5, an anonymous correspondent to Walsingham, *Salisbury Papers*, III, 403 (where the letter is wrongly dated 1589).

[55] P. 242.

Marischal's claim was just and was eventually met. But under the circumstances Maitland should not have permitted the king to give him a large part of a cupboard of plate to cover the expenses *he* had incurred.[56] Small wonder that Marischal was annoyed.

Toward the end of December James decided to go on to Denmark. On December 22 he left Oslo, and about a month later he arrived, after a long and circuitous trip which took him through Swedish territory. The king was thoroughly enjoying his holiday, and, finding Denmark rather more convivial than Norway,[57] he was easily persuaded to stay until spring, to be present at the marriage of his wife's elder sister to the duke of Brunswick. He also found Denmark intellectually stimulating. He became acquainted with the famous astronomer Tycho Brahe, and wrote him a laudatory sonnet.[58] The king's cheerful state of mind is evident in his letter of February 19 to Robert Bruce, in which he comments gaily on Danish drunkenness and closes by "recommending me and my new rib to your daily prayers."[59]

Maitland also enjoyed the company of Tycho Brahe, wrote him a couple of Latin epigrams, and commented favorably on Danish hospitality.[60] But he was anxious to get home. He had envisioned a rapid trip over to Norway and back, and had vainly opposed going on to Denmark, on the ground of the cost and also because "interview of princes produces not oft the expected fruit, but breeds rather emulation, than increase of

[56] RPCS, IV, 444-445. It is true that on November 25, 1589 Marischal had been awarded the temporalities of the abbey of Deir, now erected into a temporal lordship for his benefit. This gift was supposed to be in lieu of expenses. *Ibid.*, pp. 438-440. Since Deir was already in the hands of his family, however, Marischal evidently did not regard it as compensation. Eventually Marischal got six thousand thalers from the dowry; whether this was paid out during the stay in Denmark or just after the king's return to Scotland is not clear. BM Add. MSS 22,958.

[57] It was at this time that James wrote his famous letter to his favorite, Alexander Lindsay, promising him a barony, the letter which began, "From the castle of Cronberg, where we are drinking and driving over in the old manner," J. Stuart, ed., *Miscellany of the Spalding Club*, II, xlviii. Lindsay had lent James one thousand crowns in return for this promise.

[58] It is printed in C. Williams, *James I* (London 1934), pp. 102-103.

[59] Calderwood, v, 81-83.

[60] The epigrams are printed in J. Bain, ed., *The Poems of Sir Richard Maitland*, pp. 137, 138, 142.

amity or good intelligence." Having failed in this, he now con-
centrated on persuading James to return home as quickly as
possible, in order to save as much of the dowry as he could.[61]
The chancellor also had a personal reason for wanting to get
back to Scotland. Lady Maitland was pregnant. Later in the
year she gave birth to a daughter, named after Scotland's new
queen.

While waiting for the king to make up his mind to come
home, Maitland improved the time by holding a series of political conversations with him. The main topic was undoubtedly
how further to implement the legislation of 1587 respecting the
highlands and borders, since the commissions erected after the
king's return were the major administrative innovation of 1590.
These conversations gave rise to a good many rumors in Scotland. It was reported that Maitland would have the nobility
barred from the privy council, and not permitted to come to
court except on summons.[62] These were alleged to be "Danish
innovations"; but however much James and Maitland may have
admired the intellectual and commercial achievements of Denmark, the Danish aristocracy was just about as powerful and
undisciplined as that of Scotland, and its power had been growing in recent years. There is no evidence of the influence of
Danish models on the policy of James and Maitland after their
return.

The rumors of impending change persisted, however, and
were reinforced in April 1590 by the arrival in Scotland from
Denmark of Maitland's friend Carmichael, with orders from
the king to raise a bodyguard of two hundred men and command it himself, to the vast annoyance of the master of Glamis.
Archibald Douglas opined that the real purpose of the bodyguard was to protect the chancellor rather than the king.[63] The
result was that "the number of malcontents are so increased
by the conceit taken of the king's resolution to reform the estate

61 February 12, 1590, Maitland to Robert Bruce, Calderwood, v, 83–86.
62 Melville, *Memoirs*, pp. 372–373.
63 April 21, 1590, Archibald Douglas to Burghley, CSP SCOT, x, 278. April 16,
29, Bowes to Burghley, *ibid.*, pp. 272–276, 282–286. Carmichael, on James's orders, requested that England pay for the guard.

of his government, to the prejudice of the general and ordinary votes and presence of the nobility in councils and matters of estate, and the preparation of a guard to shoulder and maintain this innovation . . . together with the late discourting of Sir William Keith—all which are deemed to be wrought by means of [the] lord chancellor of Scotland with promise of the assistance of the estate of Denmark—as it is very likely that some fire shall be kindled shortly after the king's return."[64]

Maitland's handling of Anne's dowry was another source of annoyance to the aristocracy. He refused to be liberal with it; it was with great difficulty that Marischal was able to extract 6,000 thalers for his expenses. Since James insisted on staying in Denmark for the wedding of Anne's sister, 4,000 more was spent on a gift for her. Carmichael got 3,000 for the bodyguard, and Bellenden got 1,600 to pay the expenses of his mission to England. But no other large sums were handed out, and Maitland managed to keep the incidental expenses down. So he was able to turn over 54,000 thalers of the original total of 85,000 to the comptroller on his return.[65]

There was one other matter, besides finance and administration, much under discussion during the stay in Denmark. This was the question of a possible Protestant league. The suggestion was, that Scotland and Denmark should offer to mediate in the war between England and Spain. If, as was evidently expected, Spain rejected the offer, then Scotland and Denmark and whatever other states were associated with them would take the English side.

This plan had originally been proposed by Denmark in 1588; James now became its principal advocate. In June 1589 Marischal was instructed to discuss the plan with the Danes after he had completed the marriage negotiations.[66] When James and Maitland got to Denmark they resumed the discussions, taking care to keep Elizabeth fully informed. Maitland favored the scheme but was inclined to be cautious; he wanted to be sure

[64] April 24, 1590, Bowes to Burghley, *ibid.*, pp. 280-282. See also Bowes's letter of April 29, *ibid.*, pp. 282-286.

[65] Of this total seventy-five thousand was dowry and ten thousand a special gift from Anne's mother. Maitland's account may be found in BM Add. MSS 22,958.

[66] CSP SCOT, X, 103-105.

that England approved. But the king was sanguine; he sent Bellenden off to Elizabeth with a full report, and there was even talk of sending Maitland on a mission to Lübeck. In February 1590 Elizabeth cautiously expressed her approval.[67]

Nothing much more was done during the stay in Denmark, but in June 1590, shortly after the king's return to Scotland, he sent Colonel Stewart and John Skene on a tour of the courts of Germany and Denmark. In their instructions there was talk of peace, but it was clear that James expected nothing to come of the offer of mediation, and that his real interest lay in the league. And, indeed, such a league would be of considerable advantage to him in his quest of the English crown. In discounting the possibility of a successful offer of mediation James was undoubtedly right; but in so doing he wrecked whatever prospects his project had. The princes of Germany could see no advantage to themselves in such a league; they had no desire to be embroiled with Spain. Neither had the Danes, who from the beginning had been more interested in the peace offer than in the league. About the only supporter James had in his desire for a league was Henry IV, who was in the midst of his desperate struggle with his various foreign and domestic enemies and was prepared to welcome help from whatever source. When this became apparent to Elizabeth, she became cool to the whole project since it appeared to her that its only result would be an increase in French influence in Scotland. So James's scheme fell through. It was dead by the end of 1590, and occasional later attempts to revive it got nowhere.[68]

While James "made good cheer and drank stoutly till the springtime"[69] in Denmark, his government in Scotland was conducting itself quietly and, on the whole, rather successfully. A

[67] February 12, 1590, Maitland to Robert Bruce, Calderwood, v, 83-86. *Barnbarroch Correspondence*, ii, 447-448. February 25, Elizabeth to James, *Salisbury Papers*, iv, 12-13. The Spaniards knew all about the proposed league too. May 29, 1590, statement of Charles Boyd to Philip II, CSP SPANISH, iv, 581-582.

[68] This paragraph is based mainly on Stafford, *James VI*, pp. 124-131. Skene's very full account of the embassy of 1590 may be found in NLS MSS 2912. There is also some correspondence on this embassy in NLS Denmilne MSS, xxviii. For the attempts to revive the league in 1593 and 1594 see J. Ferguson, ed., *Papers Illustrating the History of the Scots Brigade in the Service of the United Netherlands, 1572-1782*, i, 142-143, 154-184.

[69] R. Pitcairn, ed., *Autobiography and Diary of Mr. James Melvill*, p. 277.

curious sort of calm, rather resembling the eye of a hurricane, settled over the surface of Scottish politics, a calm which Maitland attributed to the absence of himself and the king. The malcontents, he wrote, would not "detect themselves by ineffectual broils when . . . they may not possess his majesty's person . . . nor remove such as are the most impediment to their designs," namely, himself.[70] In this opinion the chancellor was doubtless correct.

By all odds the most active person in the temporary government was Bothwell. The erratic earl's powerful position alarmed some people, notably his enemy Fowler, who took refuge in Edinburgh castle and wrote to Burghley that "the chancellor thought to give the fox the geese to keep, which all this country wonders at."[71] But Bothwell behaved very well. He made a public confession of his sins and reconciled himself with the kirk, to the latter's pleased surprise.[72] He assured Elizabeth of his friendliness. The queen expressed her pleasure, but she was not prepared to trust the earl very far. When he proposed that he get in touch with Parma again, in order to supply the English with information, Elizabeth agreed only after considerable hesitation. As it turned out, nothing came of this anyway, since James after his return forbade Bothwell to go on with it.[73]

At almost any other time the king's wishes would have meant very little to Bothwell, but at this time they did. During James's absence and shortly thereafter the earl made a serious and sincere effort to be useful and loyal to the government, perhaps out of gratitude that he had not been punished for his part in Huntly's rebellion. At James's request he bustled around Scotland trying to patch up various feuds, without much success. He ended, for the moment, his own savage vendetta with the Humes. He kept his border subordinates quiet, resisting the temptation to make trouble for Lord John Hamilton, whom he disliked. He ostentatiously refused to join in any combination against

70 April 7, 1590, Maitland to Bowes, CSP SCOT, x, 267-268.

71 *Salisbury Papers*, III, 442-443.

72 November 10, 1589, Ashby to Burghley, CSP SCOT, x, 192. Calderwood was unimpressed: "The same night, or soon after, he ravished the earl of Gowrie's daughter out of Dirleton." Calderwood, v, 68.

73 April 9, May 23, 1590, Bowes to Burghley, CSP SCOT, x, 269-270, 296-300.

Maitland: he had promised Maitland that he would not, he said.[74] Yet at the same time some of his actions looked suspicious to the many people who disliked him. The rumors that he was secretly in touch with the Catholics persisted, and were fed by his consorting with Huntly and Arran, and by his support of the Catholic Graham of Fentry before the General Assembly of March 1590. "The best sort here fear the worst," wrote Fowler.[75] Some of these suspicions were shared by the king, who, when he got home took the earl to task for such things as his friendliness to Fentry. What he imagined to be the king's ingratitude irritated the earl, and he began to suspect that the chancellor was responsible for it.[76]

Underneath the surface calm, which was scarcely ruffled by Bothwell's activities, there was a deep and sinister Catholic plot—or so many people thought. There were rumors that the Catholics planned a *coup d'état* in Edinburgh; the appearance of a Spanish ship at Wigtown in January 1590 lent them credence.[77] Ashby was not unduly worried, but he did believe that the Scottish Catholics were still plotting with Spain and would move in the spring; James, therefore, should not dawdle in Denmark.[78] Bowes, who replaced Ashby as English resident in December 1589, felt much the same way.[79] In March there was a rumor of a sort of St. Bartholomew's Day, to be touched off by an assault on the master of Glamis by the earl of Crawford. The following month the story was that as soon as James returned, he would be seized and Maitland "put . . . out of the

74 April 3, 14, 1590, Richard Douglas to Archibald Douglas, *Salisbury Papers*, IV, 23-25; CSP SCOT, X, 278-279. April 16, 29, Bowes to Burghley, *ibid.*, pp. 272-276, 282-286. December 5, 1589, the council at Edinburgh to Lord John Hamilton, Hamilton MSS, box 1.

75 December 7, 1589, Fowler to Burghley, *Salisbury Papers*, III, 446-447. Among the "best sort," at whose behest Fowler said he was writing, was Lady Maitland, "who is a wise woman and half chancellor when he is at home." This is one of the very few indications we have that Lady Maitland was interested in politics. See also Calderwood, V, 86; February 7, 1590, Bowes to Walsingham, CSP SCOT, X, 842-843.

76 March 24, May 15, 1590, Bowes to Burghley, *ibid.*, pp. 258-260, 292-296.

77 Calderwood, V, 70-71.

78 November 18, 1589, Ashby to Burghley and Walsingham, CSP SCOT, X, 195-196. November 25, Hay to Ashby, *ibid.*, p. 200.

79 See his letters of February 3 and 16, 1590, *ibid.*, pp. 839-840, 847-848.

way."[80] All these rumors proved false, but they are evidence that the Protestant faction was still very nervous. Huntly's rebellion had been an unpleasant reminder that even now, thirty years after the triumph of the Lords of the Congregation, the adherents of the old religion were still formidable.

The kirk decided to do something about it. The ministers were feeling rather edgy and harassed in early 1590. They had been frightened by Huntly's near success and irritated by the government's failure to punish him. The rumors of a Catholic plot worried them still more. Furthermore, they were engaged in the first stages of what would be a long and trying controversy with the Anglican church which had been touched off by a very hostile sermon by bishop Bancroft earlier in 1589.[81] So, at the General Assembly of March 1590 the usual anti-Catholic acts were passed; much more important was the action of the privy council on March 6, taken at the behest of the ministers. The council's enactment recapitulated the legislation of 1587 and 1588 against Jesuits and seminary priests, and appointed a series of thirty-one commissions, each in a particular area, to administer it. The commissions included every prominent Protestant noble in Scotland. A second set of commissioners was also appointed, very largely composed of ministers. Each of these commissions was to have the power to compel anyone to come before it to subscribe the confession of faith of 1581 and a pledge to defend the true religion. Thus the kirk obtained legal sanction for its own investigative processes, and governmental approval of the ecclesiastical penalties it might choose to impose.[82] The results, however, were evidently rather unsatisfactory in the beginning, owing to lack of co-operation from the government. Calderwood summarizes the

[80] March 8, 1590, Bowes to Walsingham, *ibid.*, pp. 854-857. April 14, Richard Douglas to Archibald Douglas, *ibid.*, pp. 278-279.

[81] The controversy is conveniently summarized by G. Donaldson, "The Attitude of Whitgift and Bancroft to the Scottish Church," *Transactions of the Royal Historical Society*, 4th series, xxiv (1942), 95-115.

[82] Calderwood, v, 37-49, 86-89. The king approved the acts of the Assembly on April 4, 1590, *ibid.*, p. 91. Just before his departure for Denmark James had given the kirk the right to apply to the court of session for enforcement of its decisions respecting deprivations and disputed benefices. *Ibid.*, pp. 64-67.

attitude of Hamilton and Lennox, the two nominal leaders of the government, as one of "many words but few deeds."[83]

About a month after this meeting of the General Assembly Elizabeth lost one of the greatest of her servants. Sir Francis Walsingham died on April 6, 1590. He had done a great deal to cement the ties between England and Scotland, and both James and Maitland had come to have much confidence in him. His death meant that responsibility for Scottish affairs was transferred back to Burghley, and then to his son Robert Cecil. Since James distrusted both of them, relations between England and Scotland deteriorated in the 1590's, although there was never any real danger of a rupture of the alliance. Not until after Essex had passed from the scene did James form that close partnership with Cecil which was to be the dominant feature of his first decade on the English throne.[84]

Almost since the moment of his arrival in Denmark the king had been sending instructions back to Scotland with respect to his homecoming. The chief problem was the customary shortage of money. It was only under pressure that the burghs agreed to supply shipping for the return journey.[85] Finally enough ships were found, and on May 1, 1590, James and his queen landed at Leith. They were met by Lennox and Bothwell and sundry other dignitaries. James Elphinstone, a senator of the college of justice, pronounced a Latin oration, after which the royal couple went to church to give thanks for their safe arrival.[86] Almost at once a controversy arose over Anne's coronation. It centered on the question of anointing, a ceremony which the kirk looked upon as Popish. James, however, was determined to have his own way. He threatened that if Robert Bruce, who

[83] *Ibid.*, p. 86.

[84] James's relations with the Cecils and Essex in the 1590's are discussed in Stafford, *James VI, passim.*

[85] Their reluctance was justified. It was not until August 1592 that Robert Jamieson of Ayr was finally paid in full for the use of his ship, although he had obtained a favorable decision of the privy council on his claim as early as June 1590. RPCS, IV, 485. SRO, *Register of Deeds*, XL, 452. The town council of Edinburgh agreed to put up one thousand pounds for further repairs to Holyrood only on condition that it would not be put to any expense in entertaining James's Danish guests. RPCS, IV, 470-471.

[86] J. T. G. Craig, ed., *Papers Relative to the Marriage of James the Sixth of Scotland with Princess Anne of Denmark*, Bannatyne Club publication (Edinburgh 1828), pp. 37-38.

was to officiate, refused to anoint, he would be replaced by a bishop. This, to the kirk, was an even worse prospect than anointing: so Bruce performed the hateful task.[87] The coronation took place on May 17. Two days later the queen made her official entry to Edinburgh amidst elaborate and tedious ceremonial.[88]

For several weeks before the king's return Bowes had been freely predicting some sort of attack on Maitland as soon as James and his party landed. The chancellor's enemies were said to be drawing together. The earl of Errol, who had been very bitter against Maitland at the time of Huntly's rebellion, was negotiating through the master of Glamis for the hand of one of Morton's daughters.[89] Glamis's enmity to the chancellor was increased by Carmichael's appointment to command of the guard. He and Hume, both of whom were Morton's sons-in-law, urged Bothwell to join them in a band against Maitland, Hume going so far as to accuse Maitland of having suborned him to kill Bothwell. The latter was evidently not impressed; he knew that Hume needed no urging from Maitland to kill him. The earl of Montrose was incensed at the whole idea of a bodyguard, and said that whoever advised it deserved punishment.[90] Bellenden, the justice clerk, was still hostile. "[For] my own part, soon after his majesty's arrival and the departure of the strangers, I look for a marvelous confusion in this state," wrote Richard Douglas to his uncle Archibald on April 24.[91]

[87] Spottiswoode, *History*, II, 407-408. There is a detailed description of the coronation in *Papers Relative to the Marriage of James the Sixth*, pp. 49-56, and a list of the expenses involved in *ibid.*, appendix, pp. 13-22. For some months afterwards James did his best to extract voluntary contributions from his courtiers to get these expenses paid. Chambers, *Domestic Annals*, I, 199-200.

[88] *Papers Relative to the Marriage of James the Sixth*, pp. 39-42. Andrew Melvill's Latin oration on this occasion so impressed the king that he ordered it printed. Calderwood, v, 97. Maitland persuaded the king to shift the day of the entry from Sunday to Tuesday out of deference to the scruples of the kirk. *Ibid.*, p. 95.

[89] April 24, 1590, Bowes to Burghley, CSP SCOT, X, 280-282. It was rumored earlier that Lennox was interested in one of Morton's daughters. February 12, 1590, Bowes to Burghley and Walsingham, *ibid.*, pp. 844-846.

[90] April 29, 1590, Bowes to Burghley, *ibid.*, pp. 282-286.

[91] *Salisbury Papers*, III, 139-140 (where the letter is misdated 1586). See also his letter of April 9, 1590, *Salisbury Papers*, IV, 26-27.

Yet, strangely enough, none of the dire events so freely predicted took place. The movement of opposition to Maitland apparently collapsed. A formal process of mediation was arranged between Maitland and Glamis and Marischal. Bothwell, despite some annoyance with the chancellor respecting the disposition of the property of the now deceased Thomas Fowler, was friendly. Montrose was reconciled with him. All this despite Maitland's tactlessness in implying that Marischal had sought him out and made the first move, "which coming to Marischal's ear hath much grieved him."[92]

All these gestures of reconciliation were more formal than sincere. Undoubtedly they were caused in part by James's evident support of his chancellor; the king took the occasion of Anne's coronation to raise Maitland to the peerage as baron Thirlestane—the only person so honored.[93] But the fundamental cause of hostility between Maitland and the aristocracy still remained. The chancellor was still determined to reduce their power within manageable limits; and until he either succeeded in this aim or gave over, there would continue to be war between him and them. Bowes was aware of this. "Albeit that great labor is taken to compound the griefs among the nobility and towards the chancellor," he wrote on May 23, there was a design "to draw many noblemen and others into a strong party to provide that the king may govern with his nobility in wonted manner, and not by private persons hated, nor by order of Denmark, against the ancient rights and privileges of the nobility."[94] The struggle would go on, and with increased intensity and violence.

[92] See Bowes's letters of May 16 and 23, 1590, CSP SCOT, x, 292-296, 296-300.
[93] There were also fifteen knighthoods conferred. Among the recipients were the master of Glamis, James Melville of Halhill, Scott of Buccleuch, Ker of Cesford, and John Carmichael, the new captain of the guard. *Ibid.*, pp. 299-300. Maitland refused James's offer of a grant of crown lands, on the ground that they were too far dilapidated already. May 16, 1590, Bowes to Burghley, *ibid.*, pp. 292-296.
[94] *Ibid.*, pp. 300-301. One of the king's "Danish innovations," his decision to refuse the nobility completely free access to his privy chamber, as had been the custom in the past, was much resented. May 23, 1590, Bowes to Burghley, *ibid.*, pp. 298-299.

CHAPTER 10

MAITLAND'S ADMINISTRATION:
CLIMAX AND REACTION

THE YEAR AND A HALF which followed the return from Denmark comprise what might be called the second half of Maitland's administration. It was at once made clear that there was to be no change in policy: Maitland was still determined to implement the program of 1587. The first part of this period marked the apogee of Maitland's administrative accomplishment. Then, slowly at first, but with mounting speed and intensity as time went on, the aristocratic reaction set in. It was strong enough to sweep Maitland himself into political eclipse. But it did not destroy his system.

In May of 1590, however, the new-made baron Thirlestane stood at the pinnacle of political and personal success. For the first time since his accession to power there were no pressing problems of foreign policy to cope with, and he could direct the king's attention as well as his own to the domestic problems which preoccupied him. The result was a vigorous and relatively successful effort to assert and increase the royal authority.

A convention of estates was summoned for mid-June 1590. It was rather poorly attended by the aristocracy,[1] most of whom had gone home after the queen's coronation and had no mind to return to Edinburgh so soon. Its most important action was the creation of a special committee of the council to enforce the act of 1587 on the highlands and borders. The committee consisted of Maitland and six other officials; no magnates were members. It was to meet every Monday to deal with border questions, and report to the full council on the first of each month.

[1] June 9, 1590, Bowes to Burghley, CSP SCOT, x, 314-315.

The treasury was to meet its expenses, which included the salary of a special clerk and the keeping of a separate register.

The committee set vigorously to work. The basic principle on which it operated was the strict enforcement of the general band, which was copied into its special register immediately after the text of the act of 1587 on which its power rested. Border landlords were once more ordered to find surety for their dependents, and those who had released pledges assigned to their custody were ordered to come and show cause why they should not be mulcted of two thousand pounds for disobeying the king's orders. At the same time, in order to apportion responsibility properly, the committee undertook to compile a shire-by-shire list—unhappily for the historian, never completed—of the landlords of the country, a list which would be useful for tax purposes as well. In addition to the tenants-in-chief, the list included the names of all the considerable landholders who held of subject-superiors;[2] these also were to be held responsible to the government for their tenants. If this policy could be made to work, the power of the great feudatories would be seriously reduced.

From the existing records it is difficult to gauge the effectiveness of the committee's work. Entries in the special register are numerous in the first few months, and then fall off. This would argue either a high level of success or an almost total lack of it. In favor of the former hypothesis are the favorable comments of English officials on border administration in these months and the fact that, as time went on, the committee turned its attention to the highlands as well. This was not contemplated in the enactment which established the committee, but was a logical extension of the committee's activities.

The chief trouble spot on the borders was Liddesdale, chiefly owing to the fact that Bothwell was its hereditary keeper. The king attempted to solve the problem by persuading Bothwell to surrender his offices in Liddesdale, in return for an extensive grant in the Hebridean island of Lewis. In July 1590 Bothwell accepted the offer, provided James could put him in possession of the Lewis lands peacefully. In the meantime, however, he re-

2 I am indebted for this information to Sir James Fergusson.

fused to take any responsibility for Liddesdale, for which refusal he spent a night in ward in Edinburgh castle in August.
He then supplied the necessary sureties, but his administration
was as lax as ever, and since it was manifestly impossible for
James to put him peacefully in possession of the Lewis lands,
the whole transaction fell through.[3] The king, in no way discouraged, thought that if the earl could not be eliminated from
the borders, he might be turned into a useful agent of the government by being made lieutenant-general of the whole area.
Maitland prevented this by pointing out that Lord John Hamilton would be jealous and that Huntly would want similar
authority in the north.[4] So the Liddesdale problem remained
unsolved.

Elsewhere on the borders the committee's work was much
more effective. A serious effort was made by the wardens to
meet the English bills of complaint, and the government did its
best to increase the wardens' authority. One of the moves to
this end led to personal trouble for Maitland. In September
1590 the government decreed that henceforth the warden of the
middle march should also hold the office of provost of Jedburgh.
As the elder Ker of Cesford already held both these offices, this
action was not expected to cause any difficulty. But the king
and Maitland overlooked the feuds raging within the Ker family. William Ker of Ancrum surreptitiously arranged the election of another man as provost; this so infuriated the hotheaded young Ker of Cesford, Maitland's nephew-by-marriage,
that he slew Ancrum when they accidentally met in Edinburgh
in December. Maitland was "heavily troubled" by this, but he
would not condone the deed, and young Cesford had to go into
exile in England.[5] Aside from this, however, matters went well.
The steady pressure of the government was so effective that by
March 1591 Maitland felt that the need for extraordinary
measures was past. The customary meetings of the English and
Scottish wardens should suffice to provide justice, he said; any-

[3] The Liddesdale question may be traced in CSP SCOT, x, 321ff, especially pp.
321-322, 331-332, 350, 374-375, 379-383.

[4] September 4, 1590, Bowes to Burghley, *ibid.*, pp. 390-392.

[5] RPCS, IV, 529-530, 544. December 7, 1590, Ashton to Hudson, CSP SCOT, x,
433-434. January 13, 1591, Bowes to Burghley, *ibid.*, pp. 446-450. See also *ibid.*,
p. 562.

thing unusual could be referred to the councils of both kingdoms, or to a special meeting of commissioners of the two kingdoms which might be held later in the spring.[6]

The committee was much less effective in the highlands, although even here an effort was made. Early in 1591 three important chiefs, two MacDonalds and a MacLean, were induced
to come to Edinburgh, where they were promptly clapped into
ward until they found surety for their future good behavior,
in accordance with the terms of the general band. The government seems to have acted something less than honorably in this
matter, and its actions were not particularly effective.[7] The
resources of James's government were far too slender to permit
it to adopt the only policy which would effectively control the
highlands, namely, the use of armed force.

The same convention of estates which authorized this committee also undertook to reform the college of justice. This was
most unwelcome to the senators themselves. They stubbornly
insisted on the maintenance of their historic right of themselves
trying any member accused of crime, though they offered, on
this occasion only, that any senator accused of an offense
"should be tried by twelve persons chosen out of the nobility,
barons, boroughs, and church."[8] It was clear that the college
would not reform itself. A most unsatisfactory justice, John
Graham of Halyards, was charged with corruption by the
king's advocate; he was later accused of slander, treason, and
forgery; yet he remained on the bench until he was killed in a
street brawl. This was at least partly due to the unwise action
of the General Assembly in attempting to force him to appear
before it to answer the slander charge; the government felt
that it could not permit the Assembly even the shadow of juris-

6 March 9, 1591, Bowes to Burghley, *ibid.*, pp. 481-482. March 24, Bowes to
Burghley and Hunsdon, *ibid.*, pp. 485-488.

7 See the account of D. Gregory, *The History of the Western Highlands and
Isles of Scotland*, 2nd ed. (London 1881), pp. 241-244. According to Sir James
Melville, *Memoirs of His Own Life*, pp. 391-392, the men who stood caution
for the chiefs were later able to bribe their way out of Blackness for five
thousand marks. The proceedings of the committee are in RPCS, IV, 781-814.
See also Professor Masson's comments on the work of the committee in the
introduction to this volume, pp. liii-lvi.

8 June 15, 1590, the earl of Worcester to Burghley, CSP SCOT, x, 324-326.

diction over any official, and so Graham had to be protected, in spite of his misdeeds.[9]

Maitland's plan was not to attempt any wholesale changes in the present composition of the court, but to improve its quality in the future by requiring an examination of any nominee by the judges themselves. This would have the added advantage of putting an end to the growing tendency to regard positions on the court as heritable. The first examination was held in August 1590. Maitland's brother-in-law, the laird of Whittingham, retired; his son was nominated to succeed him, but he was required, for three consecutive days, to "pass . . . in company with the ordinary lords . . . in the Outer Tolbooth, and . . . make report in presence of the whole lords . . . and . . . give his opinion . . . upon each question." After he had done likewise in the Inner Tolbooth for three days, the lords would decide as to his fitness.[10] Young Whittingham was admitted. In the following year the next vacancy occurred, on the death of Bellenden of Newtyle. Before his death he had obtained the royal nomination to the vacancy for his brother, but the latter did not take the test, and evidently was never admitted to the court. In 1592, by act of Parliament, it was declared that all senators must be at least twenty-five years old and have property to the value of one thousand marks or twenty chalders of victual, to reduce the possibility of bribery. Two years later, in 1594, as a further check to corruption, it was enacted that no judge was to sit on a cause involving his father, brother, or son, or to buy land the possession of which was in dispute in the courts.[11] In 1593 the king agreed to nominate at least three candidates for all future vacancies. This procedure was not always followed, but by the later 1590's it was clearly recognized that it should be, and the procedure of resignation in favor of one's kinsman was regarded as tolerable only in very exceptional cases.[12] Maitland's revival of the court's right to ex-

[9] *Ibid.*, pp. 336, 519, 594. Calderwood, v, 133-134, 138.

[10] G. Brunton and D. Haig, *An Historical Account of the Senators of the College of Justice*, intro., pp. xl-xli.

[11] APS, III, 569; APS, IV, 67, 68.

[12] For a discussion of this whole subject see R. K. Hannay, *The College of Justice*, pp. 112-120.

amine appointees thus helped to prevent the college of justice from becoming, what the parlements of France later became, closed corporations, in which tenure of office was regarded as private property. This was of considerable importance for the future of the Scottish judicial system.

Improving the personnel of the Scottish bench might be important for the future, but the immediate problem was to prevent the aristocracy from overawing the courts by force. What could be done by legislation was done: in July 1590 the privy council decreed that an earl could take only twelve retainers with him to court, a lord eight, and a laird five, and all must be unarmed.[13] Like all such laws, this one remained a dead letter. James himself put the problem this way, in lecturing a special assize the following year: "Now I must advertise you what it is that makes great crimes to be so rife in this country, namely, that all men set themselves more for friends than for justice and obedience to the law. . . . Let a man commit the most filthy crimes that can be, yet his friends take his part, and first keep him from apprehension, and after by feud or favor, by false assize or some way or other, they find means of his escape from punishment."[14] This situation had to be remedied before the king could be truly master in his own house; but it could not be remedied by legislation, but only by superior force.

A measure of the amount of attention paid by the great lords to the royal courts at this time is provided by a letter to James from the earl of Angus in September 1590. In this letter Angus complained that one of his sons had been seized by the Scotts on account of a quarrel over some property rights in Ettrick Forest. "I hope your majesty will think this crime reves (injures) both . . . your majesty's honor and common weal, and doubts [sic] not your majesty will put order thereto according to your majesty's laws, that such contempt may be punished, for your majesty lately desired me to [com]plain of any man that did me wrong. Which I will do, but shall be loath to suffer dishonor at their hands."[15] In other words, Angus would give the law a chance; but if the king failed to give satisfaction, he

13 RPCS, IV, 508.   14 CSP SCOT, X, 523-524.
15 A. I. Cameron, ed., *The Warrender Papers*, II, 145-146.

would take matters into his own hands. And Angus, the former laird of Glenbervie, was one of the most pacific of all the earls.

The aristocracy was, as always, the government's most serious problem, but not its only one. In July 1590 Elizabeth wrote a celebrated letter to James, warning him against "a sect of perilous consequence, such as would have no kings but a presbytery."[16] James in his heart subscribed to the queen's sentiments, but for the moment, thanks to Maitland, he was on the best of terms with the kirk. At the June convention of estates it was declared once more that the ministers ought to be supported out of the teinds; but no way could be found to dispossess the present holders. "The possessors will not lose their tacks or leases, unless that upon the surrender of some part of the tithes in their holdings for [a] term of years they may have the residue in fee simple forever."[17] The ministers evidently felt that the government was doing its best in this matter, however; they were inclined to be charitable. The presbytery of Edinburgh suspended a minister who had preached against James, and the king, at the General Assembly of August 1590, delighted the assembled divines by assailing the Anglican service as "an evil-said mass in English, wanting nothing but the liftings. . . . The Assembly so rejoiced, that there was nothing but loud praising of God, and praying for the king for a quarter of an hour."[18] James's remarks were especially welcome to the kirk in that they committed him to public support of their position in their quarrel with bishop Bancroft. In June of 1591 James even went so far as to write to Elizabeth on behalf of the great English puritan Thomas Cartwright, who had recently been imprisoned. James obliged the assembly in other ways as well. A large number of religious offenders, including the masters of Angus and Cassillis, were ordered to appear before the council to answer for their faults. Archbishop Adamson remained in disgrace. The king gave the income of his benefice to Lennox; the wretched prelate had to beg his bread from Andrew Melvill and sign a humiliating confession of his errors.

16 CSP SCOT, x, 349-350.
17 June 15, 1590, Worcester to Burghley, *ibid.*, pp. 324-328.
18 Calderwood, v, 106.

Relations between James and his kirk were better than they had ever been before, or would ever be again.[19]

Elizabeth was not disturbed by James's apparent disregard of her religious advice. She was, on the whole, disposed to be friendly. She sent the earl of Worcester to Scotland after James's return from Denmark, to announce to the king his election to the order of the Garter, which greatly pleased him. So, too, did the subsidy of three thousand pounds sterling which shortly followed.[20] The king, for his part, kept the Scottish Catholics at arm's length, and border affairs went well. Early in 1591 the government risked a popular explosion by seizing a fugitive Irishman named O'Rourke and turning him over to the English authorities. This provoked a riot in Glasgow, which Bowes diagnosed as owing to fear that Scottish trade with Ireland would be adversely affected. He urged his government to see to it that Glasgow and the other western ports did not suffer as a result.[21] The general tone of Anglo-Scottish relations at this time is best expressed in James's letter to Elizabeth promising the capture and delivery of O'Rourke: "All your foes shall be common enemies to us both, in spite of the Pope, the king of Spain, and all the Leaguers my cousins not excepted, and the devil their master."[22]

Maitland shared his master's satisfaction with the state of Anglo-Scottish relations. He and Burghley exchanged sententious letters on the virtues of the chancellor's late brother and the benefits to accrue to both parties from their alliance. "If this microcosm of Britain," wrote Maitland, "separate from the continent world, naturally joined by situation and language, and most happily by religion, shall be, by the indissoluble amity of the two princes, sincerely conserved in union, the antichristian confederates shall never be able to effectuate their bloody and godless intentions."[23] Foreign affairs were going so well, in fact, that Maitland felt it possible, in April 1591, to turn over the office of secretary, which he had held since 1584, to his

19 CSP SCOT, X, 528. RPCS, IV, 521-522; XIV, 374-375. Calderwood, V, 118-127.
20 CSP SCOT, X, 344.
21 April 27, 1591, Bowes to Burghley, CSP SCOT, X, 505-508.
22 *Ibid.*, pp. 484-485.
23 August 13, 1590, Maitland to Burghley, *ibid.*, pp. 377-378.

nephew Richard Cockburn of Clerkington. Clerkington was a colorless and apparently rather unintelligent young man whose chief virtue, in Maitland's eyes, was that he would do exactly as he was told.

One of the benefits of good relations with England came in the tangible form of cash. These occasional subsidies were always welcome to the Scottish government, but they hardly solved the financial problem. James and Maitland, encouraged, perhaps, by the fact that for once they had some ready money, in the form of Queen Anne's dowry, resolved to raise the royal income, and, furthermore, to live within it. In July 1590 the dowry was lent out to various royal burghs at ten per cent interest. There was the usual recoinage. A customs duty of three French crowns was levied on each tun of wine, and Scottish merchants were ordered to stop transshipping wine between Huguenot and Catholic ports in France, but to bring it home, so that the duty could be collected. All gifts made out of the royal park lands were revoked. The report of the lords auditors of the exchequer early in 1591 revealed a debt of over eight thousand pounds, however; so the drastic step was taken of suspending payment to the government's creditors for the time being. In addition, a serious retrenchment of the royal household expenses was undertaken. The comptroller was put in charge of household expenditures, and more frequent and systematic accounting was required. The allowance for wine and clothing was cut, and a serious effort was made to live on twenty thousand marks a year. For a time the effort was moderately successful; expenses were cut down, the revenue increased, and for a short while, at least, there was what might be called a balanced budget.[24]

Maitland himself was personally interested in this financial retrenchment. His private finances were in bad condition. He had gone some two thousand pounds into debt on government business, chiefly in the financing of the voyage to Denmark, and

[24] RPCS, IV, 513-514, 526, 535-536. G. P. McNeill, ed., *The Exchequer Rolls of Scotland*, XXII, xxxiv-xxv, 162-164. R. S. Brydon, *The Finances of James VI 1567-1603*, pp. 43, 55-57. There is a list of the members of the royal household and their salaries and perquisites as of January 1591 in NLS MSS 34.2.17. See also February 23, 1591, Bowes to Burghley, CSP SCOT, x, 467-471.

his creditors were pressing him. His position was somewhat eased by the gift of various crown lands in feu, including the barony of Haddington, and by the acquisition of the wardship and marriage of Hay of Yester.[25] But if his personal finances were benefited by the reforms, his popularity was not. His policy of retrenchment for the royal household, and his use of public officials to supervise the expenditures of household functionaries and to limit the perquisites of the courtiers, raised up for him a host of new enemies, from the chamberlain, the duke of Lennox, on down.[26] These enemies were very much more dangerous to Maitland than the great nobles, because they had the king's ear. Maitland was absolutely dependent on the king's support; with James surrounded by men who were hostile to him, his position could become perilous in the extreme.

The sort of attack to which Maitland was subjected is best illustrated by the poetical allegory known as *Rob Stene's Dream*, presumably written sometime in 1591 by Stene, a member of the king's household.[27] The central figure in this allegory, the crafty and despicable Lawrence the fox, is greedy and insatiable; he is an enemy to the Stewarts and wants to advance the Hamiltons to the crown. He helped to destroy the lion's (James's) mother; his poems slander the lion; his grip must be due to witchcraft, and to the false claim that if he is removed, the ruin of the crown and the religion would result. The lion must rely upon his own family and cast off the Hamiltons and their treacherous agent. James was not likely to be influenced by any single attack, but the constant criticism of his chief minister, criticism in which the new queen joined, was bound to have a cumulative effect on his mind.

The courtiers simply added to the already impressive list of the chancellor's enemies. The aura of goodwill that surrounded the king's homecoming and Queen Anne's coronation was soon

25 February 23, 1591, Bowes to Burghley, csp scot, x, 473. February 23, Hudson to Burghley, *ibid.*, pp. 473-475. sro, *Privy Seal Register*, lxii, 11, 120-121.

26 Melville, *Memoirs*, pp. 375-376. November 7, 1590, Bowes to Burghley, csp scot, x, 415-417.

27 He is so listed in January 1591; nls mss 34.2.17. For the poem see W. Fleming, W. Motherwell, and J. Smith, eds., *Rob Stene's Dream*, Maitland Club publication (Glasgow 1836).

dissipated. The first serious trouble arose over the marriage of Errol to one of Morton's daughters. The chief promoter of this marriage was the master of Glamis, who was married to another of Morton's daughters; Maitland suspected that Glamis was attempting to organize another aristocratic coalition against him, as he had in July 1589, and the hollow truce between them fell to pieces. Glamis for his part affected to believe that Maitland was plotting with Bothwell against him. Maitland's temper was not improved by an attack of what may have been bursitis in July 1590—he was "grievously diseased with a pain in his right arm, causing him to keep his lodging and many times in the day his bed"—and he accused Glamis of complicity in Huntly's rebellion. Glamis hotly denied it. But, thanks in large measure to the intervention of the kirk, the quarrel was patched up before it went too far. Some of the ministers hoped that Errol's marriage to an impeccably Protestant lady might effect his conversion, and they asked Maitland to be charitable. The chancellor consented, and invited Morton and Glamis to dinner on the occasion of the baptism of his daughter.[28]

Trouble was stirred up again by Bothwell, who righteously aired his refusal to join a plot of Errol and Glamis against Maitland's life. Because Maitland "oppressed and dishonored the nobility," they "were minded to give him the like reward that was given to Cochrane, who serving under King James the third and offending generally all the noblemen was suddenly taken by the earl of Angus and others and hanged." This matter, commented Bowes, "is like to blow the coals betwixt the chancellor and the master of Glamis."[29] Bowes himself undertook the thankless role of a dove of peace in this tense situation, and by the first of August he had succeeded in patching up another reconciliation by threatening the recalcitrant with Elizabeth's grave displeasure. Errol apologized to the chancellor for plotting against him, and the apology was accepted.[30] Maitland and Glamis remained civil to each other for several months, in spite of Glamis' attempt to increase Maitland's growing un-

[28] July 11, 1590, Bowes to Burghley, csp scot, x, 350-353.
[29] July 11, 1590, Bowes to Burghley, ibid., pp. 354-355.
[30] July 16, August 1, 1590, Bowes to Burghley, ibid., pp. 357-359, 368-371.

popularity among the courtiers by insinuating that the chancellor was planning to be even more severe toward them than in fact he was.[31]

At the beginning of 1591 Bowes, who was seriously worried by the divisions within the Protestant party, tried to bring about a genuine reconciliation between Glamis and Maitland. He failed, and his failure made clear once again that the difference between them was as much a matter of principle as of personal rivalry. The point at issue was the composition of the governing coalition. Maitland informed Bowes that he was willing to come to terms with James's favorite courtiers, but beyond that he would not go: "the chancellor and some others do not fully allow as yet that . . . noblemen shall be added, as the master of Glamis hath . . . advised . . . that without the association and support of some well-affected noblemen he will not bear any part of the burden . . . but rather retire . . . and live privately at home."[32] So the effort at reconciliation collapsed, and the quarrel broke out all over again. Glamis attempted to win over the Campbell and Kennedy interests by promoting a marriage between his nephew, the young earl of Cassillis, and the sister of the equally young earl of Argyll. Maitland, who was in a position of authority over the two young men as long as they were minors, scotched this and promptly struck back. In mid-February 1591 the king honored him with a visit to his new house at Lauder, to be present at the wedding of Maitland's niece with the young laird of Lugton. Immediately thereafter the court of session handed down a decision in a suit between Morton and the old laird of Lugton in favor of the latter; Glamis, wrote Bowes, "is sharply pricked, and Morton mightily stormeth." Maitland also cultivated Glamis' deadly enemy Crawford, who in turn revived a recent quarrel between Glamis and the burgesses of Forfar. "The chancellor," Bowes reported, "is suspected to agree that Crawford should awake this sleeping dog to bite Glamis."[33] For the next

31 November 20, 1590, Bowes to Burghley, *ibid.*, pp. 419-422.
32 February 13, 1591, Bowes to Burghley, *ibid.*, pp. 458-460.
33 February 23, 1591, Bowes to Burghley, *ibid.*, pp. 467-471. February (13), Bowes to Hudson, *Border Papers*, I, 375-376. This letter is misdated; the probable date of its writing is February 23.

several weeks Glamis was kept busy finding cautions for his tenants and relatives that they would not attack the town,[34] and Maitland enjoyed a brief respite from his attentions.

An important consequence of this prolonged quarrel with Glamis was a gradual softening in the chancellor's attitude toward Huntly. The latter had behaved very submissively toward the government since the king's return from Denmark. His relative the laird of Auchindoun had surrendered the band of the confederacy of 1589, at James's insistence.[35] The earl became friendly with the king's favorite Alexander Lindsay, and ended his opposition to Lindsay's possession of Spynie castle.[36] Furthermore, a fierce quarrel broke out between Huntly and the young earl of Moray, the son-in-law of the late regent, a quarrel which embroiled Huntly with Athol and various other members of the Stewart family. The initial stages of this quarrel went rather badly for Huntly; it was clear that he would have his hands full. Maitland, whose relations with the Stewarts were none too good, as *Rob Stene's Dream* makes clear, may have sympathized with Huntly in this matter; at the very least, he was sure, as he told Bowes, that Huntly would be unable to plot against him. So, on December 17, 1590, Huntly was granted a remission for his part in the rebellion of 1589, and was formally reconciled with Maitland.[37] This did not mean that the chancellor relaxed his steady opposition to the Catholics as a party, however. In November he informed Bowes of an attempt to bribe him. The Catholics promised him ten thousand crowns and an annual pension, if he would grant them liberty of conscience, but he refused.[38] This offer may have existed only in Maitland's imagination, and have been invented to impress England; but, genuine or not, the kirk's chief political ally could have no truck with any policy

---

[34] RPCS, IV, 603-604, 608.

[35] July 23, 1590, Bowes to Burghley, CSP SCOT, x, 361-365.

[36] October 24, 1590, Bowes to Burghley, *ibid.*, pp. 407-411. Spynie castle was part of a tack granted to Huntly by the bishop of Moray. In November 1590 Lindsay was created Lord Spynie; in December he and Huntly signed a mutual band of manrent, printed in J. Stuart, ed., *Miscellany of the Spalding Club*, 1st series, IV, 244-245.

[37] CSP SCOT, x, 439-440. See also December 18, 1590, Bowes to Burghley, *ibid.*, pp. 434-439.

[38] November 7, 1590, Bowes to Burghley, *ibid.*, pp. 415-417.

so distasteful to the ministers as liberty of conscience. The chancellor's real attitude was demonstrated by the seizure of O'Rourke.

Then, in April 1591, there exploded the first of a series of bombshells which were destined to test to its uttermost the system of government and administration which Maitland had erected. A series of trials for witchcraft had begun in December 1590, involving a number of people who had supposedly met with the devil at Northberwick kirk. James, who was fascinated by the whole subject of witchcraft, took a personal interest in the trials, presided at many of the examinations of the accused, and, unfortunately for his reputation in the eyes of a less credulous posterity, permitted torture to be used. He learned, with a horrified fear, that some of the witches' practices had been directed against himself. Then, on April 15, 1591, came the crowning revelation. The wizard Richie Graham confessed that he had engaged in these practices at the instance of the earl of Bothwell.[39]

Bothwell's reasons for dabbling in witchcraft are obscure. The suggestion that he was hopeful of the crown in case of James's death without issue can hardly be taken seriously, even though it had the endorsement of the king himself.[40] Bothwell was irresponsible; he had curiosity; he craved excitement. Perhaps the explanation is no more profound than that. But, whatever his motives, he terrified the king, and also filled him with an unquenchable hatred. James would hear of no exculpation, no excuse. The offense was one which would not admit of pardon, and James was immediately and instinctively convinced of Bothwell's guilt. The earl's reputation made his guilt highly probable—it was generally felt in Scotland that "he was never . . . honest to God nor man."[41] All the king's

[39] April 15, 1591, Bowes to Burghley, *ibid.*, pp. 501-502. These witchcraft trials have been written up frequently. See, e.g., H. Stafford, "Notes on Scottish Witchcraft Cases, 1590-91," in N. Downs, ed., *Essays in Honor of Conyers Read* (Chicago 1953), pp. 96-118.

[40] Calderwood, v, 160-161. This idea is repeated by, among others, William Roughead, *The Rebel Earl and Other Studies* (Edinburgh 1926), pp. 27-29, and M. A. Murray, "The 'Devil' of North Berwick," SHR, xv (1917-18), 310-321.

[41] The phrase is James Melvill's; R. Pitcairn, ed., *Autobiography and Diary of Mr. James Melvill*, p. 278.

energies were henceforth directed toward punishing him for his alleged crime.

Punishing Bothwell turned out to be very difficult to do, however. Quite apart from the weakness of the evidence against him, weakness of which James was well aware,[42] there was the well-known reluctance of the Scottish aristocracy to allow any of its members to be punished for any crime—a reluctance which had been forcibly brought home to James as recently as 1589, in the aftermath of Huntly's rebellion. The king was nevertheless implacably determined that this particular crime would be punished. Bothwell's fate thus involved much more than simply the punishment of a giddy and unstable trouble-maker. It became a test of the power of Maitland's adminis-trative system, and of that of the crown itself.

At first, matters went well enough for the government. Con-trary to the impression left by many historians, anarchy did not set in at once with Graham's accusation of Bothwell. In fact the earl was promptly mewed up in Edinburgh castle and denied the privileges normally accorded a prisoner of his rank. Bothwell was angry. He refused to say anything about the charge unless he received a general pardon for all offenses save this one, and he claimed that the accusation had origi-nated in England.[43] Even at this early stage the charges against Bothwell were being represented, by his wife at least, as an attack on the aristocracy as a whole.[44] James was angered by Bothwell's recalcitrance; he was further upset by the partial acquittal of Barbara Napier, one of the accused witches. He ordered the summons of an assize of error to reverse this de-cision, a most unusual procedure in Scottish law—"a great novelty, not hitherto practiced," Bowes called it.[45] James was

[42] May 5, 1591, Bowes to Burghley, csp scot, x, 511-513.

[43] April 27, 1591, Bowes to Burghley, *ibid.*, pp. 505-508.

[44] April 30, 1591, Lady Bothwell to Lord John Hamilton, Hamilton mss, box 1. See also the defense of Bothwell which appeared shortly after his escape from Edinburgh castle in June 1591, in *Warrender Papers*, ii, 154-164. The authorship of this defense is there ascribed to Robert Bruce the minister; this seems to me highly unlikely.

[45] May 9, 21, 26, June 8, 1591, Bowes to Burghley, csp scot, x, 514-515, 518, 518-520, 521-522. The quoted remark is in the letter of May 26. It was at this assize of error that James made the speech quoted above, p. 221.

merciless where witches were concerned. "Try by the mediciners' oaths if Barbara Napier be with bairn or not," he instructed Maitland. "Take no delaying answer. If you find she be not, to the fire with her presently, and cause bowel (disembowel) her publicly." At the same time, however, it became clear to the king that no assize of nobles would find Bothwell guilty of witchcraft. A convention of estates summoned in May to deal with the earl had been so poorly attended that the matter was not even discussed. So James resigned himself to exile for his errant cousin, and ordered Maitland to make arrangements to that end—but "his absence to be no nearer hand nor (than) Germany or Italy."[46]

So, on June 21, 1591, Maitland went to Edinburgh castle and told Bothwell that James would allow him to go into exile. Bothwell indicated some disposition to bargain over terms; Maitland left him to think the matter over. Instead, Bothwell acted. That same night he escaped from the castle—through a hole in the roof, according to Bowes—and fled to his border fastnesses. James was furious. He at once invoked the sentence for treason which had been passed and then suspended in 1589. Bothwell was now an outlawed traitor.[47]

The king summoned the lieges and on July 2 departed for the borders in pursuit of the condemned man. And now the results of his and Maitland's years of steady work on border administration began to be felt. Bothwell was unable to raise a party of any size. Lord Hume, the warden of the east march, and the laird of Buccleuch, who at first sided with Bothwell, found it advisable to abandon him, submit to the government, and even agree to go into exile for a time by way of expiation. Numbers of border lairds signed bands against Bothwell.[48] Buccleuch had originally been designated to succeed to Bothwell's position in Liddesdale; but now the king was persuaded to pardon Maitland's nephew Robert Ker of Cesford and put

---

[46] *Ibid.*, pp. 508-510, where the letter is misdated April. It was written between June 14 and 19. For the convention of estates see May 8, 1591, Bowes to Burghley, *ibid.*, pp. 510-511.

[47] June 22, 1591, Bowes to Burghley, *ibid.*, pp. 534-535. RPCS, IV, 643-644.

[48] *Ibid.*, pp. 648-649, 666-667. CSP SCOT, X, 558-559. See also P. Ridpath, *The Border History of England and Scotland* (London 1776), p. 677.

him in charge of Liddesdale. The chancellor's grip on border administration was tighter than ever.[49]

Bothwell was now furiously angry at Maitland. On July 26 he appeared in Edinburgh, rode to the Nether Bow, "and cried in, desiring any man to bid the chancellor come and take him."[50] He felt that he had been betrayed by Maitland, whose support he had been hopeful of getting.[51] He and Maitland had been friendly enough in recent months; Maitland had known of his association with Graham the wizard and had done nothing about it. But now, Maitland had become the chief of his enemies. Bothwell held Maitland responsible for his failure to obtain the erection of the lands of Kelso and Coldingham into a temporal lordship for himself. It was owing to Maitland that Hume and Buccleuch had deserted him. After his escape from Edinburgh castle, Maitland would have no dealings with him at all. He was, Bothwell said, "at his [Maitland's] horn, not at the king's."[52]

Bothwell was entirely mistaken in this assertion. It was James who was determined on his ruin, and, on one occasion, when Maitland "offered some motion in behalf of Bothwell, the king was offended."[53] Anyone who ventured to deal with Bothwell was punished: both Marischal and Athol were warded briefly in the summer of 1591 on this account, the latter in spite of his plea that he had met Bothwell only by accident.[54] It must be said, however, that Maitland made no serious effort to persuade James to change his attitude. The ruin of Bothwell would make for a more orderly administration, particularly on the border, since it was a necessary preliminary to the settlement of the Liddesdale question. Maitland was prepared, therefore, to run the risk of adding to his unpopularity among the aristocracy. He did feel, however, that he might

[49] The chief source for border affairs in the second half of 1591 is Bowes's correspondence, CPS SCOT, x, 539ff. See also *Border Papers*, i, 380-388.

[50] D. Moysie, *Memoirs of the Affairs of Scotland*, pp. 86, 160.

[51] May 5, 1591, Bowes to Burghley, CSP SCOT, x, 511-513.

[52] Calderwood, v, 138. July 14, 1591, Bowes to Burghley, CSP SCOT, x, 542-544. For Maitland's knowledge of Bothwell's association with Graham see August 12, 1593, Carey to Burghley, *Border Papers*, i, 486-489.

[53] July 14, 1591, Bowes to Burghley, CSP SCOT, x, 542-544.

[54] September 17, 1591, Bowes to Burghley, *ibid.*, pp. 571-572.

have been spared the additional odium incurred by James's revocation of all grants made in his minority and in that of his mother.[55] The occasion of this revocation was the king's twenty-fifth birthday. The chancellor reasoned that such revocations seldom had any practical effects, and that the only result would be to make him more hated than he was already. It was not without cause that, after Bothwell's public challenge in July, he "waged soldiers to keep his house in Edinburgh."[56]

Since the king remained in his implacable mood, Maitland decided that he might as well derive some benefit from it. So he put it to use to bring about the fall of his enemy Glamis. It came to the king's ears that Glamis was involved in a plot with Bothwell, directed against Maitland. That was enough for James; Glamis was promptly warded, and was released only on finding caution of five thousand pounds that he would stay north of the Dee.[57] Toward the end of the year Glamis was deprived of his offices. The treasury was left in the hands of the treasurer-depute, Sir Robert Melville, who had been doing the work of the office during Glamis' tenure; Melville's nominal superior, and Glamis' replacement on the court of session, was Arran's old colleague the earl of Montrose, who thus reentered public life after six years of political eclipse. Montrose returned as Maitland's ally, which he steadily remained; he was to be Maitland's successor, some years after Maitland's death, in the office of chancellor. Maitland remained deaf to all Glamis' overtures; to the proposal that the quarrel might be patched up by a marriage between his daughter and Glamis' son he replied that "he liked better the master's ward than the marriage of his son."[58]

The eclipse of Glamis, which followed shortly on the death of Bellenden the justice clerk, another of Maitland's recent rivals, tightened the chancellor's grip on the Scottish adminis-

---

[55] June 1591, James to Maitland, *ibid.*, pp. 508-510. June 25, July 14, Bowes to Burghley, *ibid.*, pp. 535-537, 542-544.

[56] Calderwood, v, 138.

[57] July 31, August 16, September 2, 1591, Bowes to Burghley, CSP SCOT, x, 549-552, 564-565, 567-568.

[58] November 10, 1591, Bowes to Burghley, *ibid.*, pp. 583-587.

tration. Bellenden's successor as justice clerk was Maitland's friend Cockburn of Ormiston; his nephew Clerkington, the new secretary, got Bellenden's seat on the bench. The new cohesiveness of the administration in the latter half of 1591 was reflected in its steady pressure on noble law-breakers. Particular attention was paid to the west, where numerous Cunninghams, Kennedys, Montgomerys, and Boyds were summoned and ordered to find caution for their future behavior. The goods of two obstinate Papists, the laird of Fentry and the master of Angus, were confiscated, and they were ordered to leave Scotland.[59] Finally, the council tightened up the system of cautions by refusing to accept the earl of Huntly, "or any others of his degree and rank," as a cautioner in a case arising from the feud between the earl of Caithness and Lord Oliphant: evidently it was too difficult to collect from these great men if the person for whom they stood caution misbehaved.[60]

Despite all its vigorous activity, however, the government could not lay its hands on Bothwell. His fellow aristocrats did not want to see him punished. One day in October, 1591, for instance, Bothwell turned up in Leith. Rumor of his presence was soon all over the town. The news was carried to Lennox and Huntly, who were golfing on the sands. They notified the king, "who so hastily took horse . . . that he passed without boots," but before James's arrival they permitted several of Bothwell's servants to escape, and when the house in which Bothwell was reportedly staying was searched, no trace of the earl could be found.[61] Bowes, in commenting on this and other similar episodes, remarked that the king's plans to capture Bothwell were always revealed to the earl in advance; "few or none will take Bothwell's feud for the king's sake or favor."[62]

Shortly after Christmas the roles were reversed. Bothwell, from being the pursued, became the pursuer and launched

[59] SRO, *Treasurer's Accounts*, October 1591-January 1592. The master of Angus was not compelled to go, owing to the death of his father the earl in July 1591, but he had to sign the articles of religion in order to succeed to the earldom. RPCS, IV, 619, 624. July 6, September 17, 1591, Bowes to Burghley, CSP SCOT, X, 541-542, 571-572.

[60] RPCS, IV, 676, 689.

[61] October 19, 1591, Bowes to Burghley, CSP SCOT, X, 578-579.

[62] November 10, 1591, Bowes to Burghley, *ibid.*, pp. 583-587.

the first of his famous raids against the king and Maitland. On the night of December 27, accompanied by Douglas of Spott, John Colville, and several other desperadoes, Bothwell obtained entry into Holyrood through a disused stable, "not without secret intelligence with some that were about his majesty." Fortunately for James and his chancellor, Spott's chief concern in joining this raid was to release some of his servants who were being detained in Holyrood. He set about this immediately upon entering the palace, and made so much noise that the intended victims were forewarned. Maitland was having supper with Sir Robert Melville; when he realized what was afoot, he precipitately fled to his rooms and barred the door after him, leaving poor Sir Robert to shift for himself. "The door of the chancellor's chamber was manfully debated by himself, and [he] caused his men to shoot out of the windows continually, and through doors" until help came, in the persons of some citizens of the Canongate, led by Sir Andrew Melville, one of the king's household officials. As for the king, he had taken refuge in a tower over the queen's chambers. The queen's door was assaulted with hammers by Bothwell himself, but the rescuers arrived before an entry could be made. Bothwell promptly fled; some of his followers were captured and hanged the next day.[63]

The most serious consequence of this raid was the atmosphere of suspicion and hostility it created at court. It was agreed on all sides that Bothwell must have had an accomplice. It was clear who Maitland thought the accomplice was: Lennox. Lennox was a Stewart, and Bothwell's cousin. He had recently married a daughter of that earl of Gowrie whom Maitland had helped to ruin in 1584. More convincing still, to Maitland's mind, was Lennox's behavior during the raid. Lennox's rooms in Holyrood were directly over Maitland's, and there was a connecting stair between them. During the fight the chancellor came up the stairs looking for help. Lennox sug-

---

[63] This account of the raid is that of Sir James Melville, *Memoirs*, pp. 397-400. Melville was present at the raid, in Lennox's chambers. The account in T. Thomson, ed., *The Historie and Life of King James the Sext*, pp. 243-245, suggests that Spott's behavior was prearranged, and designed to warn Maitland of what was happening. This seems improbable; if Maitland had been forewarned, he certainly would have taken precautions.

gested that Maitland instruct his men to keep fighting below, and that he himself take refuge in Lennox's rooms. Maitland regarded this as a transparent attempt to separate him from his friends, and returned to his rooms to continue the fight. After the brawl was over, he had the connecting passage walled up. Lennox was furious, and was barely prevented from attempting to kill him on their next meeting.[64]

Lennox was the chief object of Maitland's suspicion, but by no means the only one. "The whole Douglases and Stewarts together with the whole town of Leith are likewise suspected," wrote Forster, on January 4, 1592. Angus, Morton, and Mar, among others, were accused of complicity in the raid. They denied it, but told James that "they were as the rest of the nobility, in word and deed contrary to the chancellor, who, they said, abused His Grace [James], the nobility, and common weal."[65] James was badly shaken by the raid, but his confidence in his chancellor and his detestation of Bothwell had not abated. He raised a bodyguard of a hundred men and wrote to Elizabeth for money to help pay for it. In mid-January, on hearing that Bothwell was in the vicinity of Haddington, he rode hotly eastward in pursuit, fell into the Tyne, and was almost drowned—an adventure which was not calculated to make him feel more kindly toward his rebellious subject.[66]

So matters stood in January of 1592, on the eve of the event that was to lead to Maitland's fall. The chancellor's great administrative work was done. His governmental machine was constructed. It was a very imperfect machine, but it proved to be strong enough to survive the coming storm of aristocratic reaction, of which Bothwell's raid was the first intimation. Maitland still had one more major legislative contribution to make, but his lease of power was almost at an end. The crash was to come, with great suddenness, in the first few months of 1592.

[64] Melville, *Memoirs*, pp. 400, 402-403. January 15, 1592, Bowes to Burghley, CSP SCOT, X, 621-623.

[65] *Border Papers*, I, 390-391.

[66] January 3, 1592, instructions for Roger Ashton, *Warrender Papers*, II, 167-170. January 5, Bowes to Burghley, CSP SCOT, X, 616-619. Calderwood, V, 144. January 1592, advertisements . . . of Scotland, *Salisbury Papers*, IV, 177-178.

CHAPTER 11

MAITLAND'S FALL

In view of the highly charged and suspicious atmosphere at court in the wake of Bothwell's raid, Maitland thought it wise to be more friendly to those members of the upper aristocracy who were not suspected of having any connection with the outlawed earl. This meant chiefly Lord John Hamilton, Montrose, Crawford, Maxwell, and Huntly, who was again playing the Protestant.[1] The king encouraged this policy as much as he could, in order to prevent further defections to Bothwell.[2] Disaster almost immediately followed. On February 7, 1592, Huntly took advantage of a vague commission of lieutenancy to commit one of the most famous murders of the century. The victim was his hereditary enemy, the young and handsome earl of Moray.

In the course of 1591 the long-standing feud between these two earls had been waged more furiously than ever. The tendency of the court was, increasingly, to favor Huntly. James liked Huntly, and apparently disliked Moray. The suggestion in the famous ballad that James was jealous of Moray's attentions to the queen may be safely discounted; a man of James's temperament would not be thus moved. But Moray's association with Queen Anne may have prejudiced him in James's eyes in another way. For Anne was sympathetic to Bothwell, and she strongly disapproved of James's implacable attitude toward him, for which she blamed Maitland. The chancellor, she said, "seeks the wrack of the king's blood."[3]

---

[1] August 11, 1591, Bowes to Burghley, csp scot, x, 559-560. By the end of the year Huntly was even permitting Peter Young and David Lindsay to "reform" his wife; November 29-30, Ashton to Bowes, *ibid.*, pp. 593-594.

[2] January 15, February 5, 1592, Bowes to Burghley, *ibid.*, pp. 621-623, 631-633.

[3] August 11, 1591, Walter Ker to Forster, *Border Papers*, i, 383-384.

And, in fact, by the end of 1591, there were definite reports that Moray had allied himself with Bothwell; these naturally prejudiced the king against him still more.[4]

By the latter half of 1591 Moray was getting the worst of the quarrel with Huntly; so, early in 1592, through the mediation of his cousin Lord Ochiltree, he signified his willingness to patch up an agreement. For this purpose he came south to Fife, to his mother's house at Donibristle, two miles from the northern side of the Queensferry. Here, on February 7, Huntly trapped him. On that day the king went hunting; he had given orders that no boats should cross the Forth. Huntly went to James with a story that Bothwell's accomplice John Colville was lurking in Fife and sought permission to pursue him. Whether James gave him permission is not clear. What is clear is that Huntly crossed the Forth with forty men under pretense of having such permission and promptly attacked Donibristle. Moray defended himself long and valiantly; Huntly finally had to set the house on fire. Moray's ultimate fate is well known: his successful sally from the burning house and his death by the water's edge. The story that Huntly personally gashed the dying man's face with a dagger, and was told that he had spoilt a better face than his own, we may take leave to doubt, as a mere romantic embellishment.[5]

This outrage, committed so close to the capital, produced an immediate and powerful wave of opinion demanding condign punishment for Huntly. "The people cry out of (at) the cruelty of the deed," wrote Bowes's agent Roger Ashton in concluding his account of the event.[6] Popular fury was kept at fever pitch by the ministers, who hated and feared Huntly

---

[4] Sir James Melville of Halhill, *Memoirs of His Own Life*, pp. 406-407.

[5] The contemporary accounts do not mention this. On the other hand, R. Chambers, *Domestic Annals of Scotland from the Reformation to the Revolution*, I, 134-137, gives an account of a murder in 1580, in which the leader of the party of murderers was compelled by his followers to stab the dead body of the victim, so that he could not disclaim responsibility later on. It is in this form—that of stabbing the dead body of Moray—that the tale is told by Archbishop J. Spottiswoode, *History of the Church of Scotland*, II, 419-420, and by the Fraser chronicler, W. Mackay, ed., *Chronicles of the Frasers*, SHS, 1st series, XLVII (Edinburgh 1905), p. 214.

[6] February 8, 1592, Ashton to Bowes, CSP SCOT, X, 635-636. Ashton was in Edinburgh at the time; his account is circumstantial and is the most reliable to be had.

and had looked on Moray as a pillar of the kirk, and by the murdered man's mother, who brought the corpse to Edinburgh two days after the murder, to show it to the king. James was not enthusiastic about this, and went hunting instead. The lady was persistent. She would not permit Moray's burial until he had been avenged.[7] She had a picture of the corpse drawn, and presented it to the king, along with one of the bullets found in the viscera.[8] James's reaction to these unwelcome souvenirs is not recorded.

Almost immediately popular opinion concluded that the king and Maitland were somehow involved in Huntly's deed. Ochiltree furiously declared that, besides himself, only the king and Maitland knew that Moray was at Donibristle; in council he "prayed the king in some rough language to show his forwardness" in punishing Huntly; "otherwise the king's self should be holden suspect herein." The story went round that "Huntly received a blank commission subscribed by the king's chancellor to cause Moray to present himself in the court, and in case he should disobey, to slay him."[9] Huntly certainly had some sort of commission of lieutenancy, for it was revoked by the privy council on February 8, the day after the murder.[10] But James and Maitland both denied that Huntly had any commission directed against Moray. "The chancellor is greatly condemned in this matter by Moray's friends. He knew the earl of Huntly was to ride and did not stay him. But the chancellor says he [Huntly] promised him he would not ride any way but [to] go to the king."[11]

Later historians have tended to accept James's exculpation. The consensus is that the lines in the ballad are generally true:

> Oh, wae worth ye, Huntly,
>   And wherefore did ye sae?
> I bade you bring him to me
>   But forbade you him to slay.

[7] He was still unburied in February 1598. RPCS, v, 444-445.

[8] Calderwood, v, 145.

[9] *Ibid.*, p. 146. February 17, 1592, Bowes to Burghley, CSP SCOT, x, 639-643.

[10] RPCS, IV, 725.

[11] February 10, 1592, Ashton to Bowes, CSP SCOT, x, 638-639.

Maitland, however, has not escaped so easily, at least not since the publication of Donald Gregory's *History of the Western Highlands and Isles of Scotland* in 1836. In this famous work Gregory connects the murder of Moray with an almost simultaneous murder on the other side of Scotland. On February 4, three days before Moray's death, John Campbell of Calder was shot by an assassin hired by some of his Campbell cousins. His death was, in the first instance, due to the fierce struggle within the Campbell family for control of the young earl of Argyll during his minority, a struggle which Calder had won. There were strong connections between Moray and Calder.[12] It was, therefore, very much to Huntly's interest to encourage the jealous Campbell cadets, the lairds of Lochnell, Glenurchy, and Ardkinglas, to revolt against Calder's control of the young earl, lest all the considerable resources of the Campbells be thrown into the feud on Moray's side. It may well be that Huntly knew of the plot which culminated in Calder's death. Gregory, however, goes much further. He assumes the existence of a widespread conspiracy, the purpose of which was to destroy not only Moray and Calder, but also the young earl of Argyll and his brother. This would result in the elevation of Lochnell to the earldom. Lochnell would then reward his accomplices, including Maitland, with various pieces of property. Maitland's share was to have been the barony of Pinkerton, in East Lothian.[13]

This theory of conspiracy, which has been accepted by virtually every historian of the period since Gregory's time, either uncritically like Lang, or cautiously like Miss Staf-

[12] The following abbreviated genealogy shows the relationship:

Campbell of Calder d. 1592	Mary Keith	regent Moray d. 1570	(1) Agnes Keith	(2) Colin 6th earl of Argyll	Margaret Campbell	Stewart of Doune
				Archibald, 7th earl (a minor, 1592)		
			Elizabeth		earl of Moray d. 1592	

Campbell of Calder = Mary Keith; regent Moray = Agnes Keith (1); Agnes Keith = Colin 6th earl of Argyll (2); Margaret Campbell = Stewart of Doune

[13] D. Gregory, *The History of the Western Highlands and Isles of Scotland*, pp. 244-259.

ford,[14] rests upon one lone document—a confession made by Ardkinglas. The circumstances were these. In June 1593 Ardkinglas and Glenurchy were formally accused in the king's court in Edinburgh of the murder of Calder. Nothing came of this immediately, but the young earl, and Calder's friends in the clan, employing the more rough and ready methods available in Argyll, tracked down and executed the actual assassin and his immediate employer, Lochnell's younger brother. Then, in May 1594, Ardkinglas was seized and threatened with torture. In his desperate effort to avoid incriminating himself too deeply, he attempted to throw the principal blame on Glenurchy, and in so doing, he told of a murder band signed by Maitland and Huntly, and by Glenurchy, but which he himself had refused to sign despite Glenurchy's repeated importunities. Glenurchy, when he heard of Ardkinglas's confession, at once repudiated it—and so did Ardinglas. After his release Ardkinglas withdrew the whole story of the murder band; it was "invented to eschew the trouble that might follow on me for Calder's slaughter," and "for eschewing of the present torture." Significantly enough, however, Ardkinglas did not deny that he had been involved in the murder of Calder, a fact which lends credence to the remainder of his statement of repudiation.

Circumstantial evidence also tells against the conspiracy theory. Quite apart from the inherent improbability of anyone of Maitland's astuteness signing so damaging a document for the sake of a reward which depended on the two murders that did *not* take place rather than on those that did, none of the contemporary accounts associates Maitland with the death of Calder. In this connection the *Historie and Life of King James the Sext* is most revealing. The author of this chronicle, probably Bothwell's accomplice John Colville, was bitterly hostile to Maitland and freely accused him of plotting with Huntly against Moray. He also accused the chancellor of influencing Moray against Huntly, through the instrumentality of Calder, who was "very familiar with chancellor Maitland."

[14] A. Lang, *A History of Scotland since the Roman Occupation*, II, 355-356. H. Stafford, *James VI of Scotland and the Throne of England*, p. 65.

Calder, then, was one of Maitland's friends in the clan; and, in fact, Maitland was associated with Calder as one of the curators of the young earl of Argyll. Furthermore, in his account of the murder of Calder, the author of the *Historie* mentions a band directed against Argyll, and signed by Huntly, Lochnell, Glenurchy, and "divers others" of Argyll's vassals—but not by Maitland.[15] The confession of Lochnell's brother, who was executed for his share in the murder, also mentions such a band.[16] There seems little reason to doubt, then, that Ardkinglas, knowing of this band, did just as he said he did, and invented the signature of Maitland, who was in a very uncertain political position in May of 1594 and still very unpopular, and of Lord Maxwell, who was conveniently dead, in order to remove some of the blame from himself.

One final circumstance may be mentioned. The last great political quarrel of Maitland's life was with the earl of Mar in 1595. Mar had been one of those who had witnessed Ardkinglas's repudiation of his confession. Nothing would have been easier for Mar than to say that he did not believe the repudiation; yet Mar, who was an honorable man, did not do so. The logical conclusion is, that Mar did not believe in Maitland's guilt.[17]

The murder of Moray resembles that of Lord Darnley twenty-five years before in many ways, and in nothing so much as its aftermath. Maitland, who was worried by the violence of public feeling in Edinburgh, urged James repeatedly to take swift action against Huntly. This was precisely what James would not do. The king was obsessed by his hatred of Bothwell; to him, Moray was simply one of Bothwell's allies who had got his just deserts. On the day after the murder James callously went hunting within view of the smouldering ruins of Donibristle. An expedition against Huntly was decided upon, and then put off until March, on the ground that

15 T. Thomson, ed., *The Historie and Life of King James the Sext*, pp. 246-249. The Fraser chronicler, who was also hostile to Maitland, also testifies to the friendship between Maitland and Calder, *Chronicles of the Frasers*, p. 211.

16 A. I. Cameron, ed., *The Warrender Papers*, II, 246-251.

17 Most of the documents in this affair, together with a convenient genealogy of the house of Campbell, are printed in J. R. N. Macphail, ed., *Highland Papers*, I, SHS, 2nd series, V (Edinburgh 1914), 142-194.

time was needed to gather the lieges; however reasonable the delay might have been, the effect was spoiled by the report that the forces thus gathered would be used first to pursue Bothwell.[18]

So James, like his mother before him, would take no action against the guilty party. He did, indeed, order that Huntly be warded; the earl obeyed with such alacrity that everyone was convinced that he was about to receive a judicial white-washing, as had Mary's Bothwell. As in Mary's case, James's inaction led to popular ferment, the product of Calvinist morality, whipped up by the preachers, and to a strong suspicion of royal complicity in the crime. Huntly, of course, could not pretend, like Mary's favorite, that he had nothing to do with the murder, and his first line of defense, that he was acting as the king's lieutenant, further implicated James.[19] But, unlike his mother, the king rode out the storm. He had a lightning-conductor, in the person of his chancellor.

That Maitland rather than James bore the brunt of the popular fury was owing in part to Bothwell. The latter chose this moment—February 1592—to address to "his loving brethren, the ministry and eldership of Edinburgh" a long and extremely skillful piece of invective against Maitland. The chancellor was accused of being "the author of all distress which honest men have sustained within this realm these ten or twelve years bypast." It was Maitland who was responsible for the deaths of the regent Morton and the earl of Gowrie; Maitland had been the servant of Spain, and only turned against that power when he discovered that Huntly had a greater share of the Spanish confidence than he; it was Maitland who had written some of the "infamous and heretical"

[18] February 11, 1592, Ashton to Hudson, CSP SCOT, x, 636. February 13, March 11, Bowes to Burghley, *ibid.*, pp. 637-638, 653-654. Calderwood, v, 144. A contributing factor to the postponement of the expedition was the usual shortage of funds. In February 1592 the members of the newly raised body-guard mutinied because they had not been paid, and seized some of Maitland's baggage, which was not released until their pay was guaranteed. *Ibid.*, p. 146, February 17, Bowes to Burghley, CSP SCOT, x, 639-643.
[19] February 13, 1592, Bowes to Burghley, *ibid.*, pp. 637-638. At one point, while he was in ward, Huntly tried to pretend that some of his enraged followers had slain Moray against his orders. March 18, Bowes to Burghley, *ibid.*, pp. 654-656. Nobody believed this.

documents signed by archbishop Adamson. And, of course, it was Maitland who had enmeshed him in the charge of witchcraft, and who had plotted the murder of Moray. And why? In order to accomplish "the overthrowing of his majesty's race and name," and of the whole nobility: "his crafty device, to cause . . . every one of us to destroy another; esteeming the destruction of . . . any one of us, should have made him elbowroom, and given an occasion to a puddock-stool of a night to occupy the place of two ancient cedars."[20]

How much impression this made on the Edinburgh clergy is difficult to say; it seems likely that they were more influenced by the behavior of James. On March 7 the Edinburgh presbytery proposed that Huntly and his accomplices be excommunicated. James, nettled by the ministers' earlier refusal to equate Bothwell's crime with Huntly's, rejoined that Bothwell and his friends were equally worthy of condemnation, "and said it would not be well till noblemen and gentlemen got license to break ministers' heads."[21] This reply led to a serious weakening in the alliance between the government and the kirk which Maitland had worked so hard to create. The ministers began to look decidedly askance at the king's casual treatment of Huntly's crime; they began to feel that perhaps Bothwell, who was posing as an impeccable Protestant, was more sinned against than sinning. Bothwell, in fact, was the real beneficiary of the murder of Moray, because it gave him a party. All those who believed that the punishment of Huntly should be the first order of business for the government—and there were many such: the kirk, the whole Stewart connection, led by Athol and the angry Ochiltree, and, eventually, the English government—came to side with Bothwell, simply because he was the symbol of the king's mistaken policy. James's obsessive hatred of Bothwell thus betrayed him into the worst tactical blunder of his entire reign in Scotland. By insisting that Bothwell be punished before Huntly, he actually delayed Bothwell's ruin, by making Bothwellians of all Huntly's enemies.

20 Calderwood, v, 150-156. For another example of Bothwell's invective against Maitland, probably written toward the end of 1592, see CSP SCOT, x, 825-828.
21 Calderwood, v, 147-148.

James and Maitland were aware of the hostility the king's policy aroused, especially among the Protestant citizenry of Edinburgh; so they decided to leave the capital for a while, in the hope that, in time, the popular temper would cool. The purpose of their departure was apparent, however, and the discontent did not abate. There was a temporary relaxation of tension early in March, when Huntly warded himself in Blackness, but in less than two weeks he was at large again, and in the meantime the king, in a long conversation with the prior of Blantyre, a Stewart, had made his policy perfectly clear. The Stewarts, he said, must renounce Bothwell before he would move against Huntly.[22]

Maitland's position was becoming more and more untenable. He had been regarded for so long as the real ruler of Scotland that the king's present policy was attributed entirely to him. This view of the situation was eagerly disseminated by Bothwell and his followers, who may have sincerely believed it. "It is . . . cried out by the servants of God," wrote one of the Bothwellians to Archibald Douglas, that "that profane man the chancellor" was responsible for Moray's murder.[23] Maitland's enemies now had an issue, and they all combined to pull him down. At their head stood the queen.

Queen Anne had several grounds for hostility to Maitland. She knew of his early advocacy of the Navarre match for James. She liked both Bothwell and Moray. Her household was filled with people who disliked Maitland and made their dislike known—people like William Fowler, her secretary till September 1591, a protegé of Bothwell's[24]—and the head of her household was the duke of Lennox. She did not care for Lady Maitland.[25] Above all, she felt that the chancellor was withholding from her something that was rightfully hers: the lordship of Musselburgh.

22 February 24, March 18, 21, 1592, Ashton to Bowes, csp scot, x, 648-649, 658-660, csp scot, xi, 74-75 (where the letter is misdated 1593).
23 May 25, 1592, Francis Tennant to Douglas, *Salisbury Papers*, iv, 201-202.
24 For Fowler see H. W. Meikle, J. Craigie, and J. Purves, eds., *The Works of William Fowler*, iii, Scottish Text Society publication (Edinburgh 1940), introduction, pp. xxi-xxvii.
25 January 26, 1592, Bowes to Burghley, csp scot, x, 625-627.

In 1589 James, as a morrowing gift to his bride, had assigned to her the temporalities of the abbey of Dunfermline. Specifically exempted from this grant was the lordship of Musselburgh, which Maitland had held since 1587. The queen had never ceased to agitate for the nullification of this exemption, and, doubtless at her instigation, the Danish government in June 1591 addressed a formal request to Maitland that he see to it that all the grants promised to the queen were in fact put into her hands. Instead of yielding Musselburgh, Maitland obtained a new charter of erection and promptly began to sell parts of the property, in an attempt to realize on the grant in case he had to surrender it at some future date.[26] The queen was very angry.

The consequence of all this mounting hostility was what might be called Maitland's "fall." On March 30, 1592, the king ordered him to leave the court and remain away until he was summoned. He obeyed, and retired to Lethington.[27] He had tried hard to avoid this command, which he had feared for some time. At the end of February it was rumored that he might go abroad, as a way of saving face; in mid-March, that he might offer to put himself in ward and stand trial "in all things to be objected against him for the slaughter of Moray," but then he was reminded that the earl of Arran had been ruined in just this way in 1585.[28] So the blow fell. Yet in a sense the term "fall" is misleading, because Maitland did not lose his master's confidence. Gratitude was never one of James's outstanding characteristics, but he knew—none better—that he, and not Maitland, was responsible for the policy for which Maitland was being blamed. James knew that Maitland's loyalty and Maitland's political objectives had not been altered. He fully intended to restore the chancellor to favor and power. It was merely a matter of timing.

26 J. T. G. Craig, ed., *Papers Relative to the Marriage of King James the Sixth of Scotland with Princess Anne of Denmark*, pp. 17-18. Sir W. Fraser, ed., *Memorials of the Earls of Haddington*, II (Edinburgh 1889), 62-64. RMS, IV, 671-672, 681-682, 686. SRO, *Privy Seal Register*, LXIII, 66-69. SRO, *Register of Deeds*, XL, 128.

27 Calderwood, v, 149.

28 February 27, March 18, 1592, Bowes to Burghley, CSP SCOT, X, 643-647, 654-656.

Maitland knew all this; he knew that his day would come again, and that he had but to wait. But he was not willing to wait. For the first time in his career, Maitland began to betray a certain impatience. It was as if he knew that the sands were running out. And so, indeed, they were. Maitland was almost fifty. It was true that his father had lived to a patriarchal age, but his brother, secretary Lethington, had died at forty-seven. Maitland also knew his master's mercurial temper and affections, and the king was now surrounded by his enemies. Every week's delay made his ultimate return less likely.

Before his departure Maitland had extracted a promise from James to hold a convention of estates in April, "at which time he will either have such a course fallen forth as may content the best sort, or else he will leave court and all."[29] In the meantime he tried to improve his political position. Through the good offices of the earl of Mar he patched up his quarrel with that other political outcast, the master of Glamis, and with Glamis' father-in-law, Morton. On the death of his old friend Cowdenknowes, he strongly urged James to give the captaincy of Edinburgh castle to Mar rather than Lennox, and James complied, perhaps owing more to the representations of England than of Maitland.[30] In all this Maitland was doing his best to remove the label which Bothwell and his followers were attempting to pin on him, that of being the "principal defender of all the Papists in Scotland."[31]

Maitland had high hopes of the proposed convention of estates; but the king speedily repented of his promise to summon such a meeting. The time was not ripe, in his view; so he avoided holding it by going north in April, ostensibly in pursuit of Bothwell. The convention had to be postponed. James was bent on the most formal possible condemnation of Bothwell, however, and this meant condemnation in Parliament; so,

[29] April 11, 1592, Ashton to Bowes, *ibid.*, pp. 667-668.

[30] April 11, May 3, 1592, Ashton to Bowes, *ibid.*, pp. 667-668, 673-674. April 22, June 6, Bowes to Burghley, *ibid.*, pp. 670-671, 684-687. The chancellor's reconciliation with Morton was helped by the settling of a quarrel between the latter and Maitland's nephew, young Cesford. RPCS, IV, 738-739.

[31] June 4, 1592, Francis Tennant to Archibald Douglas, *Salisbury Papers*, IV, 205-206.

on his return from the north early in May, he decided to proceed with the Parliament which had been planned for late in the month. He and Maitland had both hoped that the latter could return to court in advance of Parliament, but the public temper was still too hostile; so Maitland had to be content with a visit from the king, "to the chancellor's great comfort."[32]

Maitland took advantage of the king's visit to convince him of the necessity of using the forthcoming Parliament to repair the breach between the government and the kirk. This, he suggested, could best be done by a partial repeal of the Black Acts and by giving legal recognition to the presbyterian structure. James accepted this advice. Thus originated what was to be the best-known legislation of the Parliament of 1592, the series of enactments which the historians of the kirk, looking back upon them with nostalgia from the bishop-ridden seventeenth century, labelled collectively the Golden Act.

This title was an exaggeration. The enactments of 1592, in the words of two leading authorities, "made no real innovation, caused no dislocation, and cost nothing."[33] What they did was to recognize the legality of the existing structure of the kirk: General Assembly, provincial synods, presbyteries, and kirk sessions. The disciplinary and administrative powers of the presbyteries were recognized, and all presentations to benefices were to be made to them. The act of 1584 which gave administrative jurisdiction to bishops was repealed; it was further enacted that the act of the same year declaring the king's jurisdiction to be superior to that of the kirk was not to be construed to limit the power of the kirk over heresy, excommunication, collation and deprivation of ministers, or anything else "having warrant of the word of God." Any minister deprived by a presbytery automatically lost his benefice. Committees were set up, as usual, to see what, if anything, could be done about the ministers' stipends and the further "plant-

<hr>

[32] April 22, May 13, 1592, Bowes to Burghley, csp scot, x, 670-671, 674-675. May 3, Ashton to Bowes, *ibid.*, pp. 673-674. D. Moysie, *Memoirs of the Affairs of Scotland*, p. 93.

[33] W. C. Dickinson and G. Donaldson, eds., *A Source Book of Scottish History*, iii, 48.

ing" of kirks. At the same time the privy council authorized administrative cooperation with the commissioners of the General Assembly for the purpose of planting kirks, pursuing Jesuits, and inquiring into the condition of the kirk generally at the local level. In 1593 the kirk was authorized to apply to the courts for letters of horning against anyone who defied the authority of the church courts.[34]

This is what the Parliament of 1592 did for the kirk. The things it left undone were just as important. It did not repeal the "Black Acts," or the act of annexation of 1587, in spite of James's promise to the General Assembly of May 1592 that it would do both these things.[35] It did not abolish lay patronage; patrons had to make their presentations via the presbyteries, but the presbyteries had to accept the patron's nominee if he was qualified. It did not even abolish episcopacy. There were still people around after 1592 called bishops, who were distinguished from ordinary ministers only by the fact that they had a vote in Parliament. The General Assembly of May 1592 had asked, as it had in 1587, that the prelates be deprived of their parliamentary position, and that a plan be worked out whereby "the ministry should succeed . . . in the prelates' place." James was as hostile as ever to this plan, and his temper was not improved by a series of laudatory sermons on Knox, Buchanan, and the regent Moray.[36] So the question of parliamentary representation remained in abeyance. No accurate line of demarcation was drawn by this Parliament between the jurisdictions of church and state. The "warrant of the word of God" was certainly open to conflicting interpretations; and, in fact, while this Parliament was in session the question as to whether the civil magistrate had the authority to interrupt a seditious sermon was reopened in Edinburgh, and left undetermined.[37]

The "Golden Act," then, really represented the recognition of a *fait accompli* rather than a comprehensive religious settle-

[34] APS, III, 541-542, 545-547, 553-554. APS, IV, 16-17. RPCS, IV, 753-754.
[35] Calderwood, v, 159-160.
[36] *Ibid.*, pp. 156-159, 166.
[37] *Ibid.*, pp. 161-162.

ment, and it left a good many loose ends.[38] But for all that, it meant a real gain for the kirk, and the ministers knew to whom they were beholden. "The kirk is indebted to Mr. John Maitland . . . for the same, who induced the king to pass it at that time, for what respect I leave it to God, who works for the comfort of his kirk by all kinds of instruments," wrote James Melvill discreetly.[39] Calderwood was much more blunt: the chancellor's purpose, he wrote, was "to win the hearts of the ministers and people, alienated from him for his hounding out of Huntly against the earl of Moray."[40] Certainly Maitland did hope to regain his popularity, and thereby his power, by these enactments, but they represented more than mere expediency. They followed logically from his policy of the last six years, of cementing the alliance between the government and the kirk. Owing to the political exigencies of the moment, they failed of their immediate purpose. But in the story of Maitland's career they have a special significance: they stand as his last great act of constructive statesmanship. With the Parliament of 1592 the creative part of Maitland's political life came to an end.

[38] This is the judgment of G. Donaldson, "The Polity of the Scottish Church 1560-1600," *Records of the Scottish Church History Society*, XI (1955), 225-226.
[39] R. Pitcairn, ed., *The Autobiography and Diary of Mr. James Melvill*, p. 298.
[40] Calderwood, v, 162.

CHAPTER 12

THE LAST YEARS

THE last three and a half years of Maitland's life were a period of frustration and anticlimax. The chancellor tried hard to regain his once-great power and to maintain his influence over King James, but he had very little success. The king turned from him to other advisers, or more frequently, to no adviser at all. James wanted no more tutors, and after Maitland's death the office of chancellor remained vacant for three years. On the appointment of the Octavians to office early in 1596 James "was very merry, saying he would no more use chancellor or other great men in those his causes but such as he might convict and were hangable."[1]

Yet, paradoxically enough, the years which saw the decline of Maitland's influence also saw the triumph of his policy. The rebellions of Huntly and Bothwell were at bottom directed against the growing power of the crown; and James, for his own sake, could not afford to abandon completely the man who was most responsible for his own increased authority. This fact accounts for Maitland's anomalous position during these years, a position of disgrace which was not really disgrace. James kept Maitland away from court because it relieved the pressure on him when he did so; but he often rode to Lethington or Lauder to ask Maitland's advice—or to appear to do so. Maitland had very little power during these years, but he never lost his chancellorship, and his team of subordinate officials retained their positions. They were far more indispensable to the king than he was.

There is some evidence that Maitland's aristocratic foes were gradually becoming aware that Maitland's creation of

[1] January 11, 1596, George Nicolson to Bowes, CSP SCOT, XII, 116-118.

an official class was more dangerous to them in the long run than was the chancellor as an individual. Among the enactments of the Parliament of 1592 was one which forbade for the future the erection of church lands into temporal lordships, except in the case of men who were already lords of Parliament.[2] If enforced, this act would have made it impossible for the government to use permanent possession of the church lands as bait and as reward for loyal service, and would have resulted in the weakening of the official class. In this case the customary nonenforcement of Scottish statutes worked to the advantage of the crown.

James was certainly aware of the implications of this act, and it seems likely that he assented to it for the same reason that he assented to the Golden Act, namely, that it was necessary in order to assure the condemnation of Bothwell. The earl was duly declared a traitor and forfeited; his heirs were disinherited also, in order to prevent any collusive transfer of property.[3] Bothwell's reply was prompt and vigorous. On June 27, 1592, he launched his second raid against the king's person. James was at Falkland, where he had gone to enjoy the hunting after the dissolution of Parliament. Bothwell collected a group of border ruffians and the master of Gray and launched a midnight attack on the back door of the palace.[4] Fortunately, the king had been warned, Bothwell was beaten off and returned to the borders. An attempt at pursuit, launched in July, proved futile.

The aftermath of this raid produced one very revealing episode. Lord John Hamilton captured some of Bothwell's accomplices. James was anxious to hang them; Lord John wanted their lives spared, and when he failed to get the requisite assurances from the king, he simply let his prisoners go.[5] Lord John had no affection for Bothwell. The most probable cause of his action lies in the shifting attitude of the kirk.

[2] APS, III, 544. D. Masson, RPCS, 2nd series, I, intro., cxliii.
[3] APS, III, 531-539.
[4] June 28, 1592, Ashton to Hudson, CSP SCOT, x, 717-718.
[5] July 2, 4, 1592, Bowes to Burghley, *ibid.*, pp. 716-717, 718-720. See also *Salisbury Papers*, XIII, 470-472.

Lord John, after a youth of religious indifference, became steadily more devout as he approached later middle age.[6] And the kirk, at this time, was looking more and more favorably upon Bothwell. "The grudge of Moray's slaughter," wrote Bowes, "so works in the hearts of most men, and in the well affected, that they will not give their endeavors to touch Bothwell . . . they think that by the welter of the state the evil counsellors and instruments in the king's chamber shall be defeated and removed."[7] After Bothwell's raid the clergy carefully pointed the moral. Robert Bruce informed James that it was an indication of divine disapproval of his failure to punish Huntly. James was unimpressed. He replied that, after all, Bothwell's first raid had preceded Moray's murder.[8]

Bothwell's attack brought the fallen chancellor back to court once more. After the dissolution of Parliament Maitland had retired to Lethington, apparently because he was ill. While there, he heard rumors of the raid and warned James; and so the king restored him to favor early in July. But he was not restored to power; Bowes remarked that he was "not called to manage matters as he was wont to be."[9] Nor was he to stay at court very long, even in this reduced position. Early in August the Edinburgh kirk session angered the king by calling for the punishment of Huntly and the "reformation of his [James's] chamber"—i.e., the expulsion from court of Huntly's sympathizers. Maitland was unable to smooth matters over.[10] A few days later the chancellor encountered Lennox, Hume, and the master of Glamis on the road between Edinburgh and Dalkeith; "some evil countenances shewed," and a brawl was narrowly averted. Maitland hastened to the king with the tale of his perils and woes; James was not at all sympathetic. If Maitland could not even assure the friendly attitude of the kirk, he was clearly still a political liability.

6 In 1593, when the king ventured to hint at religious toleration, Lord John reacted so furiously that James had to pretend he had suggested it only to test Lord John's staunchness in the faith. Calderwood, v, 268-269.

7 June 12, 1592, Bowes to Burghley, CSP SCOT, x, 693-695.

8 Calderwood, v, 168-169.

9 July 16, 1592, Bowes to Burghley, CSP SCOT, x, 729.

10 August 6, 1592, Bowes to Burghley, ibid., pp. 745-746.

The chancellor took the rather broad hint, and retired to Lethington once more.[11]

James would not altogether abandon his chancellor, however. He sent a message to Maitland to say that he still thought well of him, and he did his best to reconcile the chancellor with his enemies. But the dominant faction at court, headed by Lennox and Queen Anne, and supported by the master of Glamis, who now returned to court, remained implacable; only the earl of Mar seemed at all disposed to be friendly. So the king decided that the best solution would be to send Maitland abroad. On September 6, 1592, a patent was made out appointing him ambassador to France.[12] Maitland was willing to go. He sent the king a long letter defending his actions and blaming his abrupt withdrawal from court on the malice of his enemies; for the sake of peace, however, he was prepared to accept voluntary exile.[13] The chancellor was in real fear of his life. By mid-September he had taken refuge in the west with his friends Douglas of Lincluden and the laird of Lochinvar.[14]

Maitland's departure made the court a good deal less contentious for James, but it did nothing to solve his political problems. The kirk grew increasingly suspicious of the king's intentions, particularly in view of the close relationship between Huntly and Lennox, who was now the dominant figure at court. In mid-November an informal convention of ministers in Edinburgh decided to proclaim a general fast for two successive Sundays in December, "that by true humiliation and unfeigned repentance, the fearful judgments of God that hang over this land may be prevented." In the ministers' view the country was being subverted to Papistry and atheism, was perishing in ignorance through lack of pastors, and was "over-

[11] August 12, 1592, Bowes to Burghley, *ibid.*, pp. 752-754. D. Moysie, *Memoirs of the Affairs of Scotland*, p. 96, attributes Maitland's departure to the hostility of Lennox.

[12] CSP SCOT, X, 769-770.

[13] This letter is endorsed "delivered the ix of September 1592," but its content indicates that it was written before the issue of the ambassadorial commission. A. I. Cameron, ed., *The Warrender Papers*, II, 177-181.

[14] September 10, 1592, Forster to Burghley, *Border Papers*, I, 405-406. October 8, Lowther to Burghley, *ibid.*, pp. 411-412.

flowing with all kind(s) of impiety . . . contempt of the Word, blasphemy . . . treason, innocent bloodshed, adulteries, witch-crafts, and other abominable crimes." Hence the fast.[15] A more practical remedy was the appointment of a committee of eight ministers which was to meet at least once a week to review the state of the kirk and to exert pressure on James.[16] For the king's further edification, a Mr. William Row preached a ser-mon in which he said that "the king might be excommunicated in case of contumacy and disobedience to the will of God."[17] A few weeks later the ministers raised a dreadful clamor at the sudden reappearance in court of their old enemy Arran, brought back, so it was reported, in order to make accusations against Maitland. James paid Arran no heed, and he soon de-parted; but the king was very angry that the ministers should have preached so violently against Arran and Huntly and said nothing about Bothwell.[18] James finally lost patience when, on the first Sunday of the December fast, the hotheaded John Davidson declared that the king had been infected since the time of the first duke of Lennox, and that no justice could be had for Moray "howbeit great severity had been used against the servants of God." James demanded, and got, a public re-traction and apology.[19] But relations with the kirk were very strained.

As ominous for James as the hostility of the kirk was the growing conviction on the part of the English government that Bothwell might be useful. England was nervous about the potential danger represented by the Scottish Catholics, who were once more rumored to be plotting with Spain.[20] James's unwillingness to crush Huntly after Moray's murder seemed an act of signal folly, or worse; and Bowes reported that Mait-land's fall had been due to his hostility to Huntly.[21] Elizabeth

[15] Calderwood, v, 179-180.
[16] Ibid., pp. 181-185.
[17] Ibid., p. 179.
[18] November 30, 1592, Bowes to Burghley, CSP SCOT, x, 818-820. Calderwood, v, 187-188.
[19] Ibid., pp. 191-192.
[20] H. G. Stafford, James VI of Scotland and the Throne of England, pp. 74-75.
[21] June 16, 1592, Bowes to Elizabeth, CSP SCOT, x, 695-698.

had no confidence in any coalition headed by Lennox. Throughout the summer and fall of 1592 she sent James a steady
stream of advice, culminating in a letter indirectly urging a
pardon for Bothwell, on condition that the latter revealed all
he knew about the Catholic plot.[22] Elizabeth had not yet committed herself to Bothwell. But she allowed him to move about
freely in north England, to James's great annoyance, and
she gave James no money.[23] She was getting ready once more
to revert to the traditional English policy of backing a noble
faction against the Scottish government.

All the worst fears of Elizabeth and the kirk were suddenly
confirmed. On December 27, 1592, George Ker, the brother
of Lord Newbattle, was seized as he was about to sail for the
continent. On his person were found a number of letters from
sundry Scottish Catholics and Jesuits to their continental con-
frères, and—much more alarming—a number of blanks signed
by Huntly, Angus, and Errol, and Huntly's chief adviser, Gordon of Auchindoun, with their seals enclosed. Under torture
Ker and his coreligionist Graham of Fentry confessed that the
blanks were for use in an elaborate plot, the chief feature of
which was to be the landing of thirty thousand Spanish soldiers in Scotland in 1593.

Thus began the celebrated affair of the "Spanish blanks."[24]
Its immediate effect was seriously to weaken the political position of the king. Both the kirk and the English government
now became partisans of Bothwell. In July of 1593 John
Davidson "prayed that the Lord would compel the king, by
his sanctified plagues [i.e., Bothwell], to turn to Him."[25] When

[22] J. Bruce, ed., *Letters of Queen Elizabeth and King James VI*, pp. 77-79.
Bothwell had been in touch with England through the master of Gray. See
also September 13, 1592, Lowther to Burghley, *Border Papers*, I, 406-408.

[23] October 4, 10, 1592, Bowes to Burghley, csp scot, x, 782-784, 787-788. October 13, James to Lowther, *Border Papers*, I, 415.

[24] This episode has been fully treated many times. See, e.g., the accounts of
Stafford, *James VI*, pp. 74-123, and A. Lang, *A History of Scotland from the
Roman Occupation*, II, 363ff. A useful older summary is T. G. Law, "The Spanish Blanks and the Catholic Earls, 1592-1594," *Scottish Review*, XXII (1893),
1-32. The recent Catholic attempt to show that the whole affair was a Protestant
plot (Francis Shearman, "The Spanish Blanks," *Innes Review*, III [1952], 81-
103) is unconvincing.

[25] Calderwood, v, 255-256.

the news of the blanks reached Elizabeth, she wrote James a blunt letter, couched in language far removed from her usual prolix style, insisting that he punish the Catholic earls.[26] To show that she meant it, she sent a special ambassador, Lord Burgh, to Scotland in February 1593 to push James in this direction and to build up the strength of the pro-English party in court and on the council. At the same time a special agent of Burghley's, Henry Lock, was sent north to get into direct touch with Bothwell.[27]

For this falling-away of the kirk and the English queen James himself was largely responsible. As in the case of Moray's murder, he refused to pursue Huntly with any vigor. Quite apart from his preoccupation with Bothwell, it seems likely that one reason for this was that James knew perfectly well that there was no real substance to the Catholic plot. James had kept in touch with the Catholic party. He knew of their plans. Among the papers captured on Ker was a memorial, drawn up in a manner reminiscent of Burghley's, in which James weighed the pros and cons of an alliance with Spain, and concluded against such a policy for the time being.[28] This memorial was drawn up in the summer of 1592; so it may be assumed that James had been aware of the plot since that time—which may well have been the beginning.[29] James therefore knew that there was no danger in the conspiracy, that it was, in Law's words, a plot "born of the brain of a dreaming and impractical priest."[30] Bothwell, on the other hand, was a clear and present danger. Furthermore, a vigorous prosecu-

26 Bruce, *Letters*, pp. 71-73.

27 Stafford, *James VI*, p. 82. February 10, 1593, instructions for Lock, csp scot, xi, 44. March 7, Bothwell to Musgrave, *ibid.*, pp. 69-70. April 4, Bothwell to Burghley, *ibid.*, p. 76. Burgh, of course, was instructed to deny that Elizabeth had ever helped Bothwell. His instructions are in *ibid.*, pp. 45-48.

28 One copy of this document, which found its way into the hands of the English government, is in Stafford, *James VI*, pp. 118-121.

29 This is suggested by a letter of Bowes, dated June 16, 1592, in which he says that Maitland had expressed some concern to him because, Maitland said, various Catholic agents, after persistent efforts to bribe him, had suddenly stopped, which gave him "just cause to think that they have found another way to the entry of their desires." csp scot, x, 696. Ker, in his confession, stated that the blanks had been subscribed in June 1592. csp scot, xi, 50.

30 Law, *op.cit.*, p. 19.

tion of Huntly would doubtless cause the Catholic earls to reveal James's connections with them.

James had to take some action, however, in order to quiet the uproar. The earl of Angus, who happened to be in Edinburgh when the plot was discovered, was warded in the castle. Graham of Fentry, whom Andrew Lang calls an "honest Catholic," was executed, possibly because the ruling faction at court was angered by Montrose's support of Maitland.[31] James even led an expedition north in February 1593 in pursuit of Huntly, who made no resistance and fled to Caithness, in part, no doubt, because he realized that the king did not have the money to keep a force in the field for long.[32] More significant of the king's true temper are the facts that Angus managed to escape from Edinburgh castle, that James apparently allowed the wives and close relatives of the fugitive earls to continue to occupy their property, and that when the presbytery of Edinburgh summoned a meeting of the clergy of Fife and the Lothians on the first news of the discovery of the blanks, James, after keeping the assembled divines and their supporters waiting for an hour and a half for an audience, berated them for meeting without his consent.[33]

Nevertheless, the king had promised Lord Burgh that he would punish the conspirators. He signed a new band for the defense of the religion, and summoned a Parliament for June 1593, to forfeit the earls. But he complained to Burgh of lack of funds, and protested at England's friendliness to Bothwell. His attitude to the General Assembly which met in April 1593 was decidedly cool, and a convention of estates which met at the end of that month produced nothing but a band

[31] On February 13, 1593, two days before Fentry's execution, another of Montrose's family, Graham of Halyards, was killed in a street brawl with Lennox and Sir James Sandilands, one of Lennox's followers at court. Halyards was a disgrace to the Scottish bench and deserves no sympathy, but Lennox's hostility to the Grahams was very marked. Calderwood, v, 223-224.

[32] Even the kirk recognized that James's financial difficulties were serious; the Edinburgh presbytery made an effort to get some money for the government in March 1593. Its circular letter to the other presbyteries of Scotland to this effect is in SRO, *Royal Letters and State Papers, 1566-1628.*

[33] Calderwood, v, 215-217. January 13, February 16, 1593, Bowes to Burghley, CSP SCOT, XI, 21-24, 57-58. March 19, occurrents in Scotland, *ibid.*, pp. 72-73. Stafford, *James VI*, p. 79.

against Bothwell.[34] With the meeting of Parliament, however, the king could no longer disguise his true intentions, and under the circumstances it is surprising that he decided to hold the meeting at all. Parliament was originally summoned for June; it was put over until mid-July, and in the interval Ker escaped from Edinburgh castle. Therefore, when Parliament met, the king's advocate informed it that the earls could not be prosecuted, for lack of witnesses. On the other hand, Bothwell's forfeiture was repeated.[35] It was perfectly clear that the king would not proceed against the earls until he had settled with Bothwell.

ii

The Parliament of 1593 accomplished very little of a public nature, but one of its private acts was of great importance to Maitland. This was the ratification to Queen Anne of the abbey lands of Dunfermline, including those of the regality of Musselburgh.[36] Maitland had just surrendered this valuable possession; by this means he effected what he hoped would be a permanent return to court.

After considerable hesitation Maitland had decided, in the fall of 1592, not to take advantage of his commission as ambassador to France. His life was in jeopardy if he remained in Scotland; but if he left the country his property would be in still greater danger. His disgruntled nephew, James Maitland, secretary Lethington's son, had petitioned the king to restore Lethington to him; the petition had the support of the duke of Lennox.[37] James decided, nevertheless, to reject it, and his rejection marks another shift in his attitude toward his harassed chancellor. By the end of 1592 the king was becoming very anxious for Maitland's return to court. The chancellor's departure had not solved the king's political problems,

34 March 19, 30, 1593, Burgh to Burghley, CSP SCOT, XI, 71-72, 75-76. March 19, occurrents in Scotland, *ibid.*, pp. 72-73. The band, dated May 1, is in *ibid.*, pp. 85-86. Calderwood, v, 232-233, 239-249.

35 *Ibid.*, p. 254. APS, IV, 8-11.

36 *Ibid.*, pp. 23-27.

37 September 23, November 10, 1592, Bowes to Burghley, CSP SCOT, X, 777-779, 812-815.

and in Maitland's absence there was no one to handle the day-to-day business of government, unless the king did it himself. This James, who was lazy and bored by the details of administration, was not prepared to do. The queen was the nominal leader of the chancellor's enemies; so "the king moved her either as party to declare his fault, or else as a principal to hear his petition; whereupon it is advised that the chancellor shall in humble wise submit and make suit to the queen for her favor and good countenance, and when this has been got, the duke and other adversaries of the chancellor shall be laid off by the king's means."[38]

This was eventually done, but it took considerable time. The queen was not easily placated, and the uproar caused by the discovery of the Spanish blanks delayed matters still further. It was not until the middle of March 1593 that James took the business seriously in hand. Pressure was then put on the queen from all sides: by James himself, by the ministers, who still regarded Maitland as a true ally in spite of Bothwell's fulminations, even by Elizabeth, who, at James's request, wrote to Anne urging her to extend her favor to the chancellor.[39] Toward the end of April the king rode off to Lethington to see Maitland; the result of the visit was a most humble letter from Maitland to Anne, asking to be informed of the cause of her anger and to be heard in his own defense.[40] Gradually the queen's resistance was worn away. Early in June the king paid another visit to Lethington, and on June 21, 1593, the basis of reconciliation was announced: Maitland would part with Musselburgh. On July 15 he surrendered his rights to the queen, and received a refund of the composition of twenty pounds he had paid the king for them. He was also required to buy up the tacks he had set during his tenure. In return, the king consented that Anne should hold Musselburgh in

[38] October 10, 1592, Bowes to Burghley, *ibid.*, pp. 787-788.

[39] April 7, 1593, occurrents in Scotland, CSP SCOT, XI, 77-78. April 19, May 20, Bowes to Burghley, *ibid.*, pp. 79-81, 89-92. For an example of Bothwell's current attitude toward Maitland, see his letter of April 12 to Patrick Galloway, where the chancellor is described as "the author of my calamity and pest of the name of Stewart." *Warrender Papers*, II, 202-206.

[40] The letter, dated April 30, 1593, is in *ibid.*, pp. 207-209.

liferent only; after her death the property was to revert to the Maitland family.[41]

Maitland's bargain with the queen was as wormwood and gall to Lennox. Quite apart from the duke's normal dislike of Maitland, the chancellor was currently enjoying the strong support of Lord John Hamilton, who was Lennox's chief rival for the succession if James should die childless. In this situation Lennox turned to his Stewart relatives, who raised a great force and drove the chancellor out of Edinburgh at the end of June, 1593. This made the king angry; he informed Lennox bluntly that he was either to make peace with the chancellor or leave court himself.[42] Lennox was in no mood to submit. He considered the possibility of bringing charges against Maitland in the forthcoming Parliament, and of attempting to have himself declared "second person" of the realm there.[43] But ultimately he decided on a much more drastic and dangerous plan. He would help the chancellor's great enemy Bothwell to lay hands on the king.

Lennox waited until after the meeting of Parliament, which Maitland, adopting the better part of valor, had not attended. Then, having assembled "a great company . . . all his special friends," he smuggled Bothwell into the Gowrie town house, with the assistance of Lady Athol, Gowrie's sister. The Gowrie house was located at the rear of Holyroodhouse, "whereby there is patent passage at all times." On the morning of July 24, 1593, Lennox flooded the palace with his dependents, which

[41] June 20, 22, 1593, Bowes to Burghley, CSP SCOT, XI, 100-103. RMS, IV, 815-816. SRO, *Treasurer's Accounts*, July 1593. SRO, *Register of Deeds*, XL, 120-122, 128-129b; XLVI, 187, 215. The question of the disposition of Musselburgh after Anne's death was complicated by a subsequent grant of all the Dunfermline holdings to her without any exception being made for Musselburgh's special status. The result was considerable confusion; as late as 1641 the Maitlands complained that they had received no income from Musselburgh since Anne's death, over twenty years before. When the chancellor's grandson, the famous duke of the Restoration, was served as heir to the earldom of Lauderdale in 1649, his rights to Musselburgh were recognized. NLS, *Balcarres Papers*, 29.2.8. J. Paterson, *History of the Regality of Musselburgh*, pp. 24-25. *Warrender Papers*, II, 232-236.

[42] June 28, July 7, 1593, Bowes to Burghley, CSP SCOT, XI, 106-107, 693-695. Calderwood, v, 253-254.

[43] July 7, 1593, Bowes to Burghley, CSP SCOT, XI, 693-695. July 13, Carey to Burghley, *Border Papers*, I, 474.

was easy enough for him to arrange, thanks to his position at court, and then, once the palace was secured, Bothwell was notified. The earl slipped into the king's presence chamber and "prepared himself on his knees, and laid his sword down before him, drawn; and when the king came forth, he cried with a loud voice, 'Pardon, and mercy for Christ's sake.' "[44] James found himself at an acute disadvantage, both physical and psychological: he had just risen from the privy, and his clothes were in disarray. Nevertheless he fought down his panic and faced his captors with courage. "The king . . . asked what they meant? Came they to seek his life? Let them take it: they would not get his soul"[45]—almost certainly a reference to Bothwell's affinity for witchcraft. Bothwell was most polite: all he wanted, he said, was justice. What this meant, it turned out, was a trial (and, of course, an acquittal) on the witchcraft charge, and the restoration of his property. In the meantime he offered to keep out of the royal presence, and also to go into exile after his rehabilitation, if the king insisted.

James had no choice but to accept Bothwell's terms, if he was to avoid rigorous captivity or worse. He met Bothwell's pretense of humility with an equally hypocritical pretense of forgiveness. The earl and his followers were relaxed from the horn, and the king had to send out some very lame letters of explanation, referring to Bothwell's "humble" bearing and his own "princely humanity," which afforded the recipients a wonderful opportunity to be merry at his expense.[46]

Bothwell was not deceived by James's play-acting. He attempted to secure his position by forcing the appointment of his ally Ochiltree as commander of the guard, and by an immediate appeal for English aid, both via Henry Lock and through a flying visit to Durham on August 2, where he saw the dean of the cathedral. "The earl maketh no question," wrote the latter, "but by her majesty's assistance (whereupon he seemeth willing wholly to depend) he shall be, with his

[44] T. Thomson, ed., *The Historie and Life of James the Sext*, pp. 270-272.
[45] Calderwood, v, 256.
[46] See e.g., Elizabeth's letter in Bruce, *Letters*, pp. 85-86. See also August 23, 1593, Elizabeth to Bowes, csp scot, xi, 153-155. For a sample of the letters James wrote, see hmc 11th report, appendix, pt. vi, 66.

friends and followers, sufficiently able to manage the estate about the king to the peace of both realms."[47]

Bothwell's coup reminded contemporary observers of the raid of Ruthven. As Sir George Carey wrote to Robert Cecil, Scotland was "not unconstant in unconstancy"; all was just as it had been before, when the king "was in ten years taken nine times by contrary factions, each time in danger of his life."[48] But the bad old days of James's minority had not returned. James was no longer the terrified adolescent of 1582, and Bothwell's high-handed behavior soon began to alienate some of his supporters. The strongest link between the plotters was hatred of Maitland and of his ally Lord John Hamilton. The pregnancy of Queen Anne, which was public knowledge by mid-August, helped to relieve the tension between Lennox and Hamilton, however; the birth of an heir would make their dispute as to the succession academic. Furthermore, the king made it clear that he was not prepared to abandon Maitland to his enemies.[49]

On August 10, 1593, Bothwell was duly acquitted of the witchcraft charge; he took advantage of the occasion to denounce Maitland again, as follows: "My lords, and you all of my jury, it is not unknown to you what long banishment and great trouble I have endured without any just cause, only by the means of some enemies who incensed the king's majesty against me—as the chancellor, who was one of the conspirators of the death of the king's father, and a special mean of the queen his mother's death, and a conspirer and special worker of all the treasons and conspiracies contrived in Scotland in his time (as I can sufficiently prove)."[50] This speech was designed as a preliminary to a legal attack on Maitland, which Bothwell was planning to launch after his own acquittal. Mait-

---

[47] July 30, 1593, Bowes to Burghley, CSP SCOT, XI, 702-705. August 2, the dean of Durham to Burghley, *Border Papers*, I, 481-484. August 5, Bothwell to Lock, CSP SCOT, XI, 705-706. For Bothwell's own account of his seizure of the king see August 10, 1593, Sir William Reed to Burghley, *Border Papers*, I, 485-486.

[48] *Salisbury Papers*, IV, 346.

[49] July 25, August 16, 1593, Bowes to Burghley, CSP SCOT, XI, 131-132, 144-147. August 20, Forster to Burghley, *Border Papers*, I, 492-493.

[50] August 12, 1593, Carey to Burghley, *Border Papers*, I, 486-489.

land was to be charged with collaboration with Spain and foreknowledge of Moray's death.[51]

On the night of Bothwell's acquittal the king made an effort to flee from Edinburgh to Falkland. Bothwell discovered the plot in time, and insisted on the dismissal of those of the king's servants who were involved.[52] James was furious, and accused Bothwell of violating his promise to withdraw from court with his henchmen after his trial. On August 14, in the presence of some members of the court of session and of the ministry who had come to try to compose the quarrel, James refused to appoint Bothwell as lieutenant-general of the kingdom in the south, and threatened to appeal to the people to deliver him from the earl by force. This threat, and the evident wavering of Lennox, made Bothwell more reasonable. A formal agreement was drawn up between him and the king. Bothwell was pardoned for his past offenses, and a parliamentary ratification of the pardon was promised. Four of his chief enemies, Maitland, Lord Hume, Sir George Hume, and the master of Glamis, were forbidden the court. In return, Bothwell himself was also to retire from court.[53]

James was bent on breaking this agreement as soon as possible. He summoned a meeting of the convention of estates for September 7 and then went west with Lennox to hunt, and to see Lord John Hamilton and persuade the two men to patch up their quarrel. In the meantime Bothwell's declared enemies settled their differences: Maitland ended his long feud with the master of Glamis.[54] For the moment Lennox held the balance of power in Scotland; his defection to the king's side was decisive. The September convention of estates held that James's promises to Bothwell, having been extracted by

[51] August 5, 1593, Bothwell to Lock, CSP SCOT, XI, 705-706. August 8, Christopher Sheperson's statement to Burghley, *ibid.*, pp. 141-142. Sheperson was Bowes's servant.

[52] August 11, 1593, Bowes to Burghley, *ibid.*, pp. 142-143.

[53] August 16, 1593, Bowes to Burghley, *ibid.*, pp. 144-147. Calderwood, v, 257-259. *James the Sext*, pp. 273-275. Lang, *History*, II, 376, suggests that Lennox's defection was owing to his dislike of Bothwell's plan of becoming lieutenant-general.

[54] August 21, 30, September 10, 1593, Bowes to Burghley, CSP SCOT, XI, 151, 159-161, 169-170.

force, were void. But Lennox was not prepared to abandon Bothwell entirely to James's fury. The king promised that Bothwell, and any accomplices he named, would be pardoned at the next Parliament, after which they would go into exile; in the meantime, Bothwell was not to come within ten miles of the king.[55] The Humes and Glamis returned to court immediately; by the beginning of October Maitland had done the same.[56] His political exile was over.

James was suddenly reminded that Bothwell's well-wishers consisted of more than a handful of Stewart artistocrats. The kirk was alarmed by Bothwell's sudden decline, by the appointment of the Catholic Hume as captain of the guard, by the return to court of Lady Huntly. It was rumored that Huntly himself might be restored to favor. An even greater cause for concern was the depressing news of the conversion of Henry IV of France, which reached Scotland in mid-September.[57] So the provincial synod of Fife, dominated by the Melvills, at its meeting in late September 1593, excommunicated the three Catholic earls, and also Lord Hume. It claimed jurisdiction over the four, none of whom lived in Fife, on the ground that they had all once been students at St. Andrews.[58]

The synod's action angered James. He was even more incensed at the report that the ministers threatened to withdraw their allegiance if he failed to punish the earls. "He said the ministers were cruel, and as they sought blood they should have it," and he talked of reviving episcopacy. He forced the election of Hume of Northberwick, an enemy of Bothwell's, as provost of Edinburgh, in order to penalize the capital and its clergy for supporting the earl. He summoned Bothwell to

<hr/>

[55] September 10, 1593, Bowes to Burghley, *ibid.*, pp. 169-170. Calderwood, v, 259-261. *James the Sext*, pp. 276-278. Bothwell objected strenuously to the requirement that he name his accomplices in order to get pardons for them. Many of them were unknown to James; they were thus in a cleft stick. Either Bothwell identified them to the king, or else they passed up the possibility of pardon and ran the risk of future prosecution if James ever did identify them. See Bothwell's protest on this point, dated September 13, csp scot, xi, 178-179.

[56] September 13, 1593, Bowes to Burghley, csp scot, xi, 170-171. October 3, Forster to Burghley, *Border Papers*, i, 410-411.

[57] September 15, 21, 1593, Bowes to Burghley, csp scot, xi, 175-177, 179-181.

[58] Calderwood, v, 262.

answer a charge of treason, and had him denounced rebel when he failed to appear.[59] With respect to the Catholic earls, he planned to summon the General Assembly and compel it to rescind the sentence of the synod of Fife on the ground that the synod lacked jurisdiction. This plan, involving, as it did, outright favor to the earls, produced an immediate reaction when it became known. Early in October Huntly's enemies gathered at Doun, the ancestral castle of the slain earl of Moray. Athol was there, and Montrose, and Gowrie, and even the young earl of Moray. James, getting wind of this gathering, collected some forces and rode to Doun in haste. The meeting at once dispersed, but the point was not lost on the king— or, perhaps, the point was made clear to him by Montrose's friend the newly-restored chancellor, who had accompanied James.[60] So, the king resolved to play the game so recently played by Bothwell. On October 12, 1593, as the king was crossing Fala moor on his way to visit Maitland at Lauder, the three Catholic earls rode up to him, knelt, and asked for justice. All they wanted, they said, was a fair trial. After some suitable play-acting James ordered them to appear before a convention of estates at Perth on October 24.[61]

Unfortunately for James, everyone knew that the Fala meeting was collusive. Bowes had heard virtually all the details of the plan before the king set out for Lauder.[62] The reaction, particularly on the part of the kirk, was immediate and extreme. The king brushed aside the ministers' demands, but he was unable to ignore the fact that both sides were preparing to come to Perth in force, in order to determine the legal points at issue in the traditional Scottish fashion. James therefore

[59] Ibid., pp. 268-269. James the Sext, pp. 282-283. Archbishop J. Spottiswoode, History of the Church of Scotland, II, 437-438. October 4, 1593, news from Scotland, CSP SCOT, XI, 188-191. SRO, Treasurer's Accounts, October 1593. RPCS, V, 100-101.

[60] October 4, 1593, news from Scotland, CSP SCOT, XI, 188-191. October 9, Bowes to Burghley, ibid., pp. 193-196. That the danger was genuine is shown by Athol's friendly letter to Bothwell, dated October 8; ibid., p. 193.

[61] October 12, 1593, Bowes to Burghley, ibid., pp. 200-201. October 16, Carey to Burghley, Border Papers, I, 506-507.

[62] See his letters of October 9 and 12, 1593 to Burghley, CSP SCOT, XI, 193-196, 198-200.

shifted the time and place of the trial, to Linlithgow on October 29. Nothing daunted, the ministers bade their supporters come to Edinburgh on the 27th.[63]

At this point Maitland intervened—his first important political act since his return to court.[64] He pointed out to the king that in the present tense atmosphere any attempt to hold a trial would simply end in a riot if not worse. He proposed that the government hold out terms to the earls, and offer them the choice of immediate acceptance or exile. So, at Linlithgow, a committee was appointed, headed by Maitland, Lennox, and Mar, to draft the terms of the offer. After considerable work the committee produced a plan which was accepted by a slenderly attended convention of estates dominated by government officials and published on November 26. By the terms of this so-called act of abolition, everyone in Scotland was required either to embrace the true religion by February 1, 1594, or go into exile. Anyone choosing exile would be permitted to retain his property, as long as he was out of the country by February 1 and stayed out. There would be no prosecutions in the affair of the Spanish blanks, provided that none of those concerned had sent pledges out of the realm. But the offer of immunity extended to this affair only, "and to no murders . . . [or] other criminal matters whatsoever." In other words, Huntly was not pardoned for the murder of Moray. Huntly and Errol were ordered to expel their Jesuit friends and relations; if they opted to stay and subscribe to the true religion, they would have to accept a minister as a house-guest. The earls were given until January 1 to inform the government of their choice, and to find surety in the amount of forty thousand pounds for their good behavior.[65]

Maitland hoped to solve a good many political problems by this act of abolition. There were three possibilities: either the earls would refuse the offer altogether, or they would accept one of the two alternatives. No matter what they did, the

---

[63] *James the Sext*, pp. 284-286. Calderwood, v, 274-275.

[64] Maitland's first recorded appearance in the *sederunt* of the privy council was on October 15, 1593. RPCS, v, 101.

[65] Calderwood, v, 277-288. Moysie, *Memoirs*, pp. 106-109.

net result would be political gain for Maitland and the government. If the earls refused the offer, it would be obvious that their real motive for rebellion against the king was political rather than religious, and James could then be persuaded to pursue them in earnest and thus regain the support of England and the kirk. If the earls accepted either of the proposed alternatives, the result would be either the departure from Scotland of three aristocratic troublemakers or else their submission to the kirk, which would almost certainly result in the kirk's abandonment of Bothwell. The plan had the added advantage of embarrassing the English government; the chancellor resented the English unwillingness to help him during his period of political exile.[66] At one point the English had suggested that the earls might be pardoned if they conformed in religion. Maitland and the king seized upon this, and in his letter to Elizabeth explaining his offer of pardon, James blandly remarked that he was simply following English advice.[67]

Personal factors were also involved in Maitland's decision. His period of political oblivion had made it painfully clear to him that he could not afford to antagonize the entire aristocracy at once, and that for the moment the man he must conciliate was Lennox. By late 1593 Lennox was willing to meet him part way, as is shown by his acceptance of Maitland's nephew Cesford as deputy keeper of Liddesdale. Bowes suggests that Lennox, who was a good enough Protestant, was becoming seriously alarmed about the threat to the religion.[68] He was certainly disenchanted with Bothwell. Maitland was delighted to be able to accommodate the duke. If Huntly and the others were truly troubled in conscience over their religion, they could live in comfortable exile without any financial loss. What could be fairer than that?

Still, it seems likely that the possibility of ending the alliance between Bothwell and the kirk was even more important

[66] October 4, 1593, instructions by Bowes for George Nicolson, csp scot, xi, 185-188. November 12, Bowes to Burghley, *ibid.*, p. 223.

[67] October 29, 1593, Burghley to Bowes, *ibid.*, pp. 211-212. December 7, James to Elizabeth, Bruce, *Letters*, pp. 95-98.

[68] October 20, 1593, Bowes to Burghley, csp scot, xi, 205-206. Lennox had become keeper of Liddesdale in October 1592; csp scot, x, 792.

to Maitland than the favor of Lennox. He knew the explosive possibilities that lay in the alliance of the kirk with a dissident noble and his friends, particularly if the combination was supported by England. The history of Scotland since the Wars of the Congregation bore witness to the power of such a coalition; indeed, Maitland himself had profited by it in 1585 to overthrow the earl of Arran. It had been Maitland's policy ever since to prevent any recurrence of such an alliance. The offer to the earls was made in order to separate the religious from the political questions involved, and thus pacify the kirk. The chancellor doubtless expected that the kirk's first reaction would be unfavorable—the government's resolute exclusion of the kirk's representatives from any share in formulating the act of abolition was enough to ensure that. His expectations were more than borne out. "Upon the Lord's day, the 16th of December, Mr. Robert Bruce in his sermon, the chancellor . . . being present, said the king's reign should be troublesome and short if he abolished not the act of abolition."[69]

Maitland was not prepared for so violent a reaction. He thought that he had made it clear to the ministers that some such solution was the best to be had, that a trial would simply result in an acquittal on the principal charge and virtually no punishment—always assuming, of course, that a trial could be held at all without degenerating into a riot. He now met with the ministers and asked them to detail their objections, which, apart from the iniquity of offering terms to Papists at all, came down to two: the indefiniteness of the clause enjoining the earls to satisfy the kirk, and the provision that, if they chose to remain Catholic and go into exile, they should retain their property. Maitland held out hope that some changes might be made, but the king was adamant. He regarded the final version of the act as his handiwork, and would not allow it to be tampered with. He did promise, however, that if the earls refused to accept the act, the next convention of estates would deal strictly with them.[70]

69 Calderwood, v, 290.
70 November 23, December 2, 26, 1593, Bowes to Burghley, csp scot, xi, 228-231, 235-237, 249-250. Calderwood, v, 289. To Bowes himself, when he came to

James was soon required to implement this pledge. The earls rejected the offers contained in the act, on the ground that they could not find the forty thousand pounds' surety required. So, on January 18, 1594, the convention of estates withdrew the act and declared that the earls would be summoned to underlie the law at the forthcoming meeting of Parliament, which would be held in April.[71] This meant, of course, that no action would be taken until after the meeting of Parliament, and such was clearly the king's intention. This was satisfactory neither to the kirk nor to England, and the chancellor, in an interview with Bowes, "promised to provide some speedy remedies."[72]

It was not easy to provide speedy remedies however. For one thing, James was preoccupied by Queen Anne's approaching confinement, which resulted in the birth of a son on February 19, 1594, an event which "was a great comfort and matter of joy to the whole people . . . bonfires were set out, and dancing and playing used in all parts, as if the people had been daft for mirth."[73] This child was the ill-fated Prince Henry. Two days after his birth he was placed in the charge of the traditional guardian of the Scottish kings' firstborn, the earl of Mar, as head of the house of Erskine.[74]

The pleasures and distractions of fatherhood predisposed the king to neglect the earls for the time being. This predisposition was strengthened by the hectoring and minatory tone of Queen Elizabeth and her special ambassador Lord Zouche, who, James protested, treated him "as if he were not a sole prince but the queen's lieutenant, who must render account

protest, James made light of the act; the earls, he said, would not accept its terms. November 30, Bowes to Burghley, csp scot, xi, 231-235.

[71] February 5, 1594, Errol to an anonymous correspondent, *ibid.*, p. 277. APS, iv, 52-53. RPCS, v, 116-117, 126-127. At this same convention a privy council was named with a membership most satisfactory to Maitland—several lairds, and a group of reliable nobles: Hamilton, Mar, Marischal, Montrose, among others.

[72] csp scot, xi, 265-266. January 20, 1594, Bowes to Burghley, *ibid.*, pp. 267-268. Calderwood, v, 291-293.

[73] Moysie, *Memoirs*, p. 113.

[74] csp scot, xi, 280.

of his dealings to her."[75] In James's view Bothwell was still the chief problem to be dealt with. Yet in the end it was a combination of English policy and the didos of Bothwell which ultimately compelled James to come around to Maitland's view and agree to take action against the earls.

Queen Elizabeth had been infuriated by the act of abolition, which seemingly spelled defeat for her whole policy. Ever since the discovery of the Spanish blanks she had been attempting to persuade or coerce James into moving against the earls by showing favor to Bothwell. Now she resolved to go much further, and, in her usual subterranean manner, to give real support to Bothwell. The old game, which had been played so many times before was to be played once again, with this difference: that this time the queen did not desire to overthrow the Scottish government, but rather to compel it to change its policy.

The queen's choice as ambassador, Lord Zouche, was not a happy one. Zouche had none of the talent for intrigue of Thomas Randolph or Edward Wotton, and his hectoring manner infuriated the king. The result was that he and Henry Lock, between them, nearly botched the job. Zouche did get James to promise in writing that he would make no bargain with the earls without asking Elizabeth's advice, and that they would be vigorously pursued unless they warded themselves immediately and without conditions—provided that the queen gave him some financial aid, without which nothing could be done. The attitude of the English government, on the other hand, was that James would get help only after he had taken forceful action against the earls. Both sides held to their positions on this question, and the interviews between the king and Maitland on the one hand, and Zouche and Bowes on the other, became increasingly bitter.[76]

If Zouche was unsuccessful with the king, he was almost too successful with Bothwell for the comfort of the English

75 March 12, 1594, Zouche to Burghley, *ibid.*, p. 289.
76 January 26, 1594, Zouche to Burghley, *ibid.*, pp. 270-273. March 12, Robert Cecil to Zouche, *ibid.*, pp. 285-287. See also Zouche's report of his audiences in late February and early March 1594, *ibid.*, pp. 288-294.

government. He and Lock sanctioned Bothwell's plan to attack the king; Elizabeth could not countenance this. There was to be no attack on James; only on his advisers and the earls. A direct attack on the king, besides putting Elizabeth in an embarrassing position, would also be bad tactics: many of Bothwell's potential allies, such as Athol and Argyll, were eager to fight Huntly, but much more chary of an assault on James. Zouche and Lock promised Bothwell money, and, apparently, gave him some. This was a mistake; Bothwell, like the king, was to receive English bounty only after he had taken the field. In brief, the English government was to be committed to as little as possible. What Zouche, not being a trained Elizabethan diplomat, did not understand was that he was supposed to commit himself personally and prepare to be repudiated if things went wrong—or, as one of the marginalia of the correspondence in which these points were discussed put it, "the queen would have her ministers do that [which] she will not avow."[77]

Maitland's position throughout all this was a most uncomfortable one, and was complicated by occasional periods of bad health and by the threatened eruption of the old rivalry with Glamis, who was treasurer again and still wanted to be chancellor. As one of Bothwell's supporters put it, Maitland and Glamis were "agreed *in odium tertii*"—that is, Bothwell—but on not much else.[78] With respect to the overriding political problem, the chancellor was required on the one hand, to carry out James's wishes in negotiation with the English representatives, and on the other, to try to convince his master of the necessity of acting against the earls. Zouche did not trust him. "I am told for certain," the ambassador wrote in January, "that the lord chancellor works underhand for the earls and receives great sums of money to that end."[79] Maitland's assurances that both he and his master were pro-English were

[77] There is an excellent treatment of Zouche's mission in Stafford, *James VI*, pp. 100-109. The relevant correspondence is in CSP SCOT, XI, 239ff.
[78] May 3, 1594, Colville to Lock, *Salisbury Papers*, IV, 523-524. See also January 15, 1594, Bowes to Burghley, CSP SCOT, XI, 262-263.
[79] *Ibid.*, p. 272.

received with a good deal of skepticism—"slippery" was the adjective Cecil used to describe him.[80] The chancellor had his personal preoccupations too, although they had a happy issue. A son was born, to carry on the Maitland name and line— the chancellor's second and last child, who one day would become the first earl of Lauderdale.[81]

The resolution of the long-drawn-out crisis began with the last of Bothwell's great escapades, the so-called raid of Leith in early April 1594. Whatever military laurels attached to this affair rested with Bothwell; the forces which Maitland, who took the lead in organizing the defense, gathered to oppose him were riven by internal suspicions and not inclined to fight. James's own role was not heroic; he left the field and "came riding in to Edinburgh at the full gallop, with little honor."[82] The really alarming aspect of this affair to James was the fact that, once again, Bothwell had found numerous allies among the enemies of Huntly: Athol, Gowrie, Ochiltree, Forbes, the master of Montrose.[83] The king also remembered that he was now a father. If his enemies could get possession of Prince Henry, they might be able to use the infant as he himself had been used against Queen Mary. The same menacing combination was in existence in 1594 as had existed in 1567: a few nobles, the kirk, and England. So at last the king decided to follow the policy which had been urged on him for so long by the kirk, by England, and by his chancellor. In St. Giles, on the morning of the day of Bothwell's raid, James publicly promised to pursue the earls in return for the help of ministers and people against Bothwell. "If the Lord give

[80] *Ibid.*, p. 297.
[81] On March 7, 1594, a recapitulation of Maitland's property holdings as Lord Thirlestane, in which his son is mentioned, passed the privy seal (SRO, *Privy Seal Register*, LXVI, 89-94) and the great seal (RMS, V, 24-26). At some time after the birth Maitland paid the very large sum of one thousand pounds for the right to hold Lethington and pass it on to his son, thus extinguishing the claims of his troublesome nephew James. SRO, *Treasurer's Accounts, 1593-1596.*
[82] Calderwood, V, 297. April 4, 1594, Forster to Burghley, *Border Papers,* I, 524-525. For Maitland's role see Moysie, *Memoirs*, p. 114; *James the Sext,* p. 302. In spite of his age, the chancellor was prepared to fight himself, according to Calderwood, V, 296. It is not recorded whether he actually did so.
[83] CSP SCOT, XI, 327-328.

me victory over Bothwell, I shall never rest till I pass upon Huntly and the rest of the excommunicated lords."[84]

James, having made his decision, set about attempting to implement it. He promised Zouche that he would pursue the earls at the end of April; and, having decided to do as Elizabeth wished, he could not resist writing her a stinging letter about her favor to Bothwell and about the behavior of Zouche, "who, although it pleased you to term him wise, religious and honest, had been fitter in my opinion to carry the message of a herald than any friendly commission."[85] The effect of this well-deserved scolding was somewhat spoiled by the simultaneous dispatch of a Scottish embassy to England to ask for money, and to invite the queen to send a representative to the baptism of Prince Henry.[86] The queen was not yet prepared to open her purse, but she was willing to give James a chance. Bothwell was warned that he must not attack the king while the latter was pursuing the earls; if he did, England would intervene forcibly to stop him.[87]

James and his council, having committed themselves to speedy pursuit of the earls, now began to have second thoughts. Since no money was available to hire soldiers, recourse must be had to the traditional summons of the lieges. Many men would be unwilling to turn out, and risk the blood-feud of the Gordons and the Douglases, unless there was a proper condemnation by Parliament. So, at the end of April, it was resolved to condemn the earls in Parliament first, and then pursue them. The northern expedition was put off—though the lieges were ordered to be ready to march on six days' notice—and a parliamentary session was planned for the end of May.[88]

Bowes at first was rather skeptical of all this; he urged James to ignore the legal niceties and launch the pursuit at once. He thought that the month's delay was to give the earls

<hr />

[84] Calderwood, v, 296.

[85] April 13, 1594, James to Elizabeth, *Warrender Papers*, II, 226-228.

[86] CSP SCOT, XI, 312-314. James also seized upon this occasion to deny once more to Elizabeth that he had had any dealings with Spain. NLS, Denmilne MSS XXI, No. 2.

[87] April 20, 1594, Burghley to Bowes, CSP SCOT, XI, 317-318.

[88] April 24, 1594, Bowes to Cecil, *ibid.*, pp. 320-321. RPCS, v, 143.

a chance to enter nominal ward or slip out of the country, and that Parliament would then be postponed.[89] Bowes was not the only English skeptic; Robert Carey wrote to Cecil at this time, "both you and her majesty shall do very well to remember that the king (although he be a king) yet he is but a king born in Scotland and so a Scotsman."[90] But toward the end of May the English attitude was beginning to change, influenced, doubtless, by the fact that Bothwell's April raid had shown that the earl's position was weaker than had been supposed. By May 23 Bowes was reporting that it really appeared that the Catholic earls would be forfeited, and, after the event, the suspicious Carey conceded that the king had personally assured the parliamentary forfeitures by overriding some opposition in the committee of the articles. The surest indication of the shift in English opinion, however, was Elizabeth's decision on May 17 to give James some immediate financial aid.[91]

As the English attitude shifted, so did that of the kirk, and for approximately the same reasons. The ministers may have regarded Bothwell as a sanctified plague, but they never trusted him.[92] So the ministers, like Elizabeth, were prepared to jettison Bothwell if it seemed expedient to do so. And, like Elizabeth, they were skeptical of the king's sincerity at first. In April of 1594, when they were asked what they would do if Bothwell attacked Edinburgh while James was pursuing the earls in the north, they said they would pray for him.[93] This was something less than satisfactory to the king. But by the time of the meeting of the General Assembly in May 1594, the atmosphere was much friendlier. True, the Assembly ratified the excommunication passed by the synod of Fife, save in the case of Lord Hume, who had submitted to the kirk. But the Assembly also deprived a minister who had actually joined

---

[89] April 30, 1594, Bowes to Burghley, CSP SCOT, XI, 321-325.

[90] Border Papers, I, 530-531.

[91] CSP SCOT, XI, 335, 343-344. June 8, 1594, Carey to Burghley, Border Papers, I, 534. It is significant that Henry Lock, now back in London, advised giving money to James. Salisbury Papers, IV, 530-531.

[92] See, e.g., R. Pitcairn, ed., The Autobiography and Diary of Mr. James Melvill, pp. 314-315.

[93] Calderwood, V, 298.

Bothwell, and, rather reluctantly, "admonished" another who had already been interrogated by the council for a sermon which could be taken as incitement to assassination of the king. The ministers also agreed to instruct their flocks not to join Bothwell, and to speak to the king privately rather than preach against him, if they had any complaints to make. Nothing was heard of the demands of the previous autumn, that the act of annexation be repealed and episcopacy completely abolished. The king was prepared to meet the kirk halfway. Only one of its important requests was refused: an ambiguous suggestion to the effect that the populace be charged to "put themselves in arms . . . as they shall be certified by his majesty, or otherwise finding the occasion urgent." James evidently regarded this last clause as opening the door to private summons to the lieges. But almost everything else was accepted. The king also had a long private conference with James Melvill which did much to clear the air.[94] Some ministers were still suspicious, and preached sermons declaring the "king's heart not to be upright," and comparing him unfavorably with Charles IX of France, the king of the St. Bartholomew massacre.[95] But by and large relations between king and kirk were so friendly that on May 30 Roger Ashton could describe the two as "all one."[96]

Thus by the time of the meeting of Parliament in May 1594 the king's political position was greatly improved. He promptly consolidated his gains by having Parliament find the earls guilty of treason.[97] The king also took advantage of the meeting to put through a number of measures which increased the administrative authority of the crown, the most important of which was an act which required the submission in advance of all proposed parliamentary legislation to a committee of the estates—which meant, in effect, a committee of the council. As James later explained to the English Parlia-

[94] For this Assembly see *ibid.*, pp. 307-328. See also *James the Sext*, p. 325; CSP SCOT, XI, 210-211, 216.
[95] Calderwood, v, pp. 329, 337-338.
[96] CSP SCOT, XI, 348-349.
[97] At the same time Bothwell's condemnation was reaffirmed. APS, IV, 56-62.

ment, the purpose of this act was to ensure that only legislation which he had approved in advance would be submitted to Parliament.[98] Parliament also attempted to deal with the chronic problem of the king's finances. The shortage of money had reached the acute stage once again, thanks to the turmoil of the last two years. The gains of the period immediately following the return from Denmark had been wiped out, and the queen's dowry, which had helped to keep the government partially solvent, had finally all been spent.[99] To meet this crisis, the usual expedients were tried; and Parliament ratified a recoinage ordered by the council in January.[100] It also ratified the lease of the mineral rights in certain lands once belonging to the abbey of Newbattle to Thomas Foulis, an Edinburgh merchant who had made extensive loans to the king.[101] James was very hopeful of the possibilities of profits from mining—so much so, that in 1592 the office of master of the metals had been created for the energetic and knowledgeable Lindsay of Menmuir. But in this direction, as in so many others, the king's hope of alleviating his desperate fiscal situation was doomed to disappointment.

Every penny that could be raised, and the king's whole attention, were now devoted to the baptismal ceremonies for his firstborn. They were finally held, after several postponements, on August 30, 1594, in the chapel royal at Stirling, with all the tiresome and elaborate pomp that was customary in sixteenth-century Europe. The high point of the festivities was the appearance in the banqueting hall of an artificial ship, eighteen feet long, with silk lines and taffeta sails, thirty-five

98 *Ibid.*, p. 69, R. S. Rait, *The Parliaments of Scotland*, pp. 426-427.

99 RPCS, V, 139-140, 145-146, 151-152. April 21, 1594, Bowes to Cecil, CSP SCOT, XI, 319-320.

100 APS, IV, 65-66, 78-79, 85-86. The government had been so hard pressed in January that it could not afford to await the profits of the recoinage; it immediately leased the profits of the mint to the town government of Edinburgh for two years and three months for the sum of 110,000 marks, payable at the rate of 1,000 marks a week. RPCS, V, 119-124. "The poor," comments Calderwood, V, 296, "were greatly endammaged."

101 APS, IV, 84-85. RPCS, V, 117-118. Foulis did not profit from his transactions with the king; by the end of the decade James owed him 180,000 marks. R. Chambers, *Domestic Annals of Scotland from the Reformation to the Revolution*, I, 295.

pieces of brass ordnance, and the pilot decked out in cloth of gold.[102] This sort of thing was very expensive, and the king was soon having to beg money again, from his nobility, from the ministers, from Elizabeth. Robert Carey reported that James was even trying to borrow from Huntly.[103] Elizabeth, who had sent the king four thousand pounds sterling in June, was not enchanted, and instructed her representative at the baptism, the earl of Sussex, to reply, if the question of money was raised, that the English government was confident that James could cope with his problems, including the Catholic earls, by himself. James had to be bailed out by a last-minute loan from an Edinburgh burgess, who also provided the wine and beer.[104] The day after the ceremony James sent a gloomy note to Maitland, who had not attended, saying that he did not have enough cash to meet household bills, and concluding, "Help now or never."[105]

Three months went by between the end of Parliament and the baptism, months during which the Scottish government, preoccupied as it was with the coming festivities, made no important political decisions, and only one serious administrative gesture. In June 1594 another attempt was made to implement the system of justice eyres planned in 1587, by employing, in addition to government officials, some reliable noblemen, such as Mar and Marischal, as judges.[106] During these months both groups of the king's rebels made mistakes which contributed substantially to their undoing. That of the Catholic earls was the less serious, since it merely intensified the king's resolution to deal firmly with them. In July a ship arrived at Aberdeen from Spain, carrying, among other things, Huntly's Jesuit uncle, Father Gordon, and some Papal gold. The citi-

102 Calderwood, v, 345. There is a long description of the baptism in *Tracts Illustrative of the Traditionary and Historical Antiquities of Scotland*, pp. 471-495.

103 July 18, 1594, Carey to Cecil, *Border Papers*, I, 541. R. S. Brydon, *The Finances of James VI, 1567-1603*, pp. 70-72. Calderwood, v, 340.

104 June 30, 1594, Cecil to Bowes, CSP SCOT, x, 538-539 (where the letter is misdated 1591); August, instructions for Sussex, CSP SCOT, XI, 407-410. RPCS, v, 167-168.

105 CSP SCOT, XI, 425.

106 RPCS, v, 754-756.

zens of Aberdeen attempted to detain both passengers and cargo. Father Gordon escaped, however, and when Huntly learned what had happened, he marched on Aberdeen in force and threatened to burn the town unless the prisoners and the gold were surrendered at once. The town had no choice but to comply. When the news reached Edinburgh, Maitland was for immediate action, and he offered to provide fifty horsemen at his own expense. His only support on the council came from Sir Robert Melville and the master of Glamis, however; so it was resolved to take no action until after the baptism.[107] But the king was now absolutely convinced that the earls were a political danger and that action was necessary. This conviction was demonstrated by the appointment of Athol, Argyll, and Forbes as lieutenants in the north, a step the government had been reluctant to take before, on the ground that it would simply perpetuate the old feuds. The appointment of Athol is significant. He was the leader of those nobles who demanded vengeance for Moray, and was guardian of the latter's minor heir. Three months before, he had been denounced rebel for dealing with Bothwell. His return to his allegiance was indicative of the growing conviction that, this time, James really would act against Huntly.[108]

Bothwell's mistake was much more serious. In fact, it was absolutely fatal. After the failure of his April raid, the earl's position became increasingly uncomfortable. English support gradually lessened; by June 1594 the English government was taking steps against his supporters on the English side of the frontier, and at the end of the month he himself was informed that he was no longer welcome in England. His tentative overtures to James, made indirectly through Maitland, were rejected out of hand, though Maitland evidently attempted to hold out some hope to him with the notion of keeping him quiet until after the baptism.[109] Furthermore, his posi-

---

107 July 21, 23, 1594, Bowes to Burghley, CSP SCOT, XI, pp. 379-382, 384-385.

108 RPCS, V, 143, 157. July 6, 28, 1594, Bowes to Burghley, CSP SCOT, XI, 367-371, 389-393.

109 June 9, 1594, Bowes to Burghley, ibid., pp. 356-361. June 28, Forster to Burghley, Border Papers, I, 537-538. July 14, Bowes to Cecil, CSP SCOT, XI, 373-374. July 17, Colville to Lock, ibid., p. 377.

tion on the border itself was becoming untenable. The famous victory of his friend the laird of Johnstone over Maxwell at Lockerby in December 1593, in what was to be the last of the great border affrays, afforded Bothwell only temporary relief, and was offset by the coalition organized by Maitland early in 1594, consisting of Hume, Cesford, and Buccleuch, aided by Lord Herries and Lord John Hamilton. This coalition was held together by little more than a desire for spoils: those of Bothwell himself, and of the earl of Angus, who for this reason was reportedly to be more severely treated than Huntly and Errol[110]—as, indeed, he had been throughout. Whatever the motive, the coalition was powerful, and with the pardon of Johnstone in September 1594, Bothwell's last major ally was gone. The border was loyal to King James.

The same thing was true elsewhere. "Bothwell's friends in Edinburgh, Leith, and parts adjoining are so discovered, wracked and terrified that they dare deal no more with him, and the gentlemen in Fife are in like case," wrote Bowes in mid-September.[111] Bothwell's countermeasures were ineffective. An attempt to seize the king in July 1594 never got properly started; an attempt in August to inveigle Lennox into a new conspiracy by working on the duke's jealousy of Maitland, proved equally abortive.[112] Under these circumstances, Bothwell took a last, desperate, supremely foolish gamble. Huntly had offered him a substantial sum of money to join the Catholic earls. Bothwell gave England a chance to meet the offer; Elizabeth, after some hesitation, refused. So, sometime in late August, Bothwell accepted Huntly's proposals.

This move exposed Bothwell for what he was: a political adventurer who stood for no principles save those of feudal gangsterism and anarchy. And, it might be added, he was an unintelligent political adventurer. Bothwell's only important sources of support were England and the kirk. By joining the earls he threw away whatever chance he had of regaining the

[110] June 9, 1594, Richard Douglas to Archibald Douglas, *Salisbury Papers*, IV, 547-549; July 6, Bowes to Burghley, CSP SCOT, XI, 367-371.

[111] CSP SCOT, XI, 445.

[112] July 8, 1594, Carey to Burghley, *Border Papers*, I, 539-540. August 20, Colville to Cecil, *Salisbury Papers*, IV, 583.

support of Elizabeth and of keeping that of the ministers. And to what end? Simply "to put in practice the lovable custom of our progenitors at Lauder"[113]—that is, the murder of the king's favorites by an enraged aristocracy. Blind hatred of Maitland might have been enough to create a political faction, but it was not enough to hold one together. Bothwell's followers, more percipient, or more honorable, than he, began to desert him in droves. The egregious John Colville, Bothwell's link with Henry Lock and through him with the English government, a man who, throughout the summer, had been spreading the most scandalous rumors about the paternity of Prince Henry, was among the first to turn his coat. With a great show of righteous indignation he wrote to Bothwell consigning him to outer darkness for his religious hypocrisy, and then addressed an obsequious appeal to the king. James was not deceived, but he pardoned Colville anyhow, for a consideration: the blood of Bothwell's brother.[114]

The accession of Bothwell to their ranks proved to be a liability to Huntly and his friends, since it made the king even more determined to punish them. James's zeal was still further excited by the capture of one of Bothwell's servants, who revealed that the new-made allies planned to capture the king and mew him up in Blackness. After some delay in order to permit the gathering of the harvest, and also to permit the king to borrow some money, including twelve thousand pounds from the useful Foulis, James started north on October 4, 1594.[115] On the next day he received some bad news. The young earl of Argyll, who had recently discovered Huntly's connection with the plot which had led to the murder of Campbell

113 This was the phrase Bothwell used in the letter he addressed to the Edinburgh presbytery attempting to justify his alliance with Huntly. CSP SCOT, XI, 429-430.

114 September 16, 1594, Colville to Cecil, ibid., pp. 440-441. Salisbury Papers, IV, 629-632. Lang, History, II, 391. The last of Bothwell's important Stewart supporters, Lord Ochiltree, also made his peace with James during September. September 28, Bowes to Cecil, CSP SCOT, XI, 452-455.

115 August 17, September 24, October 7, 1594, Bowes to Burghley, ibid., pp. 416-417, 449-452, 455-457. September 17, Bowes's instructions for Sheperson, ibid., pp. 443-447. RPCS, V, 172-173. The impeccably Protestant burghs agreed to find the money for the equivalent of a thousand footsoldiers. CSP SCOT, XI, 443.

of Calder, and who hoped to lay hands on Huntly's property in Lochaber, set out after Huntly, was met by a numerically smaller but better equipped foe at Glenlivat on October 3, and was beaten, not without suspicion of treachery within his own ranks.[116] But the victory seriously weakened the forces of the earls, who were now in no position to offer any resistance to to the king's army. It also cost Huntly the services of his ablest adviser, Gordon of Auchindoun, who was killed leading a cavalry charge. So James's expedition turned into a military promenade, albeit an expensive one; before it was over he had to send James Melvill to Edinburgh to raise some more money to pay his soldiers. The fact that the king entrusted this mission to James Melvill, and that his request for funds had the endorsement of Andrew Melvill and of two other ministers who accompanied the expedition,[117] is evidence of the vastly improved relations between king and kirk, now that James had set his face firmly against the Catholic earls. There was to be no significant change in those relations until after Maitland's death.

James accomplished little enough in the north, apart from the destruction of Huntly's mansion at Strathbogie and that of Errol at Slaines; by mid-November he was back in Edinburgh, leaving Lennox behind him in the north as his lieutenant, with a small body of soldiers and instructions to do justice and carry out the king's wishes. Just what the king's wishes were with respect to the Catholic earls was not clear, even to James, though he was prepared to be very lenient with their followers.[118] Ultimately he decided to let them off as lightly as possible. His fondness for Huntly, and Lennox's advice,[119] contributed to this decision, but the chief factor was the niggling behavior of Elizabeth. The queen had applauded James's resolution to march against his rebels, commiserated with him over Argyll's defeat, gave precise instructions that

116 See the account of Calderwood, v, 348-353.
117 *Ibid.*, pp. 353-356. *Autobiography of James Melvill*, pp. 320-322.
118 RPCS, v, 182-183. CSP SCOT, XI, 472. In the opinion of the kirk, James and Lennox were far too lenient; *Autobiography of James Melvill*, p. 319.
119 June 9, July 14, 1594, Bowes to Burghley, CSP SCOT, XI, 356-361, 375-376.

the border was to be kept quiet while James was in the north, and authorized the sending of two thousand pounds sterling to James. Then, when she learned of the king's success, and his return, she recalled the money. James was furious. The result was that on December 19 the privy council gave Lennox full powers to deal with the earls. By mid-February 1595 the bargain was made, as far as Huntly and Errol were concerned. They agreed to leave the country by March 15 and to find surety in the amount of forty thousand pounds that they would do so. The pardons of several of their followers were made contingent on their departure, so that a certain amount of clan pressure would be generated to see that they actually did leave. Their property was officially placed in Lennox's gift; the duke unofficially left it to their wives. No such consideration was shown for Angus; his property was seized and his person subsequently more or less ignored.[120]

For Bothwell, of course, there was no mercy. His lands were distributed among his border enemies, Hume, Buccleuch, and Cesford; and, at long last, James got the kirk to pronounce against him. On February 18, 1595, the Edinburgh presbytery excommunicated its "sanctified plague." On the same day his brother, Hercules Stewart, betrayed to the government by John Colville, was executed.[121] The earl skulked about in the highlands for a time, and then, in late March or early April 1595, left Scotland forever.[122] His spectacular career was over.

The almost simultaneous departure from Scotland of the two great rebels, Huntly and Bothwell, the highland chief and the border captain, represented a great personal triumph for King James. It represented an even greater triumph for

---

[120] *Border Papers*, I, 548, 550. Bruce, *Letters*, pp. 108-110. December 12, 1594, Clerkington to Bowes, CSP SCOT, XI, 492-493. February 14, 1595, Nicolson to Bowes, *ibid.*, pp. 533-534. February 22, Colville to Bowes, *ibid.*, p. 538. February 22, Ashton to Bowes, *ibid.*, pp. 540-541. RPCS, V, 192-193, 207-208, 212-213. Calderwood, V, 362-363. The wives of the Catholic earls were protected from spoliation from the beginning, by the king's order. See his letter of November 9, 1594 to Sir John Gordon of Pitlurg, J. Stuart, ed., *Miscellany of the Spalding Club*, 1st series, I, 9.

[121] Calderwood, V, 363-365. At the General Assembly of June 1595 the kirk acceded to James's request that all persons convicted of treason be excommunicated. *Ibid.*, pp. 367-368.

[122] April 10, 1595, Colville to Bowes, CSP SCOT, XI, 575-576.

the chancellor and especially for his administrative machine. As these pages have shown, that machine was neither particularly efficient nor particularly new. Maitland simply took over the old Scottish administrative mechanism and made it run, by recruiting from his own social class a group of people like himself who were willing to toil devotedly to make it work. Huntly and Bothwell, in their different ways, represented the independent power of the feudal and tribal chieftains which Maitland was determined to destroy. They were the Scottish counterparts of Warwick the Kingmaker and Charles of Burgundy, of Henry of Guise and the princes of Condé. Now, they were gone, and their departure marked a decisive turning-point in Scottish history. It marked, in fact, the final triumph of the crown in its long struggle against the forces of feudal anarchy. Never again would the royal authority be threatened by the uprising of a handful of aristocratic brigands. Maitland's machine had stood the test, and furthermore, it had won through without outside aid. James and Maitland had expelled Huntly and Bothwell without English armies and, almost, without English money. For the first time in history Scotland had an administration as distinct from a congeries of noble office-holders. This was the great contribution of Maitland of Thirlestane to his native land.

The chancellor himself took very little part in the final stages of the crisis which his administrative achievement had provoked. His health was beginning to fail, and he spent more and more time at his new house at Lauder, which was finally completed in 1595.[123] He did accompany James to Aberdeen in October 1594, however, and sometime during the course of this expedition there began the last of his great political quarrels, one which was to embitter the last year of his life, but which came to very little in the end. It was, in fact, after its opening stages, a tempest in a teapot.

Maitland's antagonist in this affair was an unlikely person, the earl of Mar. Mar, a loyal and conscientious servant of the king, his boyhood playmate, became convinced that the of-

123 A. Thomson, *Lauder and Lauderdale*, p. 178.

ficials in charge of the finances of the government, chiefly Glamis the treasurer and Seton of Parbroath the comptroller, were dishonest or incompetent or both, and he urged James to remove them. Maitland was at once on his guard. He suspected that the real instigator of this move was the ex-Bothwellite John Colville, whose pardon Mar had obtained over Maitland's bitter objections, and that the official really aimed at was himself. Once again his sharp tongue got him into difficulties; he remarked, at court, that since Mar had successfully obtained Colville's pardon, he no doubt would soon sue for that of Bothwell. Mar was naturally irritated, and open enmity between the two men resulted. By December 1594 Mar was doing just what Maitland had feared from the beginning: he was urging Maitland's removal.[124]

On the major point at issue Maitland was victorious. The entire official class closed ranks behind him at this threat to their leading members. In addition, Maitland was able to build up a powerful border coalition, headed by Buccleuch and Cesford, out of all those who had a vested interest in the spoils of the Bothwellites; in this respect Mar's patronage of Colville was costly to him.[125] James seems to have felt some sympathy for Mar's point of view, and he certainly had no love for the master of Glamis. But he was not the first king, nor the last, to be overborne by his bureaucracy. In January 1595 he decided against dismissing any of the exchequer officials; instead, a committee of twelve auditors was appointed to examine the whole financial structure. Mar was appointed to the committee, but so was Maitland, and most of the remaining members were the chancellor's friends.[126] For the moment Mar accepted his defeat; on January 24 it was reported that he and Maitland were "outwardly agreed."[127]

Maitland was not at his best in this affair. Mar was cer-

---

[124] December 12, 1594, Ashton to Bowes, CSP SCOT, XI, 494-495. For the course of the quarrel see the dispatches of the English informants from November 3, 1594 on, ibid., pp. 472ff.

[125] On this point see January 4, 1595, news from Scotland, ibid., p. 505.

[126] January 13, 1595, news from Edinburgh, ibid., pp. 509-511; January 18, February 14, Ashton to Bowes, ibid., pp. 514-516, 534-535.

[127] Ibid., pp. 520-521.

tainly right in believing the exchequer officials to be incompetent, as the succesful financial administration of the Octavians in 1596 was to show. The chancellor can perhaps be excused for defending his subordinates, who, after all, were no more incompetent than Maitland himself in money matters.[128] But it was very unwise of him to assume that Mar was really aiming at him in accusing Glamis and Parbroath; Mar, after all, had only recently helped to shield him from the wrath of Lennox. Apparently the chancellor, under the double strain of bad health and three years of unremitting harassment and fear, was losing his political judgment.

This loss of judgment became plainer in the sequel of the quarrel with Mar. Maitland's victory did not relieve him of his fear of the earl, and so, under the aegis of Buccleuch, he entered into a close alliance with his former persecutor, Queen Anne.[129] The queen also had a grievance against Mar, a perfectly natural one in a young mother whose political understanding was never very great. She wanted to have charge of Prince Henry herself, and as soon as the support of Maitland was obtained, she demanded of her husband that "she may have the keeping of the prince and the castle of Edinburgh," of which Mar was custodian also.[130] The king was very angry. He suspected Maitland of having instigated the request, and the chancellor had much ado to persuade his master and Mar that he was not responsible. He finally did so, and once again was formally reconciled to Mar in James's presence, in a curious scene "wherein neither of them spoke to [the] other, but both directed their speech to his majesty."[131]

For the moment Queen Anne dropped her demand, but the

128 At this juncture the chronic financial crisis was aggravated by the costly expedition against Huntly. The government's only solution, aside from the old one of revoking gifts of crown lands, was to try to get some money out of the Dutch. The English government blocked this; Elizabeth finally sent James three thousand pound sterling in August 1595. *Ibid.*, p. 678. The negotiations with the Dutch may be traced in *Salisbury Papers*, v, 110ff.

129 February 12, 1595, news from Scotland, CSP SCOT, XI, 531. March 3, Nicolson to Bowes, *ibid.*, pp. 543-544.

130 March 4, 1595, Ashton to Bowes, *ibid.*, p. 545.

131 March 22, 1595, Colville to Bowes, D. Laing, ed., *Original Letters of Mr. John Colville, 1582-1603*, p. 149. See also March 15, Ashton to Bowes, CSP SCOT, XI, 550-551.

grievance still rankled. After a month or two she raised the question again, much more insistently this time—in fact, rather hysterically, possibly owing to the fact that she believed herself to be pregnant once again, and was obsessed by the fear that she would lose her second child to an alien guardian.[132] And once again James, who trusted Mar and knew from experience the political value of a royal child in the hands of a dissident political faction, refused to allow the prince out of Mar's control. In July 1595 he went so far as to issue written instructions to Mar not to surrender the person of Prince Henry "except I command you with my own mouth, and being in such company as I myself shall best like of." If James should die, Mar was to retain custody of the child until he reached the age of eighteen.[133] For over two months the quarrel raged with increasing bitterness on both sides before the queen finally gave over.

Many historians, following the lead of Maitland's enemies, have pictured the chancellor as the ringleader in this affair, aggressively caballing against an innocuous nobleman in his search for greater power.[134] Almost the exact opposite was the truth. Maitland was a most reluctant plotter, who remained in the queen's coalition only out of fear for his own position should Mar become too influential. He did his best to dissuade Anne from reopening the question of the prince's guardianship, and, having failed, he foolishly attempted to carry water on both shoulders by remaining a member of the queen's faction and at the same time advising the king not to give in to her.[135] This behavior naturally aroused suspicion on all sides. Out

---

[132] If Anne was pregnant at this time, she must have miscarried; her second child, the future Elizabeth of Bohemia, was not born until August 1596.

[133] July 24, 1595, James to Mar, HMC, *Report on the Manuscripts of the Earl of Mar and Kellie* (London 1904), pp. 43-44. W. W. Seton, "The Early Years of Henry Frederick, Prince of Wales, and Charles, Duke of Albany [Charles I]," SHR, XIII (1915-1916), 367.

[134] See, for example, Lang, *History*, II, 395-396, and P. Hume Brown, *History of Scotland*, II (Cambridge 1912), 219-220. Miss Stafford, *James VI*, pp. 159-160, and D. H. Willson, *James VI and I*, p. 117, are more cautious, but neither of them mention Mar's attack on the exchequer officials.

[135] May 8, June 18, 23, 1595, Nicolson to Bowes, CSP SCOT, XI, 588-589, 615-616, 618-621. June 20, Ashton to Bowes, *ibid.*, pp. 617-618. July 24, Colville to Bowes, *ibid.*, pp. 653-654.

of fear of Mar, and of the supposed influence of Colville with Mar, Maitland clung to the queen's faction as long as he could. He evaded James's efforts to patch up a truce between himself and Mar, lest he lose his allies. But when those allies began to talk of using violence against the king, or of kidnapping him in the old fashion, the chancellor drew back. He was not prepared to jeopardize his life's work in a quarrel of which he disapproved. He braved the king's anger and told him the story, or enough of it to warn him of his danger. As Colville sneeringly put it, the chancellor "washes his hands, as Pilate did, and trusts to make stepping-stones of the rest [of the queen's party]."[136]

This act was Maitland's last public service. It effectively broke the back of the queen's faction, and doubtless would have created infinite future political difficulties for him. But by this time he was too ill to care. Late in August he took to his bed. His enemies declared that his illness was diplomatic, that it was prompted by the king's wrath and by his desire to avoid embarrassing explanations: "passato il periculo, gabato il santo."[137] James knew better. He knew that Maitland was not responsible for the renewal of the quarrel over Prince Henry, that the real instigator was the master of Glamis.[138] His anger evaporated, and he wrote the dying man a comforting, and sententious, letter wishing him a speedy recovery and assuring him that "in case of the worst (which God forbid)" he would

[136] July 12, 15, 23, 26, 1595, Nicolson to Bowes, ibid., pp. 636-637, 639-641, 651, 657-658. July 15, August 6, Ashton to Bowes, ibid., pp. 641-642, 671-672. Letters of John Colville, p. 173. A summary of the whole affair is contained in Ashton's letter of July 31, 1595, CSP SCOT, XI, 661-664.

[137] August 22, 1595, Nicolson to Bowes, ibid., pp. 686-687. August 25, news from Scotland, ibid., p. 690. September 1, Colville to Bowes, Letters of John Colville, pp. 177-178. September 10, MacCartney to Bowes, CSP SCOT, XII, 10-11.

[138] Glamis had been the original target of Mar's attacks, and Mar further infuriated him by arranging a marriage between his own cousin Agnes Murray and the young Lord Glamis without the master's knowledge. Glamis and Maitland had planned to marry the young lord to the sister of Maitland's nephew Ker of Cesford. April 24, 1595, Nicolson to Bowes, CSP SCOT, XI, 582-584; May 10, John Carey to Burghley, Border Papers, II, 30-31. The enraged Glamis struck back at Mar through the queen in order "to give Mar some other thing to think of than changing the officers of estate." July 31, Ashton to Bowes, CSP SCOT, XI, 661-664. See also June 7, Nicolson to Bowes, ibid., pp. 607-608.

protect Lady Maitland and the children, as he had the family of the long-departed Esmé Stewart.[139]

The king's letter doubtless eased the chancellor's mind, but it could do little for his body. The final illness began on September 13. By the 16th he was so poorly that Lady Maitland sent for the minister Robert Bruce. Bruce found the chancellor much concerned for the state of his soul. "He broke out in plain speeches . . . confessing that he had negligently heard the word and omitted to do that good to the kirk and commonweal which he might and ought to have done, protesting, if God gave him life, to make amends."[140] As Calderwood said, "He granted at his death, that he had greatly offended that man of God, Mr. Knox; wished often that he had builded a hospital when he builded his castle at Lauder, and cried often for mercy."[141] The kirk was disposed to look kindly on the repentant sinner. He was "in a very good estate, as appeared, for a life to come," in Calderwood's view; James Melvill regarded him as a man of "great learning, wisdom, and stoutness."[142] These judgments were, if anything, underestimates of Maitland's ecclesiastical statesmanship, if not of his personal character.

The end came on the night of October 3, 1595. Shortly before his death "the chancellor was asked what advice he would leave to the king for the managing of his estate. The chancellor said it was too late spered (asked), for his thoughts were upon another world."[143] And, indeed, it was "too late spered," though not in the sense Maitland intended. Maitland had been King James's political tutor, and, no doubt, continued to think of himself as such to the end. James, however, was now in his thirtieth year, and was fully confident of his own abilities at what he was to call "kingcraft." He knew what he owed to Maitland, and was not ungrateful. He kept his promise to look after the Maitland family, and eventually made the chancellor's son an earl. He composed a sonnet on the passing of his servant, ex-

---

[139] The letter is given in Spottiswoode, *History*, II, 463-464.
[140] September 19, 1595, Nicolson to Bowes, CSP SCOT, XII, 18-19.
[141] Calderwood, v, 382.
[142] *Ibid.*, p. 382. *Autobiography of James Melvill*, pp. 329-330.
[143] October 8, 1595, Nicolson to Bowes, CSP SCOT, XII, 39-41.

pressing his princely grief.[144] But his true sentiments were more nearly revealed in the remark he let drop when he was asked about Maitland's successor. "The king has said he will well ken who [*sic*] he chooses for that place, adding that he can have none but in short time they will presume to be equal with himself."[145] Of Maitland, as of few other statesmen, it may truly be said that he died in his time.

[144] See Appendix II.
[145] October 8, 1595, Nicolson to Bowes, CSP SCOT, XII, 39-41.

CHAPTER 13

AFTERMATH

ON THE DAY OF MAITLAND'S DEATH an English agent wrote to Robert Bowes, "The lord chancellor is fallen evil again and not like to live. . . . If he die, here will be such a change as was not this 20 years."[1] This forecast turned out to be almost completely wrong. The chancellor's death led to very little significant alteration in the policies and methods of the Scottish government, with one notable exception. For, unlike many statesmen who have held positions of eminence for a long time, Maitland had trained a successor. His successor was the king himself.

It would be rather wide of the mark to assert that his long years of intimate association with Maitland had much effect on the character of King James. His leading traits—his vanity, his laziness, his intelligence, his duplicity, even his love of theological dispute—were all present in the youth of eighteen who appointed Maitland secretary of state in 1584. Maitland's contribution lay rather in teaching the king how to govern, in showing him how to use the power which they gradually built up in the years between 1585 and 1592. What emerged was a system of government similar to, albeit weaker than, that of the Tudors, that is, government by an omnicompetent privy council run by a group of industrious and loyal officials. The personnel of the council changed somewhat, as older officials like Robert Melville retired or were driven from office because they had been too closely associated with the late chancellor—Maitland's unpopularity in aristocratic circles lived after him—but virtually all the new men who came forward after 1595 and who dominated the council and the Scottish administration generally during the next generation got their start in the chancellor's day.[2]

---

[1] CSP SCOT, XII, 33.
[2] One exception should be pointed out. Sir George Hume of Spott, who

291

During his last years as king of Scots, James governed most successfully through the council along the lines laid down by Maitland. The financial problem, indeed, proved to be beyond him, but this was not entirely his fault; the poverty of the crown reflected the poverty of the nation. James was aware of this; in the later 1590's he attempted to legislate a flourishing textile industry into existence, and he had a mercantilist's scorn for the shoddy and expensive work of the Scottish craft guilds.[3] But in this field all James's efforts led to meager results at best; temporary gains, like those of 1590-1591, were all that could be achieved. The crown remained poor. The value of the coinage continued to fall. Fiscal officials succeeded each other with bewildering rapidity after 1595; the only really efficient financial administration, that of the Octavians in 1596, lasted only a year, in part because the economies they effected irritated James's grasping courtiers. Matters reached such a pass that in 1599 the comptroller, Sir George Hume of Wedderburn, absconded rather than face the responsibilities of his office.[4] Much of James's fiscal irresponsibility and extravagance after 1603 is attributable to his grinding poverty before that date. England was as Canaan to him. "He wishes now to enjoy the Papacy, as we say," wrote the Venetian ambassador to England in 1603,[5] and enjoy it James did.

Apart from the question of money, James's administration in the years after 1595 was most successful. The amount of law and order significantly increased, even in the highlands, which were "so quiet," wrote an English observer in May 1595, "that the poor people pray for him [James] and his labors."[6] The

---

became treasurer in 1601 and, as earl of Dunbar, one of the triumvirate which governed Scotland after 1603, rose as a courtier rather than as an official. He was never particularly friendly to Maitland until the chancellor's last years, when common hostility to Bothwell drove them together.

[3] I. F. Grant, *The Social and Economic Development of Scotland before 1603*, pp. 423-424, 463-471. See also T. Keith, *Commercial Relations of England and Scotland 1603-1707*, pp. 21-31.

[4] For this affair see RPCS, v, introduction, pp. lxxxvii-lxxxviii, and G. P. McNeill, ed., *The Exchequer Rolls of Scotland*, XXIII, preface, pp. xliii-xlvi.

[5] Quoted in D. H. Willson, *James VI and I*, p. 174.

[6] CSP SCOT, XI, 589-590. A detailed discussion of James's highland policy after 1595 may be found in A. Cunningham, *The Loyal Clans*, pp. 171ff.

borders were even more peaceful, thanks to the efficient work of an Anglo-Scottish commission in 1597 and to the growing realization that James was indeed likely to succeed Elizabeth. Responsible men on both sides came to see that their long-range interest lay in keeping the peace.[7] The last great deed of border derring-do, the rescue of Kinmont Willie from Carlisle castle by Scott of Buccleuch in 1596, was a remarkable feat; but it also attracted attention precisely because such an incursion was becoming the exception rather than the rule. In these areas, as elsewhere, Maitland's administrative machine continued to function, even though its creator was gone.

In only one major matter of domestic policy did King James alter the line laid down by his great adviser. James had never sympathized with Maitland's conciliatory attitude toward the kirk, and at the first major clash with the ministers he abruptly abandoned it. The crisis came in 1596. The issues were old ones: on the one hand, the king's alleged sympathy toward Catholics, as evidenced by the fact that several of the newly-appointed Octavians had Catholic tendencies, and by the government's obvious intention to pardon Huntly and allow him to return; on the other, political sermons which frequently attacked not only James's policies but also his personal character and his family. With respect to these sermons the old issue of the right of the civil power to punish a minister for what he said in the pulpit, was revived. The resolution of all these questions came after the famous riot of December 1596, and the result was victory for the king. James might have used his victory to conciliate the clergy and work out a *modus vivendi* with the moderate majority he was able to create in successive General Assemblies in 1597 and thereafter; this is certainly what Maitland would have done. Instead, James decided to overpower the kirk by the reintroduction of episcopacy.

The king showed great tactical skill in restoring the bishops. He did not hurry, and he brought them back at first simply as representatives of the clerical estate in Parliament; it was not until after his accession to the English throne that he undertook

[7] On this point see D. L. W. Tough, *The Last Years of a Frontier*, p. 278.

to revive their ecclesiastical jurisdiction. James's reasons for acting as he did are not far to seek. In his view, conciliation had been tried and had failed; the Golden Act of 1592 had been followed by the ministers' espousal of Bothwell. As he himself explained to all who cared to read in his *True Law of Free Monarchies*, published in 1598, kings are God's lieutenants on earth; "preces et lachrymae sunt arma Ecclesiae."[8] His ideal was the submissive church of Elizabeth, and submission could be assured only by a hierarchy under royal control. So James, in the interest of his own power, imposed such a hierarchy on the Scottish kirk. He was able to succeed because, with the weakening of the power of the Scottish aristocracy, the defenders of presbytery could find no effective allies and, especially after 1603, no effective way of putting pressure on the king. Ironically enough, it was thus the very success of Maitland's policy of weakening the power of the aristocracy which now enabled the king to alter that policy in one of its essential aspects, and crush one of the chief elements in the coalition which Maitland had constructed. The kirk had served its turn; now it, too, must acknowledge the supreme authority of the crown.

James's new ecclesiastical policy had every appearance of success. It was, nevertheless, a mistake, probably the most serious error of policy James ever made as king of Scotland. Maitland had demonstrated the possibilities inherent in genuine collaboration with the kirk; the few years after the riot of December 1596 made it plain that the kirk could be controlled without bishops. Episcopacy was desperately unpopular with the earnest presbyterians; it was popular with nobody. Furthermore, the revival of episcopacy threatened to reopen the whole question of church lands. James had long since regretted Maitland's act of annexation of the temporalities of benefices; in his book of instructions for his son, the famous *Basilicon Doron*, he called it "that vile act of annexation."[9] It was repealed in 1606 with respect to episcopal lands; at the same time, in order to calm the fears of the landowning class, a number of

---

8 C. H. McIlwain, ed., *The Political Works of King James I*, p. 61.

9 J. Craigie, ed., *The Basilicon Doron of James VI*, Scottish Text Society edition, i (Edinburgh 1944), 79.

monastic properties were erected into temporal lordships. The landowners nevertheless remained nervous. Thus King James, by restoring episcopacy, accumulated a great deal of inflammable material in Scotland. The ineptitude of his successor ignited the conflagration, by precipitating the alliance between kirk and nobility against the crown which James's ecclesiastical policy had made possible. The clash between crown and kirk which resulted from the abandonment of Maitland's policy was to be the dominant political fact of seventeenth-century Scotland.

ii

"This I must say for Scotland," boasted King James in 1607, "here I sit and govern it with my pen, I write and it is done, and by a clerk of the council I govern Scotland now, which others could not do by the sword."[10] Most historians have assumed that this happy condition was owing to James's accession to the English throne, and, of course, it is true that he was vastly more powerful after 1603 than before. But it is also true that James governed Scotland by his pen before 1603, thanks to the work of his great chancellor. Never before had the royal authority stood so high. Every class in the state now looked to the king for favor and advancement. This was true even of the aristocracy—so much so that the king made some progress in his favorite project of stopping feuds; so much so that in the *Basilicon Doron* he could advise his son to use nobles as ministers, since this policy causes "least envy, contrary to that of start-ups."[11] The innocuous career of the earl of Huntly after his return to Scotland in 1596 is evidence of the weakened position of the nobility; so is the popular rejoicing manifested everywhere in Scotland at the failure of the Gowrie conspiracy. The increase in royal authority and control over the country as a whole and over the aristocracy in particular is the measure of Maitland's success—his great, and unrecognized, achievement.

Throughout his career Maitland demonstrated his capacity

---

10 Quoted in Willson, *James VI and I*, p. 313.

11 Grant, *Social and Economic Development*, pp. 194-195. *Basilicon Doron*, I, 117. If this was a reference to Maitland, it was a singularly ungrateful one.

to grow, to shed his prejudices as their danger became apparent to him. Starting out as a bitter enemy of the kirk, he gradually came round, first, to a position of compromise, then to a belief in active cooperation. He never lost his suspicion of the upper aristocracy, but he came to realize that he must cooperate occasionally with those who were willing to serve the king. His most consistent foes were the men most reluctant to acknowledge the royal authority: Huntly, Maxwell, above all, Bothwell. In foreign policy Maitland started out as the enemy of England; but he quickly became convinced of the necessity of an alliance with her, as the surest means of bolstering his master's authority at home and of achieving the coveted goal of the English succession. He insisted, however, that the alliance be a genuine partnership rather than an English-dominated affair. He disapproved of James's flirtations with the continental Catholic powers, and checked them as much as he could. During his years of power Scottish foreign policy, thanks to his influence, was one of friendship with continental Protestant states and of cool correctness, at best, with the Catholic powers. It was not until after 1595 that James began to attempt to smooth his way to the English throne by making serious use of his subterranean connections with the continental Catholics.[12] Because of Maitland's lack of subservience, and on account of his background as a former supporter of Queen Mary, the English never fully trusted him. They nevertheless recognized his usefulness to them. "Although he has his imperfections, yet he is one of the best among them," wrote Roger Ashton to Bowes a week before the chancellor's death.[13]

Maitland's fundamental political problem was twofold: he had to create an administrative machine, and he had to provide it with a political climate which would give it a chance to operate efficiently. Finding the administrators was the easier task; Maitland recruited them for the most part from the members of his own class. Maitland could have used more officials than he had,

---

[12] For an account of these negotiations see H. G. Stafford, *James VI of Scotland and the Throne of England*, pp. 146-156, 225-249, 317-321, and the authorities there cited.

[13] CSP SCOT, XII, 6-7.

and he often had to abandon or postpone a desirable reform for lack of administrative personnel; but the shortage of officials though always acute, never became absolutely crippling. The problem of creating the necessary political climate was much more difficult; Maitland arranged it by means of a coalition of the kirk and its supporters, some loyal nobles, and a large number of lairds and burgesses, all bolstered by the support and friendship of England. This coalition was most unstable; Maitland's ability to hold it together as successfully as he did was by no means the least of his achievements.

Because Maitland accomplished so much, it is easy to exaggerate his success. Much still remained to be done. The financial problem was not solved. The power of the aristocracy was limited, not broken. The administration of justice had been considerably improved, but there were still weaknesses in the judicial structure. Open violence, though declining, was still fairly common. The extent of the government's authority in the highlands was vague. And, as we have seen, Maitland's religious policy was abandoned. Not until the eighteenth century were solutions found for some of these questions. Not until then was large-scale rebellion in the highlands made impossible; not until then were the heritable jurisdictions which Maitland so disliked finally abolished; not until then, as a consequence of the act of union of 1707, did Scotland become economically prosperous; not until then did religion cease to be a dominant political issue with most men.

Maitland might have accomplished more than he did if he had been more tactful, less sarcastic, less concerned with the trappings of power. His acquisition of the chancellorship was a serious blunder; it did not add to his power, and it simply made him enemies. His determination to use his office to establish the position of his family laid him open to charges of avarice which were unfounded but damaging to his prestige. He did not understand finance, and his attempts to cope with the fiscal difficulties of the Scottish crown were uniformly unsuccessful. And yet, it was the work of Maitland which made the solution of Scotland's problems ultimately possible, because it was Maitland who gave Scotland an administration. It was not a perfect administrative machine, or even a particularly efficient one, owing partly to Maitland's own failings, partly to the immense difficulty of the problems he faced, the opposition that had to be overcome, the occasional vagaries of his royal master. But it worked. And because it worked, the indispensable groundwork was laid for the Stewart absolutism of the seventeenth century. Therefore, this half-forgotten chancellor has some claim to a place beside Thomas Cromwell and Cardinal Richelieu as one of the significantly creative state-builders of early modern Europe.

THE DISPOSITION OF THE ABBATIAL

LANDS AFTER 1587

An account of the disposition of the lands of the twenty-nine abbeys existing at the time of the act of annexation will demonstrate how the king and Maitland used the power they obtained from that act.[1] Seven of the abbeys were in the hands of the upper aristocracy in 1587 and remained there. These included the two Hamilton abbeys of Arbroath and Paisley; the two Erskine abbeys of Dryburgh and Cambuskenneth, which, along with the priory of Inchmahome, were erected into the lordship of Cardross for the benefit of the earl of Mar in 1606; the abbey of Deir, exempted from the act in 1587 for the uncle of the earl Marischal and eventually passing to the earl by inheritance; Inchcolm, held in 1587 by Sir James Stewart of Doune, father of the unfortunate "bonny earl of Moray," and erected for his second son Henry in 1609; and Jedburgh, which was in the hands of the Humes and was erected for Lord Hume in 1606. Seven more, in 1587, were in the hands of men who might be classified as officials or courtiers, and remained there: Balmerino (James Elphinstone of Innernauchtie, later Lord Balmerino), Culross (Alexander Colville; the abbey was erected for his nephew Sir James Colville of Easter Wemyss in 1589), Holyroodhouse (for the bishop of Orkney and his son, as stated in the text of the act; but a considerable portion of the temporalities were erected into a separate barony for Bellenden the justice clerk), Kinloss (the lawyer Edward Bruce), New-

[1] The material on which this appendix is based has been drawn chiefly from two sources, the register of the great seal, and the introduction by David Masson to the first volume of the second series of the *Register of the Privy Council of Scotland*. This great introduction is absolutely indispensable to any account of the question of church lands between 1560 and 1625.

battle (exempted in the text of the act and erected for Mark Ker, the master of requests), and Inchaffray and Lindores for the courtiers James Drummond and Patrick Leslie respectively. Of the remaining fifteen, the temporalities of five, Crossraguel, Fearn, Glenluce, Icolmkill, and Tungland were ultimately annexed to various bishoprics under the restored episcopal system of the seventeenth century; two of these had been held by "new" men. William Melville, brother of Sir Robert Melville the treasurer-depute, was commendator of Tungland from 1588 to 1592; he then obtained an erection in his favor of the lands of Kilwinning. Sir John Vans, son of Sir Patrick Vans of Barnbarroch the judge and ambassador, held Crossraguel from 1587 to 1616. The possession of Sweetheart abbey was uncertain in 1587, since the last Catholic abbot was still alive; eventually it was erected for Sir Robert Spottiswoode, the son of the archbishop. The remaining nine are the most interesting of all. In every case the abbey was held in 1587 by a member of the aristocracy or by a connection of a great family; in every case, the land passed into the hands of new men or of the crown. The most striking losses were those of Huntly and Bothwell. Huntly's great abbey of Dunfermline was gifted to Queen Anne upon James's marriage in 1589, and thus passed to the crown; but several large lordships were carved out of it: that of Musselburgh for Maitland, Burntisland for Sir Robert Melville, and Newburn for Andrew Wood of Largo. Alexander Seton, Lord Urquhart, in whose behalf the priory of Pluscardine was exempted from the act of annexation, became hereditary baillie of Dunfermline in 1596, and from it in 1605 he took his title of earl of Dunfermline, by which he is best known in Scottish history. Bothwell lost his holdings of Kelso, and the priory of Coldingham, although much later, in 1621, his son was restored to Coldingham, which had been erected for Lord Hume in 1606. Kelso ultimately was erected for Maitland's nephew by marriage, the turbulent borderer Robert Ker of Cesford, earl of Roxburgh; its dependent cell of Lesmahago, included in the erection for Ker, later passed to the marquis of Hamilton. Of the other seven abbeys, two, Holywood and Soulseat, were held by Johnstones in 1587, and one, Dundrennan, by a Maxwell.

Holywood and Dundrennan passed into the hands of James's great favorite and master of horse John Murray, later earl of Annandale. Soulseat went to the obscure William Adair of Kinhilt. The other great border abbey, Melrose, was in the hands of James Douglas, son of Douglas of Lochleven, in 1587; in 1609 it was erected for John Ramsay, the "hero" of the Gowrie conspiracy. Gowrie's own abbey of Scone, on which his earldom was erected, passed into the hands of the courtier David Murray. Cupur, in Fife, was held by Leonard Leslie, a connection of the great Fife family; in 1606 it was erected for the son of Lord Balmerino. Finally, Kilwinning, in 1587 in the hands of Alexander Cunningham, son of the "good earl" of Glencairn, was erected on his death into a lordship for William Melville, as has been said.

The same sort of thing happened to the lesser monastic houses, the priories and nunneries; here, perhaps, save for the highland houses, the official element was even more predominant. One exception to this statement should be noted: the greatest of all the priories, St. Andrews, was erected in 1592 for the duke of Lennox. Bishoprics were in slightly different case; here there was no question of a bishop becoming a temporal lord himself, but temporal lordships were erected out of the lands of bishoprics, as for example, that granted to James's favorite Alexander Lindsay, Lord Spynie, in 1590. A detailed study of the lordships erected out of episcopal lands would doubtless reveal much the same pattern as that shown by the abbeys.

KING JAMES'S SONNET ON

MAITLAND'S DEATH:

Thou passenger that spies with gazing eyes
This trophie sad of death's triumphant dart,
Consider when this outward tombe thou sees,
How rare a man leaves here his earthly part.
His wisdom and his uprightness of heart,
His piety, his practice of our state,
His quick engine, so verst in every art,
As equally not all were in debate.
Thus justly hath his death brought forth of late
An heavy grief in prince and subjects all
That vertue love, and vice do bear at hate,
Though vitious men rejoyces at his fall.
    So for himself most happy doth he die,
    Though for his prince it most unhappy be.

INDEX

ally of Gray, 71; and Moray's murder, 244

Athol, Mary Ruthven, Lady, 261

Babington, Anthony, 99

Balfour, Sir James, 43

Bancroft, bishop Richard, 212, 222

Bannatyne, Richard, Knox's secretary, 23, 32

Bartane, John, member of court of session, 60

Basilicon Doron, 36, 122-23, 294, 295

Beaton, cardinal David, 10

Beaton, James, archbishop of Glasgow, 106, 110, 112, 115, 141

Bellenden, Sir Lewis, justice clerk, 50n, 60, 68, 71, 73, 75, 115, 154, 208-9, 234, 299; allies with Gray, 65; mission to England, 65-66; captain of Blackness, 77; and feu of Orkneys, 160; cool to M., 190, 214; death of, 233

Berwick, 34, 96, 105, 161, 163

Black Acts (1584), 55-58, 82-83, 115, 248-50

Blackness, 55, 66, 77, 105, 219n, 245, 281

Blantyre, Walter Stewart, commendator of, 42n, 245

Blyth, barony of, 28, 32

borders, 6, 13, 98-99, 111, 128-30, 161-65, 186, 292-93; and Anglo-Scottish league, 90, 94, 96, 128-29; committee of 1590, 207, 216-19; and Bothwell's revolt, 231-32, 279-80

Bothwell, Adam, bishop of Orkney, 141, 299

Bothwell, James Hepburn, 4th earl of, 6, 28-31, 243

Bothwell, Francis Stewart, 5th earl of, 28, 106, 123-24, 149, 158n, 160, 161, 163, 201, 203, 213, 242, 251, 257, 260, 268, 294, 296; and Coldingham, 61, 78-79, 142-43, 300; hostility to Arran, 61, 71; hostility to M., 130, 155, 167-68; kills Arran's brother, 159, 164n; in Catholic plot, 181, 183, 185-87; tried for treason, 188; reconciled to M., 190, 202, 214; activity during king's absence in Denmark, 210-11; and Liddesdale question, 217-18; and M., 1590, 226; accused of witchcraft, 229-30; escapes from Edinburgh castle, 231; anger at M.,

232-33; government unable to capture, 234, 236; attack on Holyrood, 234-36; Queen Anne sympathetic to, 237, 245; attack on M., 243-45, 247; beneficiary of Moray's murder, 244; forfeited, 247-48, 252, 259; attacks Falkland, 252; kirk favors, 253, 255; captures James, 261-62; restoration of, 262-64; driven from court, 264-65; denounced rebel, 265-66; England supports, 271-72; and raid of Leith, 273-74; loses supporters, 275-76, 279-80; joins Huntly, 280-81; goes into exile, 283; significance of defeat of, 283-84

Bowes, Robert, English ambassador to Scotland, 39, 41, 42-43, 47, 51, 228, 231, 234, 253, 268, 270, 271, 274-75, 280, 291; and crisis of 1584, 52; replaces Ashby as ambassador, 211; predicts attack on M., 214, 215; arranges reconciliation between M. and Glamis, 226-27

Brahe, Tycho, 206

Bruce, Robert, Catholic agent, 167, 182

Bruce, Robert, minister, 156, 185, 192, 203, 206, 230n, 253; crowns Queen Anne, 213-14; attacks act of abolition, 269; at M.'s deathbed, 289

Buchanan, George, 32, 33, 39, 42, 59, 82, 249

Burgh, Lord, English ambassador to Scotland, 257, 258

Burghley, William Cecil, Lord, 35, 49, 154, 167, 173, 210, 223, 257; regards M. as Marian, 87; responsible for Scottish affairs, 213

Burghs and burghers, 11-12, 14, 18, 52, 95, 103n, 137, 180, 196, 200, 213, 224, 281n; M.'s policy toward, 151-52; *see also* commerce

Caithness, George Sinclair, 5th earl of, 158, 234

Calder, John Campbell, laird of: murder of, 240-42, 281-82

Campbell family, 7, 128, 227; and Calder's murder, 240-42; *see also* Ardkinglas, Argyll, Calder, Glenurchy, Lochnell

Carey, Sir George, 263

Carey, Henry, *see* Hunsdon

Carey, Robert, 105-6, 275, 278

Wars of the Congregation (1559-1560), 15, 16, 26-27, 88, 269
Wemyss of Myrecarnie, Andrew, 154
witchcraft, trials, 1590-1591, 229-31; Bothwell accused of, 229-30, 244, 262-63
Worcester, Edward Somerset, 4th earl of, 223
Wotton, Edward, English ambassador to Scotland, 65, 66, 85n, 89, 271; embassy of, 67ff; and death of Lord Russell, 72-74

Young, George, secretary of privy council, 103n
Young, Peter, 198, 237n; mission to Denmark, 193-94

Zouche, Lord, English ambassador to Scotland, 270-72, 274

LEE, MAURICE. John Maitland of Thirlestane and the foundation of the Stewart despotism in Scotland. Princeton, N.J., Princeton University Press, 1959. 314 p. illus. 24 cm. (Princeton studies in history, 11) 1. Maitland, John, baron of Thirlestane, 1543-1595. 2. Scotland—Hist.—To 1603. *Full name*: Maurice DuPont Lee. DA788.L4. (941.05.) 59-9097 ‡ Library of Congress.